No More Beyond

No More Beyond

The Life of Hubert Wilkins

SIMON NASHT

BIRLINN

This edition published in 2006 by
Birlinn Limited
West Newington House
10 Newington Road
Edinburgh
EH9 1QS

www.birlinn.co.uk

First published in 2005 by Hodder Australia
as *The Last Explorer. Hubert Wilkins, Australia's Unknown Hero*

Copyright © Simon Nasht 2005, 2006

ISBN10: 1 84158 519 2
ISBN13: 978 1 84158 519 X

British Library Cataloguing-in-Publication Data
A catalogue record for this book is available from the British Library

Typeset by Hewer Text UK Ltd, Edinburgh
Printed and bound by Creative Print and Design, Wales

*In memory of Constance Perkin (1900–2000)
and all the unsung heroes of the century*

Acknowledgments

I must principally thank two Norwegians, Trond Eliassen and Kjell Eriksen, who first introduced me to a forgotten explorer from my own country. Their enthusiasm for Wilkins was inspiring and their contribution to my research cannot be overstated. The fact checkers at National Geographic Television inadvertently sent me on a search to correct some long-standing myths, and this book is the result. Any errors however are mine.

The largest collection of Wilkins' papers is, ironically enough, held in the institute named after his greatest rival. My sincere thanks to all at the Byrd Polar Research Center at the Ohio State University, primarily Polar Curator Laura J Kissel, who has been exceptionally helpful with her time and assistance.

Professor Peter Wadhams, former director of the Scott Polar Research Institute, Cambridge, and his wife, the polar historian Dr Maria Pia Casarini, were the first to alert me to the significance of Wilkins' scientific achievements and generous in sharing their extensive knowledge.

Other collections concerning Wilkins are spread around the world and I am thankful to the many curators and archivists who assisted me, including JJ Ahern at the American Philosophical Society Library, Philadelphia; Janet Baldwin, Curator of Collections, James B Ford Library, The Explorers Club, New York; Sarah Hartwell, Rauner Special Collections Library, Dartmouth College; and the archivists of the Natural History Museum, London.

The work of Stuart Jenness, son of Wilkins' good friend from the Canadian Arctic Expedition, Diamond Jenness, has been invaluable. Stuart spent many years deciphering Wilkins' impossible handwriting and I am eternally thankful that this difficult task was accomplished at the expense of someone else's eyesight. Vice Admiral James Calvert suffered without complaint through my obvious ignorance of submarining. His moving account of Wilkins' funeral service at the North Pole is included almost verbatim.

Thomas Endrusick and former colleagues of Sir Hubert at the US Army Soldier Systems Center, Natick, Massachusetts, were diligent in collecting useful information. Climatologist Dr William Porter, a man after Wilkins' own heart, is well into his eighties and still working there, and I appreciate sharing his memories of their pioneering days together.

In Australia Ross St Clair gave valuable advice on his grandfather, aviation pioneer Garnsey Potts, and other early Australian aviators. Nick Klaasen's research into the history of the Wilkins family helped me piece together the formative years as did Dr Jeff Nicholas, president of the Pioneers Association of South Australia.

Antarctic veteran Dr Phillip Law and Stephen Martin of the State Library of New South Wales have given invaluable guidance on polar history. Alasdair McGregor, biographer of Frank Hurley, shared his immense knowledge and gave generous advice.

The Australian Antarctic Division was superb, and its choice of guide, Ian Godfrey of the Western Australian Museum, made my stay in Antarctica both safe and productive. My thanks to Don and Margie McIntyre and the crew of the Sir Hubert Wilkins for making my passage of the Southern Ocean an authentic adventure.

For their faith and patience, I am indebted to Matthew Kelly and Isobel Dixon. To my family, who endured endless retellings of Wilkins' stories without loss of enthusiasm, I am forever grateful.

Contents

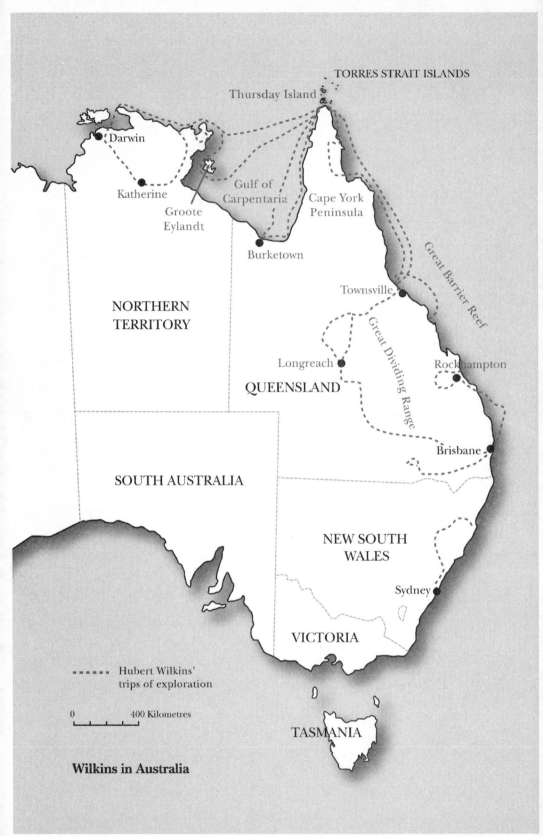

TORRES STRAIT ISLANDS

Thursday Island

Darwin

Katherine

Groote
Eylandt

Gulf of
Carpentaria

Cape York
Peninsula

NORTHERN
TERRITORY

Burketown

Townsville

Great Barrier Reef

Longreach

Great Dividing Range

Rockhampton

QUEENSLAND

SOUTH AUSTRALIA

Brisbane

NEW SOUTH
WALES

Sydney

VICTORIA

- - - - - - Hubert Wilkins'
              trips of exploration

0   400 Kilometres

TASMANIA

Wilkins in Australia

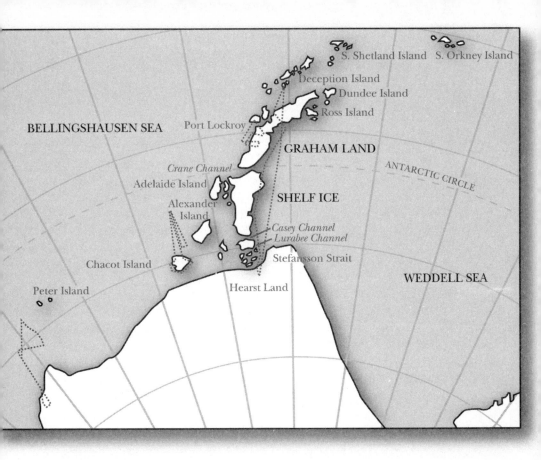

S. Shetland Island S. Orkney Island

Deception Island

Dundee Island

Ross Island

BELLINGSHAUSEN SEA

Port Lockroy

GRAHAM LAND

ANTARCTIC CIRCLE

Crane Channel

Adelaide Island

SHELF ICE

Alexander
 Island

Casey Channel
Lurabee Channel

Chacot Island

Stefansson Strait

WEDDELL SEA

Peter Island

Hearst Land

············ Wilkins' pioneering Antarctic flights from
Deception Island and Port Lockroy, 1928;
Port Lockroy and *William Scoresby*, 1929.

0   1000 Kilometres

Wilkins in Antarctica

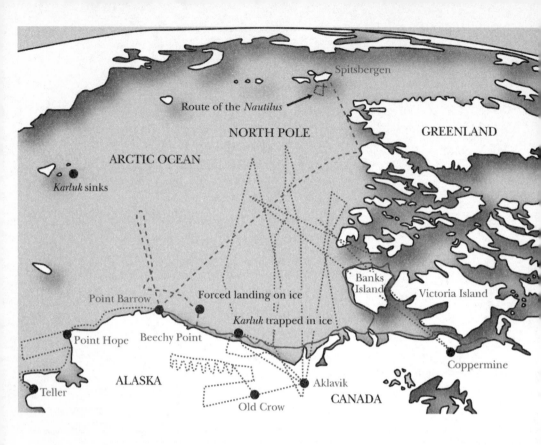

Wilkins in the Arctic

Legend:

——————— Wilkins on CAE treks 1913–17

··············· Search for Russian flyers 1937–38

- - - - - - Wilkins major flights in 1927 and across Arctic in 1928

 Route of the *Nautilus*, 1931

Wilkins in the Arctic

Introduction

Looking down from the well-trodden trails and peaks first climbed by others, we feel a mixture of awe and envy at the achievements of the past century's great explorers, the 'last of the first'. For they, unlike us, had the unknown ahead of them, challenges that tested the limits of human endurance and courage. Using only the simplest technologies and rudimentary charts – if they had any at all – these few removed the last corners of terra incognita from the maps and from our imaginations.

In the various polar and geographic institutes of Britain, Australia, Scandinavia and the United States, the same names appear again and again. We know them now as the giants of the brief, dramatic period of exploration called the heroic age: Amundsen, Peary, Scott and Shackleton, with Mawson, Nansen and Byrd just a step behind. One after another they and their kind conquered the poles, climbed the high mountains, crossed the remaining oceans and deserts, and mapped the last land. Many tried, a handful succeeded. But even those few who triumphed were often left so drained by the experience they could never savour victory. They crossed the void only to be left empty within.

Ultimately these were men of action, driven by a curious mix of ego, courage and duty, but mostly by the fear of being beaten to their prize. Though they manfully hauled back the rock samples and books full of weather data, each knew history would judge them by a simple test: did they win?

It was on a visit to the Scott Polar Research Institute at Cambridge that I was first made aware of the true significance of a man few have heard of: Sir Hubert Wilkins. While I had been fascinated by his daring and often amusing adventures, somehow it seemed disrespectful to consider him in the same light as the *great* men of the heroic age. But the institute's former director, Professor Peter Wadhams, and his polar historian wife, Dr Maria Pia Casarini, were pleased that someone had finally come to investigate further the life of a man they considered the first truly modern explorer and perhaps the finest of the twentieth century. They saw him as a visionary who realised the change that modern technology could bring to exploration and its often neglected sister, scientific research. Wilkins was the one who put to rest the notion that all that mattered was to be there a day before anyone else, and who finally reversed the heroic equation of glory before knowledge.

Wilkins did his apprenticeship in exploration the old and hard way, sledging thousands of kilometres across ice, and slogging for years on foot through deserts and tropics. He served his time on the heaving swells of the Southern Ocean and in the maze of ice passages to the Arctic Sea. But he was also the first to grasp the potential of discovery from the air, by submarine, and even from space, and once fixed on a notion he had a rare ability to make even outlandish ideas seem reasonable.

He modernised exploration while completing the chain of discovery that stretched back before history. By the beginning of the twentieth century the North and South poles were the only two regions of significance that we had not seen with our own eyes. It was Wilkins who completed the map of the world in eight glorious months of flying in 1928.

Digging deeper into Wilkins' adventures, at times I could scarcely believe them to be true, even less that a man could achieve so much yet be so little remembered. Wilkins can be ranked among the greats even if we only measure his success in terms of newly discovered square kilometres. But there is more to greatness than that, as we know; otherwise, men like Scott and Shackleton would be mere footnotes along with the other 800 or so unfortunates who set out for a pole and never returned. Wilkins too had his failures, yet setbacks never daunted him and he seemed totally untroubled by the judgment history would make of his efforts.

Therein lay the qualities that set him apart as a special case, truly innovative in his search for knowledge. In every word he wrote, every public speech, all the scratchy newsreel interviews, Wilkins never wavered. He was driven by a deep-felt need to answer a question that had formed when as a young boy he saw suffering animals and farmers hit by a devastating drought in his native Australia. Later he photographed the ferocious famine that wracked Russia after its crops failed in 1921 and made a decision to dedicate his life to preventing such disasters. He believed science could help forestall these tragedies and that understanding the climate, especially in the polar regions, was the key to predicting weather and saving lives.

As I sat in the library at Cambridge, Dr Casarini explained to me that it was not just what Wilkins achieved, it was *how* he achieved that mattered. With vision he imagined new ways of investigation, with courage he took himself where others would not dare, and with modesty he resisted the temptation for 'firsts' in favour of locations that were scientifically more valuable. It cost him fame, but he never hesitated, and it marks him as both unique among his contemporaries and the greatest of his time.

In his later years Wilkins slipped into obscurity, remembered with affection by his fellow explorers and a few others who could recall his amazing exploits. His departure from the headlines seemed not to worry him for a moment. His wife said he died with a slight smile upon his lips, and he had good reason at the end to feel pleased with his efforts. He knew the world would catch up with him eventually.

As I've followed his footsteps across the continents, from the simple stone outback cottage where it all began to the icy wastes where it ended, I've come to learn from Wilkins one of the oldest truths: that the sum of a man's life is not measured just by its accomplishments, but by how it is spent.

This then is the remarkable, at times implausible, story of George Hubert Wilkins. His was a life well lived.

Prologue

Now faith is the substance of things hoped for, the evidence of things not seen.

— Hebrews 11:1

On the Nautilus *men's hearts never fail them* . . .

— Jules Verne

T he winds were as bitter as his disappointment. Despite the half-gale blowing, Sir Hubert Wilkins stood alone on the bow of the *Nautilus*, barely moving. From time to time members of the crew came on deck, but they understood well enough when to leave a man to his thoughts. Wilkins knew the high latitudes better than any man alive and expected no solace here, no second chance.

Earlier that morning the little submarine had crossed 82 degrees north, by their reckoning as close to the pole as any vessel had ever managed under its own power.[1] *Nautilus* was adrift in these uncharted waters, well beyond hope of rescue. With engines crippled she was barely able to stay afloat, let alone dive beneath the ice. Wilkins faced an impossible choice. To turn back now would mean humiliating failure and financial ruin; to push on meant risking the lives of everyone aboard and, after the events of that morning, a mutiny too. He scanned the horizon for an answer, but the frozen ocean offered only its usual iron indifference.

In his journal of that day, 22 August 1931, Wilkins admitted it was far too late in the season to be attempting a polar expedition.

Tomorrow the sun would dip below the horizon for the first time in four months, and the long dark would begin its return. Since leaving Spitsbergen it had been all fog and storms, a sure sign the weather had turned. Deep in the icepack, manoeuvring to avoid collision with the drifting floes, they twisted and turned all afternoon, trying to stay clear of heaving ice-cakes that menaced the propellers and diving rudders. The sub was battered forward and aft, each collision reverberating through the hollow steel vessel like an exploding depth charge. The crew, nerves raw from weeks of struggle with the unreliable boat, huddled inside amid icicles and hoarfrost, trying unsuccessfully to find warmth.

They would have been better protected deeper into the pack among solid floes, but snowstorms and sleet made it impossible to see more than a few hundred metres ahead. Safest of all was probably beneath the surface, well below the treacherous ice, though no one had ever dared to find out. Jules Verne had imagined such a journey, and, inspired by his stories, Wilkins had spent years preparing for this day. He'd trudged and flown across thousands of kilometres of the unknown Arctic Ocean and was convinced a submarine could safely navigate all the way to the North Pole and beyond if necessary. Now they had no choice but to find out. He gave the order to his skipper, Commander Sloan Danenhower, to prepare the *Nautilus* for diving.

Innately cautious, Commander Danenhower had special reason to be wary of the Arctic. Fifty years earlier his father had barely survived a polar expedition that sent many good men to their deaths. He knew that underneath its new paint and bizarre modifications, the *Nautilus* was still the same obsolete hulk he had first seen in a US Navy scrapyard the previous year. Before taking it down blind into uncharted waters he insisted on a thorough inspection.

The skipper's caution was vindicated. When he tested the diving planes – the rudders vital for controlling the submarine's movement under water – there was no response. Frank Crilley, the expedition's diver, volunteered to take a look despite the risks of being crushed against the hull by the shifting ice. As they lowered him into the water, all feared what he might find. It wasn't long before there was a tug on the rope, the signal to be hauled back up, and as they lifted the heavy helmet off Crilley's shoulders, the look on his face said it all. The diving planes were gone.

At first Wilkins was more disbelieving than shocked. The loss of the rudders was a catastrophic blow to his plans. Without them the sub would be almost impossible to guide under water, like a car without a steering wheel. It didn't make sense. Though *Nautilus* had been battered by the ice, he couldn't believe the knocks had been enough to carry away heavy steel plates. Both diving planes had apparently broken off at the same time, yet the vertical rudder remained miraculously intact.

There was really only one explanation: the submarine had been sabotaged. Somewhere, probably back in Spitsbergen, at least one member of the crew and likely others had been so fearful of Wilkins' determination to continue that they had crippled the vessel to stop him.

Wilkins had gambled his reputation as a leader and visionary scientist on this expedition, standing his ground against a legion of sceptics who said it was impossible. While some newspapers attacked him, others called it the greatest adventure of all time, and the idea had captured the public imagination. In the dark days of the Depression, people were thrilled by its courage and audacity. Every day audiences tuned in to hear news by radio broadcasts carried around the world for the first time. Newspapers from Moscow to Melbourne carried front-page reports on the expedition's progress and in the United States, the Hearst press, exclusive sponsors of the submarine, put out special editions during the day to update the story. In New York a giant electronic screen had been built to carry the latest reports. To fail now because of an act of mutinous sabotage would be more than just a personal disaster; it would set back the cause of scientific investigation in the Arctic. For decades Wilkins had championed the poles as a region of immense importance to humanity, and to damage that crusade was a responsibility he could not bear.

Despite their desperate situation, this was not a reckless endeavour. Wilkins had often said adventure was just a word used to disguise unplanned surprises, and well-prepared expeditions could avoid them. He had learned the explorer's craft from other restless men like Shackleton and the Arctic pioneer Stefansson. He was friend and often rival to other renowned adventurers, Amundsen and Byrd among them. They liked and respected him, recognising a fellow traveller who was both a master of the old ways of exploring and a harbinger of the new. While slogging on sled and foot through deserts of ice and sand, Wilkins had dreamt of being the first to take motorcycles, airships and aeroplanes to unknown places. His lack of ego perplexed and occasionally annoyed his peers – one explorer complained of his 'aggressive modesty' – and he seemed to have little interest for his place in history. However, this humility cannot explain why today, despite a career of exceptional achievement, he is all but forgotten. The answer hangs on a single decision taken soon after the discovery of the missing rudder.

Nautilus anchored beside a solid floe and one by one the crew filed onto the ice for a meeting to discuss the situation. It was a relief to be out of the dank coffin of the ship, with its leaks and the rank smell of diesel mixed with bilge. Out here it was cutting too, so cold that urine arced and crackled and froze before it hit the ground. It hurt to suck in the frigid air, and the exhaled breath froze on the face, but you could move, stand upright and swing your arms. Surely, they thought, he would turn back now; what was the point in continuing?

Unwashed and unshaven, Wilkins' dishevelled crew looked more like a gang of prison escapees than sailors. Some moved with aching joints, poisoned by lead leeching into the fresh water tanks; others were yellow from unrelenting seasickness. Most had lost the will to continue and none of them had faith in the accident-prone *Nautilus*. In addition, there was something unnerving about Wilkins' obstinate resolve to push on no matter what the risks. They knew the stories about him during the war, how he had been wounded nine times and kept returning to the front, always in the hottest spot. Now that courage hung over them like a curse. There were whispered conversations on the night watch: the man would not stop until they were all killed.

It is true that Sir Hubert Wilkins had a reputation for being unconcerned with his own safety, even by the careless standards of polar explorers. Not long before leaving on the expedition, he had written 'to face death is not so very terrifying, for death is still the great adventure. The really trying ordeal is to face the uncertainty of living.'[2]

As he stood on the ice and looked into the drawn faces of his weary men, it was not uncertainty he saw. It was despair.

These were not men lacking nerve. His chief scientist, Harald Sverdrup, was the finest oceanographer of his day and had survived six Arctic winters locked in the ice with Roald Amundsen hoping their boat would drift across the North Pole. It didn't. Electrical engineers Arthur Blumberg and Ralph Shaw had spent decades in the US Navy submarine fleet, serving on the mechanised coffins since before the Great War. Frank Crilley had won the Medal of Honor after making the deepest dive in history to rescue a fellow diver trapped thirty metres below the surface. The radioman, Ray Meyers, had been at his post twenty hours a day and loyally kept silent about the increasingly alarming messages being sent back and forth. Though they knew the mission was dangerous, these and the other men aboard the *Nautilus* had willingly volunteered. Now, one and all, they regretted it.

Eighteen men stood before their leader, shuffling from foot to foot in the cold, the loneliest humans on the planet. Wilkins asked each in turn his opinion. No vote was taken as none was needed. His diary recorded the outcome:

> Without exception, the others in the vessel wanted to immediately turn back; to make no further attempt to go into the ice this year. To do so would be to admit complete failure. As commander of the expedition I ordered the trials to continue . . . I am determined the vessel will go under the ice and that as many experiments as possible will be made.[3]

It was the wrong decision, compounded by an even greater folly to come. Over the following days communications from the *Nautilus* became sporadic. On 31 August 1931 a faint signal, relayed by short-wave operators, flashed across the world. *Nautilus* would soon become the first vessel to dive into the Arctic Ocean. With just the mewing seals as her witness, she trimmed her ballast three degrees by the bow, charged towards the frozen shelf and disappeared from the face of the Earth.

1

—

In the blood

It lies beyond the farming belt,
Wide wastes of scrub and plain,
A blazing desert in the drought,
A lake-land after rain;
To the sky-line sweeps the waving grass,
Or whirls the scorching sand –
A phantom land, a mystic land!
The Never-Never Land.

– Henry Lawson, *The Never-Never Country*

Most Australians are accustomed to believing there is little worthy of note in their brief 220-year history. Against the great currents of world events, the clash of cultures and the rise of empires, Australia's slightly embarrassing origins as a British penal colony seem insignificant. Yet scratch the dusty surface and there are remarkable stories to be found, rich nuggets of human drama so peculiar they scarcely seem credible.

It was a down-on-his-luck American who first noticed the unexpected exuberance of Australian history. Mark Twain, broke and forced to make a lecture tour to restore his finances, travelled widely in Australia in 1895 and later wrote that Australia's history:

> . . . is so curious and strange that it is itself the chiefest novelty the country has to offer . . . It does not read like history, but like the most beautiful lies; and all of a fresh new sort, no mouldy old ones.

It is full of surprises and adventures, and incongruities, and contradictions and incredibilities; but they are all true, they all happened.

One of the events that got Twain thinking about the odd place he had landed in was the annual gathering in Adelaide celebrating the beginnings of the colony of South Australia. Held in high antipodean summer in the sleepy days between Christmas and New Year, most invitees found it a bit of a chore. Nevertheless, they abandoned the leftover plum cake and headed long distances to the capital for a formal luncheon with the mayor and governor. Among those pioneers present on 28 December 1895 was a sheep farmer, Harry Wilkins, rising sixty years with the wind-battered face and dark tanned hands of a man who had spent his life outdoors. His journey had taken a full day by horse and rail through the barren plains of scrub and red dirt that threatened to overrun the modest hills guarding the colony's only city. Usually he made the effort because he ranked as an honoured guest. By some accounts, Harry was the first-born son of South Australia.

Twain found the luncheon 'a stirring spectacle; stirring in more ways than one for it was amazingly funny, and at the same time deeply pathetic; for they had seen so much, those time-worn veterans and had suffered so much and had built so strongly and well'. [1]

It's likely Twain spoke with Harry Wilkins that day, and heard him tell in measured tones a story or two about the early days of the colony. We don't know if he met the youngest of Harry's thirteen children, seven-year-old George Hubert, who'd come along for what was quite likely his first trip to the city. But we can be sure that George remained proud of his father's unique place in the history of the State, because for the rest of his life he kept the faded newspaper clipping that reported the luncheon and Twain's wry observations of it.

From its inception South Australia was to be a model colony and, for a British possession, one conceived with unusually noble aims. On a crushingly hot summer's day in 1836, on the shores of the Southern Ocean, the new governor, Captain John Hindmarsh, read the proclamation establishing the Province of South Australia.

There were barely 200 settlers gathered there under the shade of strange trees amid the shrill calls of outlandish birds, standing on the edge of a distant world with little more than hope to guide them. As Governor Hindmarsh moved among the assembly, he would have spared a private word with William Wilkins and his heavily pregnant wife, Mary. The couple and their two boys had arrived some weeks earlier aboard the little brig *Emma*, one of the nine ships that had sailed from England that year as part of a grand experiment in social engineering. The professions of their carefully selected fellow passengers reflected the needs of the new settlement: carpenter, wheelwright, labourer, bricklayer, boat-builder, accountant.

Mary Wilkins had staggered ashore after five months and eleven days at sea, weakened by her confinement, the poor food and unspeakable discomforts of the fearsome crossing. She was from a farming family in Somerset, while William had come from a line of London innkeepers descended from Huguenot refugees. Like most of the settlers, William and Mary were 'respectable paupers' who, with youth and suitable references, could secure free passage on the lower decks. Their purpose was to help populate the settlement and Harry Wilkins, born just three days after the proclamation ceremony, seems likely to have been the first surviving settler child; in any case, that was the family legend. Beyond this, little is known of the couple's origins, as their papers were lost in a fire that swept through the settler tents soon after they came ashore.[2]

The Wilkins family arrived with a one-way passage and were now cast adrift, no past to return to and only the slightest hold on the vast forbidding land about them. Together with the other settlers, whose average age was just nineteen, they would build a new nation or perish trying.[3]

The Act of the British Parliament establishing South Australia is a curious document, equal parts business plan and colonial adventure. The colony was planned as a profit-making venture that might become a beacon for similar enterprises throughout the Empire. It was the only Australian colony created by parliamentary law, and optimistically included a requirement that it be developed at no cost to the 'Mother Country'. The Act established an emigration fund (to be repaid from future earnings) to assist wives and children to travel with their husbands, and, most unusually, it forbade convict transportation.

3

Britain, with its crowded cities and impoverished countryside, was in social tumult and had little interest in Australia apart from its convenience as a repository for the surplus inmates of gaols and rotting prison hulks. It was nearly fifty years since the first convicts had been transported to Botany Bay, and the sum of British settlement since then comprised little more than a handful of penal colonies on the coast and some miserable prison islands.

The colony of South Australia was therefore something quite different both in origin and intent. It began as an entrepreneurial initiative based on the untried principles of Edward Gibbon Wakefield, surely the most colourful rogue ever to call himself an economist. Wakefield was better known to the British public as a mesmerising cad who had abducted a girl of means for the purposes of securing her family's wealth and political connections.

Wakefield found his victim at Mrs Daulby's Seminary for the Daughters of Gentlefolk near Liverpool. Ellen Turner was an attractive fifteen-year-old, the daughter of a Cheshire banker and mill owner, and Wakefield devised a complicated stratagem to trick her into eloping with him. Chased around the country and across the Channel by Ellen's vengeful father and uncles, the couple was eventually apprehended on the pier at Calais and the marriage annulled by a special Act of parliament. Wakefield stood trial for felonious abduction and unlawful marriage. As described at the time in the remarkable account of notorious crimes, the *Newgate Calendar or Malefactor's Bloody Register*,[4] the trial was a sensation attended daily by fainting ladies and a series of outlandish witnesses.

Wakefield was sentenced to three years' imprisonment at Newgate Gaol, on the site of what is today London's Central Criminal Court. There, surrounded by convicts bound for Botany Bay, he had ample opportunity to consider the ills of penal settlement. Wakefield wrote a series of fictitious letters, as if sent from the evil colony of Sydney, and devised a radical social experiment which he outlined in '*A Proposed National Society, for the Cure and Prevention of Pauperism, by Means of Systematic Colonisation*'. In short it was a plan to select the most capable of the poor, sell them cheap land in the new colony and build a model society. 'The object,' he wrote, 'is not to place a scattered and half-barbarous colony on the coast of New Holland, but to establish a wealthy civilised society.'[5]

Thus, in a peculiar mixture of philanthropy, scandal and commerce, the Colonisation Commission for South Australia was born. Its chairman was the brilliant economist Robert Torrens, whose interest in colonies went well beyond the theoretical.[6] He believed the commission could build on Wakefield's theories, and proclaimed that South Australia would become the greatest rice and wool growing country of the world, and that its favourable climate could produce opium for the China trade. The opium was never tried, the rice failed, but the wool eventually did quite well.[7]

Torrens hyped the project like a burlesque barker, extolling the advantages of the far colony that he had never seen. Beyond a few cautious forays inland, the immense interior of Australia was virtually unknown to all but its native inhabitants, who were themselves equally mysterious to the early European visitors. Yet in that first year of 1836 some 546 emigrants rolled the dice on a new life, driven not by religious persecution or corrupt courts, but the simple desire to escape poverty – Australia's first economic refugees. Aboard frail ships like the little schooner *John Pirie*, which weighed barely 100 tonnes, they made the dreadful passage. Prey to pirates and often wracked by disease, these ships were undertaking the longest sea journey on Earth.

William and Mary Wilkins were taken by the ideas of the philandering Wakefield and the promised paradise of Torrens. But they would be soon disabused of any thoughts of a comfortable crossing from their old world to the new. Early accounts of the ship journey describe the suffocating heat below decks, vile food, stagnant drinking water and frequent storms from which even hardened sailors suffered.

At journey's end they found Port Misery, presumably named after the bleak tidal mudflats and mangrove swamps they had to wade through to reach dry land. Eventually it would become the port of Adelaide, named after the consort of King William IV. To the 300 native Kaurna people, the area where Adelaide stands was called Tandanya, which means 'the place of the red kangaroo'. Their reward for peacefully welcoming the Europeans was complete subjugation followed by a devastating outbreak of smallpox.[8] That William and Mary Wilkins, their two boys and unborn son all survived the journey and the first year seems, in retrospect, almost miraculous.

William Wilkins must have saved what money he arrived with from the early fire as he soon established the first hotel in the colony – a profitable business in a town that would grow to a city of more than 15 000 in just five years. He was twenty-nine and not about to waste the time he had left. A second hotel followed, and another, and at his own expense he built a slaughter yard and a bridge across the Torrens River. There were prosperous years but the impoverished administration never made good its promise to repay him for his building work, which caused William financial difficulties. He eventually died a frustrated man just ten years after his arrival. Left with six children, Mary remarried and continued to run the one remaining tavern.

Harry Wilkins was eager to make his own way and at just sixteen was drawn, like many others, to the newly discovered goldfields in Victoria. For three years, he moved about the wild, overcrowded goldfields where 70 000 hopeful 'diggers' had flocked from every corner of the Earth. They represented nearly one-third of the entire population of the colony of Victoria, distorting its economy and threatening its fragile government. The youngster had thrown himself into a wild frontier of greed and grog.

As a publican's son, Harry Wilkins would have been well aware of the influence of alcohol on the goldfields, and this may go some way to explaining his later conversion to a severe Methodist wowserism,[9] so strict that later he would not allow his musically talented son to play a piano.

He returned home wiser if not richer, to take up work as a drover, evidently saving enough money and displaying sufficient prospects to impress the proprietor of the successful Victor Harbour Guest House, who agreed to a marriage with his daughter, Louisa Smith. For four years the young couple ran the public house which still stands at the mouth of Australia's longest river, the Murray. And there beneath its corrugated iron roof and the smell of stale beer, they planned their escape.

Drawn to the outdoor life, Harry was keen to explore the lands then opening beyond the hills above Adelaide. The family loaded a bullock cart and pushed its way 200 kilometres inland, through the green hills of the Clare Valley already carrying the first vineyards, along the road that stopped at the copper town of Burra, to the tanned plains spread beneath the colony's only real mountain.

Mt Bryan is just tall enough to catch a sprinkling of snow in a harsh winter, but for the most part is barren, scarred on its sides by unsuccessful attempts at copper mining. Mt Bryan East, where the Wilkins family settled, was never a township. It was surveyed and laid out, but very few of the allotments were ever taken up. Those who did venture here were encouraged by the findings of the Deputy Surveyor General of the new colony, a young Liverpool immigrant, George Woodroffe Goyder, who in 1857 had reported with some amazement that dry lakebeds were full of fresh water and that the land was fertile. His published comments sparked tremendous interest and led to a rush for lease applications as pioneers set off to find this Promised Land. They knew nothing of the narrow margin that separated the chance of success from the certainty of disaster in Australia's capricious and brutal interior.

Among those joining Harry and Louisa Wilkins on the journey north was a young German immigrant, August Wilhelm Pohlner, and his elder sister, Pauline. The Pohlners also moved beyond the rail head at Burra, but by chance stopped a little way south of Mt Bryan. There August founded a pastoral farm, Tooralie, and it stands today still run by his descendants. Harry Wilkins went a little further on, just a few kilometres, yet all that remains of his years of struggle are ruins. Between the two farms, invisible to the eye, is a barrier as real as any wall: Goyder's Line. Still marked on some maps of South Australia, it divided the hopeless farmlands from the merely heartbreaking.

The first great drought came in 1863, quickly wiping out the first wave of pastoralists. As if to atone for his earlier optimism, Goyder returned to traverse on horseback a 5000-kilometre frontier, accurately measuring the rainfall patterns that delineated the southern boundary of the inhospitable and drought-ridden saltbush country. Below the line, rainfall exceeded 250 millimetres annually, making it suitable for farming, but above it the land could only sustain scattered pastoral use, and even then not reliably. This barrier separated Harry Wilkins from August Pohlner, and it meant that on average he could expect less than two-thirds the rainfall of his neighbour. In such marginal conditions, the distance between them, a half-hour trot on horseback, could be the difference between life and death.

The Wilkins' family Bible, received as a wedding present, records the barest details of their life together, but each date holds a story of their struggles. Their first child is entered without a name, presumably stillborn. Their second child, also named Harry, would die before his first birthday. In all, Harry and Louisa would suffer the pain of burying five of their thirteen children in this lonely new land. The nearest settlement was the little township of Hallett, nearly 20 kilometres away along a dusty track that still hasn't been sealed. It once had a rail station that connected the region to civilisation, but that was closed many years ago. Today there are a few dozen people living there and only its position astride the interior highway connecting Adelaide to Sydney seems to prevent it being blown off the map altogether. But if Hallett is unimpressive, at least it still exists – Mt Bryan East is a land of ghosts, travelling backwards in time. The settler farmers who followed Harry and Louisa Wilkins walked off the land decades ago, leaving behind their homes, some extensive with wide verandahs and parlours, others little more than a room and a fireplace. It's so isolated even the vandals haven't bothered to trouble it, and the empty homesteads stand much as they did when abandoned, windows open and gates ajar. Photos of the little church and schoolhouse from the 1940s show telegraph poles connecting the remaining community, but today even the poles are gone. The church is abandoned and roofless, the schoolhouse an overnight stop for intrepid bushwalkers. Campers are wise to use it as a marker – take a wrong turn out here and you could be lost for days.

The ruined stone cottage at Netfield also stood forgotten for more than a century until recently an effort was made to restore it to mark the birthplace of Harry's last-born child. There's a roof on it now, and a carpark built in the Australian tradition: rather larger than necessary. The simple cottage is set square to the prevailing winds and from its windows the view falls across a vacant plain to the distant low hills marking the edge of pastoral land. Beyond this lies red dirt and rock unbroken for thousands of kilometres until it eventually becomes indistinguishable from the Simpson Desert. Only the polar regions are emptier, so perhaps it is not, after all, such an unlikely place to have thrown up one of the greatest polar explorers of all time. Like an Arctic journey, the savage climate demands that anyone crossing here has their wits about them, and no one ever accused George Hubert Wilkins of being dim. Foolhardy perhaps, but never foolish.

The contemporary records reveal a few details of his early life. Hallett cemetery holds the grave of his sister who died when he was just five, newspapers tell of local cricket matches and land dealings, the names of those who came to teach in the schoolhouse, even the dramatic day when Harry Wilkins drove his trap over a road cutting, throwing six of his children roughly into the dirt. But more revealing is what is not there. Among Harry and Louisa's thirteen children only their last-born, George Hubert, has no birth certificate. It is as if he came from nowhere, and was certainly a surprise to a mother just turned fifty and a father of fifty-two.[10]

As a small child George accompanied his father and unmarried brothers as they tended the great flocks of sheep, hunting kangaroos and the dingoes that could decimate a herd given the chance. He learned skills that would serve him well on his later explorations, and became an accomplished rider and marksman. The men of the district would occasionally play a rough game of bush polo, chasing bandicoots and wallabies using one stirrup swung like a polo mallet. It took great ability to avoid the hazards of fences, rabbit holes and charging dogs. Men were often injured, or worse. George's uncle was killed in such a game, thrown from his horse and crushed against a fence post.

George also travelled with his father on visits to the temporary camps of local Aboriginal tribes. In its early history South Australia had a better record than the rest of the colonies in its dealings with Australia's original inhabitants, but the prevailing attitude was still, at best, one of paternalism. Perhaps, given his Methodist zeal, Harry Wilkins was out fishing for souls, but his son took a particular interest in Aboriginal rituals and society, and especially their mysticism. Almost unheard of for a white boy, he would camp out and hunt with his Aboriginal friends, and became fascinated by their intimate understanding of the natural world and connection with the spiritual realm beyond. He would share their food of wallabies, possums and snakes – even the sleek yellow grubs they dug from beneath the bark of acacia trees – and watch their rituals of dance and ceremony. 'Adventure enough for most boys at an age of 10 to 13,' he would later recall, 'but to me it was the routine of my existence.'[11]

Such empathy with Indigenous people stimulated his own curiosity about nature and man's place in it, and would later save his life in the Arctic. Certainly it seemed to leave a more lasting mark than the aggressive evangelism of Rev. WA Dunn at the Mt Bryan East Bible Christian Chapel. On Sundays the district crowded into the tiny church to receive Wesleyan sermons exhorting the congregation to 'spread Scriptural holiness over the land'. On hot days the doors were left open and the hymns would waft out across the empty fields, mingling with the shrill chorus of galahs that filled the gum trees planted for shade. Young George sang in the choir and displayed some musical talent, but his parents were not encouraging. Anything not related directly to the life of farming or the service of God was frowned upon as frivolous. He kept his talent to himself, but for the rest of his life would be a more than useful musician and even took a small desk organ on his polar adventures.

From his earliest years he tended towards independence of action and thought. 'I was inclined to grow up wilful, but never wild,' he wrote, 'preferring the company of my dogs and ponies to that of men and even at an early age spent many hours alone in the saddle, far from human habitation.' He was gaining the self-reliance that was the defining trait of all the great explorers: 'No doubt these things helped to build up a character which in time of trouble and distress have pulled me through.'

Each day George would walk nine kilometres to the little school-house and back. It had one room for learning and a simple attached bedroom and kitchen for the teacher, who would supervise all the district children, from six to sixteen. At one time the teacher actually lived with the Wilkins family at Netfield, paying special attention to the bright child who could already read and write by the age of five. George would have been a pleasure to teach – he was keen to know everything and was a voracious reader who could commit large texts to memory. He was once seen to hold a book with one hand and a plough with the other while working the fields. By the time he was a teenager he had read Benjamin Franklin for the physical world, Darwin for the natural and Tom Paine for the spiritual. Perhaps Paine's *Age of Reason* was a secret gift from his admiring teacher, for its dismissal of the Bible and denunciation of the church would have been otherwise unwelcome in a Methodist home. Whatever the case, George's formal education was about to be interrupted.

Of all Australia's periodic dry spells, none was more catastrophic than the 'Federation drought' of 1901. Rivers dried up and half the entire stock of sheep and cattle perished. In the cities, they feared the taps might stop flowing, and just weeks after it had been celebrating nationhood, the government declared a day of 'humiliation and prayer'. God turned a deaf ear.

At Mt Bryan East, where the dry came earlier and hit harder, the settler farmers hung grimly to the edge of the barren plains that seemed eager to be rid of them. Their stock grew progressively thinner and weaker, bleating and moaning through the scorched days and sweltering nights, the soil turned to dust by their desperate pawing for roots. Back then, before the age of bulldozers, the bodies were left to rot where they fell. Death on this scale, with the terrible stench of rotting carcasses and the plague of flies that followed, left a deep impression on young George. In later life he referred to these years of misery as 'the most depressing of any that I have experienced. Instead of spending my days at high school or college as I hoped, I was doomed to herd the starving animals and to rescue them from the mud of the waterholes. But they died in spite of all we could do. I can still shudder at the thought of these conditions . . . It was a terrible thing for an impressionable child to experience.'[12]

The devastation was so total that farmers could not *give* their stock away. At the Burra Stockyards an owner offered to give a friend 600 ewes, but the offer was refused. Soon it wasn't just the animals that were starving and Wilkins witnessed dreadful scenes that he could vividly recall more than forty years later: 'The starving animals gnawing bark from the trees, pinched, lean settlers with hollow cheeks and lack lustre eyes, sun bleached hair and gnarled hands, clothes saturated with the stench of the dead are still nightmares to me and it was such sights and the ruin of my family that gave me, even as a boy, much serious food for thought.'

Eventually the rains returned and Netfield slowly recovered from disaster. As his older siblings left to start out on their own, George remained to look after his ageing parents. By day his was a solitary life, mustering the animals in the far paddocks with just his dog and horse for company. By night it was book and Bible reading. Harry Wilkins spoke little; his silence was the sound of disappointment. Those years of struggle left scars on them all, but not without some benefit for the young boy. It taught him both humility in the face of nature and a determination to do something about it. He'd witnessed the consequences of our ignorance of the weather and he became fascinated with meteorology, and particularly the crude science of forecasting:

> I had already learned the rudiments of geography, physics, chemistry and astronomy and realized that throughout the world and all life there are natural laws, causes and effects. The stars in the heavens moved according to a plan which can be forecast; the ocean currents have been charted. We had learned the laws of chemicals, which mixed with which and to what degree. We knew from the study of geology that certain natural laws brought about fundamental changes in this earth of ours.
>
> Why should it not be possible to learn of the laws which govern the movement of the atmosphere, the conditions that bring about the seasonal rains and droughts?
>
> Gradually, as I became conscious of the need for weather forecasting, not forecasting from day to day in one locality but forecasting for the world for years in advance, I determined to devote my life to that work. Although necessity compelled me to do many other things, the one thought I have held since I was at the age of thirteen was to solve the weather problem . . . It occurred to me, as it must have to others, that while it might not be possible for man, with his limitations, to control the weather, it might be possible to learn something of its movements. With foreknowledge and forethought, one might then be able to save the dumb animals from suffering and the pioneering families from destitution.[13]

For a young man with little formal education living in the remote centre of an isolated continent it was, to say the least, an ambitious idea. But he lived in exciting times where even this preposterous suggestion might seem possible.

The dawn of the twentieth century was a period of sudden change when the old order of things was being overturned. When she came to the throne just six months after the proclamation of South Australia, Queen Victoria had no better way of communicating with her Empire than Julius Caesar – a fast horse and sailing ship. Yet by the end of her reign, swift steamers plied the oceans and a thin telegraph line snaked across the world. The theories of Darwin, Huxley and Nietzsche were revolutionising people's understanding of the world, and new technologies such as the aeroplane and the cinema were changing their vision of it. Even in Australia, the effects were being felt. Just thirty-five years after it was founded, Adelaide was a substantial city and South Australia launched an extraordinarily ambitious plan to link Australia with the outside world by telegraph. More than 36 000 telegraph poles were raised over a 3000-kilometre course to the north coast, and from there to the international line at Java. Some of Darwin's most important ideas crystallised when he came upon strange native creatures while visiting the hinterland of Sydney. And even before the Wright brothers, an Australian astronomer, Lawrence Hargreaves, had won fame by designing the first radial engine and box kites that would become the basic design of the earliest aeroplanes. Within months of the Lumière brothers' first cinema screenings, films were being made and exhibited in Australia. Even at Mt Bryan East, it must have seemed to an ambitious, bright boy that the world was within reach. George Wilkins would soon become one of the pioneers of both aviation and moving pictures, but they were only tools in pursuit of his great, lifelong passion to solve the mysteries of weather. While he would follow others in exploration, meteorology was the one field he could claim as his own.

2
—
True adventure thrills

Each incident may be verified from official records or men still living.[1]
— Hubert Wilkins' autobiographical notes

There's no one left to speak to us of their days of discovery and toil with Sir Hubert Wilkins but a little diligent searching will turn up the records of his life in libraries and archives all over the world. The official story can be gleaned from hundreds of reports and articles, photographs, a few scientific papers and even the occasional secret government memo. His name is to be found on polar maps and in the dusty shelves of museums that hold the specimens he discovered. As he predicted, they confirm the details of dates, places and events that comprised his crowded life. The most important collection – his own papers – have ended up in a corner of the vast campus of Ohio State University. There, on a back road surrounded by open fields, is a hangar-sized building that holds the archives of the Byrd Polar Research Center, North America's premier repository of all things frosty. Inside it takes a forklift truck to reach the forty rarely opened boxes of Wilkins' personal documents and keepsakes. Among the medallions and rusting film cans, the old postcards and the tax returns, are the yellowing papers that tell in his own words an amazing life.

Wilkins never finished an autobiography, though the boxes hold a few false starts. As he wrote in the introduction to one attempt, 'There are so many things that might be done and so many opportunities to do them, that it is difficult to find time even to write a summary.'[2] His was a life so full of incident that the man himself struggled to remember it all. 'Rising through the mist of years are memories thrilling and enthralling. Their very dimness ... enforces concentration ...'

By his son's account, Harry Wilkins was eventually defeated by the long and unequal struggle with the weather. On the eve of his seventieth birthday in 1905, Harry gave up the farm, selling the 400 hectares at Mt Bryan East to clear his debts. He and Louisa had just enough left to buy a modest cottage in the suburbs of Adelaide and here they kept a close eye on their youngest boy. George's teenage days were filled with work, schooling and church going.

There wasn't enough money for him to resume his studies without working too, so he was apprenticed to a firm of electrical engineers and took night classes. For a while he was enrolled at the Conservatorium of Music and also took practical courses at the South Australian School of Mines. By day he was learning the workings of steam and combustion engines, working a lathe and pounding a blacksmith's hammer. By night it was science, mathematics and technical drawing. He was a capable student, but for unexplained reasons he never sat for his final exams. Perhaps the world was too full of possibilities to hold him in a classroom. On the maps of the world there were still vast regions at top and bottom where an adventurous lad could leave his mark. In Europe, the United States, Australia and Japan, ships were filling up with eager young volunteers bound for these blank spaces. Polar exploration was the perfect science for enthusiastic amateurs because it dealt with unknowns.

So it was with a mixture of naïvety, foresight and youthful bravado that he mapped his life's mission:

> I laid out in my mind a plan of action, covering at least forty years. I would travel and study and work in out-of-the-way places of the world for at least twenty years, then spend the next twenty making use of the information gained to build up a comprehensive international weather service that would adequately include the polar regions. I was not inclined to devote my time to local meteorological work . . . there were many engaged in that, but few apparently who were looking at the subject from a global view.[3]

His plans were now settled, but all he had were big dreams and a talent for fixing things. He needed the chance to get started, and it didn't take long to appear. Adelaide, being utterly flat and laid out in a grid, was the perfect place for Australia's first horse-drawn trams, and it had many kilometres of shiny track awaiting the electric cars imported from California in 1908. At last you could see down North Terrace without a cloud of dust, and the whole town was mad for electricity.

Wilkins was soon busy laying wiring all over town, and one day, while installing new lights in an Adelaide theatre, he was approached by a man asking for help with a faulty generator. He agreed to take a look and walked over to a tent where one of the city's first motion picture shows was being screened. As he stepped inside the canvas, his life changed.

In no time at all he had the sputtering diesel motor working and he began asking questions about the picture projector. The operator took the cover off and Wilkins was introduced to the dancing shadows of motion pictures. He was fascinated, not so much by the crude apparatus, but by the possibilities it offered. The cinema eye could travel anywhere, and could bring back to audiences a world which they could otherwise never experience. He instinctively knew that these spools of spinning acetate were the beginnings of something extraordinary, and he was determined to be part of it.

The tent-cinema operators welcomed a lad with his skills and enthusiasm, and offered to take him on their travelling shows around the country towns of eastern Australia. He was soon proficient in all aspects of the business, not only with the projector but with taking motion pictures. The performances were more Vaudeville than cinema as we know it today, and the short film subjects were mixed with a song and dance act in which he occasionally performed. After eighteen months on tour he returned home, certain the camera could be his ticket to the world.

Adelaide, the city his grandfather had helped found, seemed awfully small and insignificant. He was impatient to get to Sydney, the centre of Australia's nascent film industry. Though he could well afford a ticket, young Wilkins typically decided on a more exciting way of travelling. Why pay for his passage when he could just as easily stow away? Down on the docks at Port Adelaide, where his pregnant grandmother had staggered ashore after her long journey from Britain, were any number of steamers being loaded with wool.

He waited until the night watchman left the rail of one ship and slipped silently up the gangplank, through the first open door he found – and straight into the arms of the second engineer:

> 'Where are you off to young fellow?' he asked, and in my fear I blurted out 'I wish to stow away to Sydney.' He was a kindly Scotchman, and with a broad sympathetic smile he calmed my nerves and I could not help but see the humour of the situation. He opened a door and shoving me inside told me to wait there until I was found.[4]

He was found and thrashed by the bosun, then put to work, and plenty of it, until some days later put over the side at Sydney with a warning not to try such a stunt again.

Wilkins had arrived in Sydney at an extraordinary moment when for a short time Australia led the world in the production of long silent films – more than sixty features were shot in 1911 alone – and the young cameraman was soon busy rushing from one production to the next. This was rough and ready cinema, where both the actors and the crews were making it up as they went along. As Wilkins wryly noted, the films were often 'unintentionally funny melodramas and sobering comedies because of the ignorance of the cameraman and the actors in light values, colour tones, perspective and make-up.'

He kept an irregular account of these hectic months in a little brown suede pocket diary.[5] There is no entry at all for January 1911, and then only sporadic scrawls through the rest of the Australian summer. The neat student handwriting of just three years before has been over-whelmed and in its place is the first sign of the utilitarian, often illegible script which a graphologist would later charitably describe as 'intuitive'. The hand, like the man, was in a hurry:

> We occupied a studio in North Sydney and sometimes visited country stations. We photographed race meetings and worked the scenes into our pictures. We pursued made-up smugglers and bandits in motor boats through Sydney Harbour and one day we dashed beneath the bow of H.M.S. Encounter, madly firing at the fleeing motor boat, the harbour police joined in and the unrehearsed scene that followed was the most realistic acting in the film, for I had kept my camera moving throughout the piece.[6]

Just as he hoped, the camera was opening the doors to adventure. Sometime in 1911 he met a director of the British arm of the famous Gaumont Studios. This was almost certainly Alfred Bromhead, then touring the world opening new branches of the company. With his younger brother Reginald, he'd built a production powerhouse making topical items as well as fiction films which was already bigger than its French parent. Gaumont was locked in cutthroat competition with its great rival Pathé, producing weekly newsreels of the great events of the day. Camera operators were racing one another to be first with the pictures of coronations, wars and social struggles, and by 1912 their films were being updated in cinemas twice a week. Young Wilkins, with his enthusiasm and impressive abilities, was just the type for such a job, and the Gaumont man offered him work in London as soon as he could get there.

What happened next is guesswork, as Wilkins left two conflicting accounts of his passage to England. In the more sedate retelling, he took a leisurely tour through the Orient in the company of an Italian count who later guided him through the salons and galleries of Naples and Florence. This was followed by a month of work filming the towns and desert of North Africa for a travelogue 'of striking scenes that pleased the directors of the Cinematograph Company'. All interesting enough for a young man on his first overseas trip, but rather dull compared to the alternative.

By the racier account, written in the form of an autobiographical radio series he titled *True Adventure Thrills*, Wilkins became involved in a scheme to smuggle weapons into Tunis. At the time, Italy was implicated in a dirty little war in neighbouring Libya, and her agents took part in many intrigues with local tribes keen to make money from the chaos. Wilkins was befriended by a dubious Italian noble who led him into unsavoury company. He was drugged unconscious only to awake draped across a camel, part of a caravan moving across the desert. Together with the Italian gun-runner, he was kidnapped for ransom – a rather pointless crime given that he had no money or connections.

The caravan moved through the desert from waterhole to oasis, and because there was nowhere for him to run Wilkins' abductors didn't keep too close an eye on their human cargo. He was thin and deeply sunburned, and with a fluffy beard hidden behind a burnoose could pass as a local if the inspection were not too close. The grime didn't disguise his charm, and he managed to strike a friendship with a pretty young Arab girl keen to practise her French on him. The conversation must have been limited, for Wilkins was no great linguist, but little by little he gained her confidence, and out of pity or love she agreed to help him escape. The girl delivered a local costume for disguise and described a plan to smuggle him into a pack-load bundle which would be put aboard a camel caravan heading north.

As good as her word, the girl arrived at dawn and they made for the outskirts of the camp. There, amid a jumble of packs and snorting beasts, was the loosened bundle waiting for its live cargo. He climbed in and she tightened the carpets around him. 'There had been no time for more than a handclasp with the girl,' he wrote, 'and I was beginning to wish that I could stay and be with her, but Moslem custom would not have permitted that.'[7]

It was several days before he was able to escape to freedom, moving alone at night, accepting scraps of food from wandering herdsmen, until eventually he found his way back to Biskra, an oasis town in the Sahara, and from there, eventually, to safety.

What are we to make of this extraordinary story, like something from the Arabian Nights? In a very public life of fifty years it is the one occasion when he has left conflicting versions of his many adventures, making us wonder what to believe. We may doubt it because it seems barely credible, yet white slavery along the Barbary Coast had been common for 300 years or more. Only a few years before Wilkins' escapade, a sabre-rattling Teddy Roosevelt had sent American gunboats to Morocco demanding the release of a kidnapped businessman and his son-in-law. But perhaps there is a simpler explanation for the conflicting stories. Given all the hair-raising adventures he lived through, Wilkins' confusion may have been nothing more than a trick of memory. He certainly seems to have considered the story was true; in fact, if anything, for him it wasn't exciting *enough*. In an aside to his editor he wrote in *Thrills*: 'This story, I realise, has got to be pepped up – more incidents, conversations, more drama, and a climax. But I am struck there, because it is difficult for me to get away from the facts . . .'

When he eventually made his way to London, Gaumont soon had him back on a boat again. He'd left Australia wanting to see the world, and they granted his wish. In those first eighteen months after leaving Sydney he visited twenty-seven countries, at a time when most people passed their entire lives in the place they were born. He travelled across the British Isles and Europe, finding the latest exciting pictures for a world hungry for images.[8] From Paris to Brussels and Switzerland, all through Ireland and Scandinavia, he travelled and filmed then rushed to the train once again. Wilkins filmed suffragette demonstrations in London and naval manoeuvres in the North Sea; parades, prize fights and horse races – anything that moved with sufficient speed and novelty.

The newsreel men had to struggle alone with heavy equipment through hostile crowds, face down uncooperative officials, and use lenses that left them no choice but to stand within spitting distance of their hurtling subjects. To heighten the sense of action, objects had to be filmed coming towards the camera rather than moving away from it, which made for close encounters with trains, horses and speedboats. The film stock of the time was barely adequate for anything but the sunniest weather, which made for a lot of wasted film in Britain. A career guide at the time warned that the newsreel reporter 'leads a very strenuous life, and . . . must not be a man who studies his own comfort overmuch . . . Not only is he constantly travelling, a wearing process, but the actual work involves in many cases both difficulties and dangers . . . It is quite an ordinary item in the day's work for a photographer to cover two or three hundred miles by rail, obtain the desired pictures perched on some perilous vantage-ground, and return to headquarters within forty-eight hours.'[9] Despite the dangers and low pay, the job description was just the thing for a certain type of young man keen on a life of derring-do.

The hectic newsreel offices were run by ex-newspapermen who exhorted the young cameramen and reporters to be quick, cheap and, above all, smart. As one guide for aspiring cameramen put it, the Golden Rule was to 'think, and think hard, how you can make the best picture. Nothing but the very best is good enough. There is plenty of room at the top of your profession, but you will not get there by standing about or just grinding away. Brain work is ultimately the only way to big money. And the money is there waiting for you.'[10]

By these standards, Wilkins' brain was obviously working furiously. At a time when the typical wage for a newsreel man was less than £3 a week, Gaumont put him on a two-year contract for the unheard of salary of £2000.[11] He filmed battleships and submarines, and one day, on an open field in London's distant suburbs, he witnessed the beginnings of a remarkable new technology that would once more change his life.

Hendon was the birthplace of British aviation. In 80 hectares of rolling paddocks Britain's leading aviator, the former car salesman Claude Grahame-White, built the city's first aerodrome and flying school. It rapidly became the biggest show in town, and on weekend afternoons in 1912 it was not uncommon for 50 000 people to head out to Hendon to watch the flimsy aeroplanes take to the skies. To the thump of military bands, the early pilots raced in speed handicaps and point-to-point trials. If you were game, for two guineas they'd carry you aloft on a two-lap circuit of the field, and for a fiver you could take a trip off the aerodrome to Edgeware or the Welsh Harp. Though it was only mentioned in whispers, the crowds also came to see the crashes. Six pilots were killed that year, and many others seriously injured.[12]

In 1909 Grahame-White had become the first Englishman to gain an aviator's certificate; three years later he was the most famous man in the country after the newly crowned King George V. Handsome, energetic, and rich from his prize-winning flights and the busy turnstiles at Hendon, the dashing aviator was a favourite subject for the newsreel men. Wilkins was sent to film one of these early aerial derbies and soon found himself in conversation with a tall man who apparently had something to do with the field:

> Colonial-like and country bred I did not hesitate to open a conversation . . . I volunteered the information that I had been told by several that while White was one of the foremost pilots of the day he knew it too well and was inclined to high-hat some of his earlier acquaintances.[13]

There was a slight pause in the conversation and Wilkins added that he had never met Grahame-White and would like him pointed out. 'Much to my embarrassment the man turned to me and with a smile said, "Why that's who I am."'

Fortunately the famous pilot was not lacking a sense of humour. He was, after all, the man who once dropped in to visit the President of the

United States by landing his plane on the White House lawn. Evidently amused by the brash Australian, he agreed to take him up in one of his own designs that same afternoon.

That first flight was little more than a spin around the paddocks, over and done in minutes, but it was enough to alter the course of a man's life. The engine roared and the rear lifted as the primitive plane hurtled down the field, bouncing wildly on the grass strip. As the wind rushed over the wings, the struts sang like cicadas and the whole structure quivered – a living, breathing thing. Wilkins was stunned by that first, unsettling view of the tilting horizon, as if the whole world had shifted on its axis. As the ground fell away the generations of Earth-bound existence went with it and he was swept into a new age. His heart was pumping and both fists gripped the sides, but fear soon gave way to the sheer delirious exhilaration of human flight. He knew immediately that this was the way to explore the world.

Wilkins began flying lessons, though with no particular aim in mind beyond spending as much time in the air as he could manage. Just as he had never sat those final school exams, he became a proficient flyer and expert navigator yet never sat for his pilot's licence – meaning one of history's most decorated flyers should never have had his hand on a joystick. Presumably no authority ever thought to ask.

He went up with most of the colourful early British aviators, such as Gustav Hamel and Benny Hucks: men who would enjoy brief and thrilling careers before crashing in a pile of tangled wires and broken bones.[14] One he met and liked immediately was Commander J Cyril Porte. Diagnosed with tuberculosis, Porte figured he had nothing to lose and flew accordingly. His disdain for sensible precautions came close to ending Wilkins' flying career just as it began.

The aeroplanes at Hendon in those early years were primitive designs, mostly box-kite models barely evolved from the Wright brothers' Flyer. Peculiar contraptions of canvas and wood, they resembled oversized insects; in fact, an early design was called the 'Grasshopper' (though it never actually managed to fly). It was the French who made them a thing of beauty, with graceful monoplanes streamlined and purposeful, rising from the ground more like birds than machines. But none were more elegant than those made for the rich Belgian silk merchant Armand Deperdussin.[15]

Deperdussin knew nothing about aircraft construction, but he predicted there was money to be made in aeroplanes and was canny enough to hire the most brilliant designer of the day, Louis Béchereau. One stunning model after another poured off the young designer's drawing table, all streamlined and revolutionary in their construction. Difficult to handle and deadly in inexperienced hands, they were the fastest aircraft of the pre-war years and highly sought after by a certain type of pilot.

The Deperdussin suited Porte's carefree fatalism and he was the first to bring one to Hendon. It was a high-winged monoplane made of tulip wood and ash, with slim wings braced by a skein of wires running through two king posts forward of the cockpit. In profile it had a long slender waist that made it appear rather like a young woman bound tight inside her corset. 'A frail parasol type thing,' thought Wilkins, 'that looked as if it might fall to pieces in the air.'[16]

Fragile or not, Porte believed her underpowered and was in the process of installing a 100-horsepower Anzani engine when he and Wilkins got talking. The cameraman was keen to take the first moving pictures from the air, and Porte agreed to take him up. There was one problem, however: the Deperdussin was a single-seater. Wilkins had to strap his camera to the bracing wires and climb astride the fuselage like a rodeo rider, with his nose behind the trailing edge of the propeller. Any movement forward and he would be cut to pieces – and send them both tumbling to the ground.

On a cold morning, the ground white with frost, they rolled the machine out of its hangar. The Anzani motor made a fearsome din as its fan of cylinders revved hard, threatening to wrench itself free of its mount. The aircraft was shaking as Wilkins climbed on top and Porte rather alarmingly suggested it might be necessary to wriggle backwards and forwards to balance everything. 'I don't like to chance it,' shouted Porte. 'She has too much power and not enough ballast. I don't know where to put the weight to keep her on an even keel.'

'That's all right!' screamed Wilkins over the roaring engine. 'I'll get up on the fuselage and can move back and forth if necessary.'[17]

He straddled the plane like a horse, his nose just centimetres from the propeller and Porte shouted and asked if he was ready. 'I opened my mouth to say yes and he shoved the throttle forward,' remembered Wilkins. The engine roared and he almost choked on the great gust of wind from the prop as the machine bounded over the ground. Before he could grab a breath, the plane was in the air.

'The machine, unbalanced, unstable in every direction, was twisting and turning in a crazy manner. It dipped and flipped and reared, fell off on one side and then on the other, in fact behaved like a barnyard fowl flying in a gale.'

Somehow he managed to ride the bucking craft, drawing blood from his fingers as he gripped the wires. Porte looped the aerodrome and, as fast as he could manage, brought her down to a bumpy landing. 'We had been in the air only a few minutes but time enough for me to become almost completely numb with fear and cold,' recalled Wilkins.

Porte was dripping with sweat and shaking with fear. 'We both realised that it was only a miracle that had brought us down alive, in spite of Porte being one of the greatest of the pioneer pilots.'

It was not long before Wilkins' fascination with two of humanity's finest technological achievements, cinema and aviation, would combine with that other great twentieth-century preoccupation: war.

Wilkins' willingness to take risks and his luck in surviving them made him a favourite at Gaumont and his reputation spread further afield. When the cream of Fleet Street's correspondents began assembling in 1912 to report on a war brewing in the Balkans, George Wilkins was among them. Gaumont agreed to share its star cameraman with the *Daily Chronicle*. Though still a baby-faced country-boy colonial of just twenty-three with no writing experience, the paper considered him well-suited to the job of war reporting.

Working for the *Chronicle* was a great honour. The paper was Britain's bestselling newspaper at the time, riding high on its world exclusive report that Amundsen had been first to the South Pole. It had gambled on the Norwegian beating his hapless British rival Captain Scott, and Amundsen had dutifully filed the great news from a telegraph office in Hobart before speaking to anyone else. The paper was expecting great interest in the conflict gathering in the Balkans which many saw as a prelude to an inevitable struggle between the great European powers. Though few understood the history and background to the war, it was sure to be colourful and sell a lot of newspapers.

In one aspect they were right. The First Balkan War of 1912–13 proved to be the first technologically modern conflict, with horrendous casualties caused by lethal new technologies such as machine-guns and aeroplanes. It began with an uneasy marriage of convenience between Bulgaria, Greece, Serbia and Montenegro, who agreed to put their differences aside to unite in forcing the Turks out of Europe, and ended when the victors turned on each other. The struggle was eagerly watched from the sidelines by Europe's military powers, who did little to prevent the carnage and much to encourage it. Joining them in the ghoulish spectacle was an international press corps of writers, photographers and, for the first time, newsreel men making it a media event.

Hundreds of journalists were sent to cover the fighting, among them Leon Trotsky, then working for a Kiev newspaper. Wilkins would face competition from at least twenty international newsreels, all hoping to be the first to capture scenes of real combat. The young Australian was sent to cover the Turkish side of the war and could barely conceal his glee at the prospect.

'I shall never forget the thrill of preparing for that assignment,' he wrote. 'To be a free lance at a war and in company with the bold, bad terrible Turk of the story books!' Having no concept of what a real war might look like, he begins imagining it as some exciting escapade. 'A war correspondent's life in those days, I think, offered a seldom-equalled chance for adventure, since many of the conditions were unknown. For one thing, you had to push into the danger zone to discover if the danger zone was there. Then there was the keen but friendly rivalry in getting a scoop for your paper and, for the first time, a "lead" in the moving picture war news reel.'[18]

Despite the modernisations, the correspondents still had to rely mostly on horses to traverse the battlefield. This gave Wilkins an advantage over his more experienced rivals. He had heard from his brother and cousin, both veterans of the Boer War, about the shortages of good animals in war time. Those that were any good were usually stolen, and those that weren't were shot. So he decided on a typically unorthodox approach, mounting his cameras on a motor-cycle and sidecar and driving to the front.

After bribing his way onto passenger trains and ferries across Europe, he finally wheeled the motorcycle off the wharf at Constantinople and rode it through the cobbled streets to the British correspondent's hotel of choice, the Pera Palace. He had still and movie cameras bolted between the handlebars, camping gear and tripods in the sidecar, a pistol in his holster. The old hands of Fleet Street, gathered in the gaudy lounge bar of the Palace, couldn't stop laughing at the brash Aussie and his bizarre contraptions. There were twenty-eight of them gathered there like vultures awaiting news of a fresh corpse, the finest of foreign correspondents. There was the *Daily Graphic*'s Philip (later Sir Philip) Gibbs, the first man to interview a Pope; Ellis Ashmead-Bartlett, who would later gain fame as the only man to take moving pictures of the ANZACs at Gallipoli; the peculiar Tiger Sarll, a tall, one-eyed, big-game-hunting newsreel man for Pathé, who was especially memorable for his combination of military uniform and hunting garb. Also present was fellow Australian Martin Donohoe, who'd reported every important conflict since the Boxer Rebellion, and Francis McCullagh, the soldier–reporter who would later be imprisoned by the Bolsheviks as a spy. They were men who were comfortable travelling first class with an unlimited expense account; whose many idle moments were filled playing cards while complaining about the servants and the relative merits of their preferred Grand Cru.

In such company Wilkins felt a little intimidated. 'I was only an amateur newsman far beneath the "Special War Correspondent" level of dignity because I deigned to carry a camera, which no real writer, in those days, would even dream of.'[19]

The Turkish authorities were unprepared for war, and certainly unprepared for war correspondents. They had no real idea what to do with this strange collection of English gentlemen and their outrageous demands. The last thing the Turks wanted were witnesses to the gathering collapse of the Ottoman army, and for weeks the newsmen were confined to Constantinople. Eventually the Turks concocted a ruse they hoped would bring an end to their trouble. Before being allowed to travel beyond the city, each correspondent was required to supply two servants, two horses for himself and one for each of his men, and, lest he be tempted to eat into the army's rations, two months' food supply. Given that there was barely a decent horse left in the entire city, it was an excellent means of enforcing censorship without ever admitting to it.

The Turks, however, had not counted on Wilkins' ingenuity. Soon he had managed to bribe two policemen into giving him their horses, and was being led on a clandestine tour of the city in search of a promised Arabian stallion. He found it on the sixth floor of an apartment block, where it was being hidden in a bedroom. Two hundred gold sovereigns later, he was sitting atop the finest horse in Turkey, a beautiful black-pointed bay, parading it in front of the dumbstruck correspondents at the Pera. He not only had the mount, he knew how to ride it.

'My status among the correspondents immediately went high. They had taken me perhaps for an English suburban photographer who had had the nerve to butt in on war corresponding and as such, unwelcome.'[20]

He teamed up with a young photographer for the *Daily Mirror*, Bernard Grant. Like Wilkins, Grant was a newcomer attracted to reporting for the sheer fun of travelling the world at someone else's expense. He has left us with a fine portrait of Wilkins at work, already showing the characteristics of independence and resourcefulness that would become the hallmarks of his career.

In a lull in the war at the end of 1912, Grant and Philip Gibbs jointly wrote a book of their experiences from either side of the lines in the Balkans, *Adventures of War with Cross and Crescent*. It is almost embarrassingly lavish in its praise of Wilkins, whom Grant called: '. . . one of the best companions in the world, because of his cheerfulness, his knowledge of handicraft, of horses, and of all rough work and outdoor life. He . . . has had many adventures in wild places of the world which have taught him valuable lessons, among them being the gift of leadership, instant decision in moments of peril, and a quick way of righting something that has gone wrong . . . He did all these things, not in an arrogant way, not in a bullying commanding spirit, but quietly and cheerfully, as though it all came natural to him and was part of his scheme of life.'[21]

On one occasion several correspondents were caught in a seething crowd of angry Turks fleeing from defeat on the battlefield. One of the photographers raised his camera to take pictures of them when he was suddenly bashed from behind by a man wild with anger. The confrontation threatened to turn murderous until Wilkins intervened. Grant watched while Wilkins moved decisively, 'pulled out his revolver, believing the angry Turk might try to use a knife . . . the man looked at the weapon, which had a wonderful effect in quieting his wrath.' Wilkins, he said, 'was the type of man who helps himself and does not look around for rescuers.'[22]

Wilkins turned twenty-four on 31 October 1912 and it was a day he never forgot. It was only by the merest stroke of luck that he survived to see the next morning. The date also marked the utter rout of the Turks at the battle of Lule Burgas, its army sent into chaotic retreat.

Wilkins and Grant were making their way to the frontline after a frigid night beneath ice-stiffened canvas, finally able to get near the action after the long delays in Constantinople. The morning of the 31st broke raw and fearfully cold, a driving rain intermixed with sleet-reduced visibility which made their work with the cameras a struggle.

Taking advantage of a slight rise above the action, they began to film the terrifying expanse of modern warfare below. As he ground away with his camera Wilkins filmed a Turkish artillery group blown to pieces by a heavy shell, then the attacking Bulgarian infantry being mown down by machine-guns. As the morning progressed, the thin Ottoman lines began to collapse and the Bulgars charged forward.

It is estimated that the Turks lost 50 000 men that day as they were pushed from the European colonies they had ruled for centuries. The lines collapsed so suddenly that the correspondents were caught in no-man's-land, exposed to Bulgarian artillery. As Wilkins cranked his handle on the scene, another reporter yelled a warning that the Bulgarian artillery now seemed to be sighting them.

'It is true, I know, because I have later experienced it, that the bullet or shell that hits you, you don't hear,' wrote Wilkins of what unfolded next. 'I didn't hear the one that lifted me; I had heard the one screaming as it passed scarcely over our heads, and another one that burst on the slope just below us, but as I painfully picked myself up from the dust, I saw that the third shell had buried itself directly beneath my camera . . . The shell had been, partially, a dud.'[23]

Chased by cavalry, they took to their own horses and managed to escape. But there was no rest ahead, as they were swept up in the desperate Turkish retreat. Nothing on this scale had been seen since Napoleon fled from the Moscow. The remnants of a great army, panic-stricken, leaderless and without hope, staggered past them in grim procession.

The sense of excitement Wilkins had felt at the outset of this adventure was gone. All around him men were dropping from sheer exhaustion and dying from their wounds. 'Here and there one would see a man stoop and lift up his comrade and help him along a yard or so, few words were spoken, was there need of any? There were many dead to be seen with their hands still clasped or arms entwined. My heart turned sick at the sight. Was this war? This the reward for men who had fought?'[24]

With food and warm clothes, the correspondents were in danger from these desperate men. They camped in a ditch for what Wilkins called the worst night of his life. Hundreds of hungry soldiers passed by, and he discouraged them as best he could with the only useful word of Turkish he knew. *'Yock! Yock!'* he called, meaning 'there is nothing for you'. He kept a firm grip on the butt of his revolver, fearing that any moment he might have to use it to hold off the looters. Huddling close together in the bitter cold and rain, he and Grant did not expect to see the dawn.

For several days they travelled like this, camping off the main roads to avoid confrontation and pitching their tent in darkness. One morning while preparing breakfast there was a gruesome discovery – all about them were bodies wrapped in white cloth. They had been sleeping in the middle of a makeshift cholera cemetery.

The war became a ghastly parade of nightmarish scenes. Wilkins witnessed the aftermath of a civilian massacre and once spent a long night patching up wounded men after a Red Cross surgeon collapsed from exhaustion. He passed through a village where every creature save scavenging dogs had been killed by cholera. 'As we rode through the streets the dead bodies were so thickly strewn that our horses had to carefully place their hoofs to avoid stepping on the human carcasses,'[25] he wrote. They stopped to take pictures which he hoped would bring home the horrors of war, but a passing squad of Turkish soldiers noticed them and were outraged that he should be photographing such scenes. He and Grant were arrested and held without food for six days. They were beaten and feared the worst before finally being released. It was enough for Grant, who headed home for London.

One of the innovations of the Balkan War was the use of aeroplanes. Several Turkish army officers had been sent to Britain to learn flying in 1912, and the Ottomans bought a number of Bristol two-seater monoplanes. It was these that Wilkins came across one afternoon, and he soon convinced one of the new pilots, Lt Fezil Bey, to go for a ride. Once in the air, he couldn't resist taking a look at the frontlines and, much to his Turkish pilot's horror, banked towards the fighting. They battled for control of the aircraft. 'With the two of us struggling, it was a miracle that the controls withstood the punishment. Between us, that plane was put through all manner of manoeuvres for which it was never intended, many of them neither of us had ever experienced before,' he wrote.[26]

It was only when the wings were fractured by shrapnel from the Bulgarian lines that Wilkins relented and they headed back for the landing field. Once down on the ground, though, their heated argument came to an end. Wilkins pointed out to Fezil that he had just made history by being the first to fly a plane over an enemy firing line. 'We could cook up a fine intelligence report and he would get the credit.' To seal their new friendship, Wilkins took a photograph of the young Turkish pilots standing proudly in front of their machine. He kept a copy as a reminder of his small part in military history.

Back in Constantinople Wilkins became friendly with an Ottoman nobleman, Aziz Pasha, who was deeply involved in the political intrigues that would lead to a military coup soon after the war ended. Aziz asked the cameraman to carry a message for him to the frontlines, to be personally delivered to the Turkish army commander, General Nizam Pasha. It was a request that made Wilkins a party to the conflict, crossing the line between reporter and participant.

The archives hold differing versions of what happened next. They are consistent in their details, though some are a little more colourful than others. In short, Wilkins was arrested as a suspected Bulgarian spy and roughly questioned, though the secret message from Aziz was not discovered. His demands to be taken to General Nizam Pasha were ignored. At a hasty court martial before a bullying, truculent Turkish captain, Wilkins was sentenced to a firing squad. The next morning he and fourteen other prisoners were led to the execution ground, tied to a post and the shooting began. 'One after the other men on my right went down in a hail of bullets. It was my turn next . . . then the interpreter came to speak to me; would I confess to being a spy and tell all I knew, if so my life would be spared.' Wilkins sensed a little hope – the Captain seemed to be scared to carry out the sentence, perhaps fearful that the strange foreigner might actually have some connection with the army chief. He was untied and marched back to the stockade.

The grim charade was repeated the next morning, but still Wilkins refused to buckle. While the message remained undiscovered, he had a chance to bluff his way out. On the third morning, the Captain himself approached Wilkins as he stood roped between two other prisoners. 'He was so blustering and threatening that I almost faltered. Yet something inside me made me hold out . . . I very nearly did collapse, but managed to cling to the post for support and, with the last fragment of my will, kept my knees from buckling.' When the firing squad lowered their arms, he knew it was over. Many years later when asked if this was the most frightening experience of his life, Wilkins blithely dismissed the matter. 'Of course not, I knew perfectly well they were looking for a spy, and I was just a photographer.'[27]

Now it was the Captain's turn to be nervous. He had no choice but to take Wilkins to headquarters to meet with the General, and he was fearful of the consequences. The Turkish command was in a frenzy. Wilkins learned that while he had been in captivity, an armistice had been agreed and the war went into an uneasy lull. It meant he had missed reporting the agreement but at least he was alive to see the day.

Back in London, Wilkins was received rapturously by his bosses at Gaumont, who were thrilled with his work. He was asked to address the staff, and the notes of this talk have survived, along with his dutifully completed expense records and an inventory of his returned kit (including a promise that the motorcycle might be recovered from its hiding place under blankets in a Turkish cellar). Modest and full of praise for others, he made no mention of the firing squad, though he hinted at his relief to be back alive: 'All things considered I was not sorry to leave Turkey with its dirt and filth and evil smells, but I am very thankful for having had the opportunity to experience the life of a war correspondent and would not hesitate for a moment to set out upon a similar expedition.'[28]

There was more war than even he could want in the years ahead.

3

—

An adventurer's apprenticeship

The Expedition will have two principal objects in view. First, the explora-
tion of unknown lands and seas, the second the gathering of scientific
information . . . I trust that the Expedition will have the success which it
merits, and that the members of the Expedition will return in good health
and having profited by their stay in the Northern regions.
  – GJ Desbarats, Deputy Minister of Naval Service, outlining the
  objectives of the Canadian Arctic Expedition, Ottawa, May 1913

Not all the horrors of the Western Front, not the rubble of Arras, nor the hell of
Ypres, nor all the mud of Flanders leading to Passchendaele, could blot out the
memories of that year in the Arctic.
                                      – William McKinlay, survivor

George Wilkins had just boarded a cruise ship in Barbados when
he was handed a telegram that again altered the course of his
career. For six weeks he had been filming in the Caribbean, making a
series of travelogues and commercial films on cocoa production. By his
standards it was dull work, but the surroundings were enjoyable and he
was contemplating a more adventurous trip down the Orinoco River in
Venezuela when the ship's steward handed him the envelope. It was
from the Gaumont Company in London: 'WOULD YOU GO IMPORTANT
ARCTIC EXPEDITION MEANS TWO OR THREE YEAR ABSENCE GOOD TERMS
EXCELLENT OPPORTUNITY REPLY CABLE'[1]

He felt a sudden thrill. This could mean only one thing: he was off to
join Shackleton on the great man's next journey to the South Pole. It

was only when he reread it that he realised he was not going to the *Ant*arctic, but would be heading north instead. With no telegraph on board ship, he scribbled on the back of an envelope and shouted to a friend on a launch below: 'Cable this for me as soon as you can.' It was a single-word reply: 'Yes'.

On the steamer back to London, he discovered nothing more about his mission, but never doubted he would accept whatever lay ahead. 'It suited my naturally impulsive and adventure-loving nature,' he wrote, 'to rush headlong into the uncertain.'[2] He knew Gaumont would be expecting much from him. Since returning from the Balkans he had been given all the most exciting assignments. He had sat beside Percy Lambert, filming the autoracer as he became the first man to drive faster than 100 miles (160 kilometres) per hour. On Christmas Eve 1912 he had been in the gondola of a hot air balloon with the daring aeronaut Captain Penfold over London. Penfold, dressed as Santa Claus, planned to parachute into Hyde Park and distribute chocolates to children as a publicity stunt for a confectionary company. Caught in a north-west wind, they narrowly avoided crashing into Westminster Cathedral and were last seen rising high and out of control, headed towards the English Channel. Wilkins spent a shivering night at 7000 metres before a change of wind brought the errant balloon back to the ground and a bumpy landing that left them bruised and shaken but otherwise whole.

'I found my office in an uproar,' Wilkins recalled when he got back to London. 'They thought we were lost. Steamers and tugs were searching the Channel for us. On seeing me my boss stammered, "Haven't you better sense than to take such chances when we've got no insurance on you?"'[3]

Wilkins didn't dare to ask what the premium on his life might be for his new assignment. He was to join the largest and best-equipped polar expedition in history, a massive undertaking involving numerous ships and a dozen specialist scientists in a program of exploration and research expected to last three years. Wilkins was to be the official cameraman and cinematographer, ranked with the officers and scientific staff. He could take any equipment he considered necessary, regardless of the expense, and Gaumont would pay him a bonus above his usual salary as well as a share in the profits. Once again he would be writing despatches for the *Daily Chronicle*, though these would be occasional at best – Wilkins would be beyond contact with civilisation for a year or more at a time. He had just a fortnight to prepare and say his goodbyes.

The aim of the Canadian Arctic Expedition was to explore an unknown area of 100 000 square kilometres from the Alaskan border to the unknown northern reaches of the Beaufort Sea and claim any new land found for the Dominion. This would be a grand undertaking, one of the last great journeys of discovery, unsupported by radio or aircraft, reliant on dog sleds and sweat. Its unlikely leader was an obstinate, intensely determined former divinity student, Vilhjalmur Stefansson. He was just thirty-three, already a veteran of two Arctic expeditions and a man with absolute certainty in his own genius who on occasion compared himself to Napoleon. Like many explorers, he believed discovery was the path to greatness and his lifelong dream was to find a new continent buried beneath the ice caps of the north.

Stefansson had made his name as an anthropologist, making the dubious claim that he'd found a race of blue-eyed, blonde Eskimos he believed were a missing tribe of ancient Europeans. With a gift for popular writing and often unscrupulous self-promotion, he built these thin credentials into a reputation for polar expertise that impressed important men in the cities and colleges of Canada and the United States. He had a rare skill that mixed both polar and political survival, but those who saw him at work in the Arctic were often far less impressed by this solitary and unpredictable man.

Captain Fritz Wolki, a whaler and boat owner who had been in the Arctic for twenty-six years, was deeply suspicious of Stefansson but happy to sell him provisions for the expedition at exorbitant prices. Wolki's assessment was harsh: 'A college professor who carries books in his sledge where a sensible man carries grub. Say, did you ever shake hands with him? He's got a hand soft as a woman's! I don't believe that fellow ever did a real day's work in his life. I'll eat my shirt if he ever comes back.'[4]

He underestimated Stefansson. The Commander of the CAE returned, but seventeen members of his team did not. They died from an assortment of misjudgments and bad luck; from exposure, scurvy, starvation, suicide and even, most likely, from murder. Stefansson's expedition proved to be the most chaotic and poorly led in polar history, epic in its tragedy if not its achievements. But it was the making of George Hubert Wilkins as an explorer.

When he arrived in Esquimalt, British Columbia, to join the expedition, Wilkins must have appeared slightly ridiculous in his new suit, bowler hat and spats. His first encounter was with the gruff, whisky-loving expedition doctor, Alister Forbes Mackay, who promptly asked him for money to buy a drink. Mackay had been to Antarctica with Shackleton, and he and fellow Scot James Murray, a biologist, were the only men among the scientists with real polar experience – though it wouldn't save either of them.

The sailors were little better prepared. Hastily assembled from the rough-and-tumble ports along the Pacific coast, they included an assortment of lazy and untrustworthy men, hard cases and drunks. One sailor owned nothing more than the canvas pants he turned up in; two were travelling under aliases. The cook, a young Scotsman named Templeman, was a self-confessed drug addict; the engineer was an alcoholic who smuggled piles of booze aboard. The one impressive figure was the skipper of the flagship, the *Karluk*, Captain Bob Bartlett. An ice-hardened mariner of the old school, he had sailed and sledged with Peary to the brink of the North Pole. Frustrated in his attempts to form his own expedition, he had agreed at the last minute to join Stefansson.

Looking over the *Karluk*, Bartlett was far from happy. It was a retired square-rigged whaler, in poor condition and totally unsuited for the rigours of the Arctic icepack. Before being sold cheaply to the CAE, she had been condemned by a naval expert as unsuitable even for freight carriage, much less expeditionary work. Overburdened with stores, stinking of whale oil and with her timbers creaking under the strain, for Bartlett *Karluk* spelled trouble. The day before departure, he sent a message to Ottawa warning that the ship was 'absolutely unsuitable to remain in winter ice'. Nevertheless, at sunset on Tuesday, 17 June 1913, they sailed for Alaska and the Arctic coast.

Though the expedition would rarely encounter good luck, the seeds of its disaster were already laid. The plan was to proceed along the northern coast to remote Herschel Island, where several ships would rendezvous to sort out equipment and men before splitting into two teams. A Northern Party, to be led by Stefansson, would go in search of new land to the north of Canada. A Southern Party, under the command of respected scientist RM Anderson, would investigate the far reaches of Canada's known coastline. The Southern Party was answerable not to the Navy, but to Canada's Geological Survey, and Anderson never accepted Stefansson's primacy over his operation.

This confused leadership and the conflicting demands of the two parties was the source of immense trouble, and often Wilkins would be in the centre of it as the go-between for Stefansson and Anderson, who loathed each other. Any chance of real success, however, was doomed when the *Karluk* failed to make the rendezvous, leaving both teams short of men, materials and hope.

Wilkins could imagine none of this as the *Karluk* made its way north through the Bering Strait into the Arctic Ocean. He stood on the deck entranced by the view, overwhelmed by the vast array of wildlife that funnelled through the narrow gap. Beluga whales glided in silent shoals beneath translucent sheets of thin ice, while ivory-tusked walruses and ringed seals splashed at the surface. Above him the skies were thick with flocks of every imaginable migrating bird, on their way to Siberia. Far from being overwhelmed by his first sight of the icepack, he was seduced by it:

> My first impression of the pack was of a fearsome, enticing, mocking monster; but soon it lost its fearsomeness and it seemed to beckon and call and reach out with pleading sadness that awakened sympathy. I am never unconscious of its pleading. It is a love to which those of us who knew it must return.[5]

By early August the *Karluk*, its progress unsteady due to constant mechanical failures, had lost contact with the expedition's other ships, the *Alaska*, the *Mary Sachs* and the *North Star*. It sluggishly nosed through the thickening fields of white until, on 8 August, it came to a halt. The open sea had disappeared and in its place was a solid mass of ice. They were prisoners of the pack.

For a month they drifted aimlessly back and forth with the floes. Stefansson fretted that all his plans might come to nothing and wandered the ship aimlessly. Wilkins made the most of the enforced idleness by improving his French grammar and beginning a meticulous diary of his adventure.[6] Finally, on 19 September, Stefansson came to him and suggested that they leave on a hunting trip with the anthropologist Diamond Jenness, his secretary Burt McConnell and two Eskimo companions. Though none of the scientists had any experience of ice travel, they all readily agreed. It's a decision that may well have saved their lives.

The next day the hunting party prepared to leave, sparking an argument that has continued through the decades. To Stefansson's detractors, he was abandoning the *Karluk* to its fate, knowing full well it was in great danger. The surviving records of those left behind accuse Stefansson of cowardice – or worse. Even a subsequent report by the Royal Northwest Mounted Police implied the leader's actions were suspicious. Stefansson, however, maintained that he had never intended to be gone longer than ten days.

'Stef did not return to the ship in ten days. He did not return ever,' wrote William McKinlay, a good friend of Wilkins' and a *Karluk* survivor. 'Two days after he left, the wind which had been blowing moderately from the east increased to a gale, and the next morning the ice split between the ship and the shore. We were being carried away from the land in the grip of the gale-swept icepack, moving west at the rate of thirty miles a day, leaving an ever widening expanse of Arctic sea between us and our leader.'[7]

The storm drove the *Karluk* north-west towards the Siberian coast. On 10 January 1914, the ship was crushed by the ice and sank. To the mournful sounds of Chopin's funeral march playing on the ship's gramophone, Captain Bartlett was the last to abandon her. The crew of twenty-two men, one Eskimo[8] seamstress, her two children, a complement of sledge dogs and a pet cat were left to their fate on the ice. The ship had been loaded in haste, and there was little in the way of survival equipment or adequate clothing aboard. Some of the crew, with Bartlett, eventually made their way to Wrangel Island; others, including Mackay and Murray, struck out on their own in a failed attempt to find safety. In the end eleven men died.

By the time the blizzard blew *Karluk* to its oblivion, Stefansson and his hunting party were comfortably camped on a small island in sight of the mainland. He instructed his men in the proper way to arrange their sleeping bags and how to take care of their clothes. He warned them that despite the cold, it was best to sleep naked inside their bags. Jenness and McConnell ignored the advice and stayed in their clothes, not realising their sweat would freeze and leave them chilled to the bone by morning. Wilkins did as advised and spent a more comfortable night, realising for the first time that Stefansson's years of experience in the Arctic might be sufficient to bring them to safety. The next day they learned from their Inuit guides, Ascetchak and Pyurak, how to harness and handle the dogs. It was the beginning of a long and at times painful course in the art of Arctic survival.

One of the most important lessons was to recognise different ice conditions. Wilkins' career as a polar explorer came very close to ending on its first day. Out walking on his own, he was singing a tune and paying insufficient attention to the ice when suddenly it gave off a loud hissing noise and began to sink all around him. Instinctively he made a dash for the nearest shore, 100 metres away, causing spouts of water to shoot up through the cracks. Fortunately the ice held fast just long enough to reach safety. Alone and clothed in his bulky gear, a dip in the frigid water would have meant almost certain death.

Tall, with a broad chest and particularly powerful arms, Wilkins was at home in the outdoors, but strength alone was not much use in the ice. Stefansson was a weakling by comparison, yet his long treks in the Arctic had taught him how to move with economy and precision, to save energy and stay constantly alert. It would take many months for Wilkins to attune his body to the rudiments of ice travel, to move swiftly and with economy across the surface on foot or skis. Once he mastered it he displayed remarkable stamina that stayed with him well into his sixties. Stefansson would later say of him: 'A half dozen such men would make an invincible polar expedition.'[9]

The disappearance of the *Karluk* had shattered Stefansson's plans, but not his resolve. Resilient and resourceful, he reinvented his expedition as a lightweight, mobile one that could live largely off the land with a minimum of equipment or support. He had long argued that even deep in the polar ice there were resources of food, oil and skins that could be harnessed to keep the observant man alive. Now he was determined to prove it. Abandoning any thoughts of science, he turned everything towards the search for undiscovered land. It was his only chance of salvaging prestige and countering the inevitable criticism he knew would follow if the men of the *Karluk* perished. He no longer even mentioned the ship or its crew. They slipped from his mind, even from his imagination; a ghostly presence he would not allow to become a sign of fallibility.

Stefansson announced his hunting party would head west along the Alaskan coast towards Point Barrow, where there was a trading post. Here they could discover news of Anderson and the men from the Southern Party. Stefansson's new plans would require some of their supplies and personnel.

The three-week trek to Barrow was Wilkins' first chance to pick a trail and lead the dogs, and he enjoyed it despite the cold and trouble with his feet. Stefansson was impressed at the young photographer's eager willingness and began to look upon him as a protégé.

At Barrow they learned the other expedition ships were safe and wintering at Collinson Point, some 400 kilometres to the east. Stefansson planned to meet with them before setting off in search of his mythical continent. As most of Wilkins' camera equipment had been left on the *Karluk*, officially his job was at an end. But the life of exploration appealed to him and, despite reservations about Stefansson's leadership, he volunteered to stay on.

Wilkins was ordered to accompany the anthropologist Diamond Jenness to an Inuit settlement several days away. Jenness intended to live with the Eskimo there for several months and Wilkins was to help supply him with enough fish and meat for his stay. For the first few days they travelled along the coastline in good weather and came to a wide frozen bay. His Eskimo companions wanted to avoid it but Wilkins insisted on crossing in order to save a few hours' travelling. As they moved across the bay, the wind increased and snow began to ripple across the ice, first above their ankles, and then above their knees. The Eskimos stopped the sleds and indicated they wanted to return to the shore. When Wilkins reached them he found them on their knees, crying for fear of travelling on such thin ice.

'The Eskimo did not care to go on for they said it was going to be a blizzard and wanted to go back. I did not take any heed of their advice thinking that they were only making an excuse so they would not have to face the cold wind.'[10] He would show them 'that a white man wouldn't be bothered by a little snow drift.'[11] It was a foolish decision. His impetuous arrogance put them all at risk.

Soon the ice was heaving beneath them, billowing like a sheet hung in the wind. Still unwilling to admit he was wrong and turn back with the wind behind them, Wilkins pushed on for the far shore: 'The ice might break up anyway I reasoned. If we were to be lost we might as well be lost fighting with our faces towards the danger, rather than lost while running away from it.'[12]

Now men and dogs were jumping dangerously from floe to floe as the cracks of open water became wider and the ice-cakes heaved higher. For hours they played this deadly game of hopscotch before struggling, exhausted, to the shore-fast ice.

But his lessons for the day were not complete. They had been travelling in intense cold and both Jenness and Wilkins had allowed the snow to freeze on their beards – something Stefansson had warned them to avoid. Their faces stung badly, but they paid little attention: 'These feelings, I thought, were nothing more than polar explorers had to endure to be heroes and I got quite a thrill in the belief that I was daring and surmounting the difficulties set up by the elements.'[13]

Soon the pain turned to numbness and Wilkins believed he was merely becoming accustomed to the cold. One eye was closed now, the lashes frozen together. It was too cold to stop to take compass bearings, so he navigated by turning his face into the wind to judge his direction. This only worsened the condition. His face was dangerously frozen.

They headed for an Eskimo house several kilometres further along the coast:

> When we reached the Iglu the men and women came out to see who were these foolish strangers travelling in this kind of weather, and when one of the women came to shake hands with me she started talking excitedly and commenced to rub my forehead.
>
> The cold had been bad enough, but now upon entering the warm house my face and hands and knees began to burn and smart as if somebody was holding a red hot iron to them.[14]

He later learned the weather readings that day showed the temperature was seventeen below zero and the wind speed 75 kilometres per hour. By modern measurements of wind chill they had travelled through temperatures equivalent to minus forty-eight – severe enough to cause frostbite in less than five minutes of exposure.

It was 31 October, his birthday. A year earlier, he mused, he had been 'under fire'; today he felt like he had been 'in the fire'. His face was one massive blister of frostbite. It began on his forehead, covered one eye and down to his chin. The scars took almost a year to heal. 'I am twenty-five years old today,' he wrote, 'but if I live another two times twenty-five years I do not wish to pass another such day as we have had today.'[15]

Even the agony of severe frostbite did not compare to the excruciating pain of another Arctic danger: snow blindness. In those days before proper eye protection, the debilitating effect of reflected ultraviolet light on the cornea was a constant risk. The surface of the eye was literally burnt away, causing temporary but total blindness. Wilkins likened the result to having the eyes filled with red hot, sharpened dust. Strangely, he never spoke of wearing the Eskimos' eyeshades: a carved piece of wood with a blackened interior and two narrow slits. In the absence of medicine he relied on ineffectual folk remedies, including tea leaves, fine sugar and even chewing tobacco. The only certain cure was complete rest in darkness, and this was seldom possible when travelling on the ice.

As the winter months passed and the sun returned above the horizon, Wilkins came to understand that his real teachers were his Eskimo companions. They, in turn, warmed to his willingness to join them in the daily rituals of life on the ice. He was a good shot and learned to hunt seal, caribou and wolves in the Eskimo manner. The prize, however, was the polar bear, and this led to long discussions about the days before the rifle when bears were hunted with dogs and a long sharp knife. Wilkins was fascinated by these tales, and wanted to try it for himself.

Once a bear was sighted, the procedure was to let the dogs free to chase the bear until it tired and turned to make a stand. As the dogs attacked, the hunter would wait until the bear, distracted by the dogs, would turn its back. The hunter then had to launch himself at the bear and plunge the blade deep below the shoulder into the heart. If he missed or failed to send the blade home, it was the hunter who might end up dead.

Wilkins recalled: 'It seemed to me that there was not much to that, and an agile man with a steady hand could do it, and one day I boasted that even I could do it if I had a proper knife.'[16] His companions laughed and warned him that the bears were quick and it was better for the white man to stay away. But Wilkins persisted and eventually one of the Eskimo sharpened up his long bone blade and handed it to him as a challenge.

Some days later, when a bear was seen in the distance, Wilkins had his chance to prove his hunting skills. The Eskimo brought out their best dogs, hitched them to a sled and off they went in pursuit. Once the dogs scented the animal, they pulled hard over the smooth ice for several kilometres until they were close enough to be unleashed. 'We ran on foot,' Wilkins recalled, 'to where the bear had bailed up and was dealing fairly successfully with the dogs.' One giant paw would swipe one dog, then another. Several of the inexperienced ones were sent tumbling across the ice with a yelp. The hunters approached cautiously. The Eskimo were quite emphatic that Wilkins should use his rifle and not attempt to jump the animal with his knife but he was determined to try. He dodged about the outskirts of the fight waiting for a chance.

The old bear, a giant male standing more than three metres high, turned his back on the men as he dealt with his yapping assailants. 'Now you go, the Eskimos shouted, and I dashed in and swung a vicious stab at the shaggy coat.'

But the knife did not penetrate deeply. Wilkins overbalanced and tumbled over a dog. The bear turned suddenly and took a mighty sweep with its paw that just missed him. The fall had saved him from being torn by the long claws. The dogs and the bear stamped on all around him as they battled furiously. 'I was almost winded by a dog that bounced on my stomach, and then I heard a shot . . .'

The bear fell beside him, dead. 'The Eskimo were grinning from ear to ear. "That old fellow bear, he plenty tough," they said. "You not strong enough to put knife through his skin. More better you try to kill baby bear, or seal maybe." They laughed and laughed.' So long as he was with them, he never heard the last of it, and Wilkins' unsuccessful effort was parodied in good-natured songs and stories.[17]

These generous and willing friends came to understand him well.

A colleague later recorded a conversation between two Eskimo interpreters discussing the peculiar Australian. 'When asked by another Eskimo what he thought of Wilkins, the interpreter replied: "I don't think much of this man. He doesn't know many things he must not do. He'll do almost anything and he's always doing something." '[18]

That first year in the north was difficult, often painful and frustrated by Stefansson's sudden changes of plan, which Wilkins was still too subordinate to question. He came to appreciate these were all part of a polar explorer's life, along with the strange spell the ice seemed to cast on human nature. With the cold came exposure to intense melancholy, bitter argument and, for some, an anger that never subsided. Under the stress of extreme conditions, with men huddled close together with too much free time and little to talk about, polar expeditions were bound to be riven by hostilities. The CAE, however, came close to open warfare.

Stefansson's authoritarian yet disorganised leadership was largely to blame. When he finally met with Anderson and the Southern Party, he indelicately demanded ships and men to carry him north to launch his exploring team. Anderson argued this would sabotage his own group's work. Inside the little expedition hut at Collinson Point an argument raged for seven hours. It resolved little and Stefansson would later write an official report which accused the scientists of threatening mutiny. Wilkins wisely declined to get involved.

The outcome was that Wilkins would spend winter in the hut and continue his photographic work while Stefansson travelled to the distant reaches of Banks Island – literally the end of the known world. Wilkins used this time to learn as much as he could from the assembled scientists and sailors. He mastered the basic skills of taxidermy and biological collecting. Most significantly, he was expertly tutored in navigation by the three master mariners in the hut. It was an accelerated university course in scientific exploration, and soon the microscope and sextant were as familiar to him as his cameras.[19]

In June 1914 Wilkins received a handwritten note that had taken two months to reach him. It was from Stefansson, who announced he was returning to Banks Island for further exploration. He requested that Wilkins take command of the expedition schooner *North Star* and sail it as far north as possible to reach him by the end of summer and resupply his party. It was in effect a call for help. 'Make the best arrangements you can and you may be sure that they will meet with my approval. I have seen enough of you,' Stefansson concluded, 'to have confidence both in your judgement and good faith.'[20]

To accept this uncertain mission meant Wilkins would be delaying his return to Europe and probably jeopardising his employment with Gaumont. It was dangerous and there was no certainty that he would ever find his commander even if he reached Banks Island. It would also put him squarely in the middle of the dispute between Stefansson and Anderson, who would be reluctant to release the ship.

'This is an exceptional opportunity for me,' Wilkins wrote, 'but I would rather be without it. I joined the expedition as a photographer, and it is as a photographer that I wish to make a reputation if any, not as leader of a relief party or navigator.'

Despite his reservations, Wilkins accepted the mission. Some years later, Stefansson described this dutiful response with some affection: 'There was trouble, and a man was needed to jump into the breach. He did it, not bravely or nobly, or in any of the many ways native to those who are destined to be popular heroes, but just inevitably. There seemed no one else to do it, and so it was his job.'[21]

Wilkins and three companions left for the long walk east to the point near the Alaskan–Yukon frontier where the *North Star* was beached. He celebrated his entry into Canada with a bath, only the second since he'd arrived in the Arctic. 'I didn't feel particularly dirty, although by the appearance of the water, I fear my feelings must have deceived me.'[22]

The *North Star* was attractive to the eye, a 10-metre, 10-tonne, gasoline-motored fishing schooner that drew barely a metre and was designed to bounce up on the ice and then break it with its weight on the way down. From the day he saw it, Wilkins' diaries took on a different tone. He was no longer just the expedition photographer, he was Stefansson's anointed deputy, and his writing reflects it.

Wilkins raised a solitary tent for his own use while the vessel was being prepared. Stefansson's stenographer, McConnell, who would travel with him, noticed the change. 'I rather think he believes that a Commander should not sleep with his men. I may be doing him an injustice in thinking so, but there is no doubt in my mind that a change has come over him since I last saw him.'[23]

As Wilkins might have expected, Dr Anderson intervened before he could leave. He insisted Wilkins take the larger but less ice-worthy *Mary Sachs* to find Stefansson. Its crew was surly and reluctant to take risks in search of a man they despised and considered probably dead in any case. In his biographical stories *True Adventure Thrills*, Wilkins says he had to resort to an elaborate subterfuge to get the *Mary Sachs* to sea. The fortuitous arrival of a whaling ship meant he was able to purchase a case of whisky (expensive at ten dollars a bottle) and he proceeded to get the crew dead drunk. When they finally collapsed, Wilkins and his Eskimo friend Billy Natkusiak slipped the ropes and shanghaied the crew. They were 160 kilometres out to sea by the time the crew woke up and it was too late to turn back. His engineer, James Crawford, would remain more or less drunk for the rest of the journey and Wilkins himself had to take care of the ship's constant mechanical problems. Of the rest, '. . . none of them are congenial to me and I expect to have a pretty miserable time.'[24] Despite the hostility, Wilkins continued to corral and outsmart his reluctant crew all the way to Banks Island.

When they arrived at the appointed meeting place, there was no sign of Stefansson and his two companions. Nothing had been heard of them for six months and they had left with provisions for just eight weeks. Further exploration of the rugged coast and inland proved unsuccessful. Wilkins had all but given up hope of finding his leader alive. The *Mary Sachs* was leaking badly, barely able to stay afloat; there was no alternative but to beach her and prepare a base. He did not relish the thought of spending the winter with his disagreeable shipmates.

On 11 September, Natkusiak and Wilkins were inland from the coast hunting when they noticed what appeared to be a beacon in the distance. Excitedly, they hurried towards it and discovered on the top of the grass sods a note on the back of a cartridge box written in Stefansson's unmistakable handwriting. It was undated, but the first evidence Wilkins had that his difficult mission had not been in vain.

He returned to camp in the early morning hours of the following day to find Stefansson fast asleep in his tent, his two travelling companions snoring in the focsle of the schooner. By the dim light of his lantern, 'They did not look at all emaciated, but fatter and more healthful than I had ever seen them before.'

Far from being grateful for Wilkins' efforts, Stefansson was seething with anger when they spoke, furious that his orders to deliver the *North Star* had been disobeyed. He would not accept Wilkins' explanation that he had been overruled by Dr Anderson. He was now convinced Anderson was attempting to undermine his position and had clearly believed, quite unfairly, that Wilkins – not even a government employee – would stand up to a leader appointed by the Canadian Government. It was preposterous, and Wilkins was wise enough to realise the anger had little to do with him.

By way of apology, Stefansson soon afterwards handed Wilkins a letter stating that the photographer had done as much, if not more, than any other man on staff and recommending to headquarters that Wilkins be put on the official payroll on a level equal to that of the highest paid of any of the scientific staff. Given that he had now broken his agreement with Gaumont, Wilkins appreciated the gesture.

Over the coming months, the two men spent a great deal of time together on a shared preoccupation: the hunt for food. The diet of the entire party became almost exclusively meat. Today environmentalists would be horrified by the death toll inflicted on the island's caribou herd. It was often senseless killing because the animals were brought down faster than they could be bled, cut and skinned. Foxes would reach the carcass before the hunters, making the meat good for dogs at best.

When not hunting, Wilkins worked tirelessly on his photography or collecting, prepared their camp or cooked. Stefansson was not a man who wasted words in the praise of others, but he was deeply impressed by his young protégé:

> I have never known anyone who worked harder than Wilkins. He would be cleaning the scraps of meat off the leg bones of a wolf before breakfast and scraping the fat from a bearskin up to bedtime at night. His diaries were filled with information about the speci-mens he gathered, his fingers were stained with the photographic chemical used in the development of his innumerable plates and films, his mind was always alert and his response always cheerful when a new task was proposed.[25]

Inside their snowhouse, the two men would argue long into the night about theology and philosophy, but most of all about the future of exploration. Wilkins never warmed to the long, tiring dog treks across the ice, despite his prowess, and believed aeroplanes would eventually consign the dog teams to history. One day while they were out hunting together on the coastal ice, the apprentice explorer returned to his favourite subject. Stefansson, exasperated by the younger man's naïve faith in machines, retorted: 'You cannot learn much more oceanography flying over an ocean than you learn botany flying over a botanical garden.'[26] Wilkins recalled that Stefansson, 'tired of hearing me talk of the possibilities of the airplane, announced dramatically . . . that in his opinion a submarine would be a much better vehicle for exploration of the arctic . . .'[27] A submarine could stop and stay wherever it needed, coming to the surface through thin ice or the open water between the ice floes.

The more he considered it, the more Wilkins began to appreciate it wasn't such a crazy notion. While both the submarines and aeroplanes of the day were as likely to kill their occupants as transport them, he knew these pioneering designs would be improved. It was only a matter of time, and out there, surrounded by the expanse of featureless ice with no visible line between sky and earth, time was not a pressing concern. This was a disconnected place, a looking-glass world, where anything was possible. A man could fashion a lifetime's work from just a passing thought or a good-natured argument. There, on the lip of the Earth, beneath the gathering twilight of an Arctic winter, an idea was born and Wilkins began to plan a momentous journey.

For the next two years Wilkins continued his tireless work on behalf of the CAE. He would battle wolves, a mad fox and more bears. He mastered the art of ice travel and earned the admiration of the Eskimo. He continued to act as go-between for Stefansson and Anderson, who could no longer stand to meet with each other. Now, with more maturity and confidence in his own judgment, he refused to be bullied by either of them and forced what compromises he could in the interests of the expedition. In August 1915 he did eventually bring the *North Star* to Banks Island only to discover Stefansson no longer needed it. By then he was eager to get back to civilisation and begin his real work.

He now understood that Stefansson was on a pointless dream, spending vast sums of government money for glory not knowledge. When the opportunity came, he decided, he would leave. When news of the war reached him, followed by a letter informing him his father had died, his thoughts turned to his mother. For months he had been chasing various supply boats in the hope of collecting mail he knew was waiting for him. When finally he received word that she was still alive and asking for him, he made the decision. On 1 June he wrote to Stefansson:

Dear Mr Stefansson:

You have a mother, and the love of your parents is probably no less developed in you than in most others. Imagine yourself in the position I find myself, you can if you try and I feel sure of your sympathy.

I quote a few paragraphs from my mail. 'It was our constant wish and our greatest desire your dear old father's and mine to be spared to see your safe return. I know how sad you must have been when you heard that he had passed away . . . It is comforting to have so many of my children near me but I want you my son, my baby & it is consoling to think that you will soon be on your way home. I pray that I may be spared to see you again.'[28]

In spite of the fact that it is now 18 months since the latest of these letters were written, would you in my place hesitate to choose your course of action?'

Unknown to his men, Stefansson suffered deeply from loneliness. In one year he received but a single personal letter from the outside world. He was close to his own mother, who was frail and blind. Wilkins' plea could not have left him unmoved.[29]

Stefansson continued his expedition for two further years, making some modest discoveries of new islands which he trumpeted loudly, but the search for the missing continent eluded him just as it had others. He downplayed the *Karluk* tragedy and other negative aspects of the expedition. In a letter written in 1920, he made the extraordinary statement that 'neither men nor dogs have been lost and that neither men nor dogs have suffered serious hardship.'[30]

He and Anderson continued their feud for years. When he was being considered for presidency of the Explorers Club of New York, Anderson denounced his former colleague as a 'socialist, pacifist and a coward', and accused him of deserting the expedition in the face of presumed danger. Stefansson responded by labelling Anderson's group the real deserters, despite the fact that they had successfully charted hundreds of kilometres of Arctic coastline and made valuable contributions to our knowledge of the Inuit.

The Canadian Government, deeply embarrassed by the death toll and the financial costs of the exercise, wanted the entire affair buried. It rejected calls from survivors and the scientists of the Southern Party for a royal commission. After another debacle involving an attempt to establish a commercial reindeer operation in the far north, Stefansson moved permanently to the United States, where his reputation remained unsullied.

Wilkins stayed on generally good terms with his former mentor, but now it was he who was doing the exploring.

4

—

The mad photographers

*The flickering images reveal a scene of devastation. Abandoned
vehicles litter a muddy road alongside the corpses of blasted horses.
Soldiers shuffle by with blank expressions. The film jumps, closer now, two
men are crouched by the roadside. One is a priest, the other a soldier, a
cigarette locked between his lips. They are gently raising an injured man
from the waste. From their expressions and unhurried movement it is
apparent he's close to death. They hold his hand, as if to say 'we are here
with you old friend'. All they can offer is a moment of calm before he
passes. The camera is intimate but not intrusive and the scene, even ninety
years after it was filmed, remains deeply moving. The cameraman was
Hubert Wilkins.*

On his enlistment papers for service in the Australian Imperial
Force, Wilkins was asked his 'trade or calling'. He had many
skills by now, but he summed them up in a single word:
'explorer'. It seems appropriate then that his journey to the
frontlines and fame as a war photographer was, true to his trade,
an adventure. His passage from the still of the Arctic ice to a
world in chaos covered almost 50 000 kilometres and took almost
a year to complete.

It began on foot with a 950-kilometre trek from Banks Island,
followed by a boat trip around the Alaskan coast and a train across
Canada to Ottawa. There he closed off his affairs with the CAE. The

Navy Department was sorry to see him go but insisted on having his reports, particularly his views on Stefansson's behaviour. Over the coming months of long sea voyages he wrote up his notes and delivered an honest account from which they could draw their own conclusions.[1]

There was some talk of a commission in the Canadian Navy, but Wilkins was keen to visit his family now his father had passed away, and take his chances in the Australian forces once the estate was settled. But getting home in the middle of a world war was no easy task.

He arrived in New York seeking a passage across the Atlantic, but for unenlisted men they were not easy to arrange. He eventually found a berth on a convoy of seven ships travelling together in the hope of avoiding the U-boats prowling off the coast. By the end of the first day, two of the convoy had been sunk off Nantucket and the others were scattered. His ship was filled with the wives and children of Canadian officers hoping to join their husbands and fathers in Britain. Now, with those they were able to rescue from the sea, it was dangerously overloaded.[2]

Two days later, a German U-boat found them. 'Without warning there was a terrific explosion in the bows of the ship,' Wilkins wrote The vessel listed heavily, making it difficult to launch the lifeboats:

> Two of us men slipped down the splintery ropes into the boat, the others assisted the women to the lines and practically threw them into our arms. There were many rough tumbles. Some young children were dropped to us and these we caught and placed in any arms we could find. Finally the boat was jammed full. Many on deck were pleading to be helped in, but we could take no more.
>
> We moved in and pulled aboard all we could reach and then with our boat simply jammed full and riding low, the young officer in charge ordered us to move out free from the ship.[3]

The next morning the sun rose clear on the little boat and they scanned the horizon in hope. Before she went down, their ship had sent an SOS, and others from the convoy might be looking for them. In the afternoon a cry went up – there in the distance a ship was coming towards them. A corvette had picked up the distress signal and come hurrying to their aid despite the risks. They all knew they were remarkably lucky to be rescued, as hundreds of ships were being sunk every month without trace.

For most, surviving a torpedo attack while watching others drown might be a life-changing event, certainly a ghastly moment to be remembered for all time. Wilkins left two written accounts of his travels to war, yet in one the sinking went unmentioned and in the other he dismissed it in just a few lines. This was not bravado, but when measured against what he experienced in battle, it was not an extraordinary event.

In London, Wilkins made several new acquaintances in the social circle of the flamboyant sculptor Lady Kathleen Scott. As the widow of Scott of the Antarctic, she made a point of meeting the interesting polar explorers, and at one of her soirées (sometimes conducted by her bedside) Wilkins met fellow Australian photographer Frank Hurley.

Hurley was an incorrigible wanderer who had just returned from an epic adventure in the Antarctic with Ernest Shackleton's *Endurance* expedition. Their plan had been to cross the continent from coast to coast, but the expedition never even made it to land. Trapped in the frozen ocean, their ship was eventually crushed and the party was forced to make camp on the ice. When it broke up, they took to open boats in search of a barren outcrop called Elephant Island. Here the castaways lived for months while Shackleton went on a desperate boat journey in search of help. Hurley, already a polar veteran, was tough and unflinching during their long wait, and battled against enormous odds to bring back his precious film and negatives. They made him famous.

Tall and powerfully built despite two years on a diet of penguin and seal, Hurley had an imposing forest of thick curls and huge hands which belied his delicate skills in the darkroom. Plain spoken, he was one of those men who either impressed or grated on first meetings. The much quieter Wilkins took time to get to know, but with their mutual fascination for adventure and photography, the two got along immediately. Together they reintroduced themselves to civilisation, dining and visiting the theatre and cinema in their brief time in London. That two poor, largely self-educated young men from the colonies had simultaneously spent years exploring and photographing opposite polar extremes seems, in retrospect, an unlikely coincidence. But their shared fate was still not played out – in a few months they would meet again, and their lives become inextricably bound.

After another long sea journey Wilkins finally reached Australia. He had left his family seven years earlier with hopes and grand ideas and returned, at twenty-eight, something of a local celebrity. He entertained a large crowd at the Adelaide town hall on his 'thrilling experiences in the Balkans', gave 'an illuminating talk on Arctic Canada and the Blonde Esquimaux' and, as guest of the Governor, lectured on Arctic flowers. His Excellency introduced him, to loud applause, and was 'particularly gratified to know that Mr Wilkins was a South Australian'.[4]

Wilkins' visit home was brief, barely time to see his aging mother and sign the papers regarding his father's estate. He was left with a share of the property, but, knowing he would never return to farming, passed control to his brothers. Like so many young men, he was in a hurry to get to the war.

His chance came during a visit to the Australian Flying Corps training centre at Laverton outside Melbourne. Though he hadn't flown since the Balkan Wars, 'my knowledge was on a par with those men who had been training in Australia for several months.'[5] Australia had just formed its own air force. He applied for a commission on a Thursday, received it the following Monday and within a week of signing up was on his way back to England in the newly tailored uniform of a second lieutenant. But there was one small problem: he was medically unfit for flying.

Wilkins' service records show that at his first application for a commission, on 17 April 1917, his vision was faulty. But by the time he applied for the Flying Corps two weeks later, some friendly hand had intervened and his new medical certificate avoided the issue by claiming he had been 'examined previously', and thus he was accepted for service.

Eventually officialdom did catch up with him. Several months later he was tested again and found to be almost certainly colour blind. He perceived green as red, yellow as green and could not determine dark red at all. His records were stamped as 'unfit in any capacity' to be a flying officer, but for reasons unknown they were filed away and ignored.

Wilkins always laughed this off as a misunderstanding over the precise words used to describe different colours, but from a man who could reel off the names and variations of dozens of rare Arctic plants in Esquimaux, it was an unconvincing excuse. One of the pioneers of aviation was not only unlicensed; officially, he should never have been allowed near the controls.

While he did fly often during the war, it turned out Wilkins' skill with the camera was in greater demand than his piloting. Immediately after returning to Britain, he was recommended for service in the newly established Australian War Records Section as an official photographer. It seems probable that Frank Hurley, himself newly appointed to the section, may have had a role in his friend's appointment as his assistant.

The War Records Section was created and led by a civilian who was respected by soldiers perhaps more than any man in the Australian army, the remarkable historian Charles Bean. As a newspaper correspondent, Bean had staggered ashore with the troops at Gallipoli – an ungainly, thin and shy man totally unprepared for what he was about to encounter. By the time he left eight months later, he had become a warrior with his typewriter, revered by all who knew him. His detailed and moving accounts remain some of the finest examples of war reportage of any era.

Bean was devoted to a scrupulously accurate account of the war. He called it 'the only one religion – the search for truth . . . the ultimate bedrock on which we must build the new order.'[6] As the official war historian for the Australians, he was determined that his own men should be telling it. Until Bean's intervention, Australia's role in the battles on the Western Front was largely, and irregularly, documented by the British. The High Command had little interest in recording the involvement of its Dominion soldiers, and was deeply distrustful of journalists and photographers at the front. Bean appealed directly to the British Government and was eventually granted his wish for the establishment of a records section, with Australian photographers, war artists, facilities and, most importantly, freedom of movement around the battlefield.

In Wilkins and Hurley he could not have found two better men for the perilous job of photographing the vast machinery of modern warfare. From the moment he collected them on a summer's day at Boulogne they shone for him, creating some of the most remarkable images of warfare ever seen. Bean would later call them his 'magnificent photographers', but he understood they had contrasting characters. He thought Hurley 'a rare mix of the genuine, highly sensitive artist and keen commercial man' and best suited to taking publicity pictures; while Wilkins 'sought to provide our future historians with a record of places and events so accurate they could be, and often were, relied on as historical evidence'.[7]

So they were assigned different tasks. Hurley was to take the propaganda pictures that would encourage the war effort, while the meticulous Wilkins gathered the visual record of men and events. It's doubtful if the two photographers themselves acknowledged the distinction, and in any case the thunder of battle often made it arbitrary. In practice both produced work that was arresting *and* historically valid. But the two photographers were made of different stuff, and it shows in the archives.

Hurley's photographs have an eerie sense of suspended animation – not so much a moment frozen in time as a still-life portrait. His mastery of light and composition gave his photos an incandescent quality, yet their heroic references firmly marked them with the Imperial attitudes of the time. Wilkins rarely matched Hurley for artistry, but he never aspired to. What his photos lack in exquisite construction they make up in intensity – with a lens at times so direct it seems to suck in the view. These often simple records of men at work and rest, lined up on parade grounds and rushing into battle, have a timeless humanity. He achieved what Bean asked of him: an honest account of soldiers caught in the most terrible battle in history.

Both Hurley and Wilkins took tremendous risks working the battlefield. Roaming the frontlines they were often more exposed than any soldier, and it is little short of miraculous both survived. Wilkins left only a few mentions of his wartime experience, and rarely spoke of it later. Hurley and Bean, however, kept scrupulous diaries and these, along with other eyewitness accounts, leave a vivid picture of the extreme dangers they encountered almost every day.

When they arrived together in France the trench lines had barely shifted in three years of deadly stalemate. Repeated offensives had cost millions of lives and come no closer to ending the war. Fearing that revolution in Russia might free German troops for the Western Front and desperate to disrupt the U-boat attacks launched from Belgium, the Allies needed to make headway. So began the disastrous Third Battle of Ypres, better known today after the insignificant village that became its focus: Passchendaele. The photographers landed just as the campaign began, and with characteristic understatement Bean wrote: 'Neither of them could ever come out of another time like they had at Ypres.'

Bean reasoned there was no point delaying their introduction to the front – nothing but your own eyes could prepare you for Flanders in 1917. On the day of their arrival he took them on a tour of the Australian battle line, spread out on an irregular arc of trenches just metres from the German positions. Through a sudden driving storm, one of many that sodden summer, they moved forward, seeing for themselves what Hurley described as 'the exaggerated machinations of hell'. That first day left him shocked:

Here the awfulness of the battlefield burst on one – the great howitzer and batteries were in full operation and the ear-splitting din was followed by the scream of a hail of shell which swept over our heads to the enemy lines . . . We plodded through shell craters, and shell-torn ground littered with fragments of burst shell and shrapnel, torn equipment and smashed entanglements, over the blood-drenched battlefield till we arrived at the infamous Hill 60.[8]

The hill marked the point where the great campaign of 1917 was to have begun, but the attack had been cut short by the downpours that soon turned the battleground into an impenetrable bog. In fact, little of the hill itself remained. It was now a swampy crater, all that was left of a heavily fortified German position that had taken a terrible toll on attacking Allied troops. For months Australian engineers had tunnelled beneath it from their lines, laying a massive mine under the enemy guns. When this and eighteen other mines laid along the front were simultaneously detonated, the explosion was so massive it was clearly heard by Lloyd George in his Downing Street office.

Hurley described the scene before them:

Everywhere the ground is littered with bits of guns, bayonets, shells and men. Way down on one of those mine craters was an awful sight. There lay three hideous, almost skeletal decomposed fragments of corpses of German gunners. Oh, the frightfulness of it all! To think these fragments were once sweethearts, maybe, husbands of loved sons . . . Until my dying day I shall never forget this haunting glimpse down into the mine crater on Hill 60 . . .

Deep beneath the hill were tunnels now used as a forward dressing station for the wounded. Bean and his photographers went below while above, the Australian artillery was in full roar. Inside the dim catacombs, some 75 metres below ground, were lines of injured men. The ground shook violently with the continual impact of the shells above. Hurley described the scene he found: 'Soakage trickled in through the roof or oozed through the walls, and the blackness seemed to be made blacker still by a few spluttering candles. These candles gave a convulsive jump as the reverberating shock of a near heavy gun was fired . . . one might liken it to earthquake sensations.'

Wilkins had seen battles before, but there was nothing in the Balkans that could match the sheer scale of this conflict, where a million men and ten thousand guns faced each other along a line of death that stretched from the North Sea to the Swiss frontier. He later told a writer: 'It seemed like a trip into Hell – that black night lighted by flames of guns and by signal flares, the air shaking with noise, and the earth shaking underfoot. Human beings seemed insignificant in the midst of all this. It didn't seem possible that men could go through it and live.'[9]

When the photographing was complete it was back to their quarters at Steenvorde, 10 kilometres behind the front. There, in an improvised darkroom, they worked late into the night before dropping for a few hours sleep. So ended their first day at war, and so it would continue for Wilkins every day for the next eighteen months. In that time he witnessed every battle, either in the attack line or close in support, sometimes flying low overhead in observation aircraft, at other times charging with the troops as they went over the top from the trenches. The ANZAC soldiers had the highest casualty rate of any on the Western Front and Wilkins carried the scars of these days for the rest of his life. In all, he was wounded nine times: shot, shrapnelled, gassed, blown up and blasted out of the skies. He was twice awarded the Military Cross for conspicuous acts of courage – the only Australian photographer of any war to be decorated – yet he never carried a gun. To Wilkins' great embarrassment, the commander of the Australian Corps, Sir John Monash, called him the bravest soldier in his army.

His colleague, the war artist Will Dyson, went further, claiming Wilkins was one of the bravest men who ever lived.

His near suicidal dedication defies belief. If it had not been witnessed by all around him, and visibly evident from his photographs and films, Wilkins' exploits would seem the loftiest of tall stories. Yet once the war passed, he was reluctant to speak of it, and it was left largely to others to describe.

A little of his experience can be gleaned from between the lines of dry language in the official records. Wilkins' medical papers describe the steady progress of a body that was being slowly picked apart.[10] He suffered a gunshot wound to the leg and a fractured tibia within days of arriving in August, then a broken rib and a wounded thigh two months later. A fractured thigh in October was followed by a brief repatriation to Britain to recover. He was soon back, with a wound to the other thigh and foot. And so it continued until July 1918 when a medical officer optimistically wrote that his appointment to the Australian Army should be 'terminated through wounds and sickness'. As with the eyesight test, the instruction was ignored.

During their first month in Flanders, Hurley and Wilkins roamed widely across a battlefield locked in fatal impasse. They quickly became used to the daily artillery barrages launched by both sides like some ghastly game of tennis across the trench line. The endless movements forward of men and ammunition, followed by the inevitable return of stretchers and prisoners, became a river of khaki that flowed day and night. Trees, villages and even the contours of the land itself had been altered by three years of incessant shelling. German commander Erich Ludendorff called it 'the crater-land . . . a wilderness of mire'.[11]

Across the shell-swept frontline, all vegetation had disappeared, along with the intricate irrigation channels of the Flemish lowlands. In its place was a stinking quagmire of mud. 'Sucking tenacious slime', Hurley called it. To fall from the narrow wooden duckboards meant almost certain drowning, and thousands of men and horses perished this way. At night the whole ghastly scene was lit under a shower of star shells and flashes. Hurley was as fascinated as he was fearful: 'The whole sky seemed a crescent of shimmering sheet lightning . . . it was all very beautiful yet awesome and terrible.'[12]

Most days the photographers followed a similar routine, leaving the little curved iron hut Hurley dubbed 'the Billabong' before dawn so they could capture the morning light. Though behind the lines, it was within range of enemy artillery and several times was attacked from the air. They travelled as far as possible by car, then 'truck jumped' or went on foot, usually with an assistant to help them with the cumbersome equipment of glass plates, wooden tripods and various cameras.

This was the most dangerous few square kilometres on Earth, yet they retained a grim humour. Hurley wrote that weighed down with 'rather too much equipage . . . the bursting of the Boche shells in one's immediate vicinity added to the excitement of the tramp but rather detracted from one's admiration of the surrounding desolation.'[13] Wilkins sympathised with the sentiments of a British soldier he overheard joking that he actually wanted to get wounded so that he could go back to Britain as a factory worker: 'It's no fun getting a "bob" a day over here stopping the shells when over there at home we can get a "quid" a day for making them.'[14]

The War Records Section – the photographers with their heavily laden assistant 'lumpers' trailing behind carrying gear – soon became a familiar sight to the troops, who dubbed them the 'mad photographers'. As they ran the gauntlet during the barrages it almost seemed they were enjoying it. On one occasion, while sheltering in a thin sandbag dugout at the notorious Chateau Wood, Hurley had his cinema camera trained on bursting shells. 'Then the fun began. They screamed overhead like a flight of rockets. One fell a little short and threw mud over the dugout and fell but a yard away. I owe my life to it being a dud.' Dodging from dugout to dugout, the team were 'having the excitement of our lives', he wrote. 'We puffed and sheltered for a few minutes (then) wizsh-sh-sh-sh-sh-sh – and a shell lobbed so close that had we been a few paces out we must have been hit direct. This shell was also a dud! Three times today my life has been miraculously spared.'[15]

On another occasion Hurley and Wilkins decided to get close-up pictures of the shells exploding along the only route to the front, the grim Menin Road. 'Yesterday we damned near succeeded in having an end made to ourselves,' wrote Hurley:

In spite of heavy shelling by the Boche, we made an endeavour to secure a number of shell burst pictures . . . I took two pictures by hiding in a dugout and rushing out and snapping . . . when a terrific, angry, rocket-like shriek warned us to duck. This we did by throwing ourselves flat in a shell-hole half filled with mud. Immediately a terrific roar made us squeeze ourselves into as little bulk as possible, and up went timber, stones and shells and everything else in the vicinity. A dump of 4.5 shells had received a direct hit. The splinters rained down on our helmets, and the debris and mud came down like a cloud. The frightful concussion absolutely winded us, but we escaped injury and made off through the mud and water as fast as we possibly could.[16]

Of this incident, Bean wrote in the *Official History of the AIF*: 'Many this day observed with admiration the famous pair of Official Photographers, Captain Frank Hurley and Lieutenant G.H. Wilkins, recklessly exposing themselves on the Menin Road to secure a record of the bombardment.'[17]

The war artist Fred Leist became friendly with Wilkins and claimed he had a habit of crawling over the trenches before an attack in order to get photos of the men coming over the top. After years tramping Arctic trails, it seems he couldn't get out of the habit of a morning constitutional. An Australian doctor, Arthur Joyce, heard stories of Wilkins 'walking in the vicinity of no-man's-land for exercise, quite oblivious to any danger'.[18]

Both Wilkins and Hurley succumbed to a grim but sustaining fatalism. Death had become so capricious there seemed little point in devising strategies to try to avoid it – there simply was no safe means to negotiate these desolate wastelands. 'Some days it seemed,' wrote Wilkins years later, 'no matter how intense the shelling and fighting, I entirely escaped trouble. On other days, in spite of all precaution, I got into trouble wherever I went.'[19]

Equally, they became inured to gruesome sights confronting them each day. Hurley spoke of being amazed that he could come back to the little hut after witnessing ghastly events and sit down to a hearty meal secured by his assistant from local farmers. It was, he said, as if he was returning home from the office. But one wonders if Wilkins could stomach a meal the evening after his visit to an abandoned field station where it was said human bodies were being cooked for food. 'During the investigation I took pictures of several neatly dissected bodies stewing in large cauldrons of vegetable soup.'[20] It was not the work of some deranged chef, but the outcome of a long-range shell that had fallen on an unfortunate patrol.

Wilkins could recall only one occasion that his nerve 'gave way'. In an unpublished comment to a fellow adventurer he remembered a day when he and six other men were moving single file along the wooden duckboards. A shell hit the man in the lead, blew his head off and stuck it on a post. 'All the rest of us roared with hysterical laughter, to see his head there, stuck upon the post. At the moment it seemed hilariously funny.'[21]

As he was an accomplished self-publicist, there are plentiful pictures of Hurley at work during the war, but only a handful of Wilkins. There is, however, one extraordinary series where they photographed each other amid the ruins of a blasted railway siding in early October 1917. In turn they are shown standing in the same place, holding the same pose with camera in hand, amid a group of exhausted Australian soldiers who seem more dead than alive.

In his diaries, Hurley described the scene:

> This shelled embankment of mud was a terrible sight. Every 20 paces or less lay a body. Some frightfully mutilated, without legs, arms and heads, and half covered in mud and slime. I could not help thinking that Wilkins and I, trudging along in this inferno and soaked to the skin, talking and living beings, might not be the next moment one of these things – Gee – it puts the wind up one at times.
>
> Under a questionably sheltered bank lay a group of dead men. Sitting by them, in a little scooped out recess sat a few living; but so emaciated by fatigue and shell shock that it was hard to differentiate.[22]

As a barrage of shells fell all around them the photographers stopped in this gruesome byway to take what amounted to tourist snapshots of each other. It seems likely these were private images, meant as mementos of each other's company. By now they both knew their partnership was coming to an end. For some time Hurley had been involved in a bruising struggle with Bean over his photography and earlier that week had, in an angry exchange, offered his resignation.

Hurley felt no single image could capture the vast landscape of horror, exploding shells, dismembered bodies and abandoned weaponry that were the daily experience of every soldier. So he resorted to the darkroom tricks that had always been part of his repertoire, combining images from different photographs to produce composite images that to him more accurately represented reality.

Bean, always a stickler for the facts, branded the composites 'fakes' and he demanded Hurley stop making them. It led to a heated row. Hurley tried to smuggle some past the censors, and when they were discovered Wilkins initially stepped forward to accept the blame. But his chivalry was pointless and Bean soon discovered the truth. The dispute went all the way to the High Command, and eventually a compromise was worked out that allowed Hurley to exhibit just six of the composites in London. But his time in France was over, and he was reassigned to a very different battlefield in Palestine.

We cannot know for sure what Wilkins made of his hot-headed colleague, but there is no reason to believe he felt anything but admiration. If so, it was mutual. Hurley was not a man prone to praising others, but on their last day together he passed judgment: 'Wilkins is an excellent fellow, enthusiastic, conscientious and diligent. The innumerable hair breath [sic] escapes, and our own marvellous good luck I only hope may continue.'[23]

For four months they had pushed their luck covering the increasingly hopeless struggle. Passchendaele came to represent all the horror and waste of the Western Front, remembered for its mud and the utter suffering of the soldiers. British prime minister Lloyd George called it 'grim, futile and bloody',[24] while in Winston Churchill's assessment it was 'a forlorn expenditure of valour and life without equal'.[25]

When it was over, more than half a million men were dead or wounded, and the British had moved the frontline less than 10 kilometres. The Germans were weakened but still in Flanders and their submarines continued to prowl the Atlantic from Belgian bases. Wilkins' war had only begun.

5

A man apart

If you can dream – and not make dreams your master;
If you can think – and not make thoughts your aim;
If you can meet with Triumph and Disaster
And treat those two imposters just the same;
If you can bear to hear the truth you've spoken
Twisted by knaves to make a trap for fools,
Or watch the things you gave your life to, broken,
And stoop and build 'em up with worn-out tools . . .

– from 'If' by Rudyard Kipling

It took six men to replace Frank Hurley as official photographer, but in the months it took to recruit them, Wilkins worked the desolate aftermath of Passchendaele alone. He found many subjects for his camera. For some time he had been compiling scenes for a documentary film on the long process by which men received their mail in the trenches, but had been constantly interrupted by crises at the front. Now he spent one of his leave weekends filming the mail's arrival from Australia to Liverpool and followed its rail journey to the post base in London. In a vast room, 700 women poured out the contents of the canvas sacks and somehow contrived to send letters and packages towards the right units. Some of them wore lavender water on their hands to spice the envelopes with promise. He followed the vast collection of newly sorted bags across the Channel, where on arrival they were sorted once more and sent forward to the lines. Eventually ration parties carried the letters on those last dangerous steps into the trenches. Each letter had passed through dozens of hands, all playing their part in lifting a soldier's spirits. An efficient mail service was considered vital to good morale.

Wilkins would have seen, but did not film, the growing sacks of letters that would never find their man. Even the disastrous campaign at Gallipoli couldn't match the devastating losses of the ANZAC units at Ypres. There were twice as many casualties here than in the Dardanelles campaign, lost in half the time.

He toured the casualty clearing hospitals, photographing a group of nurses taking tea in their simple tin hut, made homely with some flowers and a few magazine covers on the bare walls. Many of the Australian nurses had seen friends and family killed in the battle. Sister May Tilton had lost both her fiancé and a close cousin not a kilometre away from the hut, yet when the nursing staff was ordered away from the shelling she declined and stayed at the front.

As the snows began to fall, he photographed the exhausted battalions on parade, their ranks full of gaps like a mouthful of lost teeth. He filmed barbed wire entanglements and captured German pillboxes – small gains for such losses. In the first week of December he took one of his most historically important images: in a small commandeered cottage, a line of men were waiting their turn to vote in the second referendum on conscription.

The Australian Government had long been concerned that it could not sustain the flow of volunteers to fill its dwindling battalions. Yet the law would not allow it to conscript men for overseas service. Prime Minster Billy Hughes twice put the issue to a bruising national vote, and twice was repudiated. The votes that troubled him most, though, for they undermined every oratorical argument he could muster, were those cast by the soldiers themselves. As they wait patiently to make their mark, the men in Wilkins' photo have clearly long lost any illusions of patriotic duty. They are there for each other, not for the generals, and certainly not for politicians. The men in the trenches voted overwhelmingly against forcing their countrymen into this hell.

When the weather allowed, Wilkins made his way to the aerodrome of the newly formed Australian Flying Corps. While winter brought stalemate on the ground, in the air the battle continued, and there was nothing he enjoyed more than a hair-raising flight taking aerial reconnaissance photos. This was dangerous work, even by the standards of the time, as the life expectancy of new pilots was down to just two months. It took nerve to fly low over the enemy frontlines, particularly in the slow old RE8s flown by the Australians. Wilkins was making several flights a week.[1]

He had been told that under no circumstances was he to get involved in dogfights. Aerial photos had become a vital tool for the artillery and were considered vastly more important than engaging in combat duels. Still, it didn't prevent him coming up with outlandish alternatives. One day he approached Bean 'with a serious face' because he felt there was a gap in his photographic records: he hadn't yet managed to take a satisfactory picture of German infantry actually fighting. He planned to fill this gap by convincing some pilot to fly him so low over the enemy lines that he could get close-up pictures of the German army in action.

'I was thankful that the war ended before he induced any pilot to let him make the attempt,' wrote an incredulous Bean.[2]

Wilkins also flew with Royal Flying Corps patrols, where his skills and calm demeanour made an impression. By the spring of 1917 the British were losing more than 200 aircraft a month and the Germans were making regular bombing raids on the British mainland. Britain needed a morale-boosting strike and plans were being advanced for an audacious aerial raid on Berlin. Wilkins was keen to be involved, and Bean had to fight the bureaucracy to stop the British poaching him.

'I tried very hard to get Wilkins his captaincy from Colonel Dodds but Dodds wouldn't hear of it, tho' all the other colonial photographers are captains and he is the best, easily,' wrote Bean. 'Today Wilkins tells me he has an offer from the Royal Air Force [sic] to manage their camera department with the rank of Captain and Major within a month.'[3] It took Bean several more months to have Wilkins promoted – a lifetime by the accelerated clock of the Western Front – but he stayed with the Australians.

Wilkins and Bean now drew even closer. Like Steffanson before him, the older man became a mentor, and the admiration was returned. Years later, writing a note to Bean from a tent on one of his long expeditions of discovery, he recalled their time together in France with warm affection:

If anyone deserves the credit, it is you. We wielders of the mechanism were only agents of your influence and were it not for the fact of our great admiration of you and your outstanding example, the efforts we put forward would not have been so energetic. I look back on the war period with feelings somewhat akin to gratitude . . . I didn't mean this to be that kind of letter, but my feelings are earnest and deep.[4]

The warm feelings were mutual. Bean had witnessed many acts of courage, but in Wilkins he saw something else. The man just couldn't help himself: 'I sometimes doubted whether any course of action was for long agreeable to him unless it led eventually to danger.'[5] The historian was astounded by the risks his protégé took. When recommending him for high honours, Bean wrote:

On September 20 early in the fight forward of our old trenches he was blown up by a shell which broke some of the gear he was carrying. In spite of this he continued to take invaluable pictures of the front-line fighting; he continued his work, passing daily through the barrages without relief during a period when almost all other officers were relieved. This work has been imposed on Lt. Wilkins by his own sense of duty. His demeanour, after nearly five weeks of heavy strain, has been outstandingly gallant and has brought great credit upon his office.[6]

When not aloft in aeroplanes, Wilkins took to the observation balloons which offered an excellent, if somewhat risky, panorama of the battlefield. Their crews were sitting targets and, while heavily protected by anti-aircraft guns, became irresistible prey to the marauding German fighter planes.[7] The observers were apt to bale out as soon as they saw the enemy aircraft coming, even though the parachutes of the time were unreliable, preferring the risk of jumping to being shot in cold blood or burning should the hydrogen-filled balloons explode.

Once he joined a two-man crew in a line of five balloons that came under attack from the black-crossed German fighters. In the first strike, two of the balloons went down in flames, the occupants jumping for their lives. Wilkins looked on, horrified, as the planes dipped to fire into the floating parachutists: 'One after the other we saw [them] jerk as the bullets struck, and noticed how their heads hung forward in death.'

His balloon was also hit, but did not catch fire. Through a haze of ground fire, the marauding planes banked and came back for another strafing run. This time they killed Wilkins' observer, wounded the other and left Wilkins helplessly dangling by his arms beneath the basket. Then the fighters returned a third time to finish him off. There was a sting across his cheek, but with muscles straining he hung on while the ground crew furiously reeled him in.

'I kept my eyes raised to the gas bag. I knew that if I once looked down I would not be able to resist the urge to fall.'

Finally he felt hands on his ankles and he collapsed into the arms of the ground crew. The last thing he remembered hearing was someone saying: 'Well, this one is alive at any rate.'[8]

From the air, the devastation of war was even more apparent than from the ground. Entire villages had simply disappeared, the bricks of houses, shops and churches pulverised into red dust. All that remained was an alien crater-scape and the faint impressions where roads once ran. Amid this surreal destruction, Wilkins' thoughts often drifted back to his Arctic wanderings and his conviction that the aeroplane was the best means to explore the unmapped regions of the world.

'Some day when the world would return to normal,' he told the journalist Lowell Thomas, 'I hoped I could sail through polar skies in pursuit, not of an enemy man, but of the secrets of nature that would help conquer the natural enemies of all mankind.'[9]

As the seasons turned in 1918, both sides braced themselves for the expected spring campaign. On a misty morning on 21 March, massed artillery belched the fury of a million shells down upon the British lines, heralding the opening of Germany's great offensive to capture Paris and end the war. It was followed by the *Kaiserschlacht* (Kaiser's battle), an infantry onslaught across a 70-kilometre front rapidly capturing the ground that had been so desperately fought over for so long. In the next three months, the immense struggle lay in the balance.

Just how close Wilkins came to the action is apparent from his photographs. In his personal album of war pictures, he has kept one particularly unusual image. It is out of focus, full of smoke and the horizon line is more vertical than horizontal. He had photographed himself being blown up.

'I was looking in the viewfinder of the camera, my finger on the shutter release. The next moment I found myself in the air,' Wilkins wrote. He came down unconscious, but was picked up by the crew of a passing tank who got him to a medical station. 'I came to, badly shaken but not much hurt. I was taken to my car and drove to my own quarters.' The camera was destroyed and the image, meaningless to anyone else, put away as a personal keepsake.

He carried the legacy of these scrapes for the rest of his life. As he tramped frozen trails and desert sands, there would always be a reminder of just how close he had come to fatal injury. One military doctor later described his feet as a disgrace, and doubted that he would be able to walk for much longer. His collarbone would always remain painful, sometimes agonisingly so. But the most disabling effect of all, and the one that would plague him most seriously in later life, was creeping deafness. It would eventually leave him totally without hearing in one ear, and little but a constant drone in the other. What hearing wasn't damaged by the bombs of the Western Front was subjected to hundreds of hours of roaring engine noise in the cockpits of primitive aeroplanes. In later years Wilkins would be dependent on early electronic hearing aids. When busy, he would often turn them off to complete his work uninterrupted.

In late April the Germans pushed towards the city of Amiens, a strategic hub controlling the route to Paris. The British feared that if it were captured the war might be lost. They rushed the ANZACs into the fight to block the enemy onslaught at the village of Villers-Bretonneux. The Germans attacked with gas and tanks, capturing the village on 24 April. But that night, by the light of a nearly full moon, the Australians stormed from their trenches and counter-attacked from both the north and south, battling their way into the village and fighting house to house through the streets. By the end of the next day they had forced the Germans out. It was a remarkable victory – three years to the day since the tragic landings at Gallipoli – but the celebrations had a bizarre postscript.

With their spirits charged, many of the men had raided the fashionable dress shops in the main street of the town. When Wilkins came across them early the next morning, he '. . . found many of the men, for the fun of it, dressed up in luxurious women's clothing. Strolling about and enjoying themselves immensely.'[10] Some had the dresses over their uniforms, but others had stripped and dressed completely in women's clothes, abandoning their uniforms and equipment, letting off steam after the tremendous stress of the attack. 'They were playing about in the trenches, showing off to each other as I passed along, uninterrupted by shell fire or bullets. In fact it seemed to me that the quiet was ominous.

' "Hey you fellas," I said, "you'd better get out of them duds. Jerry is a bit too quiet this morning to please me. Ten to one he is cooking up a counter-attack and will be over here in no time . . ."

' "Ah, let him come," the men replied. "We can lick him in these clothes or even without clothes. We pushed him yesterday, alright, didn't we?"

' "Oh well," I said, "every dog has his day. It might be your turn next." They scoffed at the idea.'

At that moment a terrific barrage of shells came down upon them. There were not many casualties from the fragments, but there was much dust and smoke and a peculiar haze seemed to permeate the air.

'Soon our eyes were smarting, men dropped what they were doing, started to rub their eyes and curse and swear. "Hey what's this? Something's getting in my eyes," they said, "and it is cutting like hell." Then someone shouted "TEAR GAS" and all that could reach them hurriedly put on their gas masks. But by this time many of the men were blinded and suffering excruciating pain.'

Some of them managed to tear the blouses from their uniforms, but those dressed entirely in women's clothes were blinded and couldn't find their uniforms. Wilkins watched as 'men were lying down and writhing in agony. There was no thought of keeping a lookout to see what the Germans were doing. I was carrying . . . my gas mask at the alert and had it on before my eyes were badly damaged. Suddenly the German artillery lay down a heavy barrage on the trenches. Those of us who could see started dragging the blinded men into cover, but many of them were wounded and hardly any were in a fit condition to make a stand against the enemy, and charge they did.'

Wilkins and the few who could see arranged the walking wounded in lines, and hand-in-hand these desperate men, many still in skirts and blouses, were led back to the support lines. It was a bizarre and sad sight.

Elsewhere, he wrote, the gas was having its evil effect. 'Men who would otherwise not turn their backs on the enemy were strong bodied but entirely blind, and for the time being, helpless.'

As he made his way to safety, Wilkins turned and saw the pathetic scene. 'They were wandering in every direction, as often as not towards the advancing enemy, and many of them were before long mowed down by machine gun bullets. It was no place for me to stay around.'

The Australian forces, now united into a single corps under Australian command, played a vital role in stemming the German advance, and until the end of the war remained in virtually constant combat. In June, Lieutenant General John Monash took command and in the coming months won a series of meticulously planned battles that marked him as one of the finest commanders of the war. Wilkins was there to record them all.

Working with the photographer during this time could be a health hazard. Wilkins was quite capable of provoking a personal artillery barrage, as Bean heard one night when he came for dinner at the photographer's hut. Bean was enjoying the meal, while Wilkins was still working at the front. In his absence, the War Records staff all got around to telling their favourite Wilkins stories. Bean was so impressed with what he heard that before turning in for the night he recorded their stories in his notebook.[11] It seems they all agreed he had terrible luck – he seemed to attract trouble that passed others by:

> . . . the closest thing we ever had was on the Somme. (Wilkins was photographing several points I gave him). He put his camera up first on a trench looking down the valley. One went in there right at the foot of his tripod and didn't explode. Then he picked it up and went up the hill.
>
> Joyce [Wilkins' assistant] was getting more and more nervous and Wilkins continued moving towards the frontline. 'I thought [we] were getting pretty far forward that day. They always count it by when we pass the field guns. We passed them and went on and on. At last we came to some infantry in a sunken road. I thought they were pretty far up, but I didn't know they *were* the frontline. We went up to the top of a hill – there was beautiful long grass and no shell holes and I felt all right up there. I stood looking down into the village below, there were men and transport there, and I

saw that the men were in grey, but I thought they were just French soldiers.'

Wilkins said to Joyce: '*Give me the slide, quick.*' He doesn't often hurry himself . . . and then they started to put shells all over us. First one – like a ranging shot; then salvoes – they ought to have got us but they didn't shoot too well! . . . he picked up his camera quick and we ran quarter of a mile I think, back past that old broken white chateau . . . When we got back he says, '*I think the Germans had a good shot at us.*'

'*Could they see us?*' I asked.

'*Why, didn't you see them in the valley?*' he said.

'And I had thought they were French all the time. Why, you could have seen if one of them had a pipe in his mouth!'

Bean heard many similar stories about Wilkins' near misses, and the photographer was becoming something of a legend among the officers and troops.

One day, while returning from the front along the duckboards, Wilkins looked up to see a distant group of Canadian gunners wildly waving their arms at him as if to say 'get out of there'. Too late, the shells fell and Wilkins was once again blown off his feet into a water-filled crater. This time it was full of a hovering cloud of mustard gas. It was the camera that saved his life. The heavy Graflex half plate had fallen beneath his chest: 'When they found me, my nose and face were almost touching the water. The gunners bundled me into a wagon load of shells and took me to the dressing station from where I was taken to hospital.' Mustard gas, a vicious blistering agent that could strip the lungs of tissue, was deadly in even small concentrations. Wilkins awoke in the middle of the night, staggered out and commandeered a car back to headquarters to resume work the next day.

Luck alone was not sufficient to stay alive in this place. Survival required an unpredictable quality that few experienced but which Wilkins believed saved his life on several occasions. It was an intuition about danger, a kind of premonition. Other explorers knew of it. They usually called it 'Provenance' and the memoirs of the great adventurers often claim to have felt its presence, touching them on the shoulder ahead of some unseen danger, guiding them to safety. Wilkins recognised this presence as something otherworldly, and it planted in him the seeds of a deep spiritual awakening, a sense that if he was being protected then it must be for a purpose. His faith was both unorthodox and quixotic, but eventually deeply felt.

Wilkins calmly wandered the blood-soaked fields of Flanders, the bullets bouncing off his tunic, the shells falling at his feet but failing to explode, and, despite his quiet humility, he must have known that he was different to other men. 'I seemed to hold a charmed life,' he wrote, and those around him certainly sensed it too.[12]

His commanding officer, General Monash, led a force of 166 000 men – the largest of the twenty corps that made up the British Forces in France. As Monash liked to point out, he commanded a greater army than either Wellington or Napoleon had marshalled on these same fields. Among such numbers it would be easy to miss one man, a junior officer who carried no gun. But even Monash soon began hearing stories about the extraordinary photographer.

The General's initial encounter with Wilkins came at his very first test as commander – a small but brilliantly executed action known as the Battle of Hamel. It was launched on 4 July, in honour of the newly arrived American soldiers, some of whom were placed under his command. For the first time in history there was a coordinated attack of ground-strafing aeroplanes, tanks, artillery and infantry, and sup-plies dropped by parachute.

Wilkins moved with the first wave. 'I had decided that morning to accompany the front line infantry. The few tanks were to precede the men and clean up the trenches before the infantry arrived close behind the barrage. But what with mechanical trouble, and poor visibility, some of the tanks lagged behind and we went forward, routing the Germans from the trenches.'[12]

A nearby explosion cut Wilkins' face with a shell splinter, but, though his uniform was smeared with blood, it was not serious. He pushed on, ahead of the tanks, into the fog and smoke of the battle. The lack of visibility aided the attacking troops, but it made it difficult to coordinate the different units being thrown into the action. Wilkins stopped to help a wounded man who had been shot in the back and could not move.

'I was bending over him, on my knees, intent upon my job and paid no heed to some shouting I could faintly hear in the din. Then, again came that mysterious intuitive feeling of danger that I had several times before experienced and which had saved my life,' he wrote. Wilkins quickly turned, and there, almost upon him, was a massive Mark V tank. 'The tank driver, coming over a steep rise . . . had failed to see me and the wounded man. I barely had time to throw myself aside before the tank tracks came down upon the wounded man and crushed him beyond recognition while I lay within an inch of the tracks, gasping in horror.'

Wilkins' trials that day were not yet over. He saw another tank take a direct hit and its crew burn alive. Men were cut down on either side of him by machine-guns, and he himself was shot through the right arm and clipped on the chin. Still he carried on and under fire managed to guide a number of wounded men to safety. He returned again to try to take pictures, but his tripod was cut from underneath him. Yet still he persisted. 'I set the camera on my knee and the enemy, I believe, seeing me make the second attempt did not then try to shoot me. In fact they shouted and waved to me as I slithered back to my own trench.'[14]

In less than two hours Monash won a stirring victory at Hamel, vindicating his innovative techniques. Wilkins' extraordinary exploits that day had been witnessed and for his bravery in bringing in wounded under fire he was awarded his first Military Cross.[15]

Three days later he joined Bean for an historic visit at the Australian field headquarters at Bussy-les-Daours, near Corbie. French Premier Georges Clemenceau had come to see for himself these ANZACs who had helped turn the German offensive. Speaking to the assembled officers, he praised the Australians highly: 'I shall go back tomorrow and say to my countrymen: "I have seen the Australians. I have looked in their faces. I know that these men . . . will fight alongside of us again until the cause for which we are all fighting is safe for us and for our children." ' Wilkins set his camera and captured the moment on a colour glass plate.[16]

After a series of stunning victories that secured Paris and paved the way for Allied victory, Monash was recognised as the finest field officer in France. One afternoon Wilkins set his cinecamera on the steps of the grand chateau at Bertangles as King George V presented Monash with a knighthood, the first time in two centuries that a reigning British monarch had honoured a soldier on the field of battle. A decade later Wilkins would again meet the King and this time it would be his turn to receive the royal sword upon his shoulder.

The Australians were in combat for six months without relief, finally breaching the Hindenburg Line in October and hastening the collapse of the German army. Wilkins followed them all the way. In September he came across a band of inexperienced American soldiers who had lost their officers, and guided them through an artillery barrage to safety. It won him a bar to his Military Cross, and he received the singular honour of having the awards proudly presented by the King in a ceremony filmed by Wilkins' former colleagues at Gaumont.[17] Three days before the Armistice he was mentioned in despatches for gallantry a second time.

In 1924, on a visit to Australia, Vilhjalmur Stefansson met with Monash at a dinner in Melbourne. Naturally they got to talking about their mutual colleague, Wilkins. Monash mentioned that on returning from the war he had eulogised the photographer at a large public gathering. He later received a message from Wilkins 'begging him not to praise him publicly again'.[18]

'Sir John Monash seems to agree with me that Wilkins is so aggressively modest that he carries it to a fault,' Stefansson told the Australian papers. 'It ought to be enough to hide your light under a bushel without threatening to knock anybody down who wants to take the bushel away.'

The end of the fighting was not the end of Bean and Wilkins' work. There was one sad task still to complete. Between January and March 1919 the two of them led a mission of photographers, artists and historians to Gallipoli to gather evidence of the disastrous campaign in the Dardanelles. Bean described it as 'probably the most unadventurous expedition of his [Wilkins'] life'.

Wilkins was deeply moved by what he found. The bleached bones of his dead countrymen lay with scraps of tattered uniforms in soil that had already become sacred ground for Australians. He set up a darkroom in an abandoned water tank and worked long into the night developing his photographs.

After all their time together, Bean remained full of admiration for his assistant. Wilkins was a 'born leader . . . I used to note with amusement that, as we strode and climbed about the hills, the rest of the party unconsciously followed Wilkins' lead. If he used a certain path, climbed a cliff in a particular way, jumped a trench or even went round the left or right of a bush, the rest of us usually did the same . . .'[19]

Bean was the great chronicler of Australian soldiers at war and witness to countless acts of courage and compassion. He was scrupulously fair and loath to single one out from another. In Wilkins' case, however, he made a rare exception. Many years later, on the eve of another momentous conflict, he publicly summed up the character of Wilkins in a brief and telling tribute. Wilkins, he told his audience of war veterans, was 'the only man I know to whom every line of Kipling's poem "If" could be truthfully applied.'[20]

6

—

The great race

Several aviators are desirous of attempting flight London to Australia.
They are all first class men and very keen . . .

— cable sent from Paris, 18 February 1919,
by Australia's Prime Minister, WM Hughes

F or six months the great statesmen met in Paris, destroying the old
world and inventing the new. Beneath the glittering chandeliers
of the Hall of Mirrors at Versailles, they negotiated the treaty that all
hoped would bring lasting peace, and for a brief moment it felt as if
1919 marked the beginning of a new age.

But first there were a few scores to settle. The Peace Conference
became preoccupied with punishment, and the greedy victors took the
colonies of Austria, Germany and the Ottomans for themselves. Even
minnow nations came looking for spoils. Australia's pugnacious Prime
Minister Billy Hughes demanded Germany's Pacific territories and
insulted the Japanese by insisting there be no mention of racial equality
in the final treaty. But buried in the Versailles treaty's 440 mostly
punitive articles were a few grains of enlightenment, among them the
first mentions of global cooperation in aviation. Even though at the
time of the conference it was impossible to buy an aeroplane ticket
going anywhere, from those few words a great industry was born.

Prime Minister Hughes was no visionary, but in aviation he saw the
future. His father had been a humble carpenter, polishing the
woodwork in the House of Lords, but the immigrant son would come
to all but own Australia's parliament, setting the record as its longest-

serving politician. In his fifty-one years in national politics he won twenty-one elections, swapping parties whenever it suited but never deviating from two immovable plinths: 'Australia,' he said, 'was more British than Britain' and thus the Empire was to be supported above all else, notwithstanding that it had just cost 60 000 young Australian lives. Secondly, he knew there were no votes to be lost in promising to keep Asians out of the country. Hughes did not invent the infamously racist immigration laws known as the White Australia Policy, but he fought hard to maintain them. Now, after sixteen months in Europe negotiating the peace, he added a third pillar to his uncomplicated dictums: his nation's destiny lay with the flying machine.

Hughes had shuttled between London and Paris by primitive aircraft, and most of the time they got him to where he wanted to go. Though the only planes in Australia had arrived in boxes carried by ships, he foresaw a day when Britain and its most loyal colony would be joined by a common vein of aerial routes, reducing the six-week sea passage to a journey of just a few days. Few took his idea seriously at the time, but his faith in aviation was shared by George Wilkins, and their common interest was about to coincide in spectacular fashion.

While the diplomats in Paris remade the map of the world in the grand salons of Versailles, Wilkins sat in the humble surrounds of a Chinese restaurant in Piccadilly, planning the discovery of the places that weren't yet even on the map. His friend, an Australian ophthalmologist Dr Arthur Joyce, recalled 'one night at dinner, [Wilkins] drew on the tablecloth in lead pencil his idea of exploring the Antarctic by aeroplane and showed how he thought it could be done.'[1]

Since returning from Gallipoli, Wilkins had been adding to his singular skills by learning to navigate airships. He had joined the Royal Navy's Lighter-than-Air Command and took many flights in the R32, a cantankerous wooden-framed giant that would bend alarmingly in bumpy weather. Inside you could stand at the end of a corridor when she was in a turning manoeuvre and see a man at the other end disappear as the entire structure bent, only to come back into view when she straightened out. For Wilkins it was the view outside that mattered. He marvelled as it moved silently across the northern England landscape, low enough to smell the cooking pots in the houses below. The crew took bets on scurrying fowls in the yards beneath, so close you could almost reach out and lift them aboard. They could hear the excited words of children shouting up as they passed over, yet with the wind behind them they could outpace locomotives. This was the perfect platform for exploration, and he just knew it could take him to the poles.

In London he made a nuisance of himself, pestering the British Government, dirigible manufacturers and even the Zeppelin Company in Germany with wild ideas about taking airships to the North Pole for meteorological research. As usual, he was ahead of his time: 'Although sufficient money to finance the trip was available, not one of the owners or manufacturers of airships in England would either sell me a dirigible or allow me to use one for the purpose. They thought the idea fantastic.'[2]

More convinced than ever that the key to understanding global weather lay at either end of the earth, Wilkins began drafting a proposal for global monitoring stations for consideration by the learned societies. He made plans for expeditions by aeroplane and submarine and he talked to all who would listen about the possibilities of a new age of discovery. He was single-minded but, by Joyce's account, certainly no bore: 'I like to remember him as I knew him best, full of the joy of living, enthusiastic about everything, and a good companion.'[3]

When not making plans for exploration, Wilkins joined in the festive atmosphere that had taken hold of Britain after the grim years of conflict. With his war-artist friends, he met a colourful mix of London's avant-garde, and their favourite haunt became the Chelsea Arts Club, which had established a reputation for its raffish membership. He played the piano, singing as well as his deaf ear allowed, and made quite an impression with his Victorian floral waistcoats and high-collared coats. 'I don't know where they came from,' recalled Dr Joyce, 'but he always appeared in that garb. When he was not exploring, he really enjoyed those parties.'[4]

Like thousands of others, Wilkins was officially still in uniform. Every street in Britain seemed full of Dominion soldiers awaiting demobilisation. On a visit to wounded Australians at Cobham Hall in Kent, Prime Minister Hughes met airmen who were not so much ill as sick of waiting and keen to fly their machines home. Hughes expressed reservations about the safety of such a trip, but their determination impressed him and he made a rash decision to offer a substantial prize to anyone who succeeded.

Hughes cabled his Cabinet, insisting such a venture 'would be a great advertisement for Australia and would concentrate the eyes of the world on us' – which is exactly what horrified his colleagues and their military advisers.[5] No aeroplane had crossed an ocean, let alone the 18 000 kilometres from Britain to Australia. The first international passenger service between London and Paris was still just an idea, and pilots continued to drop from the sky with alarming frequency. There was barely a landing strip east of India and no plane with a range of more than a few hundred kilometres. The chances of survival were slim and the odds against success immense.

Despite the bureaucratic dithering, Hughes got his air race, with a prize of £10 000 to the winner – the same reward on offer for the first plane to cross the Atlantic, which he considered a mere pond by comparison. His would be the greatest air race in history, and his pilots the bravest men ever to climb into flying suits. The official announcement was made on 19 March, with the promise that the rules would be finalised shortly.

This news, however, was not met with universal acclaim at home, and Hughes took a bucketing from the Australian press. The dour Melbourne *Age* called it 'a circus flight – a poorly disguised attempt at self-advertisement at the expense of the Australian public', and demanded the ministry retract the offer. Its local rival the *Argus* rather optimistically claimed that the flight would prove so easy there was no necessity to throw away good money on the project. Meanwhile, with all the forthright charm of the Australian bushmen it represented, the *Corowa Free Press* thundered: 'They ought to carry as passengers on the experimental voyage as many Federal Members [members of the Australian Parliament] as possible and leave them somewhere else.'[6]

In an age when we take air travel for granted, it is hard to imagine the challenges facing the long-distance pilot of 1919. If the fatality rate is any guide, these vastly exceeded the risks taken by the astronauts of our age. Aviation was just a teenager and aircraft were flimsy and capricious, the best of them designed for dogfighting, not distance. Flying through stormy skies over jungles, deserts, mountains and open sea presented an endless list of potential calamities. Navigational aids barely existed, and for much of the flight the airmen would be pioneering routes that had never heard the drone of aircraft engines. It was exactly the sort of challenge Wilkins found irresistible.

In May, after consulting the Royal Aero Club, the government released the rules for the great event. The offer of a £10 000 prize would remain open from September until the end of 1920 for any Australian pilot completing the journey within thirty days. All the aircraft had to be privately financed, and British made. Each team was required to include a competent navigator and, not surprisingly, all competitors had to waive the right to claim for injuries or loss.

Two days after the announcement, amid stories of Germany's humiliation in Versailles and the push for home rule in India, the *Manchester Guardian* carried a small but significant report on the inaugural flight of Britain's first regular passenger service, a 300-kilometre journey between Hartlepool and Hull.[7] The brave passengers had climbed aboard a hastily modified wartime bomber, the Blackburn Kangaroo, surely one of the ugliest aircraft ever to fly.

The Kangaroo had none of the grace of its namesake, and could barely match it for speed. A twin-engined biplane, it was notable for the much longer span of its upper wing, and the elongated nose that jutted far forward of its centre of gravity – more anteater than kangaroo. There, poised precariously in his open cockpit, the navigator would sit in lonely vigil scribbling notes to send back to the rest of the crew far behind. Built as a heavy bomber, the plane saw some limited action on anti-submarine patrols at the end of the war, and one had actually succeeded in sinking a U-boat.

Britain's aeroplane manufacturers had looked at their maps and knew that the chances of a happy ending for the Britain–Australia air race were not good. Fearful of negative publicity while they struggled to survive in the post-war economy, most of them kept their distance. But not so the Blackburn Aeroplane and Motor Car Company of Leeds, whose founder, Robert Blackburn, had been a test pilot himself. He'd walked away from serious crashes, and he knew aviation would not progress without risk-taking. His company's entry in the race hit the desk of the organisers the day after the public announcement. Blackburn had already assembled an all-Australian crew, among them a 23-year-old lieutenant from the Royal Flying Corps, Charles Kingsford Smith.

Blackburn's entry had one small problem, however. As brave as they were, these young pilots could barely find their way out of a hangar, let alone across the uncharted route to Australia. The world governing body of aviation, the Fédération Aéronautique Internationale, ruled that the team lacked adequate navigational experience. During a break in the Peace Conference, Prime Minister Hughes met with the team for two hours to try to find a solution. When he emerged he sounded more like a concerned father than a prime minister:

I talked to the boys and found them full of eagerness. But not one of them knew anything about navigation. They admitted it. They said they had maps and would manage all right – on certain parts of the journey they would steer by coastline. But they could not see the coastline at night, and they could not find their way from India to Darwin by consulting a map. We feel we are responsible for the safety of these young fellows, and we could not allow them to start on a voyage half way around the world without any knowledge of navigation . . .[8]

The rules were bent, the race was delayed, and Hughes even offered to have the team sent to navigation school, but it was to no avail. Kingsford Smith dropped out and went looking unsuccessfully for another team to fly with. The world would hear little of him again until almost a decade later.[9]

The Kangaroo's original pilot, Valdemar Rendle, needed a navigator. It didn't take him long to find Wilkins, who put aside his Arctic plans to make a serious study of the Blackburn challenge. At thirty-one, he was by far the oldest and most experienced of the team, who were all in their early twenties. Rendle was a baby-faced flying enthusiast who at the outbreak of the war had paid his own way to Europe to join the Royal Flying Corps. After gaining his wings he was given the thankless and dangerous task of ferrying planes back and forth across the Channel, carrying some of the first airmail between London and Paris. In the transport unit he met another young lieutenant, Reg Williams, who in turn introduced the team's engineer, Garnsey St Clair Potts. All of them could fly, and all of them could work on an engine, which would be a great advantage on such an exhausting journey.

Wilkins did not consider Rendle the finest pilot, but he did think him the luckiest. He'd heard stories about the young Queenslander flying in France where he'd seemed to miraculously escape difficulties: 'I had observed that this type of pilot was often the safest in emergency; somehow their luck seemed to pull them through.'[10]

He looked over the Kangaroo and concluded she had a decent chance of success if Rendle's luck held. To improve the odds, he set about designing his own navigation instruments, among them a novel position finder built within the circular mounting where a machine-gun usually sat. With this he hoped to take a rapid solar position finding through only the briefest break in the clouds. Wilkins saw the race as an opportunity for research, and for his meteorological studies he planned to carry a range of barometers, drift indicators, thermometers and a density meter for measuring humidity. Every half-hour he would complete a log to record wind conditions, cloud formations, the height of various layers and the effects of turbulence in the tropics. For Wilkins, adventure was never useful unless it provided knowledge.

While room was made for the instruments, weight was at a premium and this precluded them carrying a radio set. Personal gear was reduced to a toothbrush, razor and a change of underwear. All entrants carried a stock of chewing gum supplied by a sponsor, often using it to perform makeshift repairs. Wilkins would leave behind his movie cameras, making it one of the few adventures of his not captured on film.[11]

What was known of the conditions beyond Europe came mostly from a series of survey flights between Cairo and India undertaken by the Royal Air Force in 1918. Piloting a lumbering Handley Page bomber on these pioneer journeys had been the remarkable Captain Ross Smith, considered by some to be the finest aviator of the day.

Smith first fought at Gallipoli and then joined the legendary Light Horse Brigade in the Middle East. On transferring to the Australian Flying Corps he proved himself to be an extraordinary aviator. Quick-witted, athletic and a born leader, he had an aura of confidence that made anything seem possible. He became TE Lawrence's personal choice as pilot, and in *The Seven Pillars of Wisdom*, Lawrence described a visit by Ross's squadron to his force as it was being harassed by German aircraft. The Australian pilots calmly interrupted their breakfast three times to down the attacking planes, returning to their bacon and tea as if they'd just stepped out to collect the morning newspaper. Amazed at their equanimity, Lawrence wrote: 'Time became spacious to those who flew.'

Two weeks after the Armistice, Smith carried two generals on the first flight from Cairo to New Delhi, and from there he accompanied Brigadier General AE Borton on a survey of potential landing strips across Asia. They travelled by sea, narrowly escaping death when their ship was destroyed by fire two days out from Calcutta. Later they both came down with malaria, but after three months they had completed their investigation, and for those pilots considering a race entry, it made sober reading. In the vast stretch from India to Indonesia, the only suitable landing-grounds were the race courses at Rangoon and Singapore. The racing authorities were duly advised to refrain from holding hurdle races on their courses and to prepare their patrons for the potential arrival of aeroplanes towards the end of the year. Such instructions must have provided immense comfort to the pilots.

Borton gloomily reported that the rest of Asia offered 'only a slight chance of a successful emergency landing'.[12] And then things got really difficult. From the last known landing area at Bandung in Indonesia to the coast of northern Australia, a stretch of more than 2500 kilometres, flyers would find nothing but jungle, rice paddy and open sea. Should they survive that, their reward for mistakenly overflying the rendez-vous at Darwin would be a vast inhospitable desert.

None of this discouraged Captain Smith, and on his return to London he and his older brother, Keith, began putting together a challenge for the race. With some cajoling from General Borton, the Vickers Company was finally convinced to allow the brothers to enter one of its Vimy bombers. The Vimy, much like the Kangaroo in scale but rather more graceful in appearance, had just proved itself on the first non-stop trans-Atlantic crossing by Captain John Alcock and Lieutenant Arthur Brown in June 1919. With new upgraded engines from Rolls Royce, Smith now became Wilkins' most serious competitor.

In seclusion, Wilkins and his crew practised 'blind flying', the first known attempt to try to navigate solely by instruments. Being able to fly through fog, cloud and darkness would give the team a tremendous advantage. Navigation and communication technologies were in their infancy, and it meant placing great faith in Wilkins' improvised instruments.

'Most of the experienced flyers scoffed at the idea,' he wrote. 'They knew how difficult it was in those days just to stay right side up and in the right direction in heavy clouds and storms. So we practised and practised blind flying in secret and depended upon this to give us an advantage over the Smith brothers whom we knew from our spying had never tried it.'[13]

It was hardly surprising the Smiths didn't waste too much time on such manoeuvres. Early altimeters were unreliable, especially at low altitudes. Variations in atmospheric pressure could give false readings that were off by hundreds of feet – more than enough to discover an unexpected mountain side. The first primitive experiments in real instrument flying were still a decade away, and it would be twenty years before they were considered successful.[14]

Potential contenders for the race came and went, but by October there were six definite starters plus one unofficial entrant from France. Etienne Poulet's challenge was in some ways the bravest of all. Unsupported and, as a Frenchman, ineligible to win the prize, Poulet and his mechanic, Jean Benoist, nevertheless committed themselves to the race and were actually the first to depart. Their aim could not be faulted, as Poulet had dedicated his flight to raising funds for the widow of his friend, the airman Jules Védrines, who had died while preparing for a round-the-world flight in April. Before any of the Australian crews were airborne, Poulet's Caudron biplane had battled through bad weather to reach the Balkans.

The Frenchman's bravery won over the sceptics, and suddenly the race came alive. The *New York Times* seemed to best grasp the immensity of the challenge:

> Success may crown it, but there is only one chance in a great many that one of the aviators who are soon to take wing will ever reach the goal. The perils in some parts of the route are so great that a man must be a visionary to face them . . . Whatever preparations have been made at some of the dubious spots on the long route must be tentative and incomplete. Columbus in his caravel did not take a tenth of the risks that these bold air pioneers will have to

face. Luck be with them, but they will be throwing dice with Death.[15]

In the coming weeks the various crews rolled the dice as they set off from Hounslow in west London. The next plane to leave was a Sopwith flown by Captain George Matthews and mechanic Sergeant Thomas Kay on 21 October. Forced north by snowstorms, they headed into Germany and damaged their plane landing in Cologne. The thirty-day time limit ticked by, but the game flyers decided to push on regardless. In dense fog they were forced down outside Belgrade and were promptly arrested as Bolsheviks and imprisoned. Both eventually escaped and after a series of adventures the Sopwith made it to Constantinople in time for Christmas. Here Matthews learned that others had won the race, but he was nothing if not persistent. The tragicomic progress continued until a mishap in a banana plantation in Bali ended their epic journey after five months of struggle.

'Battling' Ray Parer took seven months to finish his marathon journey and he became something of a celebrity for his sheer perseverance. Captain Roger Douglas and Lieutenant Leslie Ross never made it out of London. Tragically, both men were killed when their aircraft entered a spin and crashed just minutes from the start. Death also awaited Captain Cedric Howell and Air Mechanic George Fraser when their Martinsyde hit the sea off Corfu, the loss never fully explained.

With the smoke still rising from the mangled remains of Douglas' plane, Ross and Keith Smith's Vimy lifted off from Hounslow on 12 November. Their departure was a blow to Wilkins. The Kangaroo had been the first to enter, but last-minute problems meant they would be only the fourth crew to set off.

For reasons that remain unclear, Blackburn insisted on an eleventh-hour upgrade of the Kangaroo's engines, causing several days of frustrating delay. Rolls Royce had the cheek to bill Wilkins £102 8s for the unwanted overhaul, adding to the substantial personal costs that he was carrying in the venture. As a reminder, he kept the receipt as a memento – a forwarning of the avarice he would face from many suppliers to his expeditions in the years ahead.

He spent his last night alone, writing notes to those he cared for, focusing on the job ahead. Any fears he had he kept to himself; all doubts were pushed aside. It was not hubris or arrogance but quiet confidence in his preparation, and the comforting sense of purpose that came from a quest for knowledge. As many before on the eve of a great challenge, his final thoughts were for his mother:

Royal Automobile Club,
London S.W. 1 Nov 20, 1919
My dear mother,

  You will appreciate I'm sure the spirit in which I undertake this enterprise which undoubtedly has risks above the average. To your careful training I owe the trait of character that predominates even above my inclination towards the unusual . . . that occasional but forceful effort to do such things as will be useful to my fellow man.

  To you I owe everything, to you will be the credit of what success I have. You may depend I'll do my best for your sake, and whatever happens now I can't do more. We have a sound machine. My fellow officers are capable and careful men and I believe we'll get through all right. So don't worry even if you don't hear from us for several weeks. It may be that we are marooned or cut off from communication. I hope to see you soon. Much love from your loving son.

  George[16]

After days of bad weather, the morning of 21 November broke clear and crisp. Not a cloud specked the sky above Hounslow and there was barely a hint of breeze. It was a perfect day for flying. A big crowd had turned out to see them off, and telegrams were received from Prince Albert and Winston Churchill. A final photograph was taken of the crewmen beneath the Kangaroo's wing: four young men in their flying suits, impatient to be away. The big, drab-coloured machine had the words 'England to Australia' painted across its fuselage. Two spare propellers were lashed underneath. Before jumping aboard Wilkins took cinema pictures as Rendle taxied from the hangar with his new bride on board for a thrill. 'I am as keen as Val,' she told the Sydney *Sun*. 'I am sure they will land in Australia. He is full of infectious confidence.'

The *Sun* also reported Captain Wilkins' final words, a typical example of his almost too-good-to-true altruism: 'I would not do this as a stunt. I have most definite scientific reasons for going . . . She is not pretty but she is all British and thoroughly sound.'[17]

Rendle revved the engines and she lifted, climbed to 300 metres, then circled the airfield three times, Williams and Potts waving pin-sized arms from their open cockpits to the cheering crowd below. Then she turned east and headed for France. As they flew out of sight, Ross Smith was crossing the Suez Canal and heading for Basra, gaining fast on Poulet and Benoist who were laid up in India making repairs.

Smith had encountered the worst weather of his trip in the crossing to France, leaving him shaking his head and genuinely wondering why he had been so foolish as to enter the race. Now it was Wilkins' turn to suffer the violence of the Channel, the grim little stretch of water that had been cursed by sailors for centuries. The Kangaroo ran into blinding rain then dense fog as they made for Paris and they discovered that the currents of air above were just as treacherous as those of the tide below. The Kangaroo was tossed high and low by the shifting winds and left blind by thick clouds. Wilkins' instrument flying was put to the test and he managed to bring the big plane down at a military field east of the capital. The next day a heavy snowfall forced a delay. Once away, more bad weather forced them down at Lyon, then a violent thunderstorm buffeted the plane as they neared the Mediterranean. A forced landing at Fréjus almost ended the whole trip. Skirting the Roman aqueduct that juts upwards in the meadows near the landing field, Rendle struggled to bring the plane down through the storm and they almost overshot the runway, heading for a hangar at high speed.

'For Pete's sake, bring her down,' Wilkins shouted over the intercom. But still the Kangaroo floated over the rapidly disappearing strip.

Rendle shouted back, 'The throttle's jammed, I can't throttle back the engines.'

Wilkins knew they were too close to the hangar to have any chance of flying over it, so he shouted back: 'Cut the switches and let her bump and roll.' The Kangaroo smacked heavily into the ground three times as it rushed onward towards the hangar. Aircraft at the time had no brakes, and it was too late to make a ground loop. It rolled right through the hangar doors before coming to rest just metres from the rear wall.

'We climbed out to hear the French [ground crew] jabbering: "What a landing! . . . What if the doors had not been open? You were in before we could do anything."'

'But Rendle was laughing and replied in French, "Oh that's all right. We always come in like that – saves us the trouble of pushing the machine about." '[18]

Beneath the bravado they were all deeply concerned about what had forced the controls to jam. It was inexplicable, and it was not the last time on this journey they would face mysterious equipment failures. As they set about making repairs and preparing the Kangaroo for flying the next day, a group of uniformed British mechanics introduced themselves and offered to help. They were apparently part of some unit that had moved on and they insisted on assuming the maintenance duties while the crew rested. Wilkins was wary of handing over the plane to outsiders, but with his French hosts insisting on a celebration, he stepped aside and left the friendly mechanics to go to it.

When the Australians returned work was complete. They revved the engines, which wouldn't reach their normal power but seemed good enough to take off. As the weather was again threatening, there was no time to lose. On the morning of 29 November they were airborne once more, heading for Pisa.

The problems began immediately. One of the engines was danger-ously down on power, and Wilkins began searching for a spot to make an emergency landing. Once on the ground at Antibes, he discovered what appeared to be malicious damage. One of the ignition wires had been tampered with, causing a short-circuit of the magneto. It was a deliberate act of sabotage. Though the obvious suspects were the British mechanics in Fréjus, Wilkins and his team were never sure who had done it or why. It left an uneasy feeling.

The Kangaroo had not had a clear day since leaving London, and the storms continued as they headed down the Italian peninsula and out across the Ionian Sea. The engines spluttered fitfully but held the men aloft over the rocky shores of Sparta. At Suda Bay in Crete their landing field was flooded by the torrential rains, and the wheels stuck deep in the mud as soon as they came to rest.

Royal Air Force engineers worked all night digging a trench to drain the field, using Turkish prison labour to lay logs and whatever else could be found to improve the strip. They pulled the plane from the mud and at dawn were still working to fill the puddles. Despite their efforts, the Kangaroo became bogged once more as it tried to taxi and a further three days were lost.

At last, on 8 December they took off, ahead of them the daunting White Mountains of Crete, rising a sheer 2000 metres from the Mediterranean. Even carrying a light load, it would be difficult to clear them, but fully laden with petrol and supplies it was an impossible task for the Blackburn. They banked heavily to make a course around the barrier, flying low over isolated villagers and sheep herders who stared up in amazement, then turned once more and headed south-east for Cairo.

All seemed well for a time, the engine's comforting roar in harmony at last, the bracing wires tuned tightly, the dope on the giant wings shining in the winter sun. Wilkins was filling in his logbook and just about to open a box of sandwiches when Potts passed a note forward warning that oil was leaking from the port engine. Wilkins turned to look and saw a black stream spurting from the stub end of an oil pipe: 'The oil, the very life blood of the engine, sprayed into the sea below.'[19] At the rate it was leaking the tank would soon be dry.

'I had just finished a calculation as to [our] position and realised that we were then at one of the most dangerous sections of the whole flight,' he wrote. Along with the crossing from Timor to Australia, the eastern Mediterranean was the only point where they would be over open water. Wilkins made a quick estimate that they were 80 kilometres from land – the maximum distance they could hope one engine might keep them aloft.

'I instantly realised our predicament. I felt sure that we could not reach the shore. The situation seemed hopeless, we would surely be drowned, but we might as well make a fight of it.'[20]

He shouted to Rendle to pull the plane up 'and climb for dear life as long as the oil lasts'. The Kangaroo banked and turned for Crete. Wilkins scoured his map and found the nearest field was near the centre of the island on the north coast, over 100 kilometres away. The wind was against them, but as they neared the coast the currents would be rising and that might help. Between them and the landing field was the mountain range, snow-covered and barren, impossible to pass. Their only chance seemed to be to return to the main field at Canea and, if they couldn't make land, at least ditch near the beach.

Against the headwinds, their progress was slow. The four men had plenty of time to contemplate the nearly hopeless situation. Wilkins had been here before:

It had been my experience on several occasions when confronted with what seemed certain death that the mind is calm, reflecting quietly on the possibilities of post-human survival, and I was pleased to find out that this position was exemplified in my companions. There was no laughter, no ribald bluffing or whimpering. We said little to each other except to say, 'Well, looks as if we are for it. No possible chance of escape. Old Smithy will certainly win the prize and he is welcome to it.'[21]

The machine maintained altitude better than they had expected, but as Rendle switched off the starboard engine once the oil was drained, all knew there was no escape. Without parachutes there was no choice but to stay with the Blackburn until it crashed. But, as Wilkins had hoped, the coastal winds were holding them up and their spirits lifted with the breeze. There might yet be a chance.

Never an easy flyer, the Blackburn floundered on the single engine. With each air pocket it would sag alarmingly. The mountains loomed in front of them, the foam-crested waves below. To have any chance they needed to hold their altitude to reach the western end of the island, turn east and make a dash for Canea against the down drafts. The walled town, the ancient capital of the island, was built on a hill and they would have to clear it to reach the fields of Suda that lay behind. Flying at less than 300 metres altitude and dropping rapidly, it seemed as if they might crash into the town itself. Wilkins, perched at the nose and the most vulnerable of all of them, ordered a desperate manoeuvre.

'Switch on the dry engine,' he shouted over the phones, hoping a few extra turns might just carry them to safety.

Rendle flipped the switch, but the propeller failed to catch. Then, instinctively, Rendle did what all quick-witted pilots do when confronted with a stalled engine. He shoved the controls forward and forced the aeroplane into a dive to gain speed and force the propeller to turn faster.

'It looked to me, that we could not help but crash right into the roof of a two storey house on top of the hill. I gasped and clutched at the seat,' wrote Wilkins. 'Once again death seemed inevitable, and my brain quickly calmed. After all, sometime or another we must face the greatest adventure, and here it was, stark before us.'[22]

His moment of reflection ended when the engine suddenly let out a roar and a couple of backfires, and the propeller gripped the air. Rendle, the lucky flyer, yanked back the controls and the machine responded. The plane jerked as the undercarriage knocked off a chimney, but they made it to clear air. There in front of them was the landing strip.

Rendle was trying to wrangle a 3500-kilogram beast with virtually no control other than gravity. Unless he could put it down soon it would overrun the field into a deep ditch at the other end. He thrust the controls forward, but before he could kill the engine there was a boom as the dry motor seized and disintegrated, showering the fuselage with the fragments of cylinders and crankcase. The Kangaroo swung crazily into a sickening flat spin as Rendle struggled to correct its course with the rudder. He overcorrected and they were heading for one side of the strip when, with another loud bang, the machine smashed into the ground. Yet somehow the landing gear held against the impact.

At high speed they hurtled over the rough field. For once the rain was their ally, as sticky mud slowed them down a little. They hit a ditch and all fours tyres burst with a terrific bang, like cannon shells exploding. The Kangaroo bounced across the ditch and continued its groggy roll towards a two-metre-high earth embankment beside the stone walls of a lunatic asylum.

For the third time that afternoon, Wilkins felt sure he going to die. 'I remember feeling the nose of the machine rise as the wheels climbed the bank – then darkness.' The Kangaroo had come to a sudden halt, nose down and tail up, throwing Wilkins against his heavy navigator's compass and tossing him unconscious into a watery ditch.

When he came to he could see Potts and Williams high above him in the rear cockpit. 'Tears were rolling down their cheeks, but they were roaring with hysterical laughter.' Rendle had passed out in the cockpit, but his luck had held to the end and he was soon revived. Miraculously, none of them were seriously hurt.

On close examination it appeared the oil line had fractured at a fatigue point where the line had been deliberately bent backwards and forwards. Tests later showed that iron filings had been mixed into the oil supply. For the rest of his life Rendle remained convinced that the Blackburn had been deliberately sabotaged and, though less certain,

Wilkins agreed there was evidence that someone had tried to prevent them continuing. If so, it amounted to attempted murder, but none of the pilots would ever know who was responsible.

The Kangaroo, though missing an engine and most of its landing gear, was not badly damaged. The crew agreed they should try to at least finish the journey. Wilkins sent a cable to London asking for a new engine to be sent out, but he received a reply from a friend in the Air Ministry advising him he was crazy: 'You had better take a rest in that asylum you missed entering the other day.'[23]

Around the time they were dusting themselves off after the crash, Ross Smith's Vimy was leaving Timor on its way across the Arafura Sea to Darwin and a place in history. Brave Poulet, on his fifty-seventh day out of Paris, was leaving Moulmein in Burma bound for Bangkok, but he headed into heavy fog and was forced to return. Landing with a broken propeller and cracked piston, his race was over, his remarkable struggle quickly forgotten.

For the men of the Kangaroo there was one sad task remaining. The day after their narrow escape came the news that Captain Howell and Sergeant Fraser had drowned while trying to beach their Martinsyde biplane on the coast of Corfu. They had been attempting an emergency landing much like the Kangaroo, and ditched in heavy seas within shouting distance of the coast. Villagers heard the cries for help but were not able to launch boats in time to rescue the two pilots. On their way back to London, Wilkins and Rendle stopped at the island to help with the investigation. It must have been a chilling visit, a reminder of how close they had come to suffering the same fate.

7

Unsuccessfully south

I will not say that it was impossible anywhere to get in among this ice, but I will assert that the bare attempting of it would be a very dangerous enterprise and what I believe no man in my situation would have thought of. I whose ambition leads me not only farther than any other man has been before me, but as far as I think it is possible for man to go, was not sorry at meeting this interruption.[1]
– Captain James Cook, 30 January 1774, latitude 7110' south

Captain Cook was wise to turn back from the icy walls of Antarctica, which he sensed though never saw, bringing his exploration of the high southern latitudes to an end. Venturing further would almost certainly have ended in disaster. Yet his warnings of the dangers in those parts did little to deter others. Cook launched the classic age of Antarctic exploration and by most reckonings he was followed by twenty-seven expeditions, nearly all of them privately funded, led by an assortment of vainglorious and curious dreamers, genuine heroes and the occasional villain.[2] Wilkins figured prominently in the last two of these classic expeditions before returning with an aeroplane to open the modern age. He had good reason to invent a new method of polar exploration. His first visit to Antarctica, grand polar campaign number twenty-seven, was without doubt the most ridiculous of them all. If it's little remembered by history, he was pleased to keep it that way.

The magniloquently titled British Imperial Antarctic Expedition of 1920 was in fact a party of just four, all of whom disliked each other, and eight dogs with nothing to do. It had started with a plan to equip three teams of 120 men with twelve aeroplanes for a five-year circumnavigation of the continent, but ended up as little more than a cold-weather camping trip.

All the great explorers had their failures; some, like Shackleton, knew nothing else. Along with life and limb, it was the price paid for a chance at glory. Wilkins suffered more setbacks than most, and they might have discouraged lesser men, but he learned from all of them and showed a remarkable resilience. He said the only lesson to be learnt from the BIAE was in how *not* to organise an expedition. With good reason it was almost his last word on the fiasco, but enough records survive to reconstruct one of the most darkly amusing tales of polar exploration.

Still officially in uniform in London in May 1920, Wilkins met an enthusiastic young doctor, John Lachlan Cope, a man with as much passion for the poles as himself but not much burdened by either talent or scruples. Cope had been recruiting support for a voyage to Antarctica that was not so much an expedition as an all-out assault. The learned societies of London had been bombarded with his plans and he left no stone unturned in his pursuit of both financial sponsorship and official recognition. The details seemed to change regularly depending on whom he was addressing, but he and Wilkins shared a common thread of colossal ambition.

In one typical account[3] seeking help from the Royal Aeronautical Society he promised a 450-tonne specially designed ship 'at present in the course of construction' to be assisted by a smaller vessel 'ready for immediate delivery to the Expedition', six aeroplanes with spares which would fly to the South Pole, scientific equipment for an extensive program of research, and the stores and supplies for ninety personnel to last four years. No previous expedition to Antarctica had ever left with the intention of spending more than a single year in the accursed place, no aeroplane had ever flown there before, and only one party, led by Amundsen, had ever made it to the South Pole and lived to talk about it. None of this deterred Cope in the slightest.

The plans for the BIAE included establishing permanent bases. It was not so much exploration as colonisation, and if successful would have left Britain claiming three-quarters of the entire continent – the last and greatest land grab in history.

Wilkins was offered the role of deputy and chief of the aeronautical section. It was the chance to gain the Antarctic experience he needed so that his weather plans might be taken seriously. More importantly, it promised to fill in at last the vast blank space on the map of the world that so aroused his appetite for exploration. 'I was not interested in a spasmodic dash into the polar areas,' he wrote, 'but in the possibility of maintaining in them permanent stations. After studying the maps I realised that there were two large sections as yet to be explored before we could present a comprehensive plan of action. We should at least have to discover the region south of the Pacific Ocean and the one north of Alaska. I was wanting to try the south first.'[4]

Cope presented his plans to the Royal Geographical Society at its legendary headquarters, Lowther Lodge, in Kensington. But its president, Sir Francis Younghusband, was clearly not impressed by either Cope's ideas or the man himself. The official record of his response is chillingly brief and dismissive. The society, he said, ' . . . finds itself unable to approve his plans or leadership, or to give his proposed expedition its countenance and support.'[5] It would not be the society's last word on Cope and his mad plan.

It appears Wilkins knew little of this. Before leaving for a visit to Australia, he was actively supporting the project and trying to recruit others. He made a hospital visit to a colleague from the Stefansson expedition, the meteorologist William Laird McKinlay, who was recovering from serious injuries suffered at the battle of Cambria in 1917. To lift the spirits of the tough Scot, Wilkins offered to take him along with Cope. 'My leg wound made it impossible,' said McKinlay, 'but the invitation comforted and flattered me.'

If Wilkins had doubts about the expedition, he kept them to himself – a commitment had been made and for him that was a binding promise. He hurried to Australia fully expecting to be back soon to complete preparations.

At home he was decommissioned but immediately re-employed by Charles Bean to assist in the massive task of organising World War I photographs. Despite the work he made time to give public lectures and write about his plans for establishing a permanent meteorological study of the Antarctic. He foresaw a day when wireless communication between Australia, South Africa and South America would mean 'forecasting the weather for months and even years ahead . . . To read the weather signs is no longer a speculation, it is an established fact.'[6]

He urged Australian farmers to support the Cope expedition. In this age of fertilisers, telephones, aeroplanes and X-rays it was time to sacrifice the surety of the past and accept 'new fangled notions . . . the products of scientific investigations!'

His appeal fell on ears even more deaf than his own. As he would later learn, Australia's farmers were well wedded to their wasteful practices of over-grazing and poor soil management. It was the first of many cool responses he received from his fellow countrymen who rarely took well to being lectured, especially by upstart expatriates. Then came the bad news from abroad. Cope sent word that plans for the specially constructed expedition ship had been abandoned; the best he could manage for the mighty undertaking was passage aboard a whaling ship outbound from Montevideo.

In the few months Wilkins had been away the expedition had all but collapsed. His cherished aeroplanes had been ditched, along with the entire staff save two brave and foolish youngsters who had volunteered to go along without pay. Further enquiries made it clear there was a cloud over what Cope had done with the sponsorship money and there were further unspecified rumours surrounding the ambitious doctor. Of these Wilkins was circumspect, revealing only one tantalisingly scandalous snippet: 'He was denounced because of his private life to the leading scientific societies, who refused to support him for that and perhaps other reasons.'[7]

Even now, despite all evidence to the contrary, in Cope's mind the expedition was heading for triumph. Before leaving for South America, he told the New York papers he was leading 'perhaps the largest exploring expedition, certainly the largest of its kind ever organized in England, and the one from which the greatest results are expected'[8] Cope the fabulist claimed to command a fleet of ships, 120 men with $750 000 of financing and the backing of the British, Australian and New Zealand governments. The gullible American reporters believed it.

All this certainly must have been news to Wilkins. On his arrival in Uruguay things had progressed from pantomime to farce. Cope was stranded and had no money to pay for their passage, having spent what little he had securing the dogs. His personnel consisted of nineteen-year-old Thomas Bagshawe, nominally the geologist, and twenty-two-year-old Maxime Lester, who had been second mate on a tramp steamer but was now anointed the expedition's surveyor. Wilkins considered them eager enough young lads, but hopelessly unprepared for the difficulties of polar exploration.

It must have been heartbreaking for him, but having come this far there seemed little point in turning back. The Norwegian whaling magnate Lars Christensen[9] took pity on the sad little party, and found room for them aboard one of his ships travelling south. As they voyaged beyond the Falklands they were retracing the epic boat journey of Ernest Shackleton, passing the forbidding black crags of Elephant Island where Frank Hurley and his fellow castaways had been marooned for months. Shackleton had first glimpsed them at dawn, 'rose pink in the glowing sun' but for Wilkins they were fog bound and gloomy, no place to linger.

On Christmas Eve 1920 they sailed into the sunken caldera of the volcano at Deception Island, hoping to find a whaler that might take them on the last leg to the Antarctic mainland. It was said that here in 1820, at a place called Neptune's Window, the American sealing Captain Nathaniel Palmer was the first to glimpse the white continent. It lay just 90 kilometres away. The plan now was to turn the expedition into a sledge journey along the shores of the Weddell Sea. Leaving behind his camera equipment as security for their costs, Wilkins negotiated passage aboard the Norwegian steamer *Solstrejf*.[10] They weighed anchor and the putrid smells of the whaling station were left astern as they entered the pristine frozen world, bathed in the brief summer without stars or night.

Though it was not the entrée to Antarctica Wilkins had hoped for, the forbidding beauty of blue ice and thrusting mountain ridges cooled his skin and warmed his spirit. In the dazzling light the water changed from green velvet to the lightest aquamarine, and here and there were scattered emerald icebergs drifting with the currents. Emperor penguins porpoised beside the ship with amazing speed and agility, while doe-faced Weddell seals, so different from the tusked walruses of the north, lolled on the floes. In the years ahead this would become more home to him than anywhere else on Earth.

The *Solstrejf* threaded its way through the icebergs and islands of the Gerlache Strait, followed by great flocks of shags and kelp gulls after scraps. This was a thoroughfare for pods of humpbacks, and the whalers were keen to drop their passengers and get on with their gruesome business. On 12 January 1921 the party was landed at Paradise Harbour, a spot well known to whalers for its spectacular views and reliable landfall. To the west it is sheltered by two large islands, and behind are glaciers that flow into its calm waters.

Today there is a Chilean base here that receives more tourists than anywhere else in Antarctica. As they gingerly step through the gentoo penguin rookery and its slippery guano field, observant tourists will find the remains of an upturned boat and the foundations of doorposts: all that remains of the British Imperial Antarctic Expedition and its far-fetched ambitions.

The hapless team camped at what became known as Waterboat Point, a toenail of rock at the tip of a giant foot of ice cliffs. They had minimal gear and only a five-metre boat in which to explore the coast. The dogs were taken ashore but this was no place for sledging and they became little more than hungry pets.

Wilkins determined to make the most of the remaining summer weeks and immediately had the boat out investigating the myriad crags and islets along the Danco Coast. It was dangerous work in an open boat manoeuvring between the ice and the shoreline as the glacier tongues, rising sheer and solid more than 100 metres above them, were liable to calve at any moment. For the few that have seen it, the birth of a new iceberg is a staggering sight as hundreds of tonnes of ice falls from the glacier with an explosive force than can be heard kilometres away. A boat anywhere near it would be crushed or swamped, and to this day coastal exploration remains an unnerving experience.

Wilkins named one nearby glacier after young Bagshawe, but any hopes of finding a passage through the sheer cliffs to the inland were soon dashed. The mountains rose massive and impenetrable straight up from the sea, reducing the little party to mere apostrophes on the landscape.

Twice the expedition nearly ended in tragedy. Once while out in their little whale boat, Wilkins, Cope and Lester were caught in a sudden storm in Andvord Bay, a wide sweep of water and broken ice beneath some of the most rugged and spectacular glaciated mountains on the peninsula. Their boat was blown high on white-crested waves, tossed and spun towards the razor-sharp glacier tongue.

Cope and Lester were violently seasick, unable to help as Wilkins struggled with the tiller. He shouted at them to get up and pull the sails in, but they couldn't move. The boat twisted crazily in the violent sea, shipping water and likely to capsize at any moment. Through the spume and drift ahead, Wilkins could see the jagged face of the glacier, a solid wall of ice: 'It stood there before us a grim, icy, scraggy menace. The waves beat up against it with thundering shocks and it seemed as if there was no hope of our survival.'[11] Lunging forward with his sheath knife, he cut down the sail and it tumbled over them. 'I don't know why the boat did not capsize in the waves, but a well built whale boat is about the most miraculous thing in a heavy sea and our boat, even without a sail, rolled and twisted like a thing alive. I think sometimes as I recall that occasion . . . that some mysterious hand was guiding it.'

It was the current that saved them. Through the deafening roar of the thrashing waves, the backwash dragged the boat past the cliff face rather than smashing broadside against it. Once again Wilkins felt the presence of an other-worldly force: 'I grew quite calm awaiting whatever was in store. It is during such moments we sense the nearness of some outside control, some mysterious something that is guiding our fate. I was as sure as I was of sitting there that we would escape.' The boat swung around the ice-edge and behind was a little bight of sheltered water, protected from the wind and waves.

On land Wilkins and Cope had little more success. Exploring the cliffs behind their camp, they were caught in another bad storm high above the coast. Unable to climb down, they had no choice but to continue, hoping to find a safe route through the ice walls. Roped together, they struggled for hours until they reached a narrow col that offered some rest but no escape. On one side was a treacherous overhang that might collapse at any moment; on the other was a precipitous slope that disappeared in the swirling snowdrift. It was too cold to stay long on the ridge, but neither prospect presented much hope. Wilkins crawled slowly along the narrow edge, looking for a spot where they might dig in and wait out the storm. But as he moved forward the cornice collapsed under his weight, and they were both sent into a tumbling spin down the mountainside. They fell at great speed, face down at first then tumbling on their backs, over and over, unable to sink their ice-axes into the slope.

Wilkins was swept over a rise, sent clear into the air not knowing if a crevasse lay on the other side, then landed with a terrific bump. He slid on until he was yanked to a sudden stop as the rope tightened around his chest, squeezing the breath from his lungs, and he collapsed, unconscious: 'I came to hearing John yelling for help. He was screaming at the top of his voice, "Are you there? What's happened? Come and help me. Pull me out of here!"'

Wilkins slowly regained his breath and planted his axe, then crawled towards the commotion. There, through the swirling snow, Cope was suspended upside-down over the mouth of a deep blue crevasse that disappeared into darkness. Wilkins had to tear his shirt up and use it as a makeshift rope to help right him. As he pulled, Cope was able to laboriously cut footholds with a knife and haul himself up the ice-face. Eventually they navigated their way through a maze of crevasses back to solid ground and the safety of their camp. Reflecting later on their lucky escape Wilkins wrote: 'I have never really enjoyed mountain climbing since then. Every time I see a sharp ridged col, or a glacier deeply descending, I am reminded of our terrific slide and its almost fatal ending.'[12]

Cope's bumbling explorations were doing nothing to restore his reputation. Back in London, the exaggerated news reports from America were filtering back and his lies were exposed. The Royal Geographical Society wanted to distance itself from both the man and his expedition. In February 1921 its monthly journal made sure the world knew of Cope's misrepresentations:

> . . . there have been during the last few months some references in the newspapers, especially American, to the Expedition as having the support of the Society . . . It is desirable to repeat for public information that this self-styled 'British Imperial Antarctic Expedition' of a few men is not in any way whatever approved or supported by the Royal Geographical Society . . .[13]

The society hoped Cope might fade away. And he might have too, but for the stubbornness of his two young companions.

With the whaling season closing down as winter approached, Wilkins went in search of a ship to return them to civilisation. He found a Norwegian whale boat captain willing to take them all back to Montevideo, but Lester and Bagshawe said they wanted to stay on. The devious Cope, hoping to buy time that might allow him to raise more funds, encouraged them (and later ensured that no whalers returned to check on them in case they changed their minds). So there, on an islet less than 100 metres wide, suffused with the pungent aroma of guano, the young men decided to face the fury of an Antarctic winter together. Bagshawe, having a bet both ways, described their bleak patch as 'a country garden – a small prison camp'.[14]

They built their cramped hut atop the ruins of an abandoned whale boat with packing cases, coal bags and what timber could be spared from the Norwegian ship. Their supplies were limited to biscuits, baked beans, pemmican, some alcohol and sweets. But they were surrounded by seals, and the eggs and meat of the penguins they were otherwise studying. Sadly they forgot to take forks, which meant meals had to be eaten with filthy fingers; however, the gentoo and chinstraps not eaten offered much amusement and their entertainment was supplemented by a phonograph and an assortment of what became well-worn records – the original desert-island discs.

It must have been a long year. The two adventurers were not warm friends despite their shared passion for penguins. Wilkins recalled they quarrelled bitterly but managed to make up without bearing any malice: 'Any two men who can have an angry row in the morning and forget all about it by afternoon can get along anywhere for any length of time. So I sailed away with the whaling fleet, and we left young Bagshawe and Lester where they were.'[15]

It was hardly the epic stuff of Shackleton or Scott, but in his memoir of their miserable experience, Bagshawe displays the boarding-school stoicism and admirable stubbornness that built an empire: 'Everything freezes. Tonight my ink-pot has frozen-up and the mince froze as we were eating it. We sit and shiver and try and laugh at our discomfort; it's not much use to moan and groan.'[16] It took an Australian, Frank Debenham, founder of the Scott Polar Research Institute at Cambridge, to capture the true Britishness of their experience: 'These two young men possessed that quality so annoying to the great Napoleon, of not having the sense to know when they were defeated.'[17]

The Governor of the Falkland Islands was furious with Wilkins for leaving them behind, holding him responsible should anything go wrong, but the two masochists were safe enough and they passed the time in uneventful discomfort. They completed an entire year with but one bath apiece, before whalers delivered them from their exile of soot, seal oil and bird shit. Cope had promised to come back to collect them, but predictably never returned. He made a nuisance of himself on the Falklands until the authorities got him a job peeling potatoes on a Scottish steamer and sent him home, never to go exploring again.

Wilkins left for New York, undaunted and even more determined to bring aeroplanes to Antarctica. He was in negotiations with the local agent for aircraft manufacturer Junkers to lend several planes when a cable arrived from Sir Ernest Shackleton that changed his plans: 'Shackleton urged me to join him and sail completely around the Antarctic continent, carrying an airplane with us on his boat and making frequent flights from ship to the shore. This was a much more comprehensive plan that I could manage and was besides just what I wanted to do.'[18] He abandoned the idea of having his own expedition and made for London.

Shackleton had returned from the *Endurance* epic to a world that didn't need him. He was lecturing to half-filled halls while Hurley's images of his crushed dreams played on the screen behind him. Bored and frustrated, he was drinking too much and hiding a serious heart problem from doctors, friends and family. Restless to return to exploration, he persuaded a rich friend from his schooldays, John Quiller Rowett, to fund a scientific journey aboard a ship bought in Norway. Lady Shackleton named her *Quest*.

Continuing a long tradition of expedition vessels totally unsuited to the job ahead, *Quest* was a vile little sealer, just 34 metres long and weighing a mere 120 tonnes, so cramped even Shackleton's cabin measured just two metres square. She was ugly to the eye and unpleasant to sail but these sins may have been forgiven had she at least been reliable. Unfortunately *Quest* was plagued with mechanical problems and cursed with a buckled keel that only made her more unpredictable. Unperturbed, Shackleton made vague plans for two years of oceanographic studies, visits to unexplored sub-Antarctic islands and even a romantic search for Captain Kidd's hidden treasure in Trinidad.

The expedition got a good deal of attention, particularly because of one brilliant piece of Shackleton showmanship. He convinced the *Daily Mail* to run a competition for a boy scout to accompany the expedition, and the competition caught the public imagination. More than 1700 boys applied to go. Baden-Powell shortlisted ten but in the end Shackleton could not decide between the final two and brought them both along. One soon left, suffering from seasickness, while the other, Scout James Marr, an eighteen-year-old undergraduate geologist from Aberdeen, saw out the entire journey and left a touching account of his adventure. Marr went on to become one of Britain's finest polar scientists.[19]

The nucleus of the crew were veterans of the *Endurance*, including its sailing master Frank Worsley and Shackleton's deputy, Frank Wild, whose Antarctic experience went back twenty years. Most were still owed money from the last trip, but they didn't hesitate to sign up again with the man they simply called 'the Boss'. Wilkins was asked to join as naturalist and cameraman and he was enticed by the plans to collect a small aeroplane, an Avro Baby, when they reached Cape Town. Still, he was realistic enough to recognise it as 'a long, but not entirely selfish joy ride . . . a last expedition [Shackleton] was determined to have'. He was offered a salary of £600 plus expenses but for all of them the honour of serving under Sir Ernest was its own reward.

Wilkins wrote to his family shortly before leaving, outlining what was known of the route and his hopes that he might discover some unknown plant or bird life. The perennial traveller, he saw it as 'an exceptionally fine opportunity to visit most of the little known parts of the globe' but his greater hope was that it would reveal the best sites for his planned ring of meteorological stations around Antarctica.[20] For his elderly mother there was reassurance 'that we will not be going into serious danger or uncomfortable conditions', but she knew well enough by now what to make of such promises. 'I won't be sorry to get away from civilisation again,' he wrote, and not knowing if he would ever see or hear from her again, asked forgiveness for not waiting for a reply.

After much delay, *Quest* set sail on 17 September 1921 from St Katherine's Wharf. Huge crowds gathered along the Thames, and London Bridge was barely passable long before the little ship came into view. Hundreds of nurses in their white dresses waved them off as they passed Greenwich Hospital and cheers rang out from the Naval Academy. Film of the departure shows Wilkins and Shackleton grinning broadly – one man hoping to fulfil his destiny, the other perhaps knowing he would never return – both happy to be away at last.

Four days later, as they left Plymouth and the coast of England disappeared in the gathering darkness, the sea and sky turned the deep bruised colour of bad weather. A violent gale was brewing, so severe it left even the ocean veterans like Worsley pukish. The *Quest*, top-heavy and fully laden, rolled and twisted in winds of such violence that migrating birds flocked to her heaving decks for shelter. They landed exhausted, without the strength to escape the men who hand fed-them food and water. Larks and doves and little Jenny wrens fluttered above the topsail seeking a perch on the swaying mast, and soon the canvas was full of them, a sight so strange it would unnerve any sailor.

Storms blew them all the way to the Azores, where they put in for repairs, a welcome relief from the constant nausea. As the surgeon and *Endurance* veteran Alexander Macklin put it, 'It has been impossible to stand without holding firmly to some support . . . meals are a screaming comedy. The *Quest* is a little "she-devil", lively as they are made. She has many uncomplimentary things said of her, and deserves all of them.'[21]

Wilkins and his geologist colleague George Douglas shared a coffin-like space way forward in the most uncomfortable spot on the vessel, just over the rattling chain lockers, which they entered by climbing through a small hatch. As well as their bunks, the airless space included a makeshift darkroom, laboratory and storage lockers for specimens. Wilkins contrived a chute to try to funnel in some fresh air, but it rarely worked. These were the quarters he had described to his mother as 'the biggest and best accommodation for my scientific work, a comfortable cabin'.[22] He was fortunate to rarely suffer from motion sickness.

Their vile luck with the weather continued as they headed south. In 12-metre seas Scout Marr witnessed a sight he barely believed when Captain Worsley resorted to pouring oil on troubled waters to buy them some comfort: 'The gale had increased to a hurricane. We hove to about nine-o-clock and bags of oil were put down in front of the bows to keep down the sea, where the weight of the storm struck us. The effect was really remarkable. A large sea, which was likely to hit us, would fall flat about 15 yards off and slide away under the bows. Some six gallons of oil was used.'[23]

But no amount of mariner's tricks could force the stubborn *Quest* to move beyond a plodding four knots. Well behind schedule, they had to abandon plans to visit South Africa where the aeroplane and their winter gear had been sent. From now on this would be a strictly maritime expedition, and Wilkins was once again denied his chance of flying in Antarctica. As they limped into Rio de Janeiro, the ship was laid up for a major overhaul. Perhaps to make up for the disappointment, Shackleton suggested Wilkins catch a whaler to the southern islands and begin his scientific survey while the summer season still allowed.

For six weeks Wilkins forgot his frustrations amid the wild beauty of South Georgia, a mountainous finger of rock floating in the swirling currents of the Southern Ocean. Captain Cook had been the first to step ashore here, frightening the penguins with a discharge of small arms as he claimed it for Britain. Cook had hoped it was the tip of the great southern continent, and on realising it wasn't, called the southernmost point Cape Disappointment. It was an appropriately melancholy name for a site that would mark both the beginning and end of the classic age of Antarctic exploration.

Cook had thought the island savage and horrible but Wilkins delighted in its towering ranges. His notebook – part diary, part field notes – captures his elation:

> Suitably clad and with back to the wind the joy of the wild scene exhilarated and set the blood coursing through one's veins . . . In the distance is a dove, grey streak tipped with coral red, about which flashed graceful slender wings, the Arctic terns . . . Pippits, singing sweetly, soared above fluttering Wilson petrels. The Southern skua, wise in experience and scenting plunder in the presence of mankind, flew back and forth with greedy searching eyes sure of a gory feast when seals are killed . . . Scenes of slaughter haunt the vision as one stands to survey the beach; and the clean snow clad hills, severe in outline but haughty and majestic, seem to reprimand and protest against man's cruelty.[24]

He spent strenuous days collecting specimens, then carrying back his collections and heavy equipment through the tussocked hillsides:

'Dog tired I would return to the tent at night and cook a meal on the small coal stove I had brought and prepare my specimens by candle light before turning in to the sleeping bag.' Each night he took an albatross egg from a marked nest for his breakfast: 'An albatross egg is a good meal for a man; in an omelet it is delicious but when plain boiled the white is tough and leathery.'[25]

By candlelight he prepared a lonely Christmas dinner, a duck he cooked under canvas while a storm raged outside. The next day he was wracked by violent stomach cramps – in the dim light he had inadvertently mixed some of his arsenic preserving material with his dinner. For two days he writhed in agony in his tent, waiting for the pains to subside.

When the weather improved he worked furiously to extend his collection before it was time to rendezvous with the *Quest*: 'The time passed too quickly . . . my kind friends, the whalers, were pleased to find me alive and glad that what seemed to them a foolish, lonely sojourn was ended.'

He hurried towards the whaling base at Grytviken when he heard *Quest* had arrived, 'full of joyous expectation at the prospect of meeting old comrades'. He noticed a flag at half-mast, but thought nothing of it in a place where 2000 men were doing risky business each day. It was *Quest*'s navigator Douglas Jeffrey who shouted down to him from the bridge with the news: 'Shackleton is dead.'

'This meant so much that I could not at once grasp it; the dull shock numbed my senses and left my mind a void. No leader could have been more helpful; no man more generous than Shackleton had been. Without him we were as flint without steel; dull, hard things without the fire.'[26]

Quest had arrived at Grytviken the night before, eight years since Shackleton had sailed up the same fjord in *Endurance* on his way to the Weddell Sea. It was from here that he had set out to rescue his men after his epic journey from Elephant Island and many of the whalers from that time were still there. They took him ashore to celebrate his return and later that night aboard the ship he wrote in his diary: 'A wonderful evening. In the darkening twilight, I saw a lone star hover, gem-like, above the bay.' Unable to sleep, he asked his old friend Leonard Hussey to play a few tunes on his banjo and he closed his eyes to the sound of Brahms' Lullaby. In the early hours of the morning he died of a heart attack.

The men of the *Quest* were devastated by the loss, but agreed to continue on as Shackleton would have wished. At his widow's request, they buried him on South Georgia. While the other graves in the little cemetery face east towards Europe and the rising sun, Shackleton's points south to his true home.

Quest was heading there without him, exploring the frozen Weddell Sea but unable to reach land. In an eerie reminder of the doomed *Endurance*, she became locked in the ice. Wilkins, with Scout Marr as his assistant, photographed the ship in its frozen shackles, much as Hurley had done on the earlier expedition. With little coal and low on provisions, it seemed they would be forced to spend the winter where they were, a gloomy prospect for all but especially for the veterans of Shackleton's expedition. Their predicament became even worse when a giant iceberg appeared on the horizon, ploughing its way through the icepack towards them. Several kilometres long and 60 metres high, each day it came closer, driven by the strong currents beneath the ice. Its vast, threatening presence unnerved them all, and even at a distance its presence was felt as the ice squeezed its grip around the little boat until her timbers groaned and squeaked and the deck began to buckle. They assembled what emergency gear they could and prepared to abandon ship.

The *Quest* was lifted and tilted on her side as the ice piled up in giant pressure ridges around them, preventing any possible escape in the lifeboats. Wilkins was sure the ship was doomed: 'We had all we could do to keep our footing on the sloping side of the ship and clung to the bulwarks and rigging as we watched the big berg approach.'[27]

The crew gripped the gunnels, transfixed with dread and awe as the moving mountain towered above them. Then, with the iceberg less than 100 metres away, the crushing sounds stopped. For some un-accountable reason, which Wilkins likened to some mighty unseen hand taking control, its drift altered course and swung slowly away. In its wake was open water, and *Quest* slid on its keel and settled, without serious damage. They hurried to get steam up and hauled the ship by rope into the open lane to make their escape.

Frank Wild headed west cautiously on the edge of the pack, unwilling to chance another encounter with the ice, and they returned to South Georgia in April. The crew had little heart for polar exploring without the Boss. They built a cairn in his memory, high on a hill, a gateway to Antarctica. Wilkins filmed the event, and the sadness is clear on every man's face.

It was not the end of their adventures, though. The little sealer plugged on, visiting some of the least-known islands on Earth. In forgotten places such as Tristan da Cunha, Inaccessible Island and the uninhabited Gough Island, Wilkins continued his diligent fieldwork. He discovered a new variety of seabird, Wilkins' bunting, and made an important discovery of a small species of sophora tree known to exist in both New Zealand and South America, suggesting a possible ancient geological link. He also classified a new genus of finch, and for a self-taught botanist, these were significant findings that would bring him to the attention of Britain's Natural History Museum. If not working hard, he was thinking hard, and his diligence made an impression on his shipmates. 'Wilkins was a painstaking scientist,' said Jeffrey, 'and an excellent companion . . . he was always cheery, and he was always working.'[28]

Somehow this boy from sweltering outback Australia had become almost oblivious to the cold. On one of the islands he was left working alone while the others continued on. At the planned rendezvous to pick him up, Wilkins came into sight paddling towards them in an Arctic kayak he had brought along. Despite the bitter winds of the Roaring Forties screaming off the Antarctic mainland, he was dressed as if he were paddling in the South Pacific. 'His arms and legs were bare, and he had most of his frigid weather duffle in the bottom of the kayak. The cold weather didn't seem to bother him,' said Jeffrey.

By now he was also a fine sailor, who 'could furl a topsail as well as any sailor by profession'. Caught in a hurricane one day, the crew watched in horror as Wilkins was swept overboard by a giant wave. 'Somebody yelled: "Wilkie's gone!" We all gave a look and sure enough he had disappeared.' Miraculously the next wave crashed over the ship, dumping Wilkins back on deck, 'pretty wet but not at all discouraged'.

They continued on to South Africa, but it was not a happy ship. With Shackleton gone, the discomforts of the journey boiled over into frustration, and it took stern action from Wild to prevent a serious division between the scientists and the sailors. Yet, as he had with

Stefansson, Wilkins managed to remain respected in both camps. At times he amazed them all with his peculiar talents.

'One extraordinary fact about Wilkins,' said Jeffrey, 'was that he seemed to be, and regarded himself as a natural receiver of radio.' Bemused, the crew would put him to the test, and sure enough, he seemed to be able to receive signals from a distance. 'He could be far away from the radio room and pick up the radio messages as they came over the receiving sets inside the room. 'I've heard of this quality in people before, but only saw it in his case, and then he could work it only occasionally.'[29]

We can only wonder what the inventor of radio, Guglielmo Marconi, made of this bizarre talent for picking up radio signals without a receiver. The two men met in London soon after Wilkins returned, to discuss plans for a network of weather monitoring stations. Marconi, who had sent signals across the Atlantic without the slightest idea of how he succeeded in bending radio waves over the horizon, may well have believed such remote sensing was possible. In any event, he encouraged Wilkins' plans for polar stations.

Wilkins had returned with copious field notes and hundreds of specimens, enough material to write several papers for scientific journals and address the respected Linnean Society on his findings. But he had not ventured to Antarctica to become a birdwatcher or botanist. His aim in both expeditions had been to consign the days of exploration by sail and sledge to history, but he had been frustrated by events beyond his control. The white peaks still hid an unknown continent and he was certain that it held the answers he sought. Four years later he would return to the poles to pioneer the modern age of discovery, and this time he would be leading the charge. But, as always, there were distractions along the way.

8

Drought lands

And the seven years of plenteousness, that was in the land of Egypt, were ended. And the seven years of dearth began to come, according as Joseph had said: and the dearth was in all the lands; but in all the land of Egypt there was bread.

– Genesis 41:53

Joseph was just a young slave when he made history's first recorded long-range weather forecast. Hauled before the ruler of Egypt, he interpreted the Pharaoh's strange dreams as a warning of future drought and he advised urgent steps to avoid disaster. The Pharaoh put him in charge of preparations and when the rains failed just as he predicted, Joseph saved Egypt from famine. As a reward, the Pharaoh handed him the keys to the Kingdom.

When Vladimir Ilyich Lenin stepped to the podium to deliver his address to the All-Russia Food Conference on 16 June 1921, he was as powerful as any pharaoh, but *his* Joseph sat silent. Jo Stalin was biding his time while Russia slipped into a tragedy more dreadful than the revolution, more appalling than the civil war that followed. Lenin was faced with the great irony of leadership: he might control the destiny of a nation, but was powerless when confronted by the uncertainties of nature.

It was drought that had inspired George Wilkins' lifetime mission, and it was drought that would consume the next three years of his life. It would take him to Russia to witness unimaginable suffering, to a meeting with Lenin himself, and later, on foot, to a land of plenty turned to dust. If God would not deliver us another Joseph, Wilkins reasoned, humanity would need to solve the problems of weather by itself.

Since the *Quest* expedition, he had been busying himself with his naturalist's reports and cataloguing the specimen collection for the British Museum. But most of his time, as ever, was spent on his plan for a global weather monitoring system. He intended to present it for consideration by the greatest minds on weather and climate, the Royal Meteorological Society.

The society had its roots in the meetings of learned men and women in the coffeehouses of early Victorian London. Sounding for all the world like Wilkins' spiritual ancestor, the precocious writer and humanist John Ruskin was just a teenager when, in 1839, he wrote of their lofty aims in an essay:

> The Meteorological Society . . . has been formed not for a city, nor for a kingdom, but for the world. It wishes to be the central point, the moving power, of a Vast Machine . . . It desires to have at its command, at stated periods, perfect systems of methodical and simultaneous observations; it wishes its influence and its power to be omnipresent over the globe . . . to know, at any given instant, the state of the atmosphere on every point on its surface.[1]

It was fine sophistry, but the public yawned in disinterest and Ruskin's 'Vast Machine' never started. His essay failed to sell, and its publication left the young society with insurmountable debts. However, the Society was eventually revived, the astrologists removed, and by Wilkins' time it was in rude health with a royal charter and recognition that, at last, there was more science than magic to meteorology.

Despite its hard-won credibility, the further development of the discipline was restricted as long as it remained a parochial undertaking. From time to time there had been efforts in international cooperation but these were mired in differing standards and disconnected recordings. This was the central problem confronting weathermen, as Ruskin had realised: 'The meteorologist is impotent if alone; his observations are useless; for they are made upon a point . . . he would calculate the currents of the atmosphere of the world, while he only knows the direction of a breeze.'[2]

Given that he was addressing this very point, Wilkins might have reasonably hoped for a positive response from the RMS. His plan called for simultaneous occupation of a minimum of thirty-two stations in the Arctic, and a further twelve dotted around the Antarctic Circle, operated for a period of at least fifteen years. Their observations would be standardised and transmitted daily by new-fangled radio technology to a central point. In the south, the bases would be serviced by ships from Melbourne, Cape Town and Buenos Aires. He detailed at length the costs – about £2 million – and the means by which each government would pay its share. 'I hoped,' he wrote, 'it would be possible through various scientific institutions, to bring about an international bureau which would supervise the selection and training of observers for the outposts and to decide the nature of apparatus to be used at each station.'[3]

Wilkins had cannily submitted his proposal not as a report that might be easily dismissed, but as a series of interlinked questions requiring detailed responses. He was laying the groundwork for an even more extensive plan of polar investigation which he hoped would lead to an International Bureau of Meteorology, dedicated to preventing human suffering through science. It was a blueprint for global cooperation, a forerunner of coordinated research efforts such as the International Geophysical Year and the World Meteorological Organization, the UN agency founded in 1951.

The wise men of the Meteorological Society acknowledged his proposal, honoured him by electing him a fellow of the society,[4] and then reacted like all practised bureaucracies when faced with difficult questions – they appointed a subcommittee to investigate.

Judging by the membership of the committee, Wilkins' submission had been taken very seriously. The heavy guns of British meteorology were all there. Its chairman was Sir Napier Shaw, a former director of the Meteorological Office and Britain's first Professor of Meteorology (though his science was still considered only worthy of a part-time appointment). Shaw had discovered the link between polluting factories and London's ghastly pea-souper fogs, and gave science the *millibar*, the standard measurement of air pressure. He was not a man to be trifled with and his masterwork, the four-volume *Manual of Meteorology*, is remembered for the stern warning it gave to any dreamers who might propose half-baked ideas about the weather: 'Every theory of the course of events in nature is necessarily based on some process of simplification of the phenomena and is to some extent therefore a fairy tale.'

Backing him up on the committee was the respected Dr (later Sir) George Simpson, who had been on Captain Scott's tragic *Terra Nova* expedition to the South Pole. Simpson was boss of the Meteorological Office, a position he would hold for nearly twenty years. The remaining members of the subcommittee comprised two veterans of colonial administration in India and Egypt. Collectively they spent eight months carefully considering their response to the Wilkins questions.

While he waited, George was not idle. An unexpected phone call from a friend soon saw him packing his bags for Russia. Wilkins later claimed he had been 'shanghaied' into the trip after his friend had withdrawn from the project, but his protests sound unconvincing. So soon after the revolution of 1917 this was certain to be an adventure, and that was something he could not resist. Wilkins' task was to write reports and make a film about the famine relief operations being run by a religious charity, the Society of Friends. These Quakers had undertaken a massive program of emergency aid to the devastated areas of Central Europe and Russia, and they wanted a film and newspaper articles to help publicise their efforts: the more graphic, the better.

After agreeing to a three-month engagement, Wilkins was surprised by another request to accompany a young woman on this journey. She would be doing missionary work on the way before meeting up with her fiancé, a clergyman working in Moscow. It was an unusual arrangement, and if he had imagined his travelling companion as dour and pious, then he was in for a shock. Lucita Squier was petite and very beautiful, with long dark hair and olive skin, a Spanish-American from California who had experience as both an actress and writer. She had stood in as a double for Mary Pickford, America's first cinema sweetheart, and was already established as one of the few woman screenwriters in Hollywood.[5]

Squier's fragile looks disguised an iron will and a burning political passion. She was a committed socialist. Neither was her fiancé your usual village minister. Albert Rhys Williams was an outspoken journalist and Congregationalist clergyman who had been in Moscow when the Communists seized power in 1917. He'd stood with John Reed, author of *Ten Days that Shook the World*, on the steps of the

Winter Palace in St Petersburg as the Red Guards defended the revolution. He and Reed had stayed on to advise the new government on international propaganda, and Williams had served as an assistant in the Soviet Government's Commissariat for Foreign Affairs.[6] After the revolution he returned to the United States and became a vigorous campaigner for improved US–Soviet relations. Now Lucita was keen to see Russia for herself and help in its hour of need.

Perhaps it was because of Lucita Squier's politics that Wilkins received another call before leaving for Russia. The details are sketchy and he never gave away anything more than the most elliptical hints, but it seems Wilkins was contacted by British Intelligence and agreed to do some additional work beyond his filming for the Quakers. Clearly a man of his capabilities was a prize recruit, and his camera gave him access to many hidden worlds. But, on this trip at least, Wilkins was not actively involved in espionage as much as in compiling reports on the conditions inside Russia. The clearest indication of his private activities is that he met with Lenin but did not mention it in his public writings until more than twenty years later. It was not the last time he would perform such service on a freelance basis. As his fame grew, Wilkins gained access to many world leaders in the turbulent political climate of the 1920s and 1930s, and the secret services of Britain, the United States and Australia all found use for him from time to time.

As they sat together in train carriages between France and Austria, Wilkins and Lucita watched grimly as the devastation of post-war Europe slid past their window. After war had come an influenza epidemic, and now famine gripped countryside and city, an endless toll of misery that had cost millions of lives over the past eight years. It showed in the pinched faces and ragged clothes of people as much as in the broken buildings and empty factories, and the further east they travelled, the more horrible the spectacle became. They stopped often so that Wilkins could record the relief workers struggling against this tide of suffering. In all, he made four films for the Quakers, collectively called *New Worlds for Old*: a hopeful title given there were only the barest grounds for optimism.[7]

As George and Lucita continued on, transport became a problem. Often they were reduced to travelling on horse-drawn carts, and sleeping in farmhouses and barns. In Poland, where uprisings and battles continued after the Armistice, eight million refugees had fled invading armies, and Wilkins estimated some villages had changed hands fifteen times or more. At the missionary centres, more than half the children were suffering from tuberculosis and bodies were left to rot in the unploughed fields outside. Yet even this was little preparation for what lay ahead in the place the American papers called 'the Red Planet'.

'The spirit of Soviet Russia is met on the southern frontier as solid and clean cut as a wall,' wrote Wilkins. 'On one side were a few neatly uniformed Polish officials with bright buttons, cultured moustaches and military bearing keenly alert to their duty.' Across the border he found a company of round-faced youths in spattered greatcoats, standing in aimless groups and gaping at them as the train drew up to the station. 'No officer or anyone seems to be in authority and no one is conspicuous.'

The long dead hand of Soviet officialdom had descended on the two of them – briefly amusing, always tiresome and occasionally menacing:

> Over any special paper there is a general consultation, and then it is laboriously read aloud by two or more officials in concert. If it provides sufficient amusement or is sufficiently indefinite, they hand it back and in some cases it is asked for again, so that those who have been too busy before may have a chance to see it. If the paper is neatly typed and its contents state briefly and concisely what it means, it is apparently looked on with grave suspicion; its direct precise language is the mark of the Intelligentsia, and it is born in triumph from group to group and finally taken to an outside hut which is the office of the political control department.[8]

Should the papers not return by the time the train left, it meant a three-day wait in the flea-bitten border town – and the fleas were carrying typhus.

In fits and starts they made their way to Moscow, passing slowly through the treeless landscape. Their carriage was candlelit, and the steady drip of tallow added to the sense of gloom and foreboding. Villages, veiled in snowdrift, could be dimly made out on either side but there was not an animal in any field. For hundreds of kilometres it seemed as if nothing moved, a land as barren as anything he had trekked in the Arctic.

In Moscow itself, Wilkins reported at some length on the relative costs and incomes of the average Russian, where a government official and his family survived on a salary equivalent to £2 a month, eating rye bread, a little fat, sugar and an occasional meal of the cheapest meat. In the outlying villages, peasants had to fall back on supplies of edible grasses gathered during the summer, pounded in wooden troughs and mixed with rough rye flour for making bread. It seemed to Wilkins that the entire population was slowly starving, and he could only imagine the horrors that were unfolding in the distant provinces. Though the Politburo closely controlled the press, the city was rife with ghastly rumours of cannibalism and corpse robbing.

It is estimated that more than five million died during the worst two years of drought and the famine had become so serious that Lenin was forced to appeal to the outside world for help.[9] Swallowing their pride, the Communists even accepted charity from the United States. Under the arch anti-Bolshevik and future president Herbert Hoover, the American Relief Administration was feeding more than ten million Russians every day. Lenin's call had brought an assortment of missionaries, adventurers and international socialists to Russia, and when Wilkins visited the local Quaker relief office, he was given charge of another female travelling companion, Mademoiselle Laurette Citroën.

Laurette was the daughter of the French auto magnate André Citroën, and had been inspired by the Russian cry for help. She seemed to have become estranged from her father, a gambler in both business and on the gaming tables of Monte Carlo, and decided to devote herself to helping the poor. Wilkins now had two young women to escort across country as well as a difficult job, and it tested both his patience and chivalry. While he admired their courage, he would have much preferred to travel alone.

Unlike his companions, he was not greatly impressed by the progress of communism, and the deadening bureaucracy and corruption annoyed him. 'A tip or a bribe is never refused and is even asked for by those with sufficient or insufficient education,' he wrote, adding a little unrealistically that the place could do with a dose of British discipline.[10] To discourage the greedy he grew a neatly trimmed beard, looking remarkably like a young Lenin, and with his commanding presence and tailored suit must have appeared to be an important party official. For those more curious about the peculiar trio, he carried a variety of colourful government papers that seemed, with persistence and the necessary financial encouragement, to open most doors.

They rolled east across the steppes to the edge of Europe, sharing a four-berth compartment in the miserable trains. At first Wilkins hung a blanket down the centre to protect his companions' modesty, but this became pointless when they eventually had to take to droshkies – horse-drawn cabs – in which they travelled and often slept together. They crossed the Volga and finally arrived at Buzuluk, once the centre of the vast Samara grain-growing region. What they found was a scene almost beyond description.

This was the black heart of the famine with suffering on a biblical scale. Something of its magnitude can be garnered from the telegrams sent by the great Norwegian polar explorer and humanitarian Fridtjof Nansen, who also visited Buzuluk at this time on behalf of the Red Cross. Not a man prone to exaggeration, he described it as 'misery worse than darkest imagination'.[11]

Of the one million people in the region, Nansen estimated half had simply run out of food. More than ten thousand were dying every month of starvation, fatigue or disease. At the cemetery he photographed eighty naked corpses, mostly children, being buried in a common grave, their clothes stripped off to be used by the living. 'That was two days harvest of the deathcarts,' he wrote.

Wilkins set out with his camera and with his practised, inconspicuous methods filmed the gruesome scenes with both honesty and compassion. He hoped the images might provoke sympathy in the West and the last roll of *New Worlds for Old* was entirely devoted to the tragedy of Buzuluk. In the Quaker relief kitchens, skeletal children sat silently at tables, eating the food that would save their lives. One aid worker testified: 'The sight of these ragged rows of thin bodies was undoubtedly the greatest inspiration that the relief workers had.'[12]

Poor communications hampered the aid efforts, and with the horse population reduced to just a fraction of its pre-war numbers, camels were used to carry food and medicine. Wilkins filmed the lines of great hairy Bactrians, descendants of the beasts that had once brought tea along the Silk Road, spread out in columns that stretched beyond sight on the snow-blown steppes.

Travelling beyond the city was dangerous, but Wilkins and his intrepid missionaries needed to see for themselves the conditions in the countryside. On one occasion, seeking shelter in a hay barn, they narrowly escaped attack by a pack of marauding wolves. On another, their horse and cart broke through the ice on a frozen lake and they nearly drowned.

Wilkins' closest call came when he went to investigate rumours of cannibalism among the villagers. In one place it was said that down the road a group of ruffians under the leadership of an old woman had waylaid several people who had never been heard from again. Wilkins suggested they pay a visit, but no one was willing to accompany him.

'Still believing in the inordinate luck that had seen me through many an apparently hopeless situation, I set out alone, carrying what little food we could spare,' he wrote.[13] He approached the village cautiously and was edging around the corner of a house when he encountered a man 'who without hesitation delivered me such a blow on the head that I was knocked to the ground'. When he regained consciousness he found himself prostrate on a low porch, surrounded by a crowd of men and woman arguing among themselves about his fate. 'Imagine my horror when I saw on a bench the remains of several human arms and legs. The cannibal story was true after all, and I felt that at last I had been too venturesome.'

But the mood of the crowd changed when they went through the parcels that he had carried. The sight of bread and black sausage shocked them, and as they ran their hands through the flour he had brought them, they realised that Wilkins had been trying to help. 'They sat or kneeled about me with tears streaming down their faces. I could understand hardly anything of what they said, but I managed to get them to understand with the few words that I knew that I was their friend.' With gratitude the desperate villagers let him go, and he promised to send help.

With his filming completed he now had only his 'unofficial' work to do. Given his experiences, Wilkins had no misty-eyed illusions about the state of Soviet Russia as he walked through the gates of the Kremlin to meet Lenin. Ushered into a sparsely furnished anteroom in Lenin's private apartment, he wondered if the founder of modern Russia knew the truth too.

A small, elderly looking man, though only in his early fifties, Lenin was ill from the first of several strokes that would eventually kill him. Wilkins' notes of the meeting, written many years later, suggest there was little small-talk. 'Lenin told me that while he believed that he had done the right thing in bringing about revolution in Russia, after 5 years effort in communism he had come to realize that he had made a mistake in regard to the rapidity of development possible within the Soviet Union.' Lenin told him that he now knew that one could not hope to 'inject civilization into the minds of humans and get an immediate response'.[14]

This meeting was one of the last Lenin had with a Westerner and came at crucial moment in Soviet Russia's history. Just days later would come the formal founding of the USSR. But more significantly, Lenin was just about to begin composing his explosive *Last Testament*, a call for radical reform of the Communist Party and a blistering attack on the man manoeuvring to be his successor, Joseph Stalin. There is a hint in Wilkins' writings that Russia's leader revealed at least some of his frustrations, but in any event, it made no difference. Barely a year after their meeting, Lenin was dead and Stalin would begin unleashing his wave of terror.

Wilkins would later return several times to Russia, fly across its entire length by Zeppelin and was even honoured in Moscow as a hero for his attempts to rescue crashed Soviet pilots. But nothing he saw from the skies, or by land, or in the behaviour of the many Russians he met did anything to change his initial impressions of Communism. He saw it as a doomed experiment in social engineering and believed it would one day collapse under the weight of its own contradictions. When he eventually crossed the border on that first trip, he looked back at a huge but tattered Soviet flag on its bulky pole and considered it symbolic of Russia's condition: 'The mighty tree, shorn of its limbs and roots, its vital organs, greedy and grasping though they might have been, cannot live by the aid of the fluttering blood-red flag that flies this way and that as the four winds blow. Even the trunk must rot and decay unless – but it is not my province to foretell the future.'[15]

9

—

Undiscovered Australia

A few years since this country abounded with wild animals; but now the emu is banished to a long distance, the kangaroo is become scarce . . . It may be long before these animals are altogether exterminated, but their doom is fixed.[1]

– Charles Darwin, 1836

The extermination of native mammals has apparently gone much further than is generally thought . . . There are very few game laws in Australia, and no one gives any attention to the ones that are in order.[2]

– Report in the journal *Nature*, July 1920

In June 1921 the respected Curator of Tasmania's Museum, Clive Errol Lord, sent a plaintive cry for help to his colleagues at the Natural History Museum in London. Animal life was dying out in northern Australia. Charles Darwin's predictions had come to pass.

Lord was concerned that rare species might disappear before good specimens could be collected for study. 'It appears to me that it is time we got busy,' he wrote.[3] In London, the news was met with alarm. The British Museum had a varied collection of Australia's extraordinary animals dating back to the days of Captain Cook and Joseph Banks, but the collection was haphazard. There were few quality specimens from the tropical north where the extinction appeared to be the most advanced, and its reputation as the world's leading collection was under threat from the Americans. The museum had little trouble convincing the Treasury to allocate funds for a major investigation; now it needed a man to lead the expedition. George Wilkins was still in Russia when he received the telegram asking him to return to Australia on the museum's behalf.

Though he had no scientific qualifications of any kind, there could hardly have been a more skilled amateur. Wilkins' finely detailed collection from the *Quest* expedition was still keeping the museum's staff busy. What had really impressed was his absolute dedication to the often lonely work of the field naturalist. The proposed expedition to tropical Australia would be a demanding task, taking at least two years in trying and potentially dangerous conditions. The distances involved and the isolated setting meant working for long periods beyond communication. Wilkins' contract was for a modest £600 a year, the same fee he had taken from Shackleton, and he was entrusted with autonomy over the expedition's organisation and expenditure. Government approval came in December and within weeks he sailed for home.

The expedition's principal objective was to collect mammals from both sides of the Great Dividing Range, the snaking chain of mountains separating eastern Australia's narrow coastal plains from the continental interior. Wilkins would follow a criss-crossing 4000-kilometre trail from central New South Wales to the northern tip of Australia at Cape York, then head west through the tropical islands and wild Gulf country of Carpentaria. It was a distance comparable to Lewis and Clark's epic journey across the United States, in a landscape even more forbidding. The far north was an enormous frontier of forests, flooding rivers and monsoonal wetlands, thick with venomous snakes, crocodiles and fierce insects. For a century intrepid explorers had left tragic tales and thin trails through its vast interior and only its coast seemed suitable for settlement. When not in drought this region was prone to cyclones, and a particularly lethal disease, Gulf Fever, wiped out its first town. By the 1920s tropical Australia had a declining population of perhaps 5000 scattered Aboriginal people with a few hopeful white pastoralists, prospectors and missionaries. Together they fitfully inhabited an area larger than France and Germany combined. There were no roads, no railways and just a handful of telegraph stations.

Once it had been rich in wildlife. Northern Australia's immense biodiversity had evolved to survive cycles of drought, flood and fire yet this tenacity disguised a fragile order that was easily disturbed. Its Indigenous keepers had spent 50 000 years here in successful cohabitation with the environment. European settlement had taken just fifty years to upset it. Wilkins spent two and a half years trekking thousands of kilometres across this landscape, often on foot and alone, and his softly spoken record of that tremendous journey ranks as perhaps the first detailed telling of the ignorant destruction of the land he both loved and despaired for.

Wilkins was welcomed when he arrived by boat at Brisbane's New Farm in April 1923. The local paper called him Queensland's most distinguished visitor for a long time. 'A fine specimen of manhood . . . He was both tall and broad and a small beard on his strong determined face added to his somewhat exceptional appearance.' Wilkins told the papers he wanted four scientific companions from the hundreds who had applied. One of his aims was to clear up the controversy regarding the 'Queensland Tiger', a mysterious animal widely reported but still unknown to science.

The *Brisbane Courier*, and presumably much of the population, was in favour of this enterprise to gather museum specimens of Australian wildlife while they still survived. 'Game preserves might, and should, be set apart,' the paper wrote, 'but the fertile areas where the game would naturally live were the most desirable for other purposes, and the birds and mammals must go, as had their more highly developed associates, primitive man, before the inroads of modern civilisation.' [4]

In a sentence, the city's leading journal had dismissed thousands of years of human habitation and sanctioned the extermination of the nation's native wildlife.

Australia's Aboriginal population at the time of white settlement is notoriously difficult to establish. Estimates range from as high as 1.5 million to as few as 200 000. But what is clear is that by the 1920s these numbers had seriously declined, to perhaps less than 50 000 by the time Wilkins arrived. In the Gulf Country Wilkins believed there were only a few thousand remaining 'full blood' Aboriginal people.[5] A shortage of labour after World War I which saw Indigenous men employed as cheap pastoral workers seemed to stem the decline, but their survival, however, meant wholesale slaughter for native wildlife through the clearance of forests and woodland to graze introduced stock.

Within the first few decades of European settlement, the face of a continent changed beyond recognition. Never in history had so few so irrevocably altered so much, so quickly. By the 1850s more than thirty native mammal species had disappeared or were on their way to extinction, representing a third of the entire world's mammal species lost in the previous 500 years. Half the native bird species had fallen in number and 10 per cent of the freshwater fish species were endangered. An infamous menagerie of introduced pests – rabbits, foxes, cats and camels to name a few – had taken hold of the landscape. Exotic plants overran native species at an extraordinary rate and enormous areas of rainforest, grassland and shrubland disappeared in less than a single lifetime. Every year pastoralists cut down tens of millions of trees while their cattle and sheep ground the fragile topsoil to dust that blew away with the winds. In the tropical north, engineers were planning the first assaults on the rivers and creeks to irrigate new farmlands.[6] The dwindling numbers of Indigenous people stood witness to this devastation, powerless to prevent it. Wilkins had come to record the death of ancient Australia.

He found people curiously unconcerned with the calamity unfolding across their nation. When the British Museum had offered the services of a qualified scientific staff Wilkins turned down it down, confident he would find eager young assistants in Australia. However, he naïvely expected them to be young men like himself, dedicated to the pursuit of knowledge: 'I had failed to realise the average Australian's understanding of natural science,' he wrote. 'There were numerous appeals from youths seeking adventure, but each demanding pay, there were many enquiries from "dead-beats" looking for a job . . . but not one response from young biologists anxious to take advantage of the opportunity offered to see their country.' One recommended scientist had demanded payment of £1000 a year, accepted, then quit on account of the 'miserable pittance' on offer. No one seemed to share Wilkins' willingness to make sacrifices in the name of science, and he despaired at this complacency: 'Most Australians are well off in regard to creature comforts, and many of them soon reach independent means; yet the absence of the expressed desire for culture and for higher things, and their contentedness with the mediocre, make them perhaps the poorest rich people in the world to-day.'[7]

Eventually he found three companions, although only one, Russian émigré Vladimir Kotoff, had any scientific experience. They set off in a specially equipped Ford van – part caravan, part laboratory – with a general plan to travel from south to north along both sides of the Great Dividing Range. In a good year it might have been straightforward. In a drought year, it took many frustrating diversions to find what they were looking for.

The Australian bush in drought is a landscape for mystics and madmen. Wilkins met them all in the coming months: European missionaries driven half-crazy by the flies and heat; farmers who had stored away cash from the good years but lived in hovels; lonely stockmen who'd spent years with only their animals for company. Once he rode with a drover who could not complete a single sentence without cussing his animals in the same breath. Wilkins had to work hard to understand who was being abused: himself, the dog or a stubborn steer.

Each morning they set out at daybreak to lay their traps and snares, and each evening they returned with a meagre collection. It was depressing work, made worse by the painful nettles of the prickly pear which bored into their arms and legs. This nasty pest arrived on the First Fleet of settlers and convicts. At the suggestion of the botanist Joseph Banks, Captain Phillip brought the virulent cactus from South America to Botany Bay, where he hoped to establish a plantation to break the Spanish monopoly on cochineal dye, made from the insects that lived on the plant. This highly prized red dye produced the two most recognisable symbols of the British Empire: the Union Jack and the redcoat tunics of her soldiers. Banks, the great naturalist, unwittingly unleashed one of Australia's worst environmental menaces.

One night the expedition camp rose in alarm with Kotoff shouting: 'Come quickly, come quickly with a gun!' They dashed out to see a streak of something disappearing in the bush. Kotoff described the intruder as about the size of a large dog, with a bushy tail and a round, flat head, its pelt striped in wide bands.

The description fitted that of the almost mythical animal known as the Queensland Tiger, thought to be a relative of the thylacine, the marsupial then on the verge of extinction in Tasmania. Reports of the strange beast in the north persist to this day, but Wilkins suggested a less remarkable solution to the mystery. Out one night collecting by spotlight, his companions shot a cat that had run wild, its tracks identical to those found outside Kotoff's tent. They were amazed at the size of the animal, bigger than many breeds of dog. It was another member of the rogue's gallery of introduced pests that have devastated Australia's native wildlife.

Wilkins was well ahead of his time in signalling the alarm about this ecological genocide. He travelled from district to district in search of marsupials that had once been numerous but had recently vanished, and grimly recorded his findings:

> The settlers may have been responsible for the extermination of many of the native animals, and professional hunters have killed a great number, for despite the law they work ruthlessly with snares and poisons. It seems likely, however, that disease and starvation may be partly to blame for the disappearance of the animals. I was told of times when opossums and [koala] bears could be found in heaps, dead beneath the trees. The bears were usually found dead in a sitting position, with their front paws resting on the trunk of a tree as if in prayer. There is no doubt that we are witnessing the passing of these mammals, and that as far as indigenous life is concerned, Australia is in the death-throes.[8]

Wherever Wilkins went he found the settlers to be kindly and hospitable, often overwhelmingly generous, yet either unaware or unconcerned with the havoc they wrought on the landscape. It was selfishness he couldn't abide. 'After years of travel one learns to record things with dispassionate judgement, and the fact that I am the son of a father born in South Australia in 1836 has given me the courage to draw attention to some things which my countrymen may not be pleased to hear.'

He found the situation in Australia 'perhaps the most sadly depressing of any that I have experienced . . . I am reluctant to record them; I do so only in the hope that we Australians will face the facts and endeavour speedily to eliminate these conditions and to progress with earnest and organised wholeheartedness, worthy of our great country and our empire.'[9] His rallying cry was ignored.

After two months of dispiriting travel through central Queensland, the expedition looked forward to moving beyond the Tropic of Capricorn to the empty wilderness of Cape York Peninsula. They travelled by steamer towards Thursday Island in the Torres Strait, beyond the farmers and their crops, out of reach of the graziers and their European cattle. Here they expected to find virgin land teaming with wildlife.

The boat left them at a likely looking cape on the mainland, their boxes of collecting gear, hammocks and guns piled on the beach with enough flour, tea and sugar to last for two months. Nature would provide the rest. Behind the beach were slopes of turkey-bush, stringybark and acacia. Beyond, it was more or less open country. The grass and wild oats waved invitingly in the wind, small butterflies and clear-winged insects darted through the wildflowers lit by the golden sun. 'I wanted to fling away my gun and civilised paraphernalia and with a dress of leaves dance to the music of the woods,' wrote Wilkins in a rare moment of unrestrained joy. 'I wanted to linger and look for elves and gnomes and listen to the few birds in the trees, birds that, like myself, had left the jungle and bustle of crowded parts and had sought the pleasures of comparative solitude.'[10]

As so often in the Australian countryside, the bucolic scene disguised a grimmer reality. For a fortnight they hunted with indifferent success. The only animals that appeared to be plentiful were rats and mice. Ants were so numerous that any animals left in their traps overnight became unrecognisable by morning, with lips, ears and feet eaten away. Because of this they had to visit the traps two or three times a night – an unpleasant job where the grass was tall and snakes about. The nocturnal trips at least offered the chance to secure several shy sugar glider species, but the general picture was bleak. In one of his infrequent despatches to London Wilkins wrote: 'The native fauna seems to be dying out very rapidly and the natives in many parts have had to depend for some time on vegetable matter, fish and "white men's" food. I hope to have a better report when I next write.'[11]

When the steamer finally arrived to collect them, they made a queer-looking sight with their odd bundles and ragged clothes. The first thing Wilkins asked for was two bottles of whisky, which raised a suspicious eye from the crew. As he retired to his cabin carrying a bag of live squirming things, a crowd stood at his door watching in curiosity. Groans of disapproval went up when he slipped the wriggling bodies of snakes into the bottles, the whisky being the closest thing he could find to preserving spirit. 'I was never forgiven for what was termed a shocking waste,' he wrote.

For the remainder of 1923 they travelled through the drought-ridden plains of central Queensland, 'blighted by the fiery breath of some accursed dragon', struggling with the heat and flies. Finally rain arrived in December, and for three weeks it dumped on the parched country. The dusty tracks transformed into impassable mud, so Wilkins returned to Brisbane to work on the specimens in the cool basement of the local museum and plan the second year.

In a letter to the British Museum he apologised for what he considered were poor results – 'as a matter of fact I am rather ashamed of it,' he wrote – though it was clear the extraordinarily dry conditions had made his task difficult.[12] For the coming year he intended to break the team up into different districts, and would spend much of the time by himself in the far north.

On Thursday Island Wilkins waited for a mission lugger to take him west across the Gulf of Carpentaria to the eastern shores of Arnhem Land. From there he set out for a tour of the Northern Territory. It meant passing through the only town on the tropical coast, Port Darwin, to get horses and supplies. He found it a mean and unpleasant place, full of drunks and petty bureaucrats, with 'a conspicuous absence of the large and generous spirit which exists elsewhere in Australia'.[13] As long as the White Australia policy remained in force he believed the Territory would never prosper, for the white men were unwilling to do the labour. Without a north–south railway, he predicted, 'there is likely to be but slow development of this northern land.'[14] Out of curiosity he joined the annual race day at Katherine, which in reality was a three-day drunken melee. 'The brawling was continuous, the racing spasmodic as to time and place. The favourite seldom won, unless the side bets made it profitable, but in one case the favourite won by accident and all but one man were satisfied, and he was the jockey who had backed another horse.'[15]

For three weeks he and an Aboriginal guide trekked on horseback more than 500 kilometres through the Territory's wild interior to the Roper River then north towards the coast. In the stringybark stands and messmate, over sandy flats and steep-banked streams, he did some of his best collecting. Bandicoots and rat-kangaroos, crimson-winged parrots and Blue Mountain parakeets filled the saddlebags. Curious tribesmen joined them for part of the journey. Once the initial caution passed they travelled as a group, sharing food and stories and hunting together in search of rock wallabies.

Open-minded and quiet, Wilkins moved with ease in both black and white society in the rough settlements and mission stations of the north. At one mission the only accommodation available was the gaol, and, much to the amusement of all, he spent a cheerful fortnight as its only occupant. 'At night I sat about the campfires and listened to the natives singing hymns or chanting their own wild songs and dancing . . . most pleasing and graceful. It was not long before these people accepted me as a friend.'

At Milingimbi, the main island in the Crocodile Islands group, he played cricket and football with the mission children. At night they watched lantern slide shows together; on Sundays they listened to him play the little organ in the church. They liked this strange man who spent his days collecting molluscs and his nights putting them in bottles. He was unlike anyone else they had ever seen, and their innocent signs of affection deeply moved him. 'It often happened,' he wrote, 'that the black people about my camp would come and sit beside me and put their arms through mine, and sometimes when I was sitting at work two arms would steal about my neck and a dusky face would be held close to mine.'

Wilkins' skill at hunting impressed the local men. He learned to throw a spear well and gained their confidence 'by refusing the hospitable offer of their wives and the advances of the women'. They came to see him as different to the other white men they had encountered and worthy of trust. 'They had many secrets that they could not tell a "real" (usual) man; some of these they told me.'

Wilkins did not give them orders or preach, nor, for that matter, hand them food or tobacco to win them over. Few Europeans had treated them with this respect before. They called him a 'proper-white man'. Before leaving they told him: 'You come sit down 'longa camp;

no humbug (misbehaviour) longa women. You eat tucker (food) allasame black people. You no more make 'em allabout (everybody) listen when you talk; you sit down quiet and listen allatime and eyes belong you look-about, see everything. Allabout feel quiet inside when with you and allabout want to touch you.'

The fondness was mutual: 'I said goodbye to the natives and mission workers at Milingimbi with considerable feelings of regret,' Wilkins wrote.[16]

Wilkins intended his account of travels through the bush to be about natural history, but it often reads like reportage of a cultural war from which the Aboriginal people almost always emerged the losers. He wrote it quickly, dictating from field notes to a stenographer on the boat journey back to Europe. It is all the more powerful for its ungilded prose.

At Mt Wheeler in central Queensland he heard of a policeman whose enthusiasm for quelling 'Aboriginal disturbances' had become a blood lust of 'wholesale slaughter in support of the theory that no matter how good a black fellow may be, he is better dead'. The locals told him of a raid made on a nearby tribe to put fear into others in the neighbourhood.

'The sergeant and his troops drove two or three hundred – it is curious to notice that a hundred or so does not seem to matter in the estimate of numbers of victims in a tragedy – "blacks", men, women and children, up the sloping sides of Mt Wheeler and over the precipitous sides to be dashed to pieces on the rocks below.'[17]

This shocking crime went unpunished, and, more alarmingly, virtually unrecorded.[18]

As he roamed the wild spaces, Wilkins heard of many such tragedies. Returning to the tropical north from the dry plains only the colour scheme changed – the injustices continued, often with official blessing. He witnessed one of these sad sagas at close range. Today it is buried deep in Australia's past, unnoticed among the litany of similar events. For all its violence, the retribution that followed the wreck of the steamer SS *Douglas Mawson* was not exceptional. What makes it stand out is its utter pointlessness. It was not revenge for the killing of a white man or his family. In this case the tragedy was provoked by nothing more than rumours. In the tragic theatre of the bush, words alone could spark a massacre.

Sailors have never welcomed the long crossing of the Gulf of Carpentaria between Burketown and Thursday Island. The water is murky and the waves usually choppy. It is home to saltwater crocodiles and sea snakes, and is prone to cyclones. In March 1923, the wooden-hulled government steamer, the *Douglas Mawson*, was travelling be-tween the coastal settlements of northern Australia. Somewhere across the Gulf it was caught in a ferocious storm that smashed everything in its path, including the steamer. She went down with all hands lost: twenty people, including children. An extensive land and sea search followed and rumours began circulating that two women aboard had survived and been captured by Aboriginal people at Caledon Bay. On little information the press speculated that the women had born children while held captive. Hysterical reports of murder, rape and slavery led to public demands for revenge, and a punitive police patrol was assembled to track down the criminal natives.

Wilkins volunteered to join the patrol, hoping that it might give him the opportunity to continue his collecting work as well. Government officials gave him permission, but the police objected. In his writing there is the unmistakable suggestion that they didn't welcome wit-nesses.

It is impossible to be sure how many Aboriginal people were shot by the party and its seventeen volunteer vigilantes, Aboriginal trackers and assistants. It took two boats to transport them and their guns and they were primed for confrontation by the hysterical press reportage. The government set little restraint on their behaviour, and even considered sending a gunboat to indiscriminately shell the Arnhem Land coast, to what end we can only guess. If there was killing done, it was covered up. A royal commission was later held into the *Douglas Mawson* disaster, but, extraordinarily, all the reports and physical evidence connected with the enquiry have mysteriously disappeared from the Australian Parliamentary Library, and the only copy of its findings is held by the Queensland State Parliament where it remains 'eyes only' – no notes or copies may be taken of it, nothing of its contents can be published.[19]

One by one the members of the vigilante group drifted off until just two constables and their Aboriginal troopers remained. Wilkins came across one of the Aboriginal trackers, who had slipped away into the bush armed with a revolver. The man was traumatised and incoherent about what had taken place. Later, Wilkins found the remnants of the police party at Caledon Bay cowering, as if besieged: 'Although their object was to gather information, they maintained a fort-like attitude and lived in secluded independence.' After a year of searching they had successfully terrorised the Aboriginal people of the Arnhem Land coast but done nothing to solve the mystery. Wilkins noted that neither of the white policemen nor their Aboriginal troopers spoke the local language. Their interpreter was a member of the tribe suspected of murdering the survivors of the wreck and would be unlikely to implicate his clan. Wilkins concluded: 'only a prolonged and unobtrusive investigation by a trained ethnologist would be likely to bring to light any reliable evidence as to the truth of the rumour. The activities that have taken place have made the investigation of this matter extremely difficult, owing to the aggressive and hostile attitude of the punitive police expedition, who by display of arms have made the natives even more suspicious of white man.'[20,21]

Unlike the constables, he did not accept it was unsafe for whites to travel in tribal country. Before setting out on the expedition, he told the Brisbane papers a scientist with a butterfly net and collecting jars had nothing to fear. 'I have always believed that the Australian natives will not attack an unaggressive white man.'[22] He soon had the opportunity to put his theory to the test.

Few whites had ventured to Groote Eylandt, a low-lying island of tropical savannah off the Northern Territory mainland. First sighted by Dutch sailors in 1623, it was nearly 200 years before Matthew Flinders mapped its coastline, and the early Europeans, fearful of its crocodiles and fiercely independent Aboriginal people, showed little interest in exploring inland. However, Malay fishermen had been trading with the native people for centuries and the local culture, language and boat-building skills all showed signs of this long association with outsiders.

On a waning moon in a three-metre flat-bottomed wooden boat he set out with his collecting gear and a few provisions. For days he travelled with only the crocodiles and ferocious mosquitoes for company. Then one evening he returned to camp and discovered it had been disturbed, with tracks all about and items missing. He shouted friendly greetings but there was no response.

> Somewhere in the bushes I felt sure that sharp eyes were watching me, but I could not see them.
>
> It was nearing sundown, and I knew that with one deaf ear and heavy boots it would be useless for me to try and follow up the tracks in the hope of finding the blacks by stealth. I certainly did not intend to pick up my traps and run, so the only thing to be done was to put on a bold front and move about my business as if I neither feared nor cared.[23]

He took the precaution of conspicuously blazing a tree and burying a note on his situation beneath it, and then settled down to supper before crawling beneath his upturned boat and mosquito net for a nervous vigil.

> I was lying on my back getting drowsy when I snapped into life again hearing stealthy footsteps. It seemed as though there must be at least two men coming on . . .
>
> I caught my breath and then decided to lie perfectly still and pretend I was asleep. If there had been light those two warriors would have seen my hair stand with fright. A moment later two sharp, jagged spear points were pointed at my chest. The men stood on either side of me, their spear points seeming to quiver with eagerness for the kill . . .

He dared not speak for fear of provoking a sudden spear-thrust. There was utter silence but he felt sure they could hear the pounding in his chest. In his long career facing many dangers he always spoke of this moment as the one that scared him the most. For reasons he never understood, the footsteps slowly and cautiously retreated. He had heard stories that warriors would not kill men in darkness. Perhaps they would renew the attack at dawn. He settled himself to wait: 'Many watches at sea have given me the faculty of sleeping at will when tired and waking at any time I wish. So I slept and waked just before the first flush of dawn broke across the velvet darkness of the tropical sky. As the first streaks of colour were shot out by the rising sun I saw a bundle of spear shafts filtering though the bush. The men themselves were hidden by the undergrowth.'

He let out a startled yell, and a spear struck the ground a metre in front of him. There was a rustle for a second, then his attackers fled. 'I was utterly disgusted with myself for having shown so little control, but I determined now that I had seen the [A]borigines to follow them.' He rushed into the bush after them, leaving his guns behind. On the trail ahead, the two startled men met him with raised spears.

'I spent a busy half hour making motions that indicated my friendly feelings towards them,' he wrote. 'Of course I realised that they were as afraid of me as I was of them, but they could not see how shaky my knees were on account of my trousers . . . it was only after they were sure that I was a poor inoffensive white man that they calmed down and allowed me to come close to them and touch them.' [24]

From these precarious moments of first contact he established enough trust to move freely in the island's interior. He lived with the tribe for two months, his camp was never disturbed again, and his new friends brought him fish, turtle eggs and yams. The two warriors who came close to spearing him went out of their way to show their goodwill. They shared the campfire, the same shelter from the rain. It seemed to please all of them very much.

By winning the trust of many tribes across Arnhem Land, Wilkins filled his journals with their stories and customs. Of those tales, by far the most controversial was his claim that they were promiscuous cannibals.

Wilkins detailed three lengthy accounts of cannibalism among tribes in the King River, Goyder and Cape Stewart country. They included grisly details of the eating of a stillborn infant corpse. Later these reports appeared in British and Australian newspapers. Though it took little to convince Europeans that such practices might be common among Aboriginal people, Wilkins' reputation gave the claims added credibility. The *Adelaide Chronicle* was typical: 'Captain Wilkins is well known throughout the English-speaking world as an explorer and scientist of high repute, and not given to exaggeration. Therefore anything he writes bears the stamp of authority.'[25]

'These histories of cannibalism are no sordid flights of imagination or ancient myths,' Wilkins wrote with certainty some years later. 'The incidents related happened during the months of September and November 1924. The cannibals still roam the bush; unconscious of having committed a criminal act, and fearing only the disapproval of white man . . . fat starved humans sought to satisfy their appetites, and did not shrink from the flesh of their kind, because they had not learned the laws of culture.'[26]

Wilkins was not the first white explorer to make such claims, or the last. There are many accounts by European writers of cannibalism among Aboriginal people, and arguments about their veracity remains a long-running sore in race relations. The controversy continues to chafe on the faultlines of Australian politics, where it has been used to suggest an equivalency of guilt when placed against the massacres of Indigenous Australians by white men. Almost without exception however – Wilkins' included – the reports are not *eyewitness* accounts. The stories were passed on from others, usually through translators and without physical evidence.[27] Wilkins' accounts were typically second- and even third-hand, passed to him by his Aboriginal tracker, Olembek, as he openly admitted.[28]

Wilkins' accounts began as ethnographic field notes and occasional newspaper articles used to help fund the expedition, and within Australia it's unlikely they did anything more than confirm existing prejudices. When they were published in New York and London four years later, however, he was an internationally famous and widely admired aviator, and the damage done was greater. He was wise enough about the media to know it was inevitable that the claims of cannibalism – mentioned briefly in a book, *Undiscovered Australia* – would be reported in lurid detail and likely drown out his other observations. Equally he understood it would further stereotype Australia's Indigenous people as savages, hardly worthy of consideration. London's *Daily News*, once proudly edited by Charles Dickens, fell low in its headlines, but no worse than others: 'Men with Tails[29] – Sir Hubert Wilkins' Find – Cannibals from the Stone Age'.[30] It was more fuel for those convinced the passing of the Aborigine should be no more lamented than the extinction of the occasional small marsupial. Back in Australia, the reflected interest of foreigners helped to rationalise the massacres and injustice.

It was far from Wilkins' intention to contribute to this prejudice, but it was the undeniable outcome. Ultimately, he could not bring himself to deny what he believed to be the truth, no matter what the consequence for a culture he professed to admire and value.

*   *   *

After two and a half years the expedition was at an end. 'It was a sad parting when we left Groote Eylandt,' Wilkins wrote, 'for I had grown to love these people. Their simplicity, yet depth of understanding was remarkable, and to know them was in itself an education.'[31]

He arrived back at Thursday Island to discover that the world had been wondering about his whereabouts. The British and Australian newspapers feared the worst as there had been no news of him for six months. In Canberra, the Minister for Home Affairs had raised the alarm and a search party was being organised. In Adelaide, newspapers had interviewed his 82-year-old mother: 'I am not alarmed regarding my son's safety,' said Mrs Wilkins. 'I have such confidence in his ability to accomplish anything he undertakes.'[32]

These premature reports of his demise bemused the explorer. 'Those that knew me felt sure that I was safe; those that did not know me felt sure I was dead. There were many that did not worry either way.'[33]

The Wilkins Australia and Islands Expedition produced a collection of more than 5000 specimens, many unique to science; hundreds of photographs; ethnographic and geological objects; films; two human skeletons; fossils; and some interesting dinosaur bones. Though it had taken six months longer than planned, Wilkins refused additional payment and his accounts showed that it ran a mere £10 over the original budget. He donated all proceeds from his lectures, newspaper articles and book royalties to the museum.

The British Museum had rarely encountered an explorer of such dedication. Reporting to his trustees, the Director, Sir Sydney Harmer, wrote:

> Captain Wilkins has throughout treated the Museum with the utmost fairness and consideration. The work he has done has at times exposed him to great personal danger. The director thinks that the Trustees may wish him to express to Captain Wilkins their appreciation of the successful manner in which he has carried out an arduous and even dangerous undertaking.[34]

In recognition of his efforts, two new species he discovered – a rock wallaby and a small lizard – were named after him.[35] The trustees awarded him an ex gratia payment and invited him to take his pick from planned expeditions to Patagonia, Western Australia or Madagascar. Despite their praise, Wilkins continued to apologise for what he considered to be a less than satisfactory outcome: 'I feel sure that I am not returning full value in actual material for the expenditure of energy and money.'[36]

At home, the reception was less enthusiastic. Australia did not appreciate the airing of its dirty secrets. When his full account of the expedition, *Undiscovered Australia*, was published, Wilkins wrote: 'There is a golden future for Australia . . . but there is a need for them to turn at once from the expressed mediocrity, unstable democracy and independent action that are so conspicuous in Australia today.'

Reviewing his work for the *New York Times*, veteran journalist Florence Finch Kelly predicted the reaction: 'The book is likely to arouse indignation in Australia, for the people of that land are intensely sensitive, and Captain Wilkins does not spare plain-spoken criticism of the conditions and the spirit he found.'[37]

As the manuscript for the book was being completed in 1928, a white dingo hunter was murdered at Coniston, north-west of Alice Springs. In the frenzied retribution that followed, police killed between thirty and 100 men, women and children. A flawed enquiry, which refused to take evidence from Aboriginal witnesses, found the police acted in self-defence. Race relations clearly had a way to go.

For Wilkins there were no more sold-out lectures in Australia, and in the years to come he received as cool a reception from his countrymen as any he later found at the poles. He was long dead before Australia's Constitution changed to allow its Aboriginal people to be counted as citizens or be given a vote. The Indigenous population numbers have recovered since the dark days of the 1920s, but Australia's native fauna, among the most closely studied and investigated on Earth, continues to decline. Charles Darwin's clock is still ticking.

10

—

Ultima Thule

Ultima Thule! Utmost Isle!
Here in thy harbors for a while
We lower our sails; a while we rest
From the unending, endless quest.

— Henry Wadsworth Longfellow

D aniel Hudson Burnham, the man who invented skyscrapers, was driven by ambition. By the time he died in 1912 he had risen from obscurity to run the largest architectural firm in the United States, his magnificent designs, such as New York's Flatiron Building and the civic heart of Chicago, forever changing the face of the nation. 'Make no little plans,' he urged. 'They have no magic to stir men's blood.' The man never made an ordinary building or took an easy course. Sadly, Burnham didn't live to see the completion of the twin-towered, neoclassic beauty he had designed for the Dime Bank in downtown Detroit. He liked the project, as he liked the city. It was bold and impressive, representing in bricks and mortar the upstart impertinence of a sleepy town that had suddenly become an industrial behemoth.

When George Wilkins walked into the grand, sky-lit lobby of the Dime Building in 1925 he was a man after Burnham's heart. He had fantastic plans, so ambitious that no one else had dared to dream them. Upstairs waiting for him were the men who could make them happen, the newly enriched entrepreneurs who only a few years ago had been running workshops and now controlled empires.

The twenty-one members of the Detroit Aviation Society represented some of the most powerful men in the city. They were the family and friends of automotive pioneers Henry Ford and Ransom E Olds, who in just a decade had helped transform their town from a steamship stop on the Great Lakes to the capital of a vast new industry. Three out of every four autos in the world were now built in Detroit and two million workers had flocked to the city creating what was suddenly America's biggest business.

But the automobile magnates of Detroit knew this phenomenal growth couldn't last. The biggest sales were now in used cars rather then new, and the market was saturated. The auto men were turning their eyes to aviation, and the Detroit Aviation Society was charged with ensuring the city staked its claim for the new business. Congressman and former Secretary of the Navy, Edwin Denby, was Honorary President, and society members included Henry's only son, Edsel B Ford, who was passionate about aviation and had just delivered America's first all-metal airplane. William B Mayo, Ford's chief engineer, was Chairman, and another engineer, Jesse G Vincent from the Packard Company, was active too. There was George M Holley, whose carburettors have fuelled the dreams of generations of hot-rodders, and LeRoy Pelletier, the fast-talking advertising genius who was known as Ford's 'publicity engineer'. William Metzger, who had started the United States' first car dealership, was a master salesman, while Harold Emmons would later become the first head of Northwest Airways. There was William Upson, airship engineer and head of the aero division at the Goodyear Tire and Rubber Company, and William Scripps, son of the founder of the *Detroit News*. Scripps had been the first man in Michigan to own and pilot an aeroplane, and had founded the nation's first commercial radio station, WWJ.

Standing at the foot of the table before these powerful men was a tall, thin and prematurely balding foreigner who spoke calmly of his plans, but with a convincing passion built on experience. He had an understated confidence and an answer for all their questions. Perhaps he reminded them of themselves as younger men – self taught, unafraid of the unknown, an improviser. Whatever the reason, the Detroit Aviation Society quickly decided Captain George Wilkins was their man.

It was his old mentor Vilhjalmur Stefansson who had set off the chain of events that led to this meeting in Detroit. Despite the fiasco of the Canadian Arctic Expedition and other more recent disasters, Stefansson remained well-regarded in the United States and influential in government and scientific circles interested in polar exploration. He introduced Wilkins to the director of the American Geographical Society, Dr Isaiah Bowman, who liked the Australian and believed his plans would be of great scientific value. It was a crucial endorsement for an unknown foreigner, and impressed the men in Detroit.

Wilkins intended to establish once and for all whether there was land in the unexplored frigid heart of the Arctic. Since the beginning of recorded history this mission had been making fools of smart men and widows of their wives. In Plato's time, a Greek geographer, Pytheas, led a well-equipped expedition in search of a mythical land to the north that he called Ultima Thule. After six years he returned to tell of lush green fields six days sailing beyond the British Isles. The story survived, and long before the poles became objects of desire, the hidden continent in the far north was the glittering prize of exploration.

In 1906 Robert Peary, conqueror of the North Pole, peered through his binoculars and thrilled at the sight of white summits on a distant mountain range. This mirage quickened the heart of other explorers.

In 1914 an American expedition under the august sponsorship of the Museum of Natural History and the Geographical Society set out to resolve the matter. 'The new continent seems already within our grasp!' declared its colourful assistant commander, Fitzhugh Green. His expedition returned four years later much like that of Stefansson toiling on the opposite side of the Arctic at the time: hugely over budget, minus some companions and without the prize. It was clear that ships and dog sleds would never resolve the riddle.

After meeting with the men of Detroit, Wilkins wrote of his plans to Herbert Smith at the British Museum. His only regret was to be risking his life on behalf of America, not the Empire:

> It seems likely from many observations that there is a large body of high land between the Pole and Point Barrow . . . I hope to discover it and proceed safely across the Pole to Spitsbergen. It is a pity that I could not have started with English equipment but it is so difficult to get anything like adequate support in England for Arctic exploration . . .[1]

In fact the British and Australians would never be supportive. While the Empire had lost its taste for exploration he soon discovered the United States had a huge appetite for adventure – and the money to bankroll it. For the next thirty years Wilkins based himself there, always an outsider but at least a busy one. It took just a single meeting with the farsighted men of the Detroit Aviation Society to finance a year's worth of exploring.

His target was the most isolated spot on earth, the 'Pole of Inaccessibility', a point furthest from all land masses and about 600 kilometres south of the North Pole. If the mythical land existed it would be found there, on the unexplored Alaskan side of the Arctic, and it would be a great strategic prize for the United States. With little discussion the committee 'promised to provide eighty, ninety or a hundred thousand dollars if necessary,' wrote Wilkins. 'With what the North American Newspaper Alliance gave and my own fifteen thousand dollars, we had forty thousand. Thus it appeared there was no need to worry . . . "We are in the job to do it," the Detroit men said.'[2] There was, however, a catch. The men of the society wanted it done their way, and they demanded success.

What Wilkins didn't know at the time was that Edsel Ford at least was hedging his bets. A retired naval flyer, Richard E Byrd, believed he could be the first to fly to the North Pole, a dubious scientific goal but one sure to attract attention. Ford was impressed by the handsome officer, and enlisted other rich friends, like John D Rockefeller Jr, to help him. When it was announced that Roald Amundsen and his rich American sponsor Lincoln Ellsworth were also planning to reach the pole in the Italian-built airship the *Norge*, the public sensed a three-cornered race for glory. Though the teams had different aims the denials that a contest was under way were largely ignored. Inevitably the headline writers saw it as a challenge: who would be first to the Pole?

The cast of players in this undeclared race was intriguing. Wilkins had more experience in aviation than any other explorer and more knowledge of both the Arctic and Antarctic than any other aviator. Now he had serious backing he seemed ready to move first. Amundsen and Ellsworth had come close in a previous expedition by sea plane, but they were uneasily matched with the *Norge*'s third member, the Italian airship designer Colonel Umberto Nobile. Their plans to cross the Polar Sea would soon become mired in rancour and very public recriminations. Byrd was the least experienced of them all.

He was born in the same week as Wilkins, but in very different circumstances, and it seems strange that the careers of these two contrasting characters would become so closely entwined, even long after their deaths. Byrd was the son of a patrician Virginian family with roots extending deep into the seventeenth century. His plantation-owning ancestors had founded the state capital of Richmond, and a long line of relatives have been prominent in state and national politics ever since. The family had sufficient clout to manoeuvre his rise from lieutenant to admiral in only six years entirely by political promotions, including a special bill passed by President Hoover that saw him promoted *after* he had left the Navy. Byrd had an unsavoury habit of claiming credit for himself when it wasn't due and was constantly scheming against his rivals, yet he could also be charming and generous. Fame was his goal, not knowledge, and in this he was supremely successful. Immensely ambitious, undoubtedly courageous, Richard Byrd was deeply flawed, but that put him in good company with many of the polar greats. Over the years Wilkins would experience both sides of this complex man's character.

At the urging of Isaiah Bowman at the Geographical Society, Byrd was encouraged to cooperate with the vastly more experienced Australian. Wilkins offered him the position of deputy, though he really had no need for him. Byrd seemed to swallow his pride and wrote to Bowman: 'I will be delighted and honoured to serve as second-in-command. I do this unconditionally as I do not hesitate to follow the leadership and judgement of Captain Wilkins.'[3] In typical Byrd style, within two weeks he broke the commitment. He had new support from the Navy and apologised to Wilkins for the change of heart and the delay it had caused. In a simultaneous serving of Southern manners and Yankee arrogance he wrote: 'I must say to you very sincerely, that I am distressed that I won't have the opportunity to serve under you. I know it would have been very enjoyable and instructive.'[4] The Australian was not unduly surprised – he'd seen much worse behaviour in the small and jealous world of explorers – and got on with his own plans.

Wilkins had obtained what he believed to be the best flying machines for the job: two Fokker monoplanes of Dutch design. At the time there was no American-built machine to match the range or performance of either the big three-engined machine, dubbed the *Detroiter*, or the single-engine plane, the *Alaskan*. Wilkins would handle the navigation, and Stefansson had recommended a 28-year-old school teacher turned bush-flyer, Ben Eielson, as his main pilot. Ben had been making a name for himself ferrying mail, miners and medicine over wild parts of Alaska in a flimsy World War I era Jenny. From their first handshake, the two men liked each other. The young pilot was sent on to Fairbanks in Alaska to make preparations. Wilkins, meanwhile, spent his last weeks in Detroit continuing the fundraising drive that was the bane of any explorer's life. He called it 'an orgy of publicity', a whirlwind campaign of lunches, dinners, banquets and speeches, all begging for money. 'I would not have believed it was possible,' he wrote, 'that I could withstand the humiliation of accepting a luncheon in my honour and then plead for money.' It was, he said, 'the greatest hardship I have ever suffered . . . I still shudder to think of it. No one except myself seemed to mind it, and even those who were gypped a hundred dollars for my signature on a photograph, laughed it off.'[5] At the request of the committee he addressed thousands of Detroit school-children, each of them donating pennies from their piggybanks to help the cause. He told them that his planes had been fitted with special tanks that would allow a range of 3000 miles (4830 kilo-metres), much more than he needed. The planes would be modified so that the oil tanks and magnetos would be warmed by exhaust gases, and in the event of an emergency, he was confident they could safely land on the ice. In fact, he told them, he fully intended to land and take depth soundings and other measurements. Soon the world would know if there was new land in the north.

On the northernmost point of Alaska, at Point Barrow, the American continent comes to an inconclusive end. Wrapped in ice for all but a few weeks a year, it's usually impossible to tell where land ends and ocean begins. The little settlement here was named after Sir John Barrow, Second Secretary of the Admiralty and founder of the Royal Geographical Society, who sent a succession of ships to these parts in an obsessive search for the Northwest Passage – the mythical shortcut between the Atlantic and Pacific. Most of those explorers passed this spot, and few of them found any reason to linger.

When Wilkins first came this way in 1913, Barrow was a town of seven Europeans, 200 Eskimo and 800 dogs. When he returned a dozen years later, nothing much had changed. It was still 300 kilometres to the nearest bump resembling a hill, twice as far again to the nearest tree, and 800 kilometres to the nearest telephone. Mail reached the settlement just three times a year, hauled by dog teams on a month-long journey along the coast. In short, it was the type of place where Wilkins felt right at home.

For a few weeks between the bitter winter and the thick fogs of summer the little settlement was the last piece of solid ground from which to launch an assault on the Arctic. However, there were several rather daunting drawbacks: there was no runway, and no fuel, spare parts or radio. He would have to build the first and bring the rest. Given that Barrow was separated from humanity by a vast stretch of unknown land, including a mountain range of undetermined height, this was no simple task. Any expedition hoping to fly from here would first have to open up a frontier wilderness beyond the Yukon River about the size of Texas. This was enough work for a lifetime; Wilkins had four months.

In March 1926 the *New York Times* announced its sponsorship of the Amundsen-Ellsworth Expedition to fly an airship across the Arctic Ocean. In a panic, Byrd wrote to his backers and received financing to take a team of fifty men to Spitsbergen to launch an aerial assault on the pole. The *Times'* headline proclaimed: 'Massed Attack on Polar Region Begins Soon'.[6] Despite polite denials, the race was on.

The Detroit Expedition arrived in Fairbanks, last stop on the Alaska Railway, and prepared to ferry fuel and equipment 800 kilometres north-west to Barrow. In temperatures fifty-two below zero the two big Fokkers were assembled in the town's only hangar, and a big crowd turned out to see them christened on 11 March. The ceremony was the idea of the official correspondent from the North American News Agency, Palmer Hutchinson. Energetic and helpful, Hutchinson was well liked by everyone. The big launch ceremony was attended by the mayor, five priests and two ladies cracking bottles of petrol over the propeller. The festivities over, Wilkins warmed up the *Detroiter*, intending to take a brief test flight.

The plane looked clumsy on the ground, and at low speed it was difficult to steer while taxiing. Only 100 metres down the runway it came to a stop against a soft snow bank. The mechanics and a few men standing by came over to give assistance, stamping the snow forward of the wheels so the plane could get a start – a dangerous job in front of the propellers. Hutchinson was one of the first to help. The 'all clear' sign was given and the throttles were thrust open. Pathé newsreel man Will Hudson began rolling his camera to capture the first flight of the expedition. The machine had barely begun to move when Wilkins and his pilot heard a dull, sickening thud. Wilkins looked over the side and saw a splash of bright red against the ice. Hutchinson's lifeless body was lying beneath the propeller.

Hudson had filmed the dreadful scene as the reporter was cut down in an instant, stepping directly into the invisible propeller whirling at two thousand revolutions a minute. 'I was suddenly ill,' wrote the cameraman. 'I opened the movie camera, pulled out the film and let it drop – fogged – into the snow. Hutchinson's death cast a spell of gloom over our party and over the entire town of Fairbanks.'[6]

The next day, the same fate almost befell Wilkins' deputy, US Army pilot Major Tom Lanphier, who fortunately escaped with just a nick in his fur parka. They decided to leave the plane on the ground for a while and concentrate on putting the single-engined *Alaskan* through its trials. A week after the tragedy, Wilkins and Eielson sat together at the controls, gunned the throttle and made a perfect take-off. They circled Fairbanks for forty minutes, getting a feel for the aircraft, liking the way it behaved. Wilkins watched his pilot carefully, and felt confident he was the man for the difficult job ahead.

As they came in to land on the 350-metre strip, snow banks on either side, the margin for error was narrow. Everything seemed fine until they were low over the runway when suddenly the engine stalled. Eielson threw the throttle wide open, but there was no time to react. The plane came down heavily, smashing the landing gear and sliding towards the bank. The propeller twisted like a ram's horn, but the plane pulled up before the end of the runway, the two occupants shaken but unhurt. It was not a good beginning.

Ben expected to be fired right away, but there was no rebuke from Wilkins. He ordered the damaged machine dragged off the runway for repairs and told the mechanics to get the jinxed *Detroiter* ready for flight.

The next day Wilkins and Major Lanphier took the big Fokker up. It was immediately clear something was wrong. One of the engines was giving less power than the others and pulling them off course. Lanphier was forced to crawl the plane sideways to avoid the snow banks and she took off like a crab, narrowly avoiding spectators. The entire plane was shaking violently and they needed to get her back on the ground immediately or risk being pulled apart. As they circled and came back over the field, Lanphier lined up the strip; then, in the same spot as the *Alaskan* had come to grief the previous day, the tri-motor plane stalled and dropped like a stone.

'I was in a fever of fright,' recalled Wilkins. 'In an instant I knew that we would crash for we were still fifty feet in the air, and she went in nose first and with one wing lower than the other.' There was a terrific crash and rending of the air as the huge propellers dug hard into the ice. The landing gear collapsed and they swung violently to one side, then tipped until the tail was almost vertical: 'It is remarkable how one can take in every detail . . . I clearly remember looking up over my shoulder expecting the tail to flip over and crush us beneath the fuselage.'[7]

They climbed out, miraculously unscratched. 'Well fellahs,' he told the downcast mechanics, 'we have made some sort of a record anyway. Two crashes in 24 hours and we walked away from both of them.'

One man dead, the pilots lucky to be alive and $100 000 worth of aircraft wrecked in a day. Like the *Detroiter*, the expedition teetered on the edge, held together only by the leader's utter determination. 'There was nothing to do,' wrote Wilkins, 'but go on, keep faith and smile to the world while our hearts ached piteously within.'[8] It took weeks to rebuild the planes, and the time lost made it unlikely there would be any exploration flights that year. Back in Detroit, the public and his backers were losing patience.

Wilkins was under pressure to sack his pilots and get new men, but he refused. After three weeks of struggle, they had the *Alaskan* back in flying condition. The dog team was still less than halfway to Barrow with the gas and radio equipment, so there would be no weather reports from the coast to guide him. Wilkins had to chance a cargo flight if any real exploration were to be achieved that year. With a new motor specially built at the Ford Factory, he hoped to be able to lift 1300 kilograms, most of it gasoline, for the 1100-kilometre trip to Barrow. With Eielson at the controls, the Fokker lifted ponderously, climbed slowly and headed north. Ahead of them lay the Endicott Range, a snaking line of mountains supposedly no more than 1500 metres high. The closer they flew, the higher the mountains loomed in view so they climbed as high as the heavily laden machine could manage. At 2700 metres they were still beneath the jagged peaks and Eielson had to search for gaps in the mountains to thread the plane through. The glycerine in the cooling system boiled over and blew back over the windshield, making it impossible to see directly ahead, so the men had to stick their heads out into the freezing breeze through the side windows. Wilkins gasped when he saw a towering peak directly in their path, quite near. He shouted at Ben to veer left. 'I can't,' Eielson shouted back, 'there's a peak on my side too.' There was no time or room to turn as Ben desperately yanked back the controls to try to gain every inch of height. He looked grim, no longer watching out the window but concentrating on his instruments. Wilkins glanced over and saw a pile of rocks sweep by the wing tip and then felt a bump. He looked down to see one of the wheels spinning – it had glanced the snow as they crept over the peak. The *Alaskan* had escaped by the narrowest of margins.

They emerged over broad white tundra, heading towards a dull grey mass of soft floating cloud lit by distant sunlight. There was no view of a horizon, and just the slightest hint of their shadow on the ice-covered land below. The *Alaskan* was flying beyond the map, a tiny speck in a boundless world. All his life Wilkins had sought the unknown corners of the Earth, but even he had not expected the vast plains of emptiness revealed from the air. 'I am sure that we could find no situation more weird if we were to travel through space to the moon,' he wrote. 'The monotony and uncertainty of it would drive any man crazy if endured for long.'[9]

For hours they flew on through the clouds, unsure of their location. Below them the ice had become rougher, piled up in blocks like huge bales of hay. It was the familiar face of the Arctic icepack, which meant that by now they must be well beyond the coast. 'I was jubilant,' Wilkins recalled, 'we had actually started our work of exploration. Quite unwittingly, but now we were on our way, it was our chance to make a little headway.'[10] He leaned over to Ben and shouted above the engine's roar that they should continue on for a while longer before turning back in search of Barrow. Eielson was calm. 'Whatever you think is best,' he shouted back.

Wilkins brought them back to Barrow through a howling blizzard using his exceptional navigating skills honed all those years before during the Great Air Race. With nothing but uncertain compass bearings and dead reckoning he delivered them directly above the settlement. Below he recognised a familiar building – the Cape Smyth Whaling and Trading Company Station. The store was still run by Charlie Brower who had so welcomed him when he staggered out of another storm like this back in 1913. It looked good then, it looked even better now.

The *Alaskan* came in across a frozen lagoon, attempting a landing on wheels which everyone had said would be fatal on snow and should only be attempted on skis. Wilkins disagreed, and cautioned Ben to land tail down to lighten the weight on the wheels. They swept in over the ice, touching down on the crusted snow as gently as settling on a cloud. The plane came to a smooth stop, then taxied towards the trading post.

It was only when they opened the cockpit door that both men realised what they had achieved. It was weather no one would think of walking in, let alone flying. There was driving wind, drifting snow and the temperature was forty below zero. It was, they would later learn, one of the worst blizzards of the year. Charlie Brower and a few brave Eskimo came out to greet them, but it was no place to linger. They slung canvas over the engine and got inside as fast as possible. Warmed by coffee and a fire, they set up the portable radio gear they had carried with them. With Ben cranking the handle, Wilkins sent the first radio message from the north coast of Alaska advising everyone that they were safe.

There were old friends to catch up with and many stories to tell after his absence of so many years. Six white women were staying in Barrow that year, including a schoolteacher and a young writer, Edna Clare Wallace, who had come north to find inspiration for a novel. While the blizzard raged the two flyers filled the evenings with bridge parties, teas and dancing. They visited the Eskimo homes and Ben had his first uncertain taste of *muktuk* – whale skin and fat. 'I can taste it yet . . .' he wrote home. Somewhere out in the evil weather, eleven men and seventy dogs had been struggling for six weeks to bring their spares and equipment – a journey that had taken the *Alaskan* hours. Flying would transform this land and when it was all over, Ben planned to stay in Alaska and start its first real airline.

While on the other side of the Arctic Byrd and Amundsen prepared their own flights from Spitsbergen, the *Alaskan* continued to freight gasoline between Fairbanks and Barrow, each trip an adventure in its own way. Pushing off from Barrow on one flight Wilkins fractured his arm in two places but continued to fly despite the pain. Preparing for another, they discovered a young Fairbanks girl hiding inside as stowaway. Newsreel man Will Hudson had got word of it and was there when she was caught. 'On being discovered her language would have put an old sailor to shame. We shooed her from the field and she kept up her yowling until the noise of the airplane's engine drowned her out.'[11]

Every flight was taking its toll on the plane and the pilots, but there was no alternative until the big tri-motored *Detroiter* was back in action. Taxiing down the runway for another flight to Barrow, the plane rumbled but failed to leave the ground. It came to a stop at the end of the field and the ground crew ran in to assist. Eielson complained that the craft seemed overloaded and they removed some freight so the plane could turn and make another run at it. As the Fokker reached flying speed it shook then literally fell apart. The right wing flew clean off and they crashed to a stop, nose-first. Wilkins had been standing in the door to the cockpit and was pummelled across his broken arm by 20-litre gasoline cans. Some split and gas started pouring onto the engine exhaust. Ben yelled 'Hurry up and get out! She'll catch fire.' But, pinned under the cans, Wilkins couldn't move. Luckily she didn't catch and with the help of the ground crew they managed to crawl out. The plane was a wreck. Will Hudson was taking pictures: 'Had the ship left the ground that morning it would have been certain death to all onboard. So far as I was concerned, this expedition was washed out for good. I shot a splendid story about the mess of splintered wood and torn fabric.'[12] Like many, he underestimated Wilkins' determination to continue.

Within six hours of the crash the fuel was transferred to the hastily prepared *Detroiter* and they were in the air towards Barrow, Major Tom Lanphier at the controls. Wilkins hoped that in Barrow he might at last get a few hours of clear sky to go exploring rather than just transporting freight. His place in history could depend on little more than the fog lifting long enough to get their plane in the air.

Day after day the clouds stubbornly refused to part. On the other side of the Polar Sea, the weather was clear and dramatic events were unfolding.

For weeks Byrd and the rival team of Amundsen, Ellsworth and Nobile had been anxious neighbours in the little mining settlement of Kings Bay, Spitsbergen. On the surface they were cordial and Amundsen's men were quick to help out when Byrd's landing gear failed on his first attempts to fly. But the tension could not be denied.

'While I was not actually racing to be the first man to fly across the Pole,' Byrd wrote, 'I knew the public construed our relative expeditions this way.'[13] Given the criticism he had endured for racing Captain Scott to the South Pole, Amundsen was being careful not to appear churlish. He lent one of his best men, Bernt Balchen, to help repair Byrd's tri-motor Fokker, the *Josephine Ford*. If he had been unhelpful and Byrd should crash, the critics would be after his blood.

It was the American who moved first. At 2.00 am on 9 May 1926 Byrd took off, a man of little achievement whom the world hardly knew. Sixteen hours later he returned a genuine American hero, famous all over the planet. His claim to have reached and circled the North Pole that day remains one of the most controversial in exploration history. The long list of doubters included the man who sat next to him, Floyd Bennett, and the pilot on his subsequent flight to the South Pole, Balchen. Byrd's own notebook of the journey, discovered in 1996, casts serious doubts over his navigation and appears to have been doctored. He is even said to have confessed his failure in a long walk one day in 1930 with Dr Isaiah Bowman.[14] However, his powerful friends, including the National Geographic Society, which awarded him its highest honour even before examining his records, helped bury the criticism. It is a sad saga that may never be resolved and undermines the reputation of a man who otherwise achieved much.

Byrd's dubious claim had serious consequences for Amundsen, Ellsworth and Wilkins. Whatever they achieved would be tarnished by the man who said he was first. Amundsen and Ellsworth were denied the recognition they deserved, while Wilkins was represented as a loser even though he wasn't competing in the same event. Byrd's journey added not a jot to our knowledge about the Arctic, yet it is the flight that is remembered. History, as ever, was written by the winner.

Two days after Byrd returned to Spitsbergen, the airship *Norge* headed out across the Polar Sea towards Alaska. For much of the way it travelled in heavy fog, and the crew were unable to see what lay below them. They travelled 3000 kilometres from Europe to America across the pole, capturing occasional glimpses of jagged ice, but unable to sight land.

On the morning of 13 May a shout brought everyone at Barrow tumbling out of bed. There above them, floating majestically through scattered puffs of thick white cloud, was the silver-grey airship. Wilkins claims he wasn't disappointed to see it, and even sent first word of its success to the outside world, but it's hard to believe he didn't have a tinge of regret. He had, after all, first suggested flying the Arctic by airship back in 1919 and was dismissed as crazy. Now others were realising his plan. Both his rivals had achieved their aims and he was still stuck on the ground.

The flight of the *Norge* should have been a triumph, but it was treated as a postscript to Byrd's triumph. The headlines it received focused rather on a bitter squabble that had broken out between the men aboard. Amundsen was furious that Nobile had claimed credit for the journey and accused him of nearly wrecking the airship. Ellsworth added of Nobile, 'I doubt if he understands navigation.' Pushed by Mussolini, the newly promoted General Nobile shot back: 'This is the first time I have ever heard the captain of a ship criticized by one who is merely a passenger.'[15]

Ultimately, the Byrd and Amundsen flights had not proved a great deal. In its October 1926 issue, the *Geographical Review* concluded that it still had not been established whether there was land to be found in the Arctic Ocean between the North Pole and Point Barrow.[16] The great riddle remained unsolved, leaving a crack of opportunity for Wilkins to redeem his terrible year.

The men of Detroit assumed the expedition's $30 000 debt and, far from abandoning him, provided Wilkins with two new aeroplanes. This time he would be flying a pair of Detroit-made Stinson biplanes. President Coolidge, apparently overlooking Wilkins' Australian passport, sent a message of support: 'America has always been in the forefront of Arctic exploration, and it is fitting that we should strive to be the first to open the unknown lands to the knowledge of the world . . .'[17] Wilkins returned to the fundraising circuit, giving 107 lectures in a period of six weeks, sometimes making five appearances a day.

By March 1927, he and Eielson were back in Alaska with new planes and a new team. On the morning of the 29th, the two adventurers were in the air. Wilkins' target was in the deep Arctic Ocean, a point about 78 degrees north. He planned to make a landing on the ice – something never attempted before – in order to take depth soundings to determine if they indicated shallow water and the possibility of nearby land. They flew out over the broken ice, across leads of open water looking like giant blue snakes, donning their snow glasses to protect against the intense glare. To the south-west Wilkins pointed out to Eielson the area where the *Karluk* had met its fate, crushed in the shifting ice. The view from the cockpit looked 80 kilometres ahead to a broad horizon without a single distinguishing landmark.

From his navigator's seat, behind the pilot and separated by a fuel tank, Wilkins was busy taking sightings with his sextant and measuring their wind-blown drift off course. Every half-hour he struggled with the primitive shortwave radio to send their position. Occasionally the engine misfired, but Eielson revved it and skilfully worked the mixture to clear the carburettor of ice. After five hours of flying and more than 700 kilometres from the coast of Alaska, the engine began to stutter alarmingly. Then it choked a last time and stopped completely. Eielson put the Stinson into a steep dive, forcing the propeller to turn while he desperately struggled to restart the engine. It coughed and spluttered fitfully to life. Wilkins passed him a note: 'That's good ice to land on. Think we had better land and fix it?'[18]

Both Byrd and Amundsen had said it was impossible to find clear ice in the Arctic Ocean on which to land a plane. Wilkins had hoped one day to prove them wrong. Now he had no choice.

With a graceful loop, Eielson brought the plane near horizontal, gliding just above the surface, then dropped lightly onto the frozen ocean. The plane skidded gently across the ice and came to a stop, undamaged. Wilkins recalled being elated at proving his theory correct. It didn't cross his mind that he and Eielson might be the only two men who would ever know it.

The ice beneath them was dull grey and flat, blown smooth by the winds. Wilkins, his heart still pumping from the excitement, noticed the beautiful flower-like crystals that covered the surface, cut sharp and brittle as steel in the temperature of minus thirty degrees. His first thought was to take a depth sounding.

While Eielson worked on the engine, Wilkins hacked a hole through the metre-thick ice, breaking his pick in the process. A second hole, thirty paces away, had to be painstakingly chipped out with a knife. In one hole he placed a small detonator cartridge, while at the other he waited with an echo-sounder to measure the time it took for the explosion's report to bounce off the seabed and return.

> I listened for the echo. It came more than seven seconds later, indicating that the ocean was more than three miles deep. I couldn't believe it. Scientists had theorized the Arctic Ocean was shallow. I tried again, and just as I heard the second echo, Ben started the engine and as it roared, he turned to me with a grin. I was glad to know it was fixed, but I shouted: 'Stop that dammed engine. I can't hear what I'm doing. Come over here and listen to this thing.' Ben gave me a look, and hesitated, but true to our agreement, he stopped the engine and came over.

Eielson confirmed the reading. It showed they were standing alone in the middle of the Arctic, on a thin layer of ice with 5625 metres of water beneath their feet. Wilkins was delighted: instead of finding islands, he had found a deep ocean.

'Ben, we have made a great discovery,' he said, beaming at his partner.

'Well,' said Eielson in his slow Dakota drawl, 'maybe it is a great discovery; maybe the scientists will be interested. But you made me stop that engine, we'll never get it started again and we will stay here and freeze to death and no one but you and God will ever know how deep that ocean is.'[19]

Writing about this incident in *Science*[20] magazine later in the year, Byrd and Stefansson called the landing on the ice a 'deciding moment in Arctic aviation' proving Wilkins' belief that, with care and experience, the Arctic ice could be used as a landing strip for ocean exploration. They also called the sounding 'a decisive moment in oceanography'. Water so deep meant that almost certainly there could be no land in the vicinity. It is one of the great achievements of Arctic survival that Wilkins returned to reveal his discoveries.

For two hours Eielson battled with the engine repairs, using his bare hands in the stiff wind and freezing temperatures. His fingers inevitably froze and frostbite set in. When Wilkins realised his pilot's condition he asked why Eielson had not taken time to warm his hands occasionally to stop them freezing. 'I prefer losing a few fingers to losing both arms and legs and what they're fastened to,' he replied.[21] It was brave but foolish, a reminder to Wilkins that his friend had no experience in the life-threatening conditions they now faced.

After some false starts, they had the engine going again and took off towards Barrow. It was late afternoon and the wind was rising against them. This was the first chance they'd had for something to eat and they emptied a thermos of coffee and ate some biscuits and pemmican. Wilkins noted in his log: 'The food tastes good. Everything OK, but speed over the ice painfully slow.'[22] Working against a strong side wind they crabbed their way towards the coast. To the west the sun began to dip and below them the ice turned a sombre grey then disappeared altogether. Soon all they could see were the shadowy ribbons of leads and open water. It was too dark now for Eielson to observe his instruments, so Wilkins lent over the gas tank with a small torch and watched the compass, tapping his pilot on one arm or the other to keep him on course. Ahead was the dullest glow through the clouds like a pale moon on a winter's night. It was the sun skimming beneath the far horizon, leaving them to their lonely fate.

Wilkins glanced at his watch. It was nearly 9.00 pm and his calculations put them near the coast but still over the most rugged ice, snarled and broken into huge blocks. Outside the cabin a storm was blowing violently, further slowing their progress. The engine purred nicely, but any time soon he expected to hear the snap of a misfire due to the lack of gas pressure. He took a final bearing then wrote: 'What do you think; let her go on as long as she can, then drop straight down ahead?' Eielson nodded his head. No word was spoken.

At 9.02 pm the engine suddenly cut, as if turned off by a switch. There was no spluttering or gasp, but a sudden silence, only the hum of the wind in the wires told them they were still in the air. Ben desperately snapped the ignition left and right; there was no response. They could feel the sag of the falling plane, dropping from 1500 metres at 160 kilometres an hour in total darkness. Cool and skilful, Eielson steadied the machine on an even keel and an easy glide, his eyes zeroed on the turn and bank indicators.

Wilkins described his feelings: 'There seemed to be a cold hand gripping my heart and my breath came in short gasps . . . I knew what to expect, and the crashes and dead men I had seen in the past flashed through my mind . . . a motion picture of crashes in my head, and in every one I seemed to be a mangled thing that was dragged out of the wreckage. I remember being slightly relieved that there was no chance of flames following our coming exit; all our fuel was gone.'[23]

Near the ice the air was rough. The plane swerved and pitched, but Eielson remained calm and battled with the controls to correct each unsteady movement. The snowdrift swirled against the windows; they could see nothing. The left wing and the skis simultaneously struck a hard surface, accompanied by the screeching sound of fabric ripping. They swung violently to one side then the plane flopped as if being set down on a bed of feathers. Scarcely believing their luck, they came to a gentle rolling stop.

For a moment Wilkins was paralysed. 'I think the dazed feeling was chiefly due to the fact that we were still alive, when by all that was to be expected we should have been smashed, mangled, dead.'

They both crawled out of the cabin and for a few moments staggered about the ice, speechless. 'In our thanksgiving it seemed as though some unseen hand had guided our destiny,' Wilkins remembered. Driving snow filled his eyes and it was impossible to determine their situation. They climbed back into the cabin. Few words were exchanged. Courses, wind and speed were briefly discussed. The tension had left them both weak and tired. Eielson stretched out a sleeping bag on top of the empty fuel tank while Wilkins huddled in a corner. They slept like the dead.

The storm worsened overnight, and by morning it was difficult to move about for long outside. Even in the thick snow they could see how miraculous the landing had been. On three sides were high rough ridges and they had come to rest on the only patch of smooth ice anywhere in sight. Even in broad daylight a pilot would have been desperate to attempt a landing here. Wilkins dug a hole and measured the current. They were drifting rapidly east. This at least was good news – Barrow lay in that direction. He took a sun shot with his sextant and was able to fix their position at approximately Latitude 7230'; Long. 155 – around 100 kilometres from help.

'It was no use expecting to be rescued, for no one would come to look for us,' Wilkins wrote.[24] 'I had left strict orders that if we did not return the rest of the expedition should go home and forget about us; we would turn up some day.'[25] Though resigned to walking out to safety, they would have to wait until the storm passed.

For five days they were held prisoner by the wind, drifting further and further away from the coast. They drained the tanks and salvaged a couple of litres of fuel. They had good equipment and adequate food but Ben's fingers were causing him a great deal of pain. If his hands were to be saved there was no time to spare. Wilkins wrote their story on the ceiling of the cabin. Even if they never got back, the Stinson might. They sent a last hopeful radio message not expecting it to be heard: 'Walking home.'

Back in Barrow radio operator Howard Mason had been listening in vain for days for news from the missing flyers. Schedules were forgotten and there was almost always someone listening in. On the third day, some distant dashes were heard on the Stinson's wavelength, nothing they could decipher, and then the dashes ceased. An hour later it started again, a strong signal this time, the two-letter combinations coming from the automatic generator. The code stood for 'forced landing on sea ice' and 'plane damaged'. A jerky hand had begun sending a signal, putting their position about 160 kilometres from Barrow. Then silence.

They set out on Sunday, 3 April, pulling makeshift sleds made from parts of the wing. Eielson's fingers were blistered and badly swollen. They throbbed with pain but he did not complain. After five hours of steady, hard pulling they stopped and Ben watched Wilkins build a snow house. It had been twelve years since he'd made one, but necessity made the memory fresh. Once safely inside it was time for Ben to learn a few Arctic survival lessons. Out went his expensive riding breeches and woollen underwear, flyer's boots and sheepskin jacket. They would dress in native fashion: furs and reindeer-skin boots Wilkins had ordered from the skilful Eskimo seamstress in Barrow. In the coming days they pared their gear down to the minimum, disposed of one sled, and took it in turns pulling while the other broke trail.

Ben watched closely the way Wilkins would judge the ice, knowing if the cakes near open water would hold them, crossing snow bridges on all fours and sensing just where to hop across thin ice. Though he was ten years younger than the Australian, Eielson felt clumsy next to this dextrous, nimble veteran of the ice. Despite their predicament, he was confident Wilkins would take them to safety. Like Bean on the hills at Gallipoli he gladly acquiesced. 'If I had relied on my own judgement,' Eielson wrote later, 'I would have been compelled to give up. I believe he knows more about the ice, conditions of travel and living on the ice than any man living, and on trail walking I have never seen his equal.'[26]

By the fifth day leads of open water were more frequent and at timesthey had to detour kilometres off course to find a crossing. They saw the first seals and Wilkins told Ben it was a sign of being closer toland. By day eight the ice became heavier and more difficult to tramp. They abandoned the last sled and relied on carrying heavy packs. Ben's muscles, accustomed to the easy life of a flyer, were slowly growing used to the rhythms of ten steps, then a tumble. He seemed to spend more time on his face than on his feet. Each time they fell forward, their packs drove their faces deep into the ice crystals until their noses were skinned and their chins were scratched and bleeding.

Ben's fingers had blackened and shrivelled. Each fall on the ice must have been excruciatingly painful.

'Looking back on this trip,' Wilkins remembered, 'it now seems impossible. But for miles and miles we crawled on our hands and knees rather than face the risk of falling and, possibly, spraining a wrist or an ankle.'[27]

From time to time they came across great moving pressure ridges. Thrown together by the currents, two floating icepacks collided, throwing up giant blocks in tortured shapes. The action made an eerie, sobbing sound, like the wailing of a suffering child. To stand in their midst, uncertain of safety and not knowing whether the ice on which they stood would, any moment, rise and tilt, was awe-inspiring.

Once, while Wilkins was crossing a lead by stepping from one block to another, the ice gave way beneath him. He fell into the freezing water, and thrashed around to get close to the edge so he could sink his axe into a firm ice. Ben watched helplessly from the other side. There was nothing he could do and for a moment he felt a dread terror, knowing he might soon be left alone.

Wilkins struggled onto the ice, ducked behind a narrow ridge for wind cover and stripped naked. Ben thought he'd gone mad. The Australian was rubbing his clothes in the soft snow to soak up the water, then jumping up and down in a grotesque dance to keep up the circulation. There were spare boots in his pack and Wilkins squeezed as much water out of his pants and fur shirts as possible. The soaked clothes would dry fastest on his skin so the stiff material went back on. It took two uncomfortable days to get the damp out.

Hard physical work, uncertainty and anxiety meant they spoke little: only a solicitous enquiry now and then after a heavy fall. Together in silence they bonded as warmest friends. 'Absolute sympathetic companionship I had found in Eielson who had shown under conditions of the most trying nature courage and competence,' wrote Wilkins.

Each night Wilkins built their shelter, prepared their meal and took care to look after both their clothes. It involved a careful ritual, beating the snow and frost from their boots, scraping the insides then placing them outside to freeze solid. The furs needed similar care. They now shared a single sleeping bag and carefully rationed their fuel. It was used only to melt drinking water. Wilkins seemed to Ben to be in complete control of their environment and, despite his aching hands, the younger man never despaired. Wilkins advised him not to let the doubts creep in. Concentrate on each step, each session of work, each single task. Many little victories would shrink the enormity of their situation, he said. Survival in the Arctic required patience.

Hour after hour they struggled on, staggering, falling and crawling their way towards the coast. On 16 April, thirteen days and 200 kilometres from where they had abandoned the plane, the two men climbed over a high pressure ridge, a sure sign that the coast was near. Wilkins saw in the distance what looked like a pole. He pulled out field glasses and could make out the roof of a building. It was the trading post at Beechey Point. Soon a dog team was scurrying in their direction and an hour later they were in the trader's hut. It had been a remarkable escape: first Eielson's calm handling of their dark descent to the ice, then Wilkins' experience and reassuring confidence on the long trek back. Ben told others there was no better man to travel with in all the world than the quiet and resolute Australian.

An Eskimo named James Takpuk, an old friend of Wilkins' from the Stefansson days, took news of the miraculous survival to the outside world. He arrived at Barrow at 1.20 am four days later, exhausted but elated. In his hand was Wilkins' note telling the bare details of the story. His ridiculously understated version of the thirteen-day trek across the broken ice made it sound as if they had been out for a weekend ramble: 'Travelled over ice, eating biscuits and chocolate, living in snow houses. No particular hardship.'[28]

The other Stinson was sent to collect the exhausted pair and Eielson's hands were treated in Barrow. The fingers were saved except for two joints on a little finger that had to be amputated. While he recovered, Wilkins continued as best he could with a less experienced pilot, but weather and the usual mechanical problems meant there was little opportunity for another exploratory flight. The rebuilt Fokkers and the remaining Stinson were stored back at Fairbanks and by June 1927 the second season of flying ended much as the first – the mystery of the Arctic continent still unsolved.

In Barrow the Eskimos had a new name for Wilkins. From now on he was known as Anakuta. It meant 'strong wise man'.

Wilkins summed up his two years of struggle in his typically succinct way: 'We begged for money, bought machines, flew them and smashed them, rebuilt them and smashed ourselves. My crooked arm and Eielson's missing finger are mute evidence of trials endured.'[29] The fight had not extinguished his faith but it had exhausted that of his financial backers.

11

–

Over the top

Following the light of the sun, we left the Old World.
                                        – Christopher Columbus

'Vega' – A brilliant star of the first magnitude. From the Arabic for 'falling eagle'.
                                        – Webster's Dictionary

T he message from the men in Detroit was clear: their partnership with Captain Wilkins was at an end. Apart from the dramatic trek across the ice, he hadn't delivered the headlines the newspapers wanted. This withdrawal by the sponsors hardly came as a surprise, but their lack of faith rankled. For two years he had struggled against dangerous odds in their name and all he had to show for it now was a bent arm and a few battered planes. 'With one or two exceptions, I consider them my friends no longer,' he wrote.[1]

In closing the expedition, the *Detroit News* had been honourable, agreeing to cover the debts and passing ownership of the machines and equipment to Wilkins. He could barely afford the storage costs and had come to San Francisco to try to sell them.

Sitting at the desk in his room at the Hotel St Clair, Wilkins considered the remaining options. One idea he was seriously contemplating was a solo flight from Alaska, landing at the Pole of Inaccessibility, then a walk across the ice to Greenland. He had 2000 litres of fuel still in Barrow and felt that working alone might be the best way to go – he couldn't ask another man to take such risks. If he landed safely the trek to civilisation might take months, perhaps years. Friends tried to dissuade him, arguing that failure would set back the cause of Arctic aviation. Given the conditions and the navigation challenges, they said, such a flight would be a suicide mission. It would be a lonely death out there on the ice.

Only the knowledge that without a witness any important discoveries might be discounted seems to have persuaded Wilkins against the idea. He was determined to go on, but it would take a new aeroplane and he had spent almost all his money in the past two years of disappointment. He needed something small and fast, but no such plane existed. He found himself absent-mindedly sketching the outlines of such a machine on the desk blotter – wishful doodles of a rocket-shaped, single-engined, high-winged monoplane.

In what became one of Wilkins' favourite stories, he swears he was looking out the window of his hotel that afternoon when the plane of his dreams flashed into view. There was a golden gleam in the distance shooting across the sky. A sleek monoplane, it looked like a bullet as it raced through the air. He was stunned by the vision and stood there watching in disbelief as it appeared to land in the distance. He had a terrible thought that he might have been hallucinating. He hit the telephone, ringing around the San Francisco airfields, but no one had the slightest idea about the plane. So he jumped into a car with a friend, Ray Shreck, visiting half a dozen fields in the Bay area without success. Ready to give up, they made a final visit to Oakland Airport, where Wilkins had his first glimpse of the golden plane, a mirage made true.

In its own hangar at the edge of the field, watched over by a security guard, the shining machine was clearly a revolutionary design. Streamlined, without wires or exposed controls to offer wind resistance, its body came to a sharp point at the nose where an air-cooled radial Whirlwind engine sat in front and just below the enclosed cockpit. Wilkins walked around it, admiring the lines, taking in its features.

The single, shimmering cantilevered wing extended outward from the top of the fuselage and tapered slightly along the trailing edge like the wings of a swooping swallow. Perfect. A high wing avoided the obstructions of the ice. It was made of wood. Useful. This meant less interference with his instruments than a metal machine. The monocoque shell reminded him of the graceful Deperdussin racers he had seen at Hendon in 1912: two curved halves joined together to form a slender tube without the need for an internal frame. Excellent. It allowed plenty of space for additional fuel tanks in the cabin. Even on the ground it appeared a thing of eager beauty, a conceptual leap forward from anything he had seen elsewhere. Just by looking at it Wilkins knew this was the plane that could carry him and Eielson across the top of the world. On the tail was its name and its creator: Lockheed Vega, Los Angeles.

Like many of the aviation pioneers, brothers Allan and Malcolm Loughead had an up-and-down ride trying to establish themselves in the new industry. They built their first plane together in 1910 and closed their first company soon afterwards. Allan took up real estate, but never lost his love for flying machines. In 1926 he teamed up with the legendary designer Jack Northrop, changed the company name to read like it sounded (he was sick of being called log-head) and formed the Lockheed Aircraft Corporation. Their first plane was the golden flash Wilkins had seen in San Francisco, made to order for George Hearst, son of the owner of the *San Francisco Examiner*. Wilkins immediately put in a bid for the next one off the line. These two orders were the beginning of a company that would eventually become the biggest aerospace business in the world.

Wilkins didn't have the money to pay for his Vega, but he was working on it. Two Australian flyers, Charles Kingsford Smith and Charles Ulm, were in town, looking to buy a plane that could get them across the Pacific. Smith had come on somewhat since being kicked out of the England–Australia air race because he couldn't navigate. Wilkins was keen to help him and offered a good price on his Fokker tri-motor, the *Detroiter*. It was more than Smith could afford but he eventually found a backer. Rebuilt with the wing from the *Alaskan* it was renamed the *Southern Cross* and soon flew into history as the first plane to cross the widest ocean. Today it sits in a glass case at Brisbane airport, an Australian national treasure, the connection with Wilkins long forgotten.

At Lockheed's small factory in Hollywood, Wilkins pored over the blueprints and followed every step of the construction of the plane he called his 'bird of paradise'. This time he was determined to keep the expedition small and nimble, becoming his own business manager, labourer, mechanic and navigator. He would do without media sponsorships which might cloud the decision-making, though out of gratitude for their previous support he generously called his new venture the '*Detroit News*–Wilkins Expedition'. The paper gave cautious thanks but offered no money.

The Vega was modified to his own needs, with two large gas tanks separating the navigator's cabin from the pilot's cockpit. Wilkins could squeeze forward if necessary, but most communication with Eielson would be done by shouting or passing a note on a stick. He installed extra windows for the pilot and two glass windows in the floor of the cabin for making ground speed and drift observations without the need to open a trap, letting in a rush of freezing wind.

The Wright J-5 engine had already proved itself in long-distance flight, taking Byrd to the Arctic and Lindbergh across the Atlantic. It required a few modifications for flying in intense cold, which Wilkins, now a more than useful mechanic, supervised. He also designed a tray he could fit beneath it to warm the fuel lines before taking off. The final item of special equipment was the latest shortwave radio from the firm of Heintz and Kaufman. Aircraft radios were expensive and still quite a novelty. On previous expeditions, Wilkins had been disappointed with the results.

The wooden exterior was painted in lacquered coats of deep orange, making it easier to spot on the Arctic ice, and finished with a final flourish on the tail, marking it as Lockheed's third experimental Vega, X3903. Wilkins hoped it would be a case of third-time lucky. The plane he had seen through his hotel window in San Francisco had flown in a race to Hawaii and disappeared, and the second had crash-landed while Wilkins watched.

There had been longer flights and some just as dangerous, but none as difficult as he was now planning. Sometime in early April they would leave Barrow to take advantage of the brief break in the fogs, set out towards the unexplored regions north-east of the pole then dogleg towards Green Harbour in Spitsbergen across the other side of the Earth. It was journey of more than 3500 kilometres that would pass through ten time zones.

By not flying directly across the pole, he was adding hundreds of kilometres to the journey. More significant than the distance, however, were the complications of flying east through 171 degrees of long-itude. This was no straight-line course, like Lindbergh's route across the Atlantic, but an immensely challenging navigation, which, due to constantly shifting magnetic variations, required more than twenty course variations during a flight Wilkins expected to last as many hours. Byrd and Amundsen had merely followed a single meridian line north then south, while Wilkins' irregular route would see his compass shift through more than 300 degrees of compass variation. The process of plotting this course would be daunting even today.[2]

Every hour he would need to make a series of brief sightings of the sun with his sextant as they travelled at speed and bounced through turbulent air. From an average of these momentary 'spots' he would then estimate their altitude and allow for refraction of the sun's light through the atmosphere. The magnetic forces at such high latitudes could vary a compass reading by as much as a degree in just a minute, so he needed to adjust compass bearings using a complicated list of tables prepared by the American Geographical Society.

Wilkins' calculations would also need to allow for wind drift and changes in speed. One mistake in his readings, the slightest error in his arithmetic, could send them careering at 190 kilometres per hour in the wrong direction, missing their target and likely to run out of fuel far from any hope of help. Roald Amundsen reputedly told Wilkins: 'What you are trying to do is beyond the possibility of human endeavour.'[3]

Pilot and navigator accompanied the Vega on its sea journey from Seattle to Seward in Alaska. Leaving nothing to chance, Wilkins practised his morse code and pored over the sextant and astronomical tables until they became a solid image of figures in his mind. 'When, as leader of an expedition,' he wrote, 'one has to turn his hand to many different things, even in an amateurish sort of way, it is easy to forget a mathematical principle or to lose temporarily one's skill in an opera-tion.'[4] He practised mental calculations until he was satisfied that even without pencil and paper he could accurately process the dozen calculations needed to set their course across the Arctic.

On the eve of his departure for Barrow, Wilkins penned a final note to his friend Herbert Smith at the British Museum, knowing that if successful he might very well beat the letter's arrival. 'If I reach London we can discuss the problems we share; if we are delayed, it might be for years or forever . . . I have a good machine and a good pilot. But I have had such each year and met with set-backs. This year I think we will get through.'[5]

On 19 March 1928, Eielson taxied the Vega into position on the icy runway at Fairbanks ready for its first Arctic flight. She was fully loaded with 45 litres of extra oil and 130 more of gas. With their survival equipment and spares, the plane was carrying double its weight. Ben gave her the gun and they quickly gathered speed along the polished strip. Well short of the end, the Vega lifted from the snow as smoothly as from a concrete highway and banked towards Barrow. Two hours later the Endicott Mountains, such a danger in previous years, were crossed with ease. It was a clear day and below they could see every detail on the tundra. Here and there were caribou tracks, and Eielson, looking west towards the Bering Strait, caught the magnificent sight of a herd of thousands of animals on the move. A maze of woven rivers covered the landscape. Without incident and greatly encouraged, they arrived at Barrow, their second home.

Wilkins prepared their stores and equipment for the trip with previous contingencies in mind. He took a carton of cigarettes 'to while away the time should we meet with temporary injury' and a supply of chewing tobacco: 'I have found from experience that the nasty taste of it sometimes helps one forget other things.'[6] They carried two Mannlicher rifles and 350 hollow-point cartridges, good enough to bring down a polar bear with a straight shot. He added an ivory Inuit blade used for scraping hides and a bar of coarse soap for tanning and softening skins. 'Should we land on northern Grant Land or Greenland and spend many months or years walking home we might need these.'

The plane had been pulled by a dog team to the Elson Lagoon which ran along the eastern shore eight kilometres north of the settlement. Three attempts to take off from the lagoon failed because the Vega was too heavy and the runway too short. For days a team of thirty-five Eskimo had been paid to shift tonnes of snow and ice to fashion a makeshift runway that was now nearly two kilometres long. They were ready to go.

Apart from a brief message sent to the *New York Times* announcing they might soon be in touch with some news and a cable to Isaiah Bowman at the American Geographical Society, the world had no idea the two men were attempting the greatest adventure of their lives.

They were unencumbered by expectations, free to make whatever decisions circumstances may require.

With the plane's engine warmed and ready, the ground crew lifted the tail and shoved the machine off the wooden blocks that kept the skis from freezing to the ice. Eielson opened the throttle and the heavily laden plane began gathering speed, its tail swinging alarmingly from side to side across the narrow strip.

'Eielson kept his nerve,' Wilkins observed. 'I prayed. Sixty, seventy miles an hour. We lifted, swung sickeningly, touched the ice again – then soared smoothly into free air. Never has there been a more fervent prayer of thanksgiving than the one I uttered.'[7]

The Vega climbed fast, buoyant and willing like a thoroughbred horse let off the bridle. Wilkins was moved too in heart and spirit. 'I thanked God for the understanding of the man who designed her; for the honest, conscientious men who had built her and for the skill and wisdom of the man at the controls. I was conscious of the great privilege of guiding her on her course.' Unnoticed by the world, the bright orange bullet set out over an endless white expanse.

In light winds with good visibility, they made easy progress for the first few hours. Wilkins busied himself laying out his charts, testing his sextants for index error, setting the wireless and ensuring the drift indicator was registering true. Each snow drift and ice ridge revealed clues to him about the direction of the winds and currents, the depths of the ocean and temperature on the ground. It would have been easy for an inexperienced eye to assume the rounded hummocks glistening in the sunshine below were terra firma, part of the mysterious hidden continent. Wilkins, however, noticed the signs of narrow irregular cracks in the surface, evidence that perhaps only a few weeks earlier this solid ice had been open leads of water. No one wanted to find land more than he did, as it would be the site of his planned meteorological station. The facts, however, suggested otherwise. Centuries of speculation could now be laid to rest.

They had been flying for eleven hours. It was past midnight, but the polar sun – almost due north now – was still low above the horizon. As they sped along Wilkins struggled to take an accurate fix. Bouncing in the turbulent air, it was proving impossible to keep the sun centred in the bubble of his sextant. At high latitudes the sun's rays bend wildly as they pass through the deep blanket of the atmosphere, and this refraction is greatest when the sun is low on the horizon. Flying at altitude only intensifies the effect. Wilkins would have to wait before he could fix their position.

Eielson was concerned that the fuel was burning faster than expected, leaving little margin for error. While Wilkins was reasonably confident they were on course, visual confirmation would be comforting. According to his reckoning they should be very close to Grant Land, the northernmost point of Ellesmere Island, where Peary had set out for his dash to the North Pole. Ahead he could see a barrier of high cumulus clouds in motion, their tops blown over by wind. This was an unmistakable sign that landfall was near. But just when they expected to catch a glimpse of the mountains, Eielson was forced to change course to go around the mass of threatening clouds. It was taking them away from a possible sighting, so they banked and tried once more to weave a path through the maze. The clouds enveloped the tiny plane and smothered them in mist. It was difficult flying but they were rewarded when Ben shouted out that he had glimpsed the mountains of Grant Land.

'Clouds always tell a true story,' wrote the British meteorologist Ralph Abercromby, 'but one which is difficult to read.'[8] Wilkins was an expert nephologist, and his reading of the clouds was as useful a tool as any of his navigation instruments. By observing their frequency and the way the winds sculpted their form at different altitudes he could predict the weather that lay ahead. Looking forward he saw the first menacing signs of a vast wall of cumulonimbus, their base several kilometres across, rising thousands of metres into the atmosphere where the high winds sheared off their top like an anvil. Magnificent structures, the largest complete object we can witness on this Earth, these giants are feared by aviators. Inside, swirling torrents of vertical currents rise and fall with enough energy to tear a small aircraft like the Vega to pieces. The vaporous curtain hid a raging snowstorm, perhaps even an Arctic cyclone, and blocked their passage to Spitsbergen.

Wilkins sent a hastily scribbled note forward to Ben. 'There are two courses open: We are above storm now. Down there we can land and wait until it's over. Can we get off again? If we go on, we will meet storm over Spitsbergen, and perhaps never find land. Do you wish to land now?'[9]

Perhaps Eielson remembered Wilkins talking about a two-year trek across the ice if they landed in the unexplored region, a prospect that filled him with more dread than a quick demise in the storm. 'I'm willing to go on and chance it,' he replied.[10]

Wilkins huddled in the cramped cabin with his charts, logs and protractor, drawing a curve over a celluloid sheet, plotting a new course turning sharply from the current heading. He passed another note forward on his long stick, instructing Ben to steer 15 degrees east. Because the pilot's compass was unsteady, he had to hammer on the gas tank to let Ben know they were on the right track. Steadily the Vega rose higher, a tiny speck against the great masses of swirling vapour, but still the clouds towered thousands of metres above them. It was useless to try to fly above them so Eielson threaded his way through the feathery mountains, mindful that every detour burned more precious fuel and took them off their set course. Turbulent air shook the plane hard. They had been flying for more than eighteen hours now, every moment of it requiring intense concentration, and each sudden plunge strained their nerves. Time and again Wilkins' charts and tables were thrown from his little desk, and his stopwatch had succumbed to the blows.

Wilkins was making a mass of complex calculations for hours on end, most of them in his head, and knowing there were potentially lethal consequences if he made an error. Later, when scrutinising the flight log book, the American Geographical Society's chief surveyor commented 'he accomplished a feat in navigation which can be confidently declared unparalleled in the history of flying.'[11]

The radio generator had been playing up and Wilkins was fairly certain that none of his hourly signals was being heard. He sent a final message: 'Now within a hundred miles of Spitsbergen. We are in bad situation. Heavy clouds about us. Have two hours gas but will not be able to see land. All open water below.'[12] As he repeated the message, anxious about their chances, he caught sight of two sharp mountain peaks. He tapped a postscript: 'Spitsbergen in sight. We will make it.'

Visibility was down to 100 metres and it was impossible to locate the settlement at Kings Bay or any other landmark. Their greatest fear now was running into a mountainside, so Eielson took her low in the hope of getting beneath the storm and sighting the coast. Empty of fuel, the *Vega* bucked like a bronco in the currents. Eielson struggled at the controls to hold her and they came down fast. He pulled up just a few metres above the ice-strewn water. Furious winds whipped salt spray from the sea and covered the cockpit windows with rime.

The blizzard made it almost impossible to fly along the edge of the land and equally impossible to see the land when they kept out to sea. Eielson noticed a smooth, snow-covered clearing, but before he could investigate it a mountain loomed dead ahead. Barely able to see through the ice and frozen oil on his windscreen, he swerved adroitly, missing the rock face by a narrow margin and sending Wilkins tumbling about the cabin. With their tanks nearly dry there was no chance to wait it out. Back they turned towards the rocks, searching desperately for the briefly glimpsed patch of smooth ice.

Twice they passed over it too fast to put down. On the third attempt Eielson levelled the ship and lowered her gently into the swirling snow. For once the fierce wind was their ally, as it brought the plane to a sudden halt. They were down and still in one piece.

Wilkins leapt outside to drain the oil tanks before they froze solid. Both men stamped the snow over the skis so it would freeze and locked the Vega tight against the howling blizzard and then threw a canvas over her engine, securing it as best they could. They climbed back inside the cabin, their ears still ringing from the flight while the plane rocked and trembled in the wind.

In an eerie reprise of the miraculous escape the previous year, they munched chocolate and pemmican, smoked a cigarette and took a swig of coffee from the thermos, but barely spoke. The immensity of what had been achieved and the tension of the past hour – the past twenty hours – was beyond any words. Last year they had fallen out of the black sky without fuel, powerless to influence their fate. This time they had fought every inch of the way, anxious, uncertain, never quite helpless but ever against tremendous odds. Slumped exhausted against the fuselage, Wilkins whispered thanks. 'I cannot say which year, this or the last, our prayer of gratitude was more earnest. Both times it was sincere.'[13]

Across the Arctic Ocean, Leon Vincent was straining to decipher the faint signals. The teacher at Barrow's little school and a radio enthusiast, he had been listening for twelve hours straight on the receiver his friend Captain Wilkins had left behind.

The weak morse signals merged with the background atmospheric noise, making it impossible to discern entire messages. The fragments he could decipher gave hope. 'The principal thing was to know that the plane was still in the air and things were all right,' he recalled.[14] For all his hours of dedicated listening, his entire log of messages amounted to just half a page. At 2.00 am the message was two words: ' . . . our tanks . . .'. Two hours later there was just transmitter buzz which gradually faded to silence.

Given the extraordinary events of the previous year, no one was giving them up for dead. Still, the silence was worrying. Vincent was convinced the Vega had reached its goal, or at least been very close, because the final message came at a prearranged time and faded slowly. Someone was working the transmitter hard at a time when the Vega would have been near to running out of fuel.

For five days and nights the blizzard raged and the two flyers were pinned down inside the Vega's cabin. On brief forays outside, Wilkins thought he could make out what looked like buildings on a distant mountain. He concluded it was nothing more than cruel mirage. His sextant readings put them somewhere on the west coast, but he was unsure how far they were from any settlements. He would later discover they had landed on the appropriately named Dead Man's Island.

Inside the cabin they shared two cigars – half each over a couple of days – and went through the cigarette supply. They had food for a month and the plane appeared undamaged apart from some bending to the skis. Carefully draining the fuel tanks, they counted 90 litres – enough for about an hour of flight assuming they could take-off.

When the winds finally subsided, they worked like madmen for six hours, shovelling snow and cutting back the drifts to construct a runway. Eielson warmed the engine then gunned the throttle, but the unloaded machine didn't budge. Wilkins jumped out and shoved the tail, and the plane took off down the improvised strip – with the Australian unable to clamber aboard. Eielson, not realising, took off.

Top. Pioneering parents. Harry Wilkins was the first European born in the new colony of South Australia. Louisa Smith would bear him thirteen children. George Hubert was their last born, when both parents were over fifty. (*All photographs courtesy of the Byrd Polar Research Centre, Ohio State University*)

Above. The simple stone cottage at Mt Bryan East on the edge of the Australian Outback where Wilkins was born. His parents were the first settlers in this marginal landscape that proved susceptible to withering droughts. It eventually forced his family to abandon the farm and sent Wilkins on a life-long quest to uncover the mysteries of climate forecasting.

Top. A ticket to the world. Wilkins was fascinated by the camera and its possibilities for a life of adventure. He is seen here in Sydney around 1922 working on an early Australian feature film.

Above. The worst retreat since Napoleon was turned back from Moscow. Wilkins took this picture of the defeated Turkish army, thrown out of Europe by the Bulgarians after the battle of Lule Burgas. It is estimated that they lost as many as 50,000 soldiers on a single day, October 31 1912. Wilkins too barely escaped with his life.

Top. 'Wilkins of the cinematograph, one of the best companions in the world.' Just back from his hair-raising experiences in the Balkan Wars, Wilkins reads the glowing tributes written by famous war correspondent Bernard Grant.

Above. Vilhjalmur Stefansson (*front row with bowler hat*) called his account of the doomed Canadian Arctic Expedition 'The Friendly Arctic'. In all seventeen men would die, including five of the scientific staff pictured here in June 1913. Wilkins is top left.

'A half dozen such men would make an invincible polar expedition,' wrote Stefansson of his young protégé. Wilkins began as an official photographer of the Canadian Arctic Expedition (1913-17), and ended as a skilled exploration scientist and second in command.

A boat to nowhere. Wilkins learnt his polar craft the old-fashioned way: sledging and man-hauling across 3000 miles of the Canadian Arctic and later in Antarctica. It was back-breaking work. Confronted with ice barriers like these, he often dreamt of the possibilities of using new technology to explore such regions. Later he would return with both aeroplanes and submarines to explore the last unknown corners of the globe.

Top. Wilkins always felt great empathy for Indigenous people wherever he encountered them. Projecting the first movies in the Arctic, Christmas 1913.

Above. Vilhjalmur Stefansson was accused of abandoning the men of the *Karluk* in pursuit of his own ambitions. Here Wilkins' camera captures his controversial leader in typically determined style, dragging a seal back to their camp in Northern Alaska, 23 March 1914.

Left. Though a late-comer to World War One, Wilkins soon made up for lost time. The young officer became a legendary and much-decorated official war photographer in the bloody battles of Europe's Western front. Though he carried a camera instead of a gun, he was twice awarded the Military Cross.

Below. A photo taken on his very first day at the Western Front in the later summer of 1917, Wilkins entered what his photographer friend Frank Hurley described as the 'exaggerated machinations of hell.' Here, right on the front-line but buried deep underground, Wilkins photographed patient soldiers waiting to receive medical attention.

Top. Only stumps remain of what was once thick forest. Cut down to supply timber by both sides of the conflict, the landscape of Flanders was devastated by war. Wilkins often flew above these fields and towns and noted that nothing remained except the merest hint of buildings and roads that had been pulverised into dust by four years of artillery barrages.

Above. 'The bravest man in my army', said Lt General Sir John Monash of his young photographer. Here Wilkins is typically upright as he works in no-man's-land, while others run for cover from menacing German artillery fire.

Top. Often attributed to his better-known colleague and fellow polar explorer, Frank Hurley, it is now thought likely that this famous image was actually taken by Wilkins. It shows Australian troops making their way back through the notorious mud-fields of Passchendaele during the disastrous Third Battle of Ypres. It cost half a million lives, in Winston Churchill's assessment 'a forlorn expenditure of valour and life without equal.'

Above. The remains of the once magnificent town square of Ypres, Belgium, after constant shelling by German artillery in 1917. Amazingly the town was the head quarters of Australian and British forces fighting to hold the line against repeated offensives across the Flanders battle-front. Wilkins took many such images.

Top. The crew of the *Blackburn Kangaroo* on the morning of their departure from London for the race to Australia. They were attempting the longest flight in history, and relying on Wilkins' uncanny navigation skills.

Above. Hopes of victory in the England–Australia Air Race of 1919 come to an end in a ditch just meters from the stone wall of a Cretan asylum for the insane. Miraculously, there were no casualties.

Top. One of the last known photographs of the legendary polar explorer, Sir Ernest Shackleton. Wilkins took this picture in South America as he and 'The Boss' set sail aboard the *Quest*, Shackleton's last adventure. Sir Ernest greatly admired the young photographer, and considered Wilkins his natural successor.

Above. 'Our farewell to the Boss'. Wilkins' camera captures the dejected crew of the *Quest* at the cairn they built commemorating their leader, Sir Ernest Shakleton, above the whaling station at Grytviken, South Georgia, April 1922.

Beginning in 1923, Wilkins trekked for thousands of kilometres through tropical Australia on behalf of the British Museum, recording the devastation caused by European settlement on Indigenous people and fauna. He called his homeland 'the poorest rich country on earth' – and was never forgiven.

Camel trains were common means of transportation through the deserts of Australia. Imported from Asia along with their Afghan handlers, the camel teams helped open up vast areas of Australia's little-known interior. Wilkins encountered this one during his own epic expedition across Northern Australia in 1923-26.

Top. First contact. Most indigenous Australians were still living traditionally when Wilkins went exploring the tropical north on behalf of the British Museum. Though there were some frightening encounters, he generally got on extremely well with tribal groups, and became a keen observer of their practices and mythology.

Above. 'We begged for money, bought machines, flew them and smashed them, rebuilt them and smashed ourselves.' For two years Wilkins tried gamely to cross the Arctic by aircraft. In one twenty-four-hour period the tri-motor Fokker, *Detroiter*, was destroyed…

Top. ... followed the next day by a narrow escape from the single-engine *Alaskan*. By 1928 Wilkins had exhausted the support of his sponsors, and his hopes looked very forlorn.

Above. Undaunted, Wilkins and Ben Eielson returned with their streamlined Lockheed Vega, and unannounced set off on the first flight from America to Europe across the Pole.

Wilkins and Eielson prepare to leave from the lava strip on Deception Island on the first Antarctic flight, 1928. Despite the emergency equipment, the chances of surviving a forced landing were minimal.

The wild Southern Ocean was the inevitable welcome for any Antarctic explorer. Here Wilkins' two Lockheed Vegas are strapped precariously to the deck as they make their way south to Deception Island in an attempt to make the first flight in Antarctica.

No man saw more of our planet than Sir Hubert Wilkins. This was the view that greeted Wilkins and his American co-pilot, Ben Eielson as they flew across 1200 miles of previously unknown land. It was the first flight in Antarctica, December 20, 1928, one of the greatest days in the history of exploration.

Left. The *New York Times* called it 'the greatest flight in history'. Wilkins and Eileson were greeted with a hero's welcome after their epic trans-polar flight.

Below left. The former actress Suzanne Wilkins described herself as the 'loneliest wife in the world', enduring years of solitary vigils as she waited for her husband to return from his many adventures. In fact their twenty-nine-year marriage was highly successful.

Below right. 'I only have eyes for you', wrote Wilkins in this publicity shot he sent to Suzanne shortly after their meeting in New York in 1928. At her request, the US Navy spread Suzanne's ashes at the North Pole where they joined those of her husband.

Top. Adventuring in style. Luncheon aboard the *Graf Zeppelin* on its history-making round-the-world flight in 1929. Wilkins sits opposite Dr Hugo Eckener at the Captain's table.

Above. Inside the belly of the beast. Wilkins captures his journalist colleague Lady Grace Hay-Drummond-Hay and a friend inspecting the hydrogen tanks of the mighty *Graf Zeppelin*. Together they would make the historic 1930 round-the-world flight that would take just 21 days.

Above. The view from the bridge of the *Graf Zeppelin* as it floats just a few hundred feet above the surface of the earth. It was close enough to hear sounds from the ground, and even smell the cooking as they passed over Japanese villages. And also close enough to encourage some gunfire from terrified Siberian shepherds.

Left. The extraordinary flight of the Zeppelin was greeted with a rousing ticker-tape parade in New York. It was the second such celebration for Wilkins in less than a year. At the peak of his career he was one of the most famous men in the world.

Top. At the edge of the known world. Wilkins took a dilapidated WW1 submarine into the Arctic, further north than any vessel had ever managed under its own power. But his hopes of crossing the last uncharted ocean were dashed by a terrified crew who sabotaged the vessel to force his return.

Above. In his cramped quarters aboard the submarine, Sir Hubert writes his daily quota of a thousand words for the Hearst press empire. A picture of Suzanne and an Australian flag are above his bunk.

Top. Wilkins and his chief scientist Harald Sverdrup (*left*) conduct their experiments aboard the *Nautilus* – the first ever studies to be made of the deep Arctic Ocean.

Above. The submarine *Nautilus* adrift in the Arctic ice floes in the late summer of 1931. Wilkins' extraordinary plan to take the submarine under the ice of the North Pole was dubbed 'the Suicide Club' by a sceptical press. Despite being plagued by mechanical problems, the expedition collected valuable scientific data – but it would be 25 years before anyone would dare attempt to follow in their wake.

Top. Chief radio operator Ray Meyers at the periscope. Privy to the private communications between Wilkins and the Hearst editors, Meyers was a close confidant of his leader, and was convinced the submarine has been sabotaged.

Above. Crippled without its rudders, the *Nautilus* was at the mercy of the drifting ice. Wilkins faced an impossible dilemma: turn back and face ruin or push on to meet the demands of his media sponsors.

Top. 'It was far too late in the season to be attempting an Arctic expedition.' The *Nautilus* was dogged by bad weather and faulty equipment, pushing its crew to the brink of mutiny.

Above. Dashing pilots were the rock stars of their age, and Wilkins was courted by celebrities, dictators and kings. Here he and fellow-flyer Bernt Balchen meet Walt Disney and Mickey Mouse on a trip to Hollywood.

Top. Return to Antarctica. In 1933 Wilkins once again headed south as organiser of flying expedition for the American millionaire Lincoln Ellsworth who was attempting the first aerial crossing of the continent. Though vastly better qualified than his employer for such a task, Wilkins' logistical skills and planning eventually made it possible for Ellsworth to achieve his aim.

Above. Wilkins refuels his Soviet-built Catalina during his tireless search for missing Russian flyers over thousands of kilometres of uncharted Arctic Ocean in 1937. He used the mission as an opportunity to test his theories of extra sensory perception.

Left. Friends and occasional rivals. Millionaire Lincoln Ellsworth (*left*) and his pilot Bernt Balchen prepare for their flight across Antarctica. Wilkins had prepared the entire expedition, as Ellsworth had little interest in the details of exploration. Balchen had also flown with Wilkins' great rival, Richard Byrd, and considered the American a fraud.

Below. Shortly before his death, Wilkins visited Commander (later Admiral) James Calvert aboard the nuclear-powered submarine USS *Skate*. He urged an attempt to surface at the North Pole in mid-winter.

Top. The *Skate* surfaces at the North Pole through a frozen lake, 17 March 1959. At the height of the Cold War, it was a highly secret mission. The US Navy had carried the remains of a submarine pioneer to his final resting place.

Right. Even well into his sixties, Sir Hubert could out-ski much younger men in the field. He made his last trip to Antarctica in his seventieth year, and lived to see many of his ideas, once thought crazy, proven correct.

When he turned he saw his partner forlorn on the ice, circled and landed. They tried again, this time fastening a rope to the cabin door for Wilkins to hang on to.

Eielson revved the engine while Wilkins pushed. He grabbed the rope but his numbed hands couldn't hold it and in desperation he grabbed it with his teeth. Eielson, feeling the weight on the tail, assumed his friend was aboard and took off, whacking Wilkins with the tail and sending him tumbling into the soft snow. He was uninjured except that his front teeth were all loose. Once again the pilot circled and came down to a rough landing on the bumpy ice.

'The sight appalled me,' said Wilkins. 'It struck the snow and bounded over the ridges like a frightened deer. The skis . . . bounced and wobbled. They wouldn't stand many more landings on snow like that.'[15]

For the third attempt they lifted the tail onto a block of snow to put the machine in flying position. Wilkins sat with one leg out the cabin door and pushed with all his strength while Eielson shoved the throttle wide open. For a full minute they hung in suspension, the engine roaring. Then suddenly the plane lurched forward and Wilkins tumbled into the bottom of the cabin, utterly exhausted.

The Vega lifted fast over the mountain peak that had nearly been their end a few days earlier and on the other side the view opened to a wide, ice-strewn bay. There, less than 10 kilometres away, were two tall radio masts and a group of houses: Green Harbour. They circled the little coalmining outpost and came to a gentle landing beneath the masts, a pair of barking dogs their welcoming committee. After more than two years of struggle the epic journey was finally complete.

'Whatever else we may have accomplished through our efforts,' Wilkins wrote, 'we will only learn as time goes on. Eielson and I have learned, at all events, the sincerity of friendship.'[16]

The Norwegian miners were kind hosts. The government radio station was put at their disposal. Wilkins' first message was a coded signal to Dr Isaiah Bowman at the Geographical Society: 'No foxes seen', meaning no land had been discovered.

Confident of his arrival, the *New York Times* had left a message requesting an account of the flight. He asked if they wanted 500 words or so. The response was eager and immediate: 'Send all you can.'[17] The paper splashed the unexpected news in huge type across its front page while it awaited Wilkins' own account. He wrote this in longhand on the back of scrap paper, which the *Times* ran verbatim over the following three days. Its straightforward, restrained prose remains a classic of exploration reportage.[18] In an editorial the paper called his flight 'an amazing victory of human determination amounting to genius'.[19] It was, the newspaper claimed, the greatest flight in history.

For days the radio operator at Green Harbour was busy transcribing hundreds of congratulatory telegrams from around the world. Wilkins' rivals and colleagues among the exploration community were generous in their praise. Amundsen, who knew better than anyone what Wilkins had achieved, said: 'No flight has been made anywhere, at any time, which could be compared with it.' Byrd and Stefansson agreed. Fridtjof Nansen, perhaps the greatest explorer of them all, called it a splendid achievement for which he had the highest admiration. For forty years the American Geographical Society had seen no reason to award its highest honour, the Samuel B Morse gold medal. On the evening of 24 April its council unanimously agreed to grant it to Wilkins – the first of more than fifteen medals and awards he would receive from scientific bodies around the world.

The two men, exhausted but exhilarated, were swept up in a global outpouring of congratulations. Their tour began with a giant welcome in Norway and a meeting with the King. Amundsen hosted them at his country home, then at a banquet in their honour. That evening he received word that Nobile's airship, the *Italia*, had disappeared in the north. Though supposedly retired, the conqueror of the poles immediately volunteered to lead a rescue party. Wilkins and Eielson offered to go too, but the veteran explorer told them not to bother, he would find the Italian. Amundsen left soon afterwards and never returned.

In Germany a squadron of fifteen planes escorted them on the final leg of their flight from Denmark, and in Berlin a crowd of 10 000 awaited their arrival. 'I had to do the talking for us both,' said Wilkins, as the shy Eielson was overwhelmed by the reception. 'He could not stand the night after night round of entertainments put on for us in

Berlin, under the direction of none other than Herman Goering.' Goering at the time was a minor member of the Reichstag and the government director of entertainments for VIPs. After a week of nightlife with Berlin's idle rich and movie stars, Ben got into the habit of propping himself up against the piano used by the band and dozing off. 'He would wake up with a start every time the band started playing,' Wilkins recalled.

On to Paris, where the two fliers were honoured guests of the French Aero Club and were dined to the point of exhaustion. In Amsterdam on 4 June, Wilkins received word he should come to London immediately. Waiting for him on arrival at his hotel was a letter from Buckingham Palace. The King, it announced, was pleased to honour his brave airman with a knighthood 'for 15 years of consecutive work in the interest of science and national service'.[20]

Wilkins was humbled by the honour to the point of embarrassment. He had met King George V during the war, and had filmed the battlefield ceremony where his commanding officer, General Monash, had been knighted, but he certainly did not expect the very warm greeting he received from the monarch in their private meeting. The King was a great supporter of aviation, and his sons had all learnt to fly. He seemed genuinely pleased to see Wilkins again and said he had been following his career in recent years with much interest. At the last moment the aviator made a request to be known by his middle name, Hubert. His Majesty asked, 'Well, George, why Hubert?' [21] Wilkins mumbled something about not presuming to use the King's name and so for the rest of his life was known formally as Captain Sir Hubert Wilkins.[22]

After years of ignoring him, Britain now reclaimed its famous son. The Colonial Secretary, Leopold Amery, hosted an official dinner at the Savoy Hotel in his honour. Amery was an old-style imperialist who saw it as Britain's destiny to claim and conquer new lands and was thrilled by the flight. As a younger man he had been the tub-thumping *Times* correspondent during the Boer War and knew the value of a good attention-grabbing quote. To the assembled audience of leading scientists, soldiers and politicians he beamed with reflected glory while introducing Sir Hubert: 'Not since Balboa stood on a peak in Darien and saw for the first time the broad Pacific, has so significant a new view of the world been spread before human eyes in one day as when

Wilkins and Eielson flew in twenty-two hours across the unexplored Arctic Ocean from America to Europe.'[23]

Sir Samuel Hoare, Secretary of State for Air, was only slightly less exuberant but accurate in his forecast. The flight had proved the air could be the greatest highway between the continents, he said. Wilkins had 'reduced the North Pole to the dimensions of Piccadilly Circus which now can be crossed without the aid of a policeman. No one can foretell how much human communication has been expedited by this daring flight.'

While still in London, Sir Hubert met with his countryman and the acknowledged master of Australia's interests in Antarctica, Sir Douglas Mawson. Wilkins proposed that the older man become the first leader of his proposed International Weather Monitoring Service. Mawson, with the tenured professor's disdain for the gifted amateur and perhaps more than a little envy, was dismissive. He wrote that he considered Wilkins' plans 'crazy'. Over the coming years he took every opportunity to undermine his colleague's credibility at home and abroad. 'Wilkins knows nothing about science . . . It is unthinkable that the Government should ever make arrangements for Wilkins to direct Meteorological work in the Antarctic,' he wrote in a typically negative letter soon after their meeting.[24] It was unbecoming and dishonest treatment motivated by the aging master's own plans for taking aircraft to Antarctica. Wilkins, by contrast, continued to treat Mawson with utmost respect.

In his adopted home of the United States Wilkins found only praise. Six weeks after the flight, his arrival in New York was still front-page news and the city welcomed him like a returning hero. Though not on the scale of Byrd's triumphant reception, it was genuine and heartfelt, a wonderful tribute to a man who, after all, came from an obscure country far away. A special tugboat, the *Macon*, had been sent to meet their steamer and bring the flyers ashore to Manhattan. Planes and airships circled overhead in his honour and Mayor Jimmy Walker had organised a ticker-tape parade and big reception at City Hall. There was barely time for breakfast before the stewards called to collect his bags and take him aboard the harbour boat. Another big day of celebrations lay ahead.

*　　*　　*

For a country girl from the far side of world, Suzanne Bennett had reason to be proud. She'd arrived in New York like thousands of girls before her with hopes of making it on the Broadway stage. Now, just three years later, she was headlining in a show called *Cyclone Lover* at the Frolic Theatre. From her Brownstone apartment on 50th Street she had a view across Fifth Avenue to St Patrick's Cathedral, money in the bank, and good friends among New York's theatre set.

Born in the little Australian goldmining town of Walhalla, her singing talents were discovered early. She studied at the Conservatorium in Melbourne and met Dame Nellie Melba, who encouraged her to follow a career in opera and study in Italy. But en route to Europe she stopped in New York and set her sights on Broadway and musical theatre. When her attorney rang that July morning she had never heard of Hubert Wilkins. By the following night they would be in love.

The attorney's suggestion was simple enough. Suzanne had been invited to join a party aboard the *Macon* to welcome a famous flier to town. He was Australian, and she was the only pretty Australian anyone could think of to greet him. There'd be lots of cameras, her friend added, so it was worth the effort.

'I agreed to go with some misgivings,' said Suzanne, 'got up at the atrocious hour of 5 am, made a cup of tea and dashed off to the Battery where the *Macon* was waiting in the fresh morning air.'[25] She dutifully handed Sir Hubert his flowers, posed for the camera and then he totally ignored her. Later on, as they drove along Broadway to the Waldorf Hotel in a motorcade, he didn't say a word, which Suzanne found rude. She was about to leave the hotel when the Australian Consul asked her to say goodbye to the explorer. Sir Hubert said he was sorry she was not staying for lunch, and that unfortunately he was expected at an official dinner that evening, but could they meet again soon?

'Without thinking how it might sound, I suggested he telephone me at midnight. Hubert smiled faintly and asked me what my number was. I hadn't mentioned that I was an actress and was rarely home before midnight.' She realised he was was just shy, not arrogant, and decided she wouldn't mind getting to know this man better after all. She went off and did her homework before their supper meeting.

He called on the dot at midnight and invited her to the St Regis where they danced until the early hours. 'He was a good dancer too,' she recalled. 'I mentioned it, which pleased him, as I wondered where he had time for the lighter side of life with all his adventures. Not in the Balkans war, the Arctic, the war, the Antarctic, the Arctic again, surely, I asked? He beamed to think I had found out this much about him, and replied that he had taken a lesson between the time he 'phoned me and the time he called for me.' The next night Wilkins went to see her play, a gangster musical set in a Chicago speak-easy with plenty of loud action in the second act. He moved to the front row after intermission.

'I could see his tranquil expression all through the gunfire that followed. He never budged or showed the least concern about the mayhem that was going on onstage. I knew he had nerves of fine steel, but I didn't know he had been deafened in the war, and so a bit of noise did not bother him. In fact, he heard even better when a motor or engine was running.'[26]

Soon after, Wilkins left on a lecture tour with Eielson, flying the Vega across the country. He promised to return soon, but neglected to mention he was contemplating another startling adventure.

After his triumph in the north, Wilkins found he had little trouble finding support for his new plans. He intended to take two planes and a small team to Antarctica to make not only the first flight there, but also to solve some major geographic puzzles that had defeated the best efforts of the sledge-pulling expeditions. If all went well, he would complete the season with a spectacular flight of more than 3000 kilometres from the Antarctic Peninsula south of Cape Horn to the Ross Sea on the coast below New Zealand. This would cross a huge area of undiscovered territory – the first time new land had been seen from the air. It would be the culmination of his years of work, the ultimate conquering of the coldest, windiest, driest and most mysterious land on Earth.

The news came as an unpleasant shock to Richard Byrd. The hero of the North Pole flight had assumed the mantle of polar master for himself. 'Someone has to explore [the Antarctic],' he said, 'and it is the job I have picked out for myself.'[27] It was remarkably presumptuous. He had never even seen Antarctica, never crossed the wild Southern

Ocean. He had, however, previously come up against Hubert Wilkins, and he knew he was in for the fight of his life.

Byrd knew only too well that Wilkins could out-fly him, out-navigate him and, if it came to it, out-survive him. The Australian had already been twice to Antarctica, and possessed a well-proven aircraft with a superb pilot.

Wilkins was at pains to point out he was not in a race with Byrd as they would be exploring different sectors of the continent. The more he denied it, the more suspicious Byrd became and he sent inter-mediaries to Wilkins to try to discover more about his intentions. This time it was Wilkins who kept his options open. The two explorers wrote cordial letters to each other, professed mutual admiration, but neither was giving much away.

Like Byrd and Lindbergh, Wilkins had become a celebrity, part of what Byrd called 'the hero business'. Unlike the others, Wilkins never employed a publicity agent, yet barely a day went by without a story about him in one of the major papers. He gave radio talks and speeches across the country, and published articles in leading scientific journals. He was asked to do cigarette commercials, appear on quiz shows and open sports events, most of which requests he declined. He and Suzanne were spotted in the society pages. It was the age of flying heroes and Amelia Earhart's publicist (and future husband), George Putnam, rushed into print with Wilkins' account of his triumph, *Flying the Arctic*. It was well-reviewed and much admired. The public liked him, as they liked the other brave flyers. They were a more wholesome role model than those other headline-grabbers of the day, the gang-sters. Perhaps the intense fascination with both was because the relationship was usually brief. The previous year, no less than thirty pioneering aviators had died trying to cross the Atlantic. What odds on surviving a flight across the Antarctic?

The modest Australian with the noble ideas of using planes to benefit society came to the attention of William Randolph Hearst, often called the most influential individual in America. Hearst commanded a daily audience of 20 million Americans through his synergistic conglomerate of newspapers, radio stations and magazines. Hearst's editorial manager, TV Ranck, came to Wilkins with a proposition: $40 000 for exclusive press rights to the Antarctic expedition, and a further $10 000 if Wilkins made it to the SouthPole, a flight Wilkins had always denied he was interested in. Ranck reported back to Hearst: 'Wilkins intimated confidentially that he might attempt the Pole flight . . . He could see no reason he said why he should not try it if he gets down there and finds Byrd hasn't gone over. At the same time he did not pledge himself to do it.'[28] It was close enough to what Hearst wanted – a headline-grabbing race to the pole. Byrd meanwhile signed a deal with the *New York Times*. Hearst was unconcerned. His money was on the Australian. The following day his stable of newspapers across the country proudly announced the plans of the Wilkins–Hearst Antarctic Expedition. It was the beginning of a fateful relationship between the mogul and the pilot.

Byrd now had even more reason to be concerned. Wilkins seemed well funded and his small team, just five men, was ready to go. Meanwhile, Byrd's own vast operation, costing twenty times that of his rival, was mired in delay. The logistics of preparing an expedition of fifty men, three planes, ninety-five dogs, a ship and provisions for up to two years were immense. Byrd was a perfectionist and he insisted on arranging every detail – right down to the handcuffs and straitjacket he was taking in case any of his men became unmanageable. Three of his pilots died in crashes while he delayed, including his deputy and good friend Floyd Bennett, who had been with him on the North Pole flight. The secret of the disputed North Pole was buried with Bennett at Arlington National Cemetery. His widow was reported as saying her husband's death was 'the luckiest thing that ever happened to Byrd'.[29]

By the time he returned to New York, Wilkins had a second Vega and a second pilot, Eielson's best friend from Alaska, Joe Crosson. Like Ben, he was a fearless bush pilot and he delivered the new plane, dubbed the *San Francisco*, from Lockheed's factory in California to the east coast. The existing plane was renamed *Los Angeles*. Joining the flyers were a mechanic and a radio operator. The team's full salary was paid in advance and while Byrd was contemplating buying expensive ships, his rival had arranged transport from South America to the ice with Norwegian whalers. It was Wilkins' dream expedition: small, well-equipped and fully funded. Now all they needed was good weather.

He had just enough time to catch Suzanne in another play, invite her to supper at the Waldorf, and propose. Two days later, 22 September 1928, she saw him off on the *Southern Cross* to

Montevideo. The next day's papers inevitably played up the story about the lovers separated by Antarctic adventure.

For several months the British Embassy in Washington had been sending despatches about Byrd's plans back to London, concerned that the American might be planning to make territorial claims in Antarctica. The reports disappeared into the deep abyss of the Foreign Office, unnoticed until the middle of the year when complaints from the governments of Australia and New Zealand finally prompted action. The Australians wanted the Americans told in no uncertain terms to back off and be reminded that the Empire had already laid claim to great swathes of useless ice courtesy of Shackleton, Scott and Mawson. The mandarins of Whitehall concluded that this might only inflame American passions and were looking for another solution.

Finally, in mid-October 1928, the penny dropped that British interests in Antarctica were under threat. An interdepartmental conference was held to decide what could be done to thwart any land grab by Byrd. One proposed measure was to deliver the Americans an offer of help for Byrd – a diplomatic way of announcing they considered he would be visiting British territory. Just how they intended to assist from thousands of kilometres away was anyone's guess.

Australia's representative in London, Richard Casey, suggested the best means of countering Byrd was to beat him at his own game. Major Casey had witnessed first-hand Wilkins' courage on the Western Front and believed Sir Hubert should be encouraged to get in first. It seemed a neat solution, the only problem being he had already departed, though he was expected to land briefly on the British Falkland Islands in the South Atlantic. The Governor there was sent a secret message urging him to speak confidentially with Wilkins on his arrival in Port Stanley and coopt him into the land grab.

Reading back through the dusty records of this clandestine affair, there is an element of farce in the haphazard way the plan was concocted. The British, who for years had ignored Wilkins, now needed him to assert their dubious sovereignty in the south. His little party of privateers was to take on the might of Byrd's grand expedition. Yet they weren't even sure whose flag the mercurial Wilkins was flying.

Sir Hubert arrived in the Falklands aboard the Norwegian factory ship *Hektoria* on 29 October and was immediately ushered into a meeting with the acting Governor, JM Ellis, who handed him a cable from Casey. It urged him to do the right thing on behalf of the Empire. Ellis duly reported back to London:

> Sir Hubert stated emphatically that while he received generous support for the venture from friends and sympathisers in the United States he is beholden to no one ... He added that although an internationalist in his ideas at heart he remained a Britisher and would therefore be glad to assist so far as he could in furtherance of the cause of Empire by dropping or planting British flags in the manner suggested.[30]

A slight difficulty was Wilkins only had one British flag (and for that matter only one American flag, which he had purchased as an after-thought in Montevideo). In the contorted syntax of the career bureau-crat, Ellis 'caused him to be furnished with a number of Union Jacks', authorised him to take possession of any newly found lands, asked him to keep his mouth shut and sent him on his way.

Before departing they celebrated Wilkins' fortieth birthday on Halloween in fine style. The *Hektoria* had started life as a White Star liner, and its grand salon was left intact.[31] As Ben Eielson noted, for a man like Wilkins to live this long was quite a milestone. Never much of a drinker, he raised a toast to his friends and retired early. The Norwegian whalers reciprocated by getting his team dead drunk.

Antarctica was still 800 kilometres away through the Southern Ocean, its swirling currents unbroken by land as they circled the planet. For days the ship battled through ice until Wilkins caught sight of the volcanic mountains of Deception Island which he had first seen in 1920 on the ill-fated adventure with Cope. So much had happened since then, he scarcely considered himself the same person. He'd received news en route that his dear mother had died in South Australia, and while saddened he was pleased she had lived to hear of his success in the north. More than anything he was content that she had not lived to receive news of the death of her youngest child on some distant shore. As he did quite often now, he said a private prayer in her memory then turned once more towards the white cliffs of the southern continent.

Through the narrow gates called Neptune's Bellows they entered the hidden world of the flooded caldera, surrounded on all sides by high volcanic cliffs. Wilkins was not pleased to see the *Hektoria* progress so easily through the ice. It was unusually thin, too weak to serve as a runway. This was rotten luck. Records made by the whalers showed that in the last fourteen years the ice in the bay had averaged more than two metres thick and usually remained solid until Christmas. The sharp cinders of the black beach would tear rubber tyres to pieces, and finding a landing field above the steep cliffs of the island was unlikely. They had brought pontoons for the planes but this would limit their range and would be dangerous to use in ice-strewn seas.

The *Los Angeles* was slung on the end of a long boom and lowered onto the water on its pontoons. Wilkins searched for a possible runway onshore and settled on an unpromising hillside of volcanic tuff covered with a thin layer of snow. It was short, which meant they could not load the planes with fuel for a long flight. For days the weather fogged in, then, on 16 November Eielson and Wilkins took off for a brief exploratory flight, looking in vain for a better base – the first flight ever made in the Antarctic. Shortly after, Ben Crosson took the other Vega up in a different direction but he too had no success searching for an alternative strip.

As Wilkins readied his machines and searched for a suitable runway, Byrd was arriving with his fleet of ships in New Zealand. They had fortuitously landed just days after the end of the pious nation's experiment in prohibition and drank the place dry. In Wellington, Byrd met for the first time with Sir Douglas Mawson who was visiting on business. Doubtless they discussed their common interest in the man one dismissed and the other distrusted.

Over the coming weeks the temperature rose to unseasonably high levels, melting the snow and making them prisoners on Deception. One of the planes fell through the weakened ice in the bay and only the efforts of twenty men from the whaling station, working solidly for eighteen hours, managed to save it.

Tours of the neighbouring islands revealed only solid ice cliffs or broken pack ice, nothing from which they could launch a heavily laden aeroplane. There was no choice but to make the best of what they had, so they set about clearing volcanic rock on the hillside at Deception. Even with the Norwegians helping it took days of hard labour to hack out the semblance of a usable strip. It was the strangest runway ever built and included two 20-degree bends like a dog's hind leg, two small hills, and three ominous ditches. Worst of all, it was just 550 metres long. Crosson the bush pilot said he had seen worse.

The next morning at 4.00 am Ben carefully guided the *Los Angeles* round the bend, down the hill, over the bump and into the air while Wilkins held his breath beside him. They circled for a while and came down safely. The next day they would leave for real.

Both of them knew that by taking off on wheels they were severely limiting their chances of landing safely in any kind of emergency. The plane was stocked with a two-month supply of food and the usual survival gear, but realistically their chances of using it were slim. They either came back or they crashed. They wrote final letters to loved ones that night and Wilkins instructed Crosson that he was not to use the other plane to search for them if they did not return. The next morning, 20 December 1928, they were off.

Loaded with enough fuel for a flight of over 2000 kilometres they set out across the Bransfield Strait which separates Deception from the Antarctic mainland. Beneath them was a 1200-metre peak on Trinity Island and just ahead the spectacular iceberg alley of the Gerlache Strait. The massive cliffs of the Danco Coast, which had so frustrated Wilkins in 1920, slipped by in moments. Never in his life had Wilkins been so exhilarated by the sheer heart-pumping excitement of exploration. Over in the west he could make out the Bagshawe Glacier and Waterboat Point, where his two young friends had spent their uncomfortable year. Giant bergs, some blue as emeralds in the reflected light, were reduced to mere distractions. 'Giant loafs of sugar,' Wilkins called them.[32]

They crossed the coast at the grim Forbidden Plateau and flew across the long strip of mountainous Graham Land itself. From here in every direction they were flying over territory that no human eyes had ever seen before. While the Indigenous tribes of the Arctic could claim the Yukon tundra which Eielson and Wilkins had been first to cross by air, this flight was the first time land had been discovered using an aeroplane. Wilkins had fulfilled his youthful boast to Stefansson by consigning the dog sledge to history.

Flying along the east coast of Graham Land he noticed what appeared to be a cavernous channel slicing through what previous ship-bound explorers had assumed to be a peninsula. He named the mysterious ice-filled fjord the Stefansson Strait. It appeared to run from the Weddell Sea in the east to the Bellingshausen Sea in the west. Graham Land was thus an archipelago, separated from the main body of the continent. He saw other deep channels slicing into the mountains but for now there was no time to explore them further. Ben looked down at the chasms below and thought they could easily swallow the tallest skyscrapers; he was not eager to linger. If they were channels cutting the peninsula into islands it meant there would be no walking home should they be forced to land.

Photographing and sketching every landmark, Sir Hubert distributed geographic names as fast as he could think of them. A glacier was named after the *Hektoria*, a plateau for the city of Detroit. Ben felt a shiver. This had none of the beauty of the north, with its forests, snaking rivers and caribou. This was a lifeless place, forbidding and alien. As they flew to the limit of their range, beyond the Antarctic Circle, the mainland proper loomed impressive and frightening before them. Wilkins named the vast plateau that spread to the horizon Hearst Land.

With no maps to guide him, he took their position by dead reckoning and sextant. At the final moments of their outward leg, Wilkins opened his floor hatch and with the frigid air rushing in dutifully dropped a Union Jack and a written claim to British sovereignty. It tumbled into the swirling clouds below, never to be seen again. He estimated their turning point to be 7120' south and 6415' west, and the British flag had never rested upon a more desolate spot.

On the return flight they could see storm clouds ahead and Wilkins' hopes of further investigating the mysterious channels were dashed. All their fuel would be needed to reach Deception against the gathering bad weather. It was a pity he never got the chance to fly the deep fjords, as he would have discovered he was wrong. There was no strait separating Graham Land from the mainland, and in the years to come the mistake was used by others to belittle his achievement.

They flew into the storm but as ever Eielson held it steady through the turbulent air while Wilkins guided them to safety. Nine hours and twenty-five minutes after they'd left they circled above *Hektoria*, having flown over more than 1000 kilometres of unknown territory. They'd left after breakfast and were safely back for dinner in the ship's fine dining room after making another of the great flights in aviation history.

In his despatch to Hearst's papers, syndicated around the world, Wilkins closed out his report of the amazing flight: 'Tonight, after having had no sleep for 40 hours and after a flight of 1200 miles, we are tired and weary; but our successful flight has enabled us to prove that our luck still holds.'[33]

Wilkins was contracted to write a long series of articles on his expedition. It became something of meditation on the nature of exploring, on the character of explorers and the bitter-sweet nature of success. His predecessors Amundsen, Shackleton and Peary had all commented on just how fleeting any sense of triumph was for those who devoted their lives to discovery. Wilkins was no different. There was always another mountain to climb, another unexplored corner of the Earth to reveal. He spoke for them all in what amounted to a lamentation of the explorer's peculiar sickness, the 'why' of their being and the realisation that it would never be enough:

> And what were our feelings after such a journey? Were we thrilled with the knowledge of success? For my part I was sadly disappointed. We had passed through the gamut of human experiences. Through faith in the worthiness of our project, through hope for opportunity and kindly treatment by the elements, through anxiety when things seemed utterly against us, through labour and physical exhaustion in preparation, through adventure brought about by necessary risk and indifferent judgement, through extreme danger by choice, for fear of greater hazard, through reverent joy and exhilaration at danger passed and opportunity afforded, through boundless, absorbing interest in new scenes unfolded, through extreme satisfaction with the knowledge of expressed theories proven, through thrills beyond measure with new discoveries and solemn thankfulness with the knowledge of preservation for further effort. Yet did that bring happiness?

Positively, no . . . Our machines await us at Deception Island. Nearly two thousand miles in a bee-line awaits to be discovered.[34]

On the other side of the Antarctic, Commander Byrd was still aboard ship making his way to the coast. A fine student of philosophy, he too had much to ruminate on after a long struggle to fund and organise his expedition. His reaction to the news of Wilkins' flight is not recorded. Being beaten into the air was a blow, but the main prize of a flight to the pole remained to be won. His hope now was that Wilkins' planes did not have the range for such a trip, for the man surely had the courage. He sent a message of congratulations and an invitation for Wilkins to come and visit him at his base in the Ross Sea. It travelled from ship to New York to San Francisco and back to Deception Island, a distance of more than 30 000 kilometres – surely the longest insincere invitation ever broadcast.

In January Wilkins stored his planes and headed back to civilisation. Byrd, encamped at his new base, Little America, hunkered down for the long dark winter. The race would resume in nine months' time.

12

—

Around the world in twenty-one days

Captain Wilkins has done what few men of his generation have been permitted to do: he has changed the face of the known earth.
— *New York Times* editorial, 12 January 1929

O n 25 January 1890 a diminutive young lady calling herself Nellie Bly stepped off a train in New Jersey into the most intense public acclaim ever showered upon a woman in the United States. For two and a half months the world had followed her every move and at that moment perhaps only Queen Victoria herself was better known anywhere on Earth. A cheering crowd, thumping bands and firework displays greeted Nellie on her return from a magnificent journey. She had travelled around the world in seventy-two days, six hours, eleven minutes and fourteen seconds – faster than anyone else in history.

Nellie Bly, real name Elizabeth Cochrane, was the star reporter of Joseph Pulitzer's *New York World* newspaper whose readers were thrilled to read the latest episodes in her career of amazing 'stunts'. She had invented a hugely popular brand of investigative journalism, insinuating herself into the hidden corners of society to reveal its sordid secrets. Fearless, Bly had gone undercover to report on the shocking conditions inside a women's asylum and had herself gaoled to expose the horrors of US prisons. She had uncovered scandals in factories and the oppression of domestic workers and single mothers. And now she had pulled off the biggest stunt of all – a race against time to beat Jules Verne's fictional character Phileas T Fogg's record for travelling around the world in eighty days.

Pulitzer's papers held a competition to see who could guess the time it would take Bly to cross the globe. More than a million people entered. Each day they bought the papers to read her latest reports from exotic locations in Europe and the Far East as she raced alone against the uncertainties of Italian trains and Egyptian camels. She travelled by steamer, sampan, rickshaw and donkey, carrying just a single bag and a heavy pot of cold cream, her trademark chequered coat and, for a woman just twenty-five years old, a giant slice of pluck. In her male-dominated age she was a sensation. 'I would rather go back to New York dead than not a winner,' she declared, and the public loved her for it. On her arrival, a week inside the 'record', the *New York Herald*'s banner headlines shouted out a brave prediction: 'THE STAGE-COACH DAYS ARE ENDED! THE NEW AGE OF LIGHTNING TRAVEL HAS BEGUN'.

A popular song of the time was closer to the truth when it predicted the method the coming age of travel would employ:

I wonder when they'll send a girl to travel 'round the sky,
read the answer in the stars, they wait for Nellie Bly

Nellie never took up the offer to go flying, preferring to marry a rich factory owner. In fact it would be thirty-five years before the first circumnavigation by air was completed. In 1924 a US Air Force team managed to coax two Douglas Cruiser biplanes around the world in a staccato journey that took six months and six days – more than twice as long as young Nellie had managed by steamboat and train. The age of lightning-fast intercontinental travel still seemed the stuff of a Jules Verne novel.

It was left to another 25-year-old to change all that. On 21 May 1927, at 10.24 pm, Charles Lindbergh slowly glided down onto a field outside Paris, a flash of white across a dark sky. Waiting for him was a wildly excited crowd of 150 000. He had flown non-stop from New York, a distance of 5817 kilometres, in a little over thirty-three hours. In that instant, as one historian put it, 'everything changed – for both the pilot and the planet.'[1] Aviators had become heroic celebrities, and Sir Hubert Wilkins had joined the pantheon. Locked in the icy embrace of the polar winds for most of the past three years, Wilkins had avoided the surging waves of celebrity and it embarrassed him on his return to civilisation. Now, heading back to New York from his pioneering Antarctic flight, he wondered what awaited him.

None of the public's new-found fascination with aviators was lost on William Randolph Hearst. He instinctively understood the value of a hero in those grim days of the Great Depression. They could feed his media empire with the stories people wanted to distract them from the daily burdens of struggle and disappointment. In hard times with little good news to report, the aviators were gold dust, but they needed to be owned, not shared, spread carefully through his vast collection of papers, radio stations, newsreels and movie studios.

On Lindbergh's return to the United States Hearst invited him to a private meeting at his magnificent New York house on Riverside Drive. There he offered Lindbergh the starring role in a picture for Hearst's movie studio, playing opposite his mistress, Marion Davies. The fee would be $500 000 up front and 10 per cent of the gross receipts. There would be more money from articles and appearances, setting the flyer up financially for the rest of his life.

With immense courage, Lindbergh looked Hearst in the eye and refused, actually tearing up the contract when the mogul dared him. The man and the morals he represented were not to Lindbergh's liking. Hearst, he wrote, 'controlled a chain of newspapers from New York to California that represented values far apart from mine . . . They seemed overly sensational, inexcusably inaccurate, and excessively occupied with the troubles and vices of mankind.'[2]

For Hearst, not used to being refused, it was a rare humiliation that he was determined would not be repeated. In future he would need exclusivity and the deals would need to be signed up in advance. The word went out to his editors that 'stunts' were to be encouraged, but he wanted to know about them *before* they happened so he could dictate the terms.

Sir Hubert Wilkins' success on his first flights in Antarctica had been the model for such a deal, and for a relatively modest outlay Hearst had not only sold newspapers, he had also ended up with a chunk of the continent named for him. He kept his eye on the impressive Australian, but what he really wanted was something so big it would take the world's breath away.

So it was that Hearst came to be involved in a flight potentially more momentous than even Lindbergh's crossing of the Atlantic. Hearst's Nellie Bly was the remarkable Englishwoman Lady Grace Hay-Drummond-Hay, chief European correspondent for his newspaper group. The elegant and engaging Lady Hay was heir to a Scottish title and a family fortune. Not content to lead a life of leisure, she had gained a reputation for both fearlessness and colourful writing which made her a favourite with the Hearst readers. In October 1928, while Wilkins and Eielson were heading towards Deception Island, Lady Hay was covering what was quite literally the biggest story in the world.

The mighty *Graf Zeppelin* airship can only be described in superlatives. Like a giant silver cigar, it was, at 236 metres long, only slightly shorter than the *Titanic*. From top to bottom it rose ten storeys high and a football field would have sat comfortably across its waist. On the ground, constrained within a massive hangar, it dwarfed the observer into insignificance. In the air, driven by its five powerful Maybach engines, it cast a moving shadow the size of a mountain. It was the most magnificent application of the human imagination since the Pyramids, the creation of Count Ferdinand Graf von Zeppelin.

The count had died in 1917 before seeing his dream fulfilled. During the war and against his wishes, his glorious inventions were turned into weapons, with little success and high casualties. In his darkest hour he had turned to Dr Hugo Eckener to carry on the cause of airships after his retirement, and Eckener did not disappoint.

On the morning of 11 October 1928, the *Graf Zeppelin* was ready to depart for its initial flight across the Atlantic to New York, the first passenger-carrying flight from the Old World to the New. On board were forty crew, twenty passengers – mostly journalists and official guests – and 66 000 items of airmail. Despite containing 111 000 cubic metres of highly volatile hydrogen gas, the *Graf* was a smooth and comfortable flying machine under the command of an expert in Eckener. The doctor was always cautious, placing the safety of his passengers above all other considerations. He had a genius for predicting the subtle changes of wind and pressure that lay ahead, and no man or woman who ever flew with him felt anything less than absolutely secure.

After a journey of almost 10 000 kilometres lasting just 112 hours, the *Graf Zeppelin* landed on American soil and, as with Lindbergh, a seismic ripple reverberated around the globe. Sequestered in a penthouse suite at the Waldorf Astoria, Lady Hay filed the final instalment of what her editors called the 'biggest story since the Armistice' and, rather disparagingly, 'the finest story ever written by a woman'.[3] More importantly for Hearst, she informed her boss that Eckener had in mind an even more amazing plan, nothing less than the ultimate flight – a journey around the entire world.

Eckener knew the value of such a challenge. If successful, it would secure him the finance he needed to launch a global network of passenger-carrying Zeppelins, criss-crossing oceans and nations in swift luxury.

Thrilled at the commercial value of the venture, Hearst immediately began negotiating media rights to the trip. The flight was vastly more expensive than the Zeppelin Company could manage from its own resources, which were always stretched. With typical flamboyance, Hearst proposed the solution. He was prepared to offer two-thirds of the cost, close to $5 million in today's money, in return for exclusive rights to the story. Eckener could not accept excluding German media from the event – he would be harshly criticised at home for such an agreement – so Hearst agreed to cover half in return for the US and British Empire rights. It was a deal. The rest of the costs were covered by German papers and newsreels, passenger tickets at $9000 a head and the highly valuable cargo of stamps and letters sought after by collectors all over the world. Hearst set one condition: as he was paying for it, the journey was to begin and end in New York with a flight around the Statue of Liberty. Eckener agreed, while fully intending to continue on to Friedrichshafen for a point-to-point journey from the Zeppelin's home base.

Arriving back in New York from Antarctica on 13 March 1929, Wilkins and Eielson were once again greeted by Mayor Jimmy Walker's Committee for Distinguished Guests. Suzanne was there too, happy to have her stranger-fiancé back safe. But even before there was time to discuss the future, a Hearst representative pushed forward to inform Wilkins that 'the Chief' wanted him in Europe soon to join the *Graf Zeppelin* on its journey around the world . . . He had about six weeks to prepare, but most of that was already committed to speaking engagements and meetings devoted to the next summer of Antarctic flights. Suzanne was learning what it meant to love an aviator.

While Eielson was in Washington receiving the Distinguished Flying Cross, Wilkins continued to press forward with his global weather plan, predicting it would lead to a vast improvement in the accuracy of forecasts. Like no other explorer, he mapped out a strategy of investigation with direct economic importance to all nations.

Addressing a meeting of influential British and American business-men in New York, he said:

> You might be interested to know just why we go back from time to time to these regions, and why there is a direct connection between our work and yours.
>
> If we can forecast conditions so that the agriculturalists, the primary producers will know what type of crops to plant, when to plant them, whether it will be an early season or a dry one; if graziers can know just how much stock they can carry on a certain acreage in a certain year, it is going to do a great deal toward the stabilization of prices and it will mean a great deal to everyone of us here, whether we are concerned with science, industry or commerce. I am sure that any one of you can realize the tremen-dous advantage.

He estimated it would cost $10 million for a ten-year study, the burden to be shared by every government in the Southern Hemi-sphere, plus the United States. 'I have had the good fortune to meet some of the world's greatest meteorologists,' he said. 'They assure me they are willing to place on record that if we can establish these stations as proposed in the North and South we can improve in one year our meteorological forecasts by nearly 50 per cent.'

Wisely, he did not promise the Earth, admitting it might be many years before further improvements could be expected. 'It will be possible, not next year, or perhaps in five years maybe not in ten years, but some time in the future we believe that our efforts will enable us to forecast the seasonal conditions.'[4]

Before leaving for Europe to meet the *Graf Zeppelin*, Wilkins attended the opening of the new headquarters for New York's Explorers Club. Its official predecessor was created by survivors of a shipwreck off Greenland, and then, as now, it was a refuge for those restless adventurers who for most of the time had no permanent home. Wilkins was elected just its sixteenth honorary member – before even Byrd. To this day the club retains many mementos from Wilkins' career, including a sledge he hauled across the ice, which sits at the feet of an impressive stuffed polar bear on its wood-panelled staircase. It's that kind of place.

With all the hectic meetings, there was little time to see Suzanne, who was herself busy in a new production. If she had hoped they might be able to set a date for the wedding, she was to be disappointed. While Hubert was as charming as ever, he was still an enigma to her, and she must have begun to wonder if this second-date engagement had been a good idea. He seemed reluctant to put a wife through the pain of being married to an explorer, and for her part she was not yet ready to give up her life on the stage. They parted very much in love, but unsure of their future together.

Dr Eckener had the *Graf Zeppelin* scheduled for one more rapid trans-Atlantic trip before the round-the-world flight, part of his plan to establish his airship as a reliable passenger service. As well as paying customers and reporters like Wilkins and Lady Hay, it would be carrying cargo. As the *Graf* was prepared for its 15 May departure, Eckener's experts were grappling with the problems of carrying a pair of young gorillas to an American zoo. Also being stored for transport was a priceless Reubens portrait and a grand piano.

Wilkins had been fascinated by airships since the days he spent just after the war with the British Lighter-than-Air Command. He saw them as a potentially excellent platform for exploration – a belief he shared with Eckener and hardly anyone else. But he also knew that without adequate meteorological information to guide them safely through storms and wind currents, they were vulnerable.

While ocean-going ships need to deal mostly with resistance through the water, an airship moves in three dimensions, with a constantly changing payload of fuel and ballast. As it flies through the air, lift is generated over the control surfaces and speed can change suddenly. The delicate balance between these forces can be dramatically altered by any number of variables ranging from temperature to altitude. More than any vessel since the age of sail, an airship is at the mercy of the winds and weather. The Zeppelin bends and twists under static and aerodynamic loads, its superstructure of girders shift and creak – all the while carrying a volatile payload of 100 000 cubic metres of hydrogen, the most flammable gas of all.

Before the age of super computers, the interaction between these variables was only dimly understood, though the evidence from a series of disastrous events in the United States, France and Britain was plain to see. To pilot and navigate an airship was a remarkably complex skill requiring experience, uncanny instinct and a measure of luck. No pilot in the brief history of airships had more of these attributes than Dr Hugo Eckener.

Wilkins stared up at the giant craft squeezed into the hangar at Friedrichshafen with just half a metre of headroom to spare. It was so much more purposeful and streamlined than any airship he had seen before. Its five massive engines hung suspended like pilot fish beneath a ghostly whale. Among the twenty passengers assembled for the trans-Atlantic crossing, he was the only one familiar with the demands of airship navigation and flight. His task was to report on the technical and scientific aspects of the trip, while Lady Hay covered the colour and a third renowned Hearst correspondent, Karl von Wiegand, wrote whatever was left. Standing with Wilkins in shared awe was Merian Cooper, adventurer, fighter pilot and filmmaker. 'Ain't she grand?' he asked of no one in particular. During the flight he was greatly interested in the gorillas, and would soon start making the movie *King Kong*. Other passengers included two counts, a pair of millionaires, and a German diplomat who would later plot to assassinate Adolf Hitler.

In the still dawn air on 16 May the *Graf* slowly lifted into the skies over Lake Constance, the delicate colours of sky, land and lake reflected on its shimmering skin. Over Switzerland's Alps, it turned due south to pick up the mistral streaming down the valley of the Rhône and was pushed by the winds to more than 140 kilometres per hour, a perfect start. Soon the blue Mediterranean stretched beneath them, magnificent in the clear spring air, and the stewards began setting the tables with crisp linen for a light lunch. Wilkins was with Eckener in the control gondola when they heard a sudden metallic clatter. The main shaft in the port forward engine had shattered. It was a shock, but it could be repaired while they were under way and presented no threat. Then, almost in unison, two more engines seized. Wilkins looked at the indicators. The huge airship had lost all forward speed. Continuing was out of the question and Eckener ordered that they swing about and return to base. They would somehow have to force their way back against the mistral on just the two remaining engines.

The situation was serious. France's largest airship, the *Dixmunde*, had mysteriously broken up over the Mediterranean not far from where the *Graf* now hovered, the entire crew of fifty lost. Four of the five Zeppelin engines had all been overhauled at the same time, apparently with faulty parts. As they feared, it was not long before the fourth Maybach failed. It was unthinkable to attempt to climb over the Alps on the remaining engine. The best they could hope for now was an emergency landing in France.

'The passengers of course had heard the noise,' recalled Wilkins, 'and came crowding in to ask what the trouble was, but none showed great alarm, for in the cabin of the great airship it seems so safe and comfortable.'[5] Lady Hay remained in her cabin, bashing away on her Remington. Von Wiegand and Wilkins tried to send despatches, but the officers were desperately trying to contact the French for assistance and there was no time for the reporters.

Fighting against the winds appeared useless, as they were being pushed backwards towards the French Riviera. Beneath them cars rushed and crowds gathered apparently aware that the Zeppelin was in trouble. In the command cabin, Dr Eckener pulled every trick he could conjure, going low to take advantage of a hill for shelter, then rising above it to catch the downdrafts on the other side. He knew that in a forced landing there would be little chance of saving the ship, and passengers would be at risk. Alone, without a trained ground crew to control her, the Zeppelin would buck and bounce uncontrollably unless the crew could rip open the gas bags quickly enough to force the huge frame to settle. One spark, and the entire vessel would be alight in an invisible flash of burning hydrogen. The passengers were told to assemble inside the cavernous envelope, in preparation to abandon ship.

There was one slim chance, and Eckener risked it. Outside Toulon at the little village of Cuers was the old hangar of an airship delivered by Germany as part of the reparations for the war. It was empty but in good condition. Crawling between the narrow valleys and hills behind the coast, Eckener and his crew masterfully navigated the massive Zeppelin towards the base. Just as twilight set in they reached the field, where a small army of hastily assembled French soldiers was waiting. Captain Ernst Lehmann, Eckener's most trusted officer, parachuted down to direct the rescue efforts and the *Graf* was soon efficiently walked into the hangar. The only drama came later when Wilkins and von Wiegand, trying to send despatches on their safe arrival were caught sneaking off the base while it was locked down by the suspicious French authorities. After all, the last Zeppelin landing in France had been a war machine. The reporters aboard had been greatly impressed by Eckener's calm handling of the crisis and little unfavourable publicity ensued. It is only on reading Wilkins' notes that the true potential for disaster becomes clear.

With the Zeppelin's world tour delayed, Wilkins made his way to London and bad news: a message from New York that Suzanne was seriously ill. She wrote suggesting an end to the engagement as she feared she might become a burden to him. The next day he left on another of his many rushed trips across the Atlantic to be with her.

In the 1930s rheumatic fever and its attendant heart problems remained the number one killer of children in the United States, and those who survived the childhood illness often relapsed as adults. It 'licked the joints and bit the heart', according to one saying, and the pain it caused could be so intense that some patients could not bear to be covered by even a sheet. In those days before antibiotics, the only treatment was bed rest and aspirin. Suzanne was very weak by the time her fiancé arrived, though out of immediate danger. For the next month he hardly left her side, and it was the making of their relationship, a love affair that survived almost thirty years, refreshed rather than weakened by his endless travelling.

*　　*　　*

In the early morning hours of 1 August 1929, the mighty *Graf* was finally ready to start its round-the-world trip – or rather the preliminary crossing to New York where Hearst had insisted it officially begin. The twenty passengers, many employed by one news organisation or another, climbed the steps known as the 'stairway to heaven' into the gondola, thrilled to be finally on their way. The passenger list was like something from the ultimate 1920s house party with minor royalty, raffish Americans, cosmopolitan writers and handsome soldiers. They came from ten different nations, and the King of Sweden was there to see them off, along with ambassadors and dignitaries. They were permitted a meagre 20 kilograms of luggage each, and most brought dinner suits. Lady Hay, the only woman travelling the entire journey, was given her own cabin, while the others shared. Though most were sponsored, officially their tickets cost $12 000 each and there were hopeful faces at the airfield ready to pay up if anyone cancelled – the world's first stand-by passengers. Wilkins received an offer of $30 000 to give up his seat, but declined the offer.

A mere ninety-five hours later they were in Lakehurst after a faultless Atlantic crossing, and Eckener was impatient to be off again for the real thing. The journey back to her base in Friedrichshafen took just fifty-five hours, regaining the blue riband from the new passenger steamship, the *Bremen*. Even today, no passenger ship has made the crossing faster than the *Graf*.

If the Atlantic crossings had been publicity-fuelled joyrides, the round-the-world trip was going to be treated very differently. The next stop after leaving Friedrichshafen would be Tokyo, a journey of more than 10 000 kilometres across Russia and Siberia – the longest non-stop flight ever attempted and most of it across land that had never been traversed by air. It was, said Eckener, a genuine expedition, and he insisted that the flamboyant young American millionaire Billy Leeds remove his gramophone player from the vessel out of respect for the seriousness of the undertaking. Leeds, who was (briefly) married to the Russian Grand Duchess Xenia Romanov, daughter of the assassinated Grand Duke Mikhailovich Romanov, smuggled it aboard regardless.

Dr Eckener now had a challenging record to beat. Two American pilots, Captain Charles Collyer and John Mears, had made a circumnavigation the previous year, flying their Fairchild over land while transporting it across the Atlantic and Pacific by ship. They raced the new moon all the way, finally returning to New York after twenty-three days and fifteen hours.[7] Asked at the final press conference what he believed the *Graf* was capable of, Eckener estimated that with favourable weather it might be possible to complete the journey in seventeen days of flying, not counting rest stops in Tokyo and Los Angeles.

One reporter looking for an angle asked: 'Don't you reckon at all with having to defend yourselves against Asiatic hordes should you be compelled to descend and make repairs?'

Eckener replied without elaborating: 'We are prepared even for such eventualities.'[8]

Despite the weight penalty, the *Graf* was carrying an arsenal of weapons for protection and hunting if it were forced down over the ice of Siberia, plus emergency gear for trekking.

In the velvet darkness of a moonless summer evening, 7 August 1930, the *Graf* was led out of its hangar. As ever it left an indelible impression on those who saw it. According to Eckener, it was:

> a fabulous silvery fish, floating quietly in the ocean of air and captivating the eye just like a fantastic, exotic fish seen in an aquarium. And this fairy-like apparition, which seemed to melt into the silvery blue background of sky, when it appeared far away, lighted by the sun, seem to be coming from another world and to be returned there like a dream . . .[9]

Nose to the wind, they dragged her into position, stumbling and slipping in the damp sand, holding steady in the light breeze and waiting for the command, *'Taue los!'* – 'Let go the lines!' The ascent was so smooth it seemed from on board that it was not the Zeppelin lifting so much as the world falling away beneath their feet. In the gondola there was virtually no sound, the engines just a distant rumble, no wind noise at all. As the nose pushed its way through the currents, a layer of air cocooned the entire vessel as if wrapped in glass. It was an unearthly feeling, which one of the passengers described as like being lifted to heaven by angels.

Wilkins, however, was less concerned with the romance of the journey than the practical challenges of manoeuvring and navigating a machine the size of a skyscraper. While not immune to the drama unfolding below, the aviator in him was fascinated by Hugo Eckener's skill in navigating by meteorology. The master pilot spent more time studying his radio weather reports than looking at maps, for success in commanding a Zeppelin depended on an exceptional understanding of the weather.

The *Graf* used what navigators call flexible path routing, a constant series of small adjustments to find the most favourable winds. Like the clipper ships of the past, Eckener went in search of the weather systems that could push them along at speeds much greater than if they'd merely travelled the most direct route. This required not only calculations of the ship's location at any time, but also careful adjustment for wind drift. Weather forecasts from stations en route were studiously examined and the flight plan modified to take advantage of tail winds, even if it meant taking a wide detour. Drift was calculated by manoeuvres once an hour that turned the ship from its heading and then back again to measure the movement against flags dropped into the breeze below. It was a tiring, exacting exercise that took immense concentration from the crew.

Calculation alone was not enough, for there was art as well as science in navigating over such vast distances. It took instinct to read the clouds beyond and the snow and seas below, and iron nerves to take decisions that to less skilled navigators might seem unwise. Wilkins and Eckener shared a special bond. They were men who could confidently feel their way across even unknown routes by their wits and a few simple instruments.

When not in the control room with Eckener, Wilkins took a seat by one of the salon windows and hardly moved, fascinated by the scenes below. He brought a prototype cartographic trimetrogon camera with him, partly of his own design. It took three simultaneous images of the land below, one vertical, the others at oblique angles. The result was an image that gave a true representation of the surface features, and this method remained the primary form of aerial mapping until supplanted by satellite photography decades later. As ever, he also carried a moving picture camera, recording the flight for history.[10]

For four days they glided slowly across the entire Soviet Union, beyond the villages Wilkins had seen devastated by famine, above the endless, awesome Russian forests, over the Urals to the monotonous steppes of Siberia. 'If we didn't know it was impossible,' Wilkins reported, 'we might almost think the Zeppelin had flown to the moon or Mars. The view is positively unearthly.'[11] They could travel for hours without seeing a single soul, then come across an isolated village where the inhabitants stared up at them in horror.

With no heating on board, it was cold, and even Wilkins was forced to don an overcoat. But the meals were good, the company agreeable and the time passed quickly. There was enough fuel aboard to continue all the way across the Pacific, but their arrival was eagerly awaited in Japan and they planned to stopover for several days.

Wilkins wrote of their arrival, 'It is impossible to imagine that people as undemonstrative as the Japanese should show such emotion. Admirals in uniform danced and shouted like schoolboys. High-ranking officials tossed their hats into the air. The ground crew clapped and clapped. Thousands of people roared *Banzai!*'[12] They cheered not just for the giant airship, but for what it represented: the end of their geographic isolation. In a stroke, the fastest journey from Europe to Japan had been reduced from a month-long haul by train and steamer to a few days of luxurious flying.

Wilkins was thrilled for Dr Eckener's success, but both of them knew the future belonged to aeroplanes not airships. They had played their part as pioneers and soon enough the skies would be patterned by the slim white contrails of a thousand aircraft crossing the continents every day.

They sailed serenely on to the United States, arriving first at San Francisco then travelling down the coast. The only dark spot they noticed was the magnificent palace of Randolph Hearst at San Simeon. As they circled the estate in tribute, not a light showed from any of its 165 rooms, the one place on Earth that seemed unmoved by their arrival. Then suddenly the grounds and houses lit up in a magnificent display of dazzling intensity. Arriving over Los Angeles, the entire city was a blaze of lights, another magnificent sight. 'It seemed to me,' Wilkins wrote, 'as if we were close up to the Milky Way, each light on the ground was as a twinkling star that stretched on every side to the horizon.'[13]

The round-the-world record was theirs for the taking, and Dr Eckener was keen to push on to New York, as much to avoid the welcoming banquets and ceremonies as for the record. 'We sail tonight,' he announced, and the planned three-day visit was cut to a few hours. Randolph Hearst, however, would not be denied, and his grand banquet that evening was brought forward. Sometime during the evening Eckener slipped away, returning to the airfield where the watch officer, Max Pruss, appeared gravely worried. For some un-accountable reason, the ship was too heavy and wouldn't rise.

Every piece of baggage and freight had been meticulously weighed, and the correct amounts of fuel and gas taken on board, but she refused to budge. An inversion layer of cool air just above them pinned the Zeppelin to the surface. As there was no more hydrogen available to add to the cells, they were forced to reduce weight. Six disappointed crewmen were sent on to New York by rail. Eckener's only alternative was to take off at speed, hoping the air flow over the rudders would be sufficient to lift the craft like an aeroplane. At the end of field was a line of high-tension power lines and to hit them would mean the likely death of them all. Yet Eckener, flustered by the milling crowds and impatient to be away, insisted that they leave immediately rather than wait for a change of conditions.

The United States' leading airship pilot, Lieutenant Commander Charles Rosendahl, was in the gondola with Wilkins, and was horrified. 'This will be the end of us. Sure as little apples we'll hit those wires and the ship will go up in flames.'[14] The ground crew pulled the vessel down low then flung it into the air with a terrific heave, the engines gunned full throttle. The crowd gave a roaring cheer and the Zeppelin rose five metres, then hung suspended, gathering speed towards the edge of the field but not rising. As Wilkins recalled the ghastly moment, Rosendahl lost his composure and shouted: 'Doctor, bring her down, you can't get above those wires. BRING HER DOWN!'

Eckener seemed lost in thought. 'The wires, yes, the wires . . .' Then he came out of his trance. 'Stop forward engines,' he ordered. 'Drop all forward ballast. Full astern rear engines.'

Hundreds of litres of water from the bow ballast tanks was dumped on the crowd beneath and the nose of the *Graf* rose so steeply that the tail section ground into the field with a sickening thump . . . 'Full ahead both forward engines,' ordered Eckener. 'Drop all stern ballast.

Stop rear engines.' The crew threw overboard everything they could get to hand, and the crowd on the ground scattered like rabbits.

Looking up in horror was Wilkins' old friend from Barrow, the newsreel man Will Hudson, who had just finished packing away his cameras and was directly beneath the struggling airship. 'If I live to be a thousand years old I shall never forget it,' he said. Next to him, a policeman quietly called, 'Well, good-bye Hudson. If she's going to tangle with those wires this is the end of us.'

There were three wires strung along the top of the power poles, and the Zeppelin's great tail fin pushed against the top wire and threatened to break it. 'One slip would have caused a blinding short circuit,' said Hudson. 'A short would have been the end of the Zeppelin, her crew and passengers, and several hundred folks on the ground under the big bag of deadly hydrogen.'[15]

More water drenched the farewell band and the tail of the machine rose from the field. In the gondola they stood frozen as the nose of the ship cleared the power lines with just a metre to spare. But what hope was there of the stern rising above them? The tail rudders lagged nearly 200 metres behind and Eckener was attempting to hurdle over the wires. He nodded to his son, Knut, who manned the elevator wheels, and he spun the controls madly to force the nose down and the tail up as they passed over the lines. Someone yelled: 'Look, look she has caught fire See the sparks rippling up. We are done for!' They weren't on fire; it was droplets of ballast water caught in the beam of spotlights.

A telephone call came from the engineer in the emergency steering station deep in the stern. They had cleared the wires. Eckener's impatience had put them all in jeopardy, but his incredible flying ability had prevented a disaster. Leaving behind a trail of boxes, vegetables and cans, the *Graf Zeppelin* lifted skywards, while beneath them a cacophony of car horns honked farewell. An inspection showed that the stern had suffered only superficial damage and it was safe to proceed. Without ballast it would be difficult to control and risky to attempt a crossing of the high Sierras, but Eckener felt confident they could make it on a southerly route across the Arizona desert and Texas. It had been close, but they were headed to New York with the record within reach.

There was no water left in the tanks so as they flew across the entire United States, still thirsting under its Prohibition Law, all they had to drink was wine and champagne. For five days they washed themselves in eau de cologne and made do with a reduced menu, but there were no complaints.

Flying through the low cumulus clouds above Arizona, the rising air was hot and the turbulent currents buffeted them. The giant ship bucked like a wild horse. It wasn't comfortable, but the scenery beneath them made it worth the ride. From the air, New Mexico offered the most beautiful landscape of the entire journey. The colours of the desert and sky burned with intensity, tawny sands and cactus filled the ground below and in the distance they could see flat-topped mesas marked out by deep blue shadows. Over Texas some cowboys took a shot at them with rifles and ripped holes in the gas bags, but these were easily fixed.

On 29 August the round-the-world flight came to an end after twenty-one days, five hours and thirty-five minutes. The actual flying time across three continents had been completed in just over twelve days (another record) and Eckener considered it conceivable that a circumnavigation might be possible in as little as ten days. Though the achievement would soon be overtaken by aeroplanes, nothing could match this first flight for style or excitement. As the passengers climbed down from the gondola in the hangar at Lakehurst, they were nearly mobbed by the crowd. Lady Hay considered herself 'the luckiest woman in the world', while playboy Billy Leeds said he was 'absolutely thrill drunk', and looking forward to a warm bath – he'd managed only three since leaving. Another passenger claimed the flight had taken twenty years from his age of sixty.

For Sir Hubert it was business as usual, and he told waiting reporters that now the trip was over he could get to work on his own plans, including a new expedition to the Antarctic. 'It was a fine trip,' he said, 'and I liked the start of it better than I do the end, but I'm glad it's over and I can start my own work.'[16] First, though, he had a little private business to attend to.

*   *   *

The day after his return, Hubert invited Suzanne to accompany him on a trip to the first Cleveland National Air Races, an annual event that would become the showpiece of American aviation for the next twenty years. It was hardly a romantic interlude. As she recalled many years later, it was probably only his appreciation of her sense of humour that prompted him to invite her to a trade show, then 'buy a tractor and then to marry me, in that order. He talked all the way to Cleveland about the races, and the tractor, so I wasn't at all sure whether he'd marry a new plane, a Caterpillar or me. But I won finally and entered a new world.'[17]

They were married in the Cleveland registry office by a Justice of the Peace, without fanfare or ceremony, though the papers found out and made a fuss. His diary for the day, 30 August 1929, records the event with a single word entry, 'married', though one of the few witnesses, John Caine, said he 'had never seen a bridegroom so nervous'. The flyer's hands shook so much that he fumbled when trying to put on the ring. 'Finally the justice told the bride to put it on herself.'[18] Wilkins was forty, his new wife twenty-eight.

In many ways their marriage was as remarkable as any of Sir Hubert's adventures. By Suzanne's reckoning, in the first eight years after their honeymoon they spent just three months together and things barely improved after that. Yet almost alone among the leading modern explorers, he had a lasting and loving marriage. Amundsen had a frozen heart which even his affairs could not warm. Peary and Stefansson strayed, producing children with Indigenous women neither acknowledged. Shackleton found no solace with either his wife or his mistress. Byrd married his childhood sweetheart but, though it lasted, he was so driven by ambition that he rarely found contentment. Sir Douglas Mawson's marriage was both long and successful, but he turned to an academic life while still a comparatively young man. Only Wilkins sustained both his adventures and his marriage to the end, and for this Suzanne deserves most of the credit.

From the beginning she accepted that she could neither change nor compete with him. Many times she called herself 'the loneliest wife in the world', though in reality she was rarely on her own while her husband was away. Flamboyant and gregarious she surrounded herself with friends to fill the void. Considered one of the beauties of the Broadway stage, there would certainly have been suitors and who could blame her if there were affairs? But if so she was discreet, and nothing shook her marriage or her love for her husband. Thirty years after their wedding the letters between them remained touchingly affectionate, evidence of a resilient relationship. They had no children. Suzanne's health forced her to leave the stage, so she changed paths to become an exhibited painter and many times filled in for Sir Hubert at functions he could not attend. Her lectures and talks were filled with a collection of humorous anecdotes and popular songs. She never sought pity and in any case was far too exuberant to convincingly play the abandoned wife. Certainly the life of an explorer's wife was not easy, and fear of bad news was ever-present. 'There are many drawbacks, many heartbreaks,' she wrote, 'yet there is always a fascination with the work that my husband has given his whole life to create. Therefore, if in some small way I can be instrumental in helping him to achieve the ultimate goals, I shall not feel my sacrifice has been in vain.'[19]

While Wilkins was enjoying his leisurely journey around the world, his great rival Richard Byrd had been buried in the long winter night of Antarctica. When the sun finally rose over his base, Little America, on 22 August, it was not a moment too soon. The expedition was fraught with problems. His men were suffering from depression and the group was riven with tensions. Bouts of drunkenness had led to fighting, and Byrd himself had been carried to his room dead drunk on occasions. One of his aeroplanes had been torn apart by a storm and his first season of flying had been severely restricted. In New Zealand, the expedition's business manager was found to be mentally unstable and had committed suicide. Byrd had become more suspicious than ever, and instituted a secret society of trusted insiders who were sworn to a bizarre oath of medieval loyalty.

The worst news of all was that Wilkins was planning his return. The men at Little America considered it an invasion of their territory. One of Byrd's trusted offsiders indignantly reported that the news of the Australian's plans was received 'in a spirit of rage'. One of Byrd's closest confidants, the former boy scout Paul Siple, noted in his diary that the commander became angry when discussing the interloper who they believed was out to steal their glory. 'There is no doubt that [Wilkins] means to race to the pole.'[20]

Writing to his manager in New York, Byrd revealed his deep concerns: 'You must not forget that Wilkins is out to lick us . . . he can start early and he is going to make every effort to beat us to it. Don't forget that he was offered $50,000 by Hearst to beat us to the South Pole . . . In spite of this we have got to be sports and have got to be square with him, but do not give any information as to when we start flying. If he thinks we are going to start early he will naturally hurry the more and make it very difficult for us.'[21]

Back and forth went telegrams, as an increasingly fretful Byrd sought information on Wilkins' intentions. He appealed to their mutual friend, Dr Isaiah Bowman at the Geographical Society: 'Since we are publishing our plans, it is only fair that he should give us his. If he is going to fly to the South Pole, I want to know it. Please make urgent requests to him for his plans.'[22]

The return of the sun above Little America had done little to dispel the gloom.

Within a month of his wedding, Wilkins was off again to the Antarctic, returning to the work of the previous summer. His ground-breaking flight had added nearly 2000 kilometres to the map of the world, and he intended to continue his exploration along the uncharted coastline. Somewhere along the towering ice cliffs he hoped to find bays that would allow access to areas suitable for building permanent bases. Only then could his real work of constantly monitoring polar meteorology begin.

While heading south, the expedition picked up a special radio show of Suzanne singing farewell. Although once again flying under his own flag, this time Wilkins went with considerable support from the British, who were increasingly concerned not only about Byrd's plans but also the growing incursion of Norwegian whalers into Antarctic waters.

The Colonial Office voted Wilkins £10 000 and the services of the research vessel *William Scoresby* to act as a floating base if required. Rather than a hurried memo written by a minor official, this time he carried a charter, signed under the Great Seal by the King.[23]

Eielson had stayed behind to develop his plans for an Alaskan air service and he recommended Parker Kramer as the replacement pilot, with a Canadian, Al Cheesman, as his deputy. They retrieved the Lockheeds unharmed on Deception Island, but exceptionally high temperatures meant that once again the ice was unsuitable to use as a landing strip. It barely held the weight of a man.

Loading one plane aboard the *William Scoresby*, they sailed south in search of potential landing strips on the Antarctic coast, but were continually frustrated by storms. Wilkins was amazed to record that the floating ice field had receded by almost 1000 kilometres from the previous year. Looking back on these conditions later, he told journalist Lowell Thomas, with some prescience, that he believed this ice warming to have had a long-range effect on climatic conditions throughout the world.[24] The ice melt that southern summer year was followed by an extensive drought in the United States. Decades before the world became aware of ozone holes and global warming, Wilkins was recognising the links between Antarctic conditions and climate change.

There was no option other than to fix pontoons to the plane and once more roll the dice on take-offs from the ice-ridden seas. With no certainty that by the time they returned there would still be open water it was a tremendous gamble. There were several lucky escapes from serious damage and it proved impossible to land safely on the rugged coastal ice.

Wilkins' frustrations turned to gloom when he received news by radio that his great friend Ben Eielson was lost in the Arctic. Typically, Ben had been on a rescue mission when his plane disappeared. Wilkins insisted on daily radio updates on the search for his friend. The days turned to weeks until the report he had been dreading was received: Ben's plane had been found smashed.

By now Wilkins had lost count of the good friends killed in those pioneering days of aviation. Ben's death, at just thirty-two, was an especially heavy blow. Together, north and south, they had flown over more than half a million kilometres of the Earth's surface that had never been seen before. The world had lost a fine pilot and Wilkins had lost a great companion. In his tribute to the brave airman, Stefansson blamed international politics for Eielson's death. A break in diplomatic ties meant the Russians and Americans were not sharing meteorological reports, 'forcing Eielson and other Alaskan pilots to fly blind'.[25] It was deeply depressing to Wilkins to know that his friend had been lost for lack of the international cooperation he had so long advocated.

Despite the setback, he continued the campaign, knowing Ben would have wished it. They made a number of exploratory flights and some modest discoveries, including confirmation that Charcot Land on the western shore of the peninsula is in fact a large island. He dropped a document claiming the discovery for the King. Today the frozen passage bears the name Wilkins Sound.

Suzanne must have been concerned when for a period of three weeks there was no radio contact from the party. The newspapers published a letter he had sent from South America to his brother in Adelaide that only added to the anxiety: 'You may not hear from me for 12 months. If nothing is heard . . . you will know I am lost and it will be then too late to send out a rescue party. I have fine fellows with me in whom I have every confidence . . .'[26] Two days later, the human compass reappeared, the silence having been nothing more than radio problems.

Wilkins' presence in the Antarctic continued to trouble Byrd, who was gearing up for a second summer of flying. He made a successful exploratory flight in November but did not radio news of the milestone to New York for fear that the report might spur on his rival. Finally, on 28 November, with a crew of four and Bernt Balchen as his pilot, Byrd took off for the pole. Early the next morning they circled the long sought-after goal and nursed their plane back to safety.

In reality it had been a phantom race. Despite his feints, Wilkins had never intended a flight to the pole and his hopes of crossing the continent from the Atlantic to the Pacific coast was always reliant on the vagaries of Antarctic weather. The struggle was David versus Goliath, with Wilkins and his itinerant team of four piggybacking on borrowed vessels against Byrd with his permanent base and team of fifty men, fleet of support vessels and huge financial resources.

On the last day of 1929 Wilkins added another 500 kilometres to the map before returning to Deception Island – just in time for a massive earthquake that shook the volcanic lake and killed one of the whalers. While, by Wilkins' standards, this had been a modest campaign, it would be years before any flying in the Pacific regions of the Antarctic would come close to matching his efforts.

On a March morning the team landed at New York's Pier 97 at the foot of West Thirty-Fourth Street, Wilkins scorning an overcoat despite the chill breeze. Reporters were waiting and he declared that he was through with flying. Was it Eielson's death that had made up his mind, or his frustrations with primitive aeroplanes that could not support his imagination and gumption? The truth was there was little more he could achieve with an aeroplane. The third act of his boyhood plan, putting his theories into practice, could not be achieved from the air.

Since his triumphant return from Dead Man's Island, Sir Hubert had travelled at breakneck speed for fifteen months, covering more ground than even the *Graf Zeppelin*. He'd led flying teams to both poles – twice to Antarctica – discovering more uncharted land than any man in history. He had crossed the Atlantic four times by air, circumnavigated the globe and twice sailed the deep South Atlantic. He had been feted on two ticker-tape parades along Broadway, been knighted by the Kings of England and Italy, and criss-crossed three continents giving lectures and holding talks on his grand weather plan. After nursing Suzanne back to health, he'd even found time to get married. He had also received the singular recognition of being the subject of three glowing editorials in the *New York Times* – even though much of the time he'd been working for its arch rival.

In the month of Wilkins' return, the citizens of the five boroughs were surprised over their morning coffee by an unusually glowing editorial in the *Times*. Taking time out from thundering about the British in India and the ever worsening economic crisis, the paper rhapsodised at length about a farm boy from outback Australia who had captivated the world with his courage and humanitarian dream. It was headlined 'The Work of Wilkins' and in part it read:

> A few years ago there appeared a new planet in the explorer's firmament, and since then its course has been plotted and its weight and luminosity determined with scientific precision. 'WILKINS' is now a permanent figure in polar exploration. He has an assured place in that great company of dispellers of dark traditions . . . Like all great men, he knows when to take the last desperate chance and win; he is wise enough to skirt the edge of the abyss without falling

in. Of him HUGH ROBERT MILL, author of *Siege of the South Pole*, said quite recently: 'I consider it one of the greatest triumphs that he made sure of his return,' but this reflects the security of success viewed after the event, rather than the daring when, in December 1928, a forced landing over almost any part of the Antarctic Archipelago would have meant almost certain destruction . . .

WILKINS has a quiet voice with steel in it and the strong hands of a man who can master more than material things . . . He is a charter member of those to whom boastfulness is abhorrent. His first report to the American Geographical Society, after traversing 2,100 miles of unexplored Arctic territory on the flight from Barrow to Spitsbergen, was simply 'No land was seen.' His first published story was widely acknowledged as the finest account of its kind ever written, although it was scribbled on telegraph blanks and the backs of envelopes and transmitted by radio without the slightest revision. BEN EIELSON was devoted to him, 'I'll go wherever the Captain wants me to go.' . . .

The airplane has made it possible to secure large profits in investments in scientific geography – this is the way WILKINS puts his case. Location by him of a dozen accessible points at which meteorological stations could be established is his proof . . . The weather-breeding areas are the big game of this scientific hunt. Extraordinary connections of cause and effect have been discovered in recent years . . . it is Captain Sir HUBERT WILKINS' main object . . . The impetus which his spirit has given to later systemic study exceeds the power of current estimation.[27]

Wilkins kept the clipping, but he was not one for looking back with nostalgia while there was work to be done. Much to Suzanne's astonishment, there *was* a belated honeymoon and certainly one to remember. The couple were set to sail to Britain with Nobel Prize winning dramatist George Bernard Shaw in the summer of 1930. At the last moment Hearst rang and suggested Wilkins take his bride to Europe on the *Graf Zeppelin* instead. So, Sir Hubert and Lady Wilkins left Lakehurst on the Zeppelin's seventh Atlantic crossing. Eckener was pleased to have his old friend aboard and they discussed plans for taking the *Graf* to the Arctic the following year. Good winds and smooth air blessed the trip all the way to Friedrichshafen . . . Suzanne, however, said flying made her nervous and she preferred sailing.[28]

The millionaire explorer Lincoln Ellsworth was waiting for them on arrival to take them to his castle in Lenzburg, Switzerland. For six weeks they walked and hiked in the Alpine air, and Suzanne slowly regained her health. Ellsworth and Hubert were often deep in conversation, obviously making plans, and Suzanne realised that this would soon lead to a new separation. Making their way down on the funicular from Mount Pilatus, the spectacular Alpine vista lay open below them yet it hardly seemed to register with her husband. 'His mind,' Suzanne sensed, 'was far away at that moment and his eyes were seeing the ice and snow of the top of the world, not the white-capped mountains around us. It was evident I would have to accustom myself to sudden surprises and constant fear of what the future might hold for him, and me.'[29]

Hubert would never stop wandering. Though there was no more land to find, there remained one last magnificent challenge. To the north lay a last uncrossed ocean, a barrier that had defeated every brave and foolish sailor that had attempted it. And only Wilkins knew how to beat it.

13

The suicide club

'Ah! Sir,' said Captain Nemo, in an ironical tone, 'you will always be the same. You see nothing but difficulties and obstacles. I affirm that not only can the Nautilus *disengage itself, but also that it can go farther still . . . Yes, Sir; it shall go to the Pole.*

— from Jules Verne, *Twenty Thousand Leagues under the Sea*

On a sweltering summer's day in June 1930, Wilkins and Commander Sloan Danenhower drove up from Washington to the Philadelphia Naval Yards. They had spent the morning in the capital finalising one of the most peculiar transactions ever conducted by the US Naval Shipping Board. For the mighty annual sum of $1, they had just leased themselves a military submarine.

Danenhower was a former navy man and engineer, now in partnership with the American submarine pioneer Simon Lake. When they heard about Sir Hubert's latest plan, they were quick to offer their services. The back channel at the Navy Yard was full of old submarines soon to be scrapped, and Lake had designed and built most of them.

Waiting at the dock beside the Delaware River was a jostling contingent of journalists and newsreel cameramen, for everything Wilkins did these days was news.

The explorer made a brief statement, announcing that after much delay and frustration, President Herbert Hoover had personally approved his plan for taking one of the Navy's surplus submarines under the ice to the North Pole.[1]

He was proposing a surface voyage from New York to London, a dive beneath the pole from Norway to Alaska, then a return cruise down the West Coast of the United States, through the Panama Canal and back to Brooklyn. In today's era of satellites and nuclear-powered icebreakers, the voyage may not seem so remarkable. At the time, however, it was almost inconceivable. The 5000-kilometre journey beneath the Arctic Ocean would take at least two months in a vessel built for brief coastal patrols. Designed during the Great War, Lake's submarine had a submerged range of less than 200 kilometres, so every day it would need to hunt for an opening in the uncharted ice to come up for air and recharge its batteries. The Arctic Ocean was an area one and a half times the size of the United States, 14 000 000 square kilometres of obscure emptiness. Only its extreme edges had been charted; its currents, depth and the thickness of the ice remained a mystery.

The Arctic's flat areas of ice, the floes, were like heavy blocks sometimes kilometres wide, and where they butted up against each other huge pressure ridges were created, plunging jagged spikes downward or shooting upwards in massive piles that had been the torment of Arctic explorers since they'd first attempted surface exploration. By ship they could do little more than lock themselves in the pack ice and slowly drift, sometimes for years. No icebreaker invented had ever forced its way far inside, and they dared not follow the shifting, treacherous channels that led to the unknown interior, the deep Arctic basin.

While the High Arctic remained a blank space on the map, it had long filled the imagination of humanity and inspired some of the most grimly fateful episodes in exploration. No ship had been within 800 kilometres of the pole and survived, and though hundreds had died trying, by Wilkins' time just a handful of men had ever reached the deep interior.

The few visits to the far north were fleeting and yielded little of scientific value. Wilkins now proposed turning his submarine into a floating laboratory, manning it with some of the greatest scientists of his time, and in a single magnificent journey, unlocking the secrets of the least explored ocean. Virtually nothing was known about the contours of the Arctic sea bed, its currents, temperature, or salinity. The way it interacted with the North Atlantic and Pacific was a mystery. The effects of the magnetic pole on radio waves and compasses were little understood, likewise the influence of solar radiation on the ice cap – Wilkins listed these and a dozen more areas of groundbreaking investigation for the submarine scientists. But above all the expedition would contribute greatly to his lifelong passion for knowledge about the influence of the poles on global climate and his quest to fill in the last unknowns on the map. By crossing the Arctic Ocean he would be writing the final page in the story of maritime exploration, a link to the sailors of prehistory and the days when Magellan, Columbus and Cook set sail for uncharted seas.

'Is it the primitive thirst for adventure,' Wilkins asked, 'the desire to penetrate the unseen and the unknown; to experience the thrill that comes from the presence of danger and the satisfaction one feels at facing and narrowly cheating death that takes me again and again to the polar regions? Yes, it is, to a certain extent, but the experienced know there is a thrill greater than that of adventure. It is the thrill of worthy accomplishment.'[2]

Just weeks after Wilkins' announcement in Philadelphia a sobering discovery was made. Sealers from Norway had gone ashore to hunt walrus on a dot of rock east of Spitsbergen. On a rocky hill they found the skeleton of a man, half-buried in the snow and ice, the top half partially eaten by polar bears. A monogram on the jacket identified the body as being that of Salomon Andrée who in 1897 had attempted the first balloon flight to the North Pole. Still in the pocket of his coat was a diary and a camera loaded with film. Not far away were the relics of his camp and the well-preserved bodies of his two young companions. More than one newspaper noted that Wilkins and his submarine were destined for a similar fate.

To some extent Wilkins had only himself to blame for the necessity of such an undertaking. It was he, after all, who had finally established there was no land in the Arctic Ocean, and therefore no place to ground a permanent weather station. With the plan for global climate monitoring still his driving force, the submarine seemed the only viable alternative for studying high latitudes.

Weather remained a realm of perpetual change and eternal motion, the 'infinite mystery' he called it. Millions of tonnes of air surged about the globe, its cause and effect unknown. 'What must we know in order to take full advantage of its enormous power?' he asked, and as ever he sought the answer at the ends of the Earth.[3]

Once again he felt a hand guiding him towards a predetermined fate: 'It was the stern relentless dominating force of mysterious nature that fashioned the thoughts which later controlled my destiny and brought me to the point of undertaking what many considered the most foolhardy of all risks – a journey by submarine beneath the Arctic seas.'[4]

Like his wartime colleagues, Suzanne too was beginning to understand her husband had an uncanny gift for prescience. 'I began to realise Wilkins had insight into the future, and was not incapable of casting coming events with what turned out to be some accuracy. It was almost a little frightening at times. If he was that good I wanted him to let me know when he ought to stay home, and 'discover' me some more ... However I saw by the time the submarine expedition came up after two years of marriage that nothing and nobody would hold this man down. He had a restless urge to move and act.'[5]

Jules Verne had also suggested a submarine visit to the poles in his novel *Twenty Thousand Leagues under the Sea*:

> ... was it not a mad enterprise, one which only a maniac would have conceived? It then came into my head to ask Captain Nemo if he had ever discovered that pole which had never yet been trodden by a human creature?
>
> 'No, sir,' he replied; 'but we will discover it together. Where others have failed, I will not fail.'

Verne was an old man when he heard of the first successful open-sea run by a submarine, the *Argonaut*. The bizarre little vessel, with its wagon wheels that drove it along the bottom of the sea, made its history-making voyage from Norfolk to New York in 1898. It was the creation of an eccentric genius, Simon Lake, who as a boy had been inspired by the story of Verne's Captain Nemo and his amazing craft the *Nautilus*. With a sense of pride and pleasure, Verne cabled his congratulations:

> While my book *Twenty Thousand Leagues under the Sea* is entirely a work of the imagination, my conviction is that all I said in it will

come to pass . . . This conspicuous success . . . will push on under-water navigation all over the world.[6]

Lake was waiting for Wilkins and Danenhower at the Naval Yards on that summer afternoon in Philadelphia, and together they went down into the rusty hull of the Lake-built O-12. When they emerged, they told the waiting newsmen it would be transformed into the *Nautilus*.

The O class submarine was a twenty-year-old design that was never meant for ocean-going service. Just 53 metres long, the subs were claustrophobic and notorious for their instability while travelling on the surface. Sailors disparagingly called the early submarines 'pig boats' for their strange shape and unpleasant living conditions. They were meant to be a weapon, and the comfort of the crew was never much considered. For thirty-five men there was a single toilet or head: an unsheltered steel bowl mounted between the two diesel engines where, according to one naval veteran, 'it took great powers of concentration to be successful.'[7] Meals were taken standing up and the design was plagued by poor ventilation which led to serious problems with condensation. Sometimes it seemed to be raining on the inside. After struggling for years to get a Navy contract, building the O class had bankrupted Lake's company.

The Navy said Wilkins could take his pick from the scrapyard. The O-13 was in the best condition and had a fine record, having once made the deepest dive in history, but it was considered an unlucky number. Letting superstition overcome logic, they settled on the O-12. It was a mistake. In an unpublished manuscript Wilkins revealed he had misgivings about the vessel from the very beginning:

> I was appalled at the amount of work which would have to be done to put the boat in shape for the seas . . . On the day of our first inspection the weather was hot and sweat rolled off our brow as we emerged from the steel hold of the vessel. We were smothered in grease and oil and I almost decided then and there that the task of refitting the O12 was beyond anyone's power. To live in a thing of that kind for several months seemed appalling . . .
>
> After seeing the boat I realized it was no wonder that the officials in the Navy Department thought we were crazy to attempt to do anything with it. But after we had struggled for so many days and had

implicated so many of our official friends in getting the vessel I could hardly go to the Shipping Board and say that we did not after all want the boat. People thought it would take great courage to go underneath in a submarine but I can assure you that it took more courage and even more than I had to go back on our word. We had put our hand to the plough, it was necessary to go on.[8]

The superstructure was eaten away with rust. The central control compartment was a maze of valves, gauges, levers and switchboards all torn apart. The engine room had a scribbled note pasted to the wall: 'to avoid trouble you must scrap this engine room machinery and instal a new single unit.' As his manuscript noted, 'These words haunted me throughout the expedition.'

Using her diesel engines with care while surfaced, the *Nautilus* had a cruising radius of 11 700 kilometres. Once submerged, however, and running on her electric motors so as not to poison the crew with fumes, this range was drastically reduced. She could travel at three knots – a brisk walking pace – for little more than a day completely submerged, and the maximum radius before being forced to surface was just 200 kilometres. It took eight hours to recharge the batteries, so the long passage from Spitsbergen to the Bering Strait, a journey of at least 3300 kilometres, would be an interrupted one. Allowing for a zigzagging course through heavy ice floes, it would take a minimum of forty-two days, and possibly much longer.

The greatest challenge would be to find open spaces in the polar pack through which they could surface daily to recharge the batteries and replenish the air supplies. For this, they must have faith in Wilkins, who was the one man aboard who had seen the deep Arctic Ocean.

In a cheerful manner, Commander Danenhower set out the risks: 'Should we fail over any extended period to get air, even by using our emergency drills and dynamite, our batteries would lie dead and useless, we could not move, we could not breathe, we should die. Not a nice picture! I don't like it myself, but the possibility is there.'[9]

The press and public response to the *Nautilus* expedition was staggering, and was divided evenly between those who considered him crazy and those who believed it was a noble undertaking in the great tradition of courageous exploration.

The critics gave the expedition the unfortunate title 'the suicide club', and though Wilkins listed more than twenty detailed areas of scientific investigation, nothing could convince them it was anything less than a self-promoting publicity stunt. The *Washington Post* editorialised:

> Sir Hubert Wilkins has tried hard to justify his proposed jaunt under the polar ice on scientific grounds, but the public still regards it as a rash adventure by one who had decided that there are no more worlds to be conquered on the surface of the water or in the air . . . The chances of meeting with disaster are incalculable. Everyone admires Sir Hubert's dauntless spirit, but the popular opinion of his judgement just now is far below par. It is no small responsibility to imperil the lives of 22 men on what appears to be a hopeless quest. Unless Sir Hubert proves it otherwise, he's liable to face a permanent charge of needlessly imperilling life in a dare-devil feat.[10]

Richard Byrd, now an admiral, damned the expedition with faint praise: 'If anyone can come through and accomplish the impossible, my friend Wilkins can . . . I prefer doing my exploring above the ice instead of below it.'[11] Wilkins' old friends at the *New York Times* were more open-minded: 'Sir Hubert Wilkins has been a dauntless explorer,' wrote Henry Armstrong. 'He is a man of adventures almost too numerous to count, and the event has proved that he is exceptionally intelligent. It seems foolish to talk of luck in the case of such a man . . . He has been taking chances all his life. Fate has let him alone, as if he were invulnerable.'[12]

Meanwhile, the Hearst empire negotiated a $150 000 deal with Wilkins for exclusive news rights to the expedition. Hearst had sold a lot of newspapers on the back of his previous sponsorships with Sir Hubert and cannily structured the deal so the bulk of the money would be withheld until *after* the *Nautilus* had made it to the North Pole.[13] His vast audience was being prepared for what was billed as 'the greatest adventure of all time'. Wilkins was uncomfortable with the demands of Hearst's media machine, but he knew the deal was necessary to help meet the immense cost of the venture.

A similar agreement was concluded with the *News Chronicle* in Britain. Paramount was granted the exclusive film rights and it appointed a cameraman to the expedition – an old friend of Wilkins' from the Arctic flying days, the energetic Emile Dored. These exclusive deals angered rival outlets, whose pages soon filled with criticism of the venture.

The most damning assessment came from the former commander of the US Fleet in Europe during the Great War, Admiral Hugh Rodman, who dismissed the venture out of hand: 'What benefit of any sort can be derived from it; what new data can be collected which can be beneficially utilized? Who cares seriously about the Arctic depths of unnavigable waters? I do not believe anything practical or useful can be obtained by diving under the ice.'[14]

The argument raged on, most of it hot air, for no one really knew what lay in store for the *Nautilus*. Bemused, Wilkins looked on as 'the controversy between the credulous and the incredulous [that] has been smouldering burst forth now in a campaign of ink spilling'.[15] Partly to calm things down, and partly to help raise money, he took the unusual step of releasing the expedition book *before* he set sail. Published in April 1931 by his friend and supporter George Putnam, *Under the North Pole* was a collection of essays by Wilkins, Lake, Danenhower and his supporters written to establish beyond doubt the scientific credibility of the venture. Stefansson contributed a long chapter, as did the wealthy adventurer Lincoln Ellsworth who had generously given the expedition more than $70 000 and backed it with further personal loans to Wilkins.

Now officially called the Wilkins–Ellsworth Trans-Arctic Expedition, the project had the endorsement of the American Geographical Society, the Carnegie Institution, the new Woods Hole Oceanographic Institution, the Cleveland Museum of Natural History and the Norwegian Geophysical Institute, as well as a growing list of commercial sponsors. By far the most important vote of confidence, however, came from the appointment of Professor Harald Sverdrup as the chief scientist. This quietly spoken Norwegian was acknowledged as the finest oceanographer of the day, and arguably the most influential of all time.

When it came to science, Sverdrup was everything the Australian was not. He had trained with the great meteorologist Professor Vilhelm Bjerknes, responsible for the modern theories on weather forecasting so close to Wilkins' heart, and eventually followed Bjerknes as head of the famous Bergen School of Meteorology. Sverdrup had spent nearly seven winters intentionally locked in the ice aboard the *Maud* with Roald Amundsen. They were testing theories of Arctic drift and currents, hoping to eventually float across the pole, and although that never happened the expedition gathered a wealth of valuable data.

Sverdrup had since gone on to a brilliant international academic career, but the opportunity to return to the far north was irresistible.[16] He agreed that a well-prepared submarine was the perfect platform for Arctic investigation, offering the opportunity to penetrate further and move more freely than any other vessel. Though Wilkins had none of his qualifications, the Norwegian recognised a kindred spirit and together they began developing an ambitious research program which, while not as headline-grabbing as a trip to the pole, was infinitely more important to science.

Sir Hubert's insistence on science before glory was both his most admirable quality and his greatest failing as a professional explorer. Heroic deeds were what the public wanted, not reams of esoteric data. As a foreigner in the United States he lacked the national constituency of a home-grown hero like Byrd, whose family connections and military friends were able to pull strings and loosen purses. What allies Wilkins had in politics and academe came solely from admiration for his courage and ideas. There were no old school friends to make the introductions. His greatest sponsor, Randolph Hearst, was at best a fairweather friend whose only interest was in selling newspapers. Wilkins was an outsider attempting the near-impossible, but that had been the pattern of his life and it hadn't stopped him before.

Lincoln Ellsworth became his most important supporter. The two men, both dreamers, would form a long and sometimes difficult relationship, and because of Ellsworth's great wealth it was never an equal partnership. Ellsworth's father had made a fortune from mining and finance, but the son was more interested in adventure than business. Obsessed with the Wild West of America and fascinated by the wild south of Antarctica, he became a benefactor for many explorers. He used his inheritance to fund expeditions of his own and helped finance others, once saving Roald Amundsen from bankruptcy. Now he did the same for Hubert Wilkins, of whom he later observed: 'He was a man exactly to my taste. Had he lived in our West during the pioneer days, he would certainly have been a frontier marshal two-gunning some wild district into law and order.'[17]

At a press conference Ellsworth signed over a large cheque and gave Wilkins one of his favourite good-luck tokens: a shoe from Marshall Wyatt Earp's horse. While supportive, he obviously had some doubts about the efficacy of the horseshoe. In his autobiography he later wrote: 'I consented to attach my name to the submarine expedition as scientific adviser, though I had no intention of accompanying Wilkins on his voyage.'[18]

As Wilkins was a foreigner, the US Navy was not prepared to charter the submarine to him directly, so the contract was officially made with Lake and Danenhower's company. Wilkins shook hands with Simon Lake and agreed the inventor would have the final say on the special apparatus to be installed during the refit. With some bitterness, Wilkins looked back on these arrangements as the beginning of the end of his chances of success. Wilkins had hugely underestimated the cost of transforming the ugly duckling O-12 into the beautiful swan *Nautilus* and Lake was bleeding him dry with his crazy ideas, yet there was little he could do about it. 'The public demand for so-called safety devices and Mr Lake's desire to install most of his own inventions resulted in the installation of much equipment considered inadequate and unnecessary . . . The vessel became so crowded it was a marvel of inconvenience, and the administration of the commander [Danenhower] was not always of a manner conducive to maximum efficiency.'[19]

For months the money poured out though little progress seemed to be made. Wilkins had to insist the O-12 be moved from the government Philadelphia Naval Yard to a private dock in New Jersey where progress improved – whenever Lake could be kept offsite. He was an impractical tinkerer, who by some accounts was unable to keep his hands off a design even when a boat was almost finished.[20] Wilkins would have been horrified to discover that Lake's first submarine for the US Navy in 1909 was delivered two years, five months and fifteen days late. The Australian had broken his own hard-learned rule about keeping control of the expedition planning. There were ominous echoes of John Cope and the Imperial Trans-Antarctic fiasco.

Simon Lake had first patented plans for an under-ice submarine in 1898. The complicated wooden carapace now being built over the

Nautilus superstructure was another patent of his. When it was issued in 1924 – US patent number 1 500 000 – the Patent Office declared a holiday. Lake had been keeping them gainfully employed for decades and now all those dreams long dismissed as impractical by the Navy could be tried out on the hapless Wilkins.

Stripped of its wartime equipment and extensively rebuilt, *Nautilus* was now almost unrecognisable as a military submarine. The new hollow wooden topside, adding around a third to its original size, was designed to serve as a working platform while the vessel was on the surface. Arching above the superstructure, running from end to end of the vessel, was a 'sled deck' to slide against the bottom of the ice, protecting the submarine from damage. At her bow was a hydraulic cushioning bowsprit to telegraph gently into any obstructing ice. But in case of a heavier collision, the torpedo muzzles were blocked with heavy steel plates and the nose filled with concrete.

The interior had a light sheet metal inner wall covered in wooden and cork panels in the manner of German U-boats. There was no heating on board and in fact Wilkins had suggested that it might be necessary to chill the vessel artificially to prevent condensation.

Through a watertight bulkhead was the Central Control Compartment. This was where Sloan Danenhower would navigate the submarine 'blind' beneath the ice. This little room, three metres long, was the equivalent of the pilot house of a surface ship. It was a maze of valves, gauges, wheels and recording instruments for controlling the submarine both above and below the surface.

The compressed air tanks on board were enough to keep the crew of eighteen alive for up to three days while submerged. In an emergency, the use of soda lime to remove carbonic acid gas, and oxygen to regenerate the air supply might stretch the possible living time to six days, but these were only academic figures. In an emergency they all knew there could be no hope of rescue.

Lake had designed a series of complicated drills that he hoped would be adequate for allowing escape to the surface if *Nautilus* could not find a break in the ice. They never worked. He had insisted on a complicated jack-knife periscope that would bend if it hit obstructions. It fogged up and filled with water. Atop the *Nautilus* was a massive, hydraulically lifting steel arm with a wheel at the tip. The sub was meant to use this to 'skate' its way along the underside of the ice. Even

Danenhower knew this was only likely to snag them in the uneven surface and it was never used.

Wilkins kept his doubts private, hoping that, as in the past, everything would be all right on the day. Meanwhile, he had a new surprise to announce to the public. *Nautilus* was planning a rendezvous at the pole with the *Graf Zeppelin*. It was stunning news, splashed around the globe by a carefully orchestrated Hearst press campaign and sufficient to briefly drown out the sceptics.

Under the banner headline 'Greatest Adventure in History' the Hearst papers detailed the plan for an exchange of mail and personnel between the submarine and the airship at the most remote spot on Earth. This would be the ultimate triumph, humanity's complete and utter domination of the natural world. No mention was made of the huge deal Hearst had made to finance *Graf Zeppelin*'s journey.

Dr Hugo Eckener had been reluctant at first, doubting the *Nautilus* would ever make it to the pole. Still, he was pleased to take Hearst's money and wished his friend Wilkins well.

As usual, however, the devil in a Hearst deal was in the detail. Like his contract with Wilkins, he ensured the Zeppelin contract was conditional. For exclusive news rights he was prepared to pay a *total* of $150 000 if the airship and submarine met at the North Pole and exchanged mail and passengers; only $100 000 if they just met at the pole; and just $30 000 if there was merely a meeting somewhere in the Arctic.[21]

The *Graf Zeppelin*'s luxurious interior was stripped out in preparation for the flight, replaced with the sparse furnishings more in keeping with a scientific venture. Like Wilkins, Eckener prepared his scientific team to be led by the Russian Arctic specialist, Professor Samoilovich, and began trials of the huge airship in the cold air of Iceland. He was sure he could make his end of the bargain, but could Wilkins?

Wilkins was lecturing day and night to earn as much as he could to pay the mounting costs.[22] There was an endless stream of letters to be written to contractors, scientific bodies, potential sponsors – and begging letters to friends. In March 1931 alone he dictated more than 500 letters, a secretary following him wherever he went.

Throughout his struggle to raise money and organise the expedition, Wilkins was buoyed by an immense show of public support. Wherever he went on his fundraising lectures he was greeted as a hero. Though people had little cash to spare, they were generous in their praise – and their criticism. He received mail from all over the world, and he kept the best and worst of it in his private collection.

The Archbishop of Ottawa gave benediction to a medal of St Christopher and a crucifix and posted them to Wilkins to protect him on his journey. An eager-eyed girl from Minnesota sent a four-leaf clover to match the ones she had previously sent Admiral Byrd and Charles Lindbergh. Daniel Green sent forty-two pairs of comfy slippers from his shoe store on Madison Avenue. Frank Stern of the Stern's Patented Safety Stacking Coffee Cup Company sent 144 of his space-saving devices.

An Australian living in California sent Wilkins a small Australian flag, which he placed above his cramped little desk inside the submarine along with portraits of Suzanne and his mother. Although the Australian papers followed the project avidly, officially he was still not forgiven for his earlier criticisms and there was no government support. But a wartime friend sent a note: 'They will wake up in Australia some day and know what a great Australian Wilkie is.'[23]

The response wasn't entirely uncritical. In a neat hand 72-year-old D Cameron MacDonald wrote from Canada: 'I presume the whole civilized world is discussing your proposed trip . . . my judgement is dead against it . . . I deeply regret to see a man of your outstanding ability deliberately throw away his life in a useless cause. You will pardon my plain talk, but I only write as I think, and not being an Irishman, cannot flatter you.'

Despite the well-advertised risks, there was no shortage of applications to join the crew. Literally thousands poured in from all over the world, including many from women. They ranged from highly experienced to the utterly bizarre. One man requested to be taken to the Arctic and let out in a barrel – as long as Wilkins would pay the life insurance. Many men were looking for adventure: 'Dear Sir Hubert: Two air force officers mentally fit desire join expedition. We fear neither God nor man but would like to have a round or two with death. We are rearing to go.'[24]

Danenhower would command the vessel under Wilkins' direction. He'd been many years in the Navy, but was not an expert submariner. However, he had an appropriate pedigree for a polar mariner. His father had been Master of the *Jeannette*, an American vessel crushed in the ice in 1881. Most of the expedition members had perished, but John W Danenhower, sent blind and close to madness, survived. Some years after his son joined the Navy, he committed suicide.

Many of the crew knew each other from previous service. Ralph Shaw, the Chief Engineer, had been riding pig-boats since 1916 and was close friends with the head electrician, Ray Meyers, a legend among radio operators. Chief Petty Officer Arthur Blumberg was a veteran of fifteen years' service aboard US Navy submarines and took leave of absence from the Navy so he could make the trip. All of them knew master diver Frank Crilley – everyone did. Crilley was considered the greatest diver in the US Navy, winner of the Medal of Honour and holder of the world record for deep diving. They signed on for $160 a month plus expenses, but most of them would have done it for the adventure alone. Wilkins left Danenhower to fill the minor crew positions, another oversight.

The Hearst papers ran a series of daily profiles on each crew member. The assistant engineer, John R Janson from Chicago, seemed typical of the excited seafarers. 'Why this expedition is something new. Nothing like it has ever been attempted by men in any century. Nothing like it has been imagined except in the pages of fiction. I never asked about my rank or pay. I'd be willing to go without any pay at all – just for the chance to become part of an adventure that will be one of the splendid adventures of all time.'[25]

In fact, Ralph Shaw had already had words with Janson, who had been grumbling about his low pay and working conditions. He and another young assistant, Harry Zoeller, became known as the 'black gang'. Together these two otherwise lowly crewmen would play a decisive role in the drama ahead.

Wilkins had always insisted this was much more than a mere adventure, and he was determined to ensure it had true scientific credentials. Sverdrup had enlisted Dr Bernhard Villinger as his assistant and ship's surgeon. Villinger had been on the opposite side to Wilkins during the war on the Western Front, working as a doctor, and, like the Australian, had come there from an Arctic expedition. He had traversed Greenland with Helmer Hansen, a veteran of Amundsen's successful South Pole expedition, and then forged a new career as a respected chemist. He was a fine addition to the expedition. The Carnegie Institution lent one its best young researchers, Floyd Soule. Trained as an electrical engineer and physicist he would operate many of the complicated recording devices being carried aboard. His time on the *Nautilus* inspired him and he went on to a distinguished career in oceanography for the Coast Guard as a specialist in ice studies.

Each crewman was required to sign a contract indemnifying Lake and Danenhower and the Expedition against damages, 'including particularly claims for death' The release, signed by all, was kept aboard the submarine for the entire journey.[26]

By March 1931 the major structural work had been completed and *Nautilus* headed for the Brooklyn Navy Yard for fitting out – and tragedy. Entering New York harbour on a day of high winds and choppy water on the ebb tide, a huge wave suddenly crashed over the low deck. The quartermaster, Willard Grimmer, was picked up and lifted bodily into the water. Thrashing his arms about, he was swept away. He had been trying out his heavy Arctic kit and had no chance of swimming back. Grimmer was twenty-seven and recently married.[27]

Despite the loss, there was no time to delay. A major public event had been planned beneath the Brooklyn Bridge to christen the vessel, and the ceremony went ahead as planned on Tuesday, 24 March before a crowd of more than 800 people and a large press contingent. The guest of honour was Jean Jules Verne, grandson of the author, who had come from Paris for the event. He stood beside Wilkins and in halting English proclaimed: 'What man can imagine, man can do! My grandfather told me that, and I transmit it to you . . . I wish to express my admiration for you in attempting this feat. It almost surpasses anything that my grandfather dreamed of. I am sure you will succeed.'[28]

Sir Hubert then introduced Simon Lake to the audience, but the old man could barely speak as he choked back tears. 'I never expected to see this day when . . .' He stepped back, overcome with emotion.

A Navy band played the national anthems of the United States, France and Britain, and the crowd dipped their hats. As the last notes echoed over the water, Lady Wilkins pulled a rope attached to a special silver bucket full of ice – champagne being out of the question in those days of Prohibition. As the flags were raised on the yardarm, and a national audience crouched around their Radiolas, Lady Wilkins spoke out clearly in her best Broadway voice: 'Ship, I name you *Nautilus*. Go on your wonderful adventure. In your heart is great treasure. Bring that treasure safely back to me.'[29]

The next few weeks were spent in a furious effort to make the submarine seaworthy for an attempt on the pole during the brief Arctic summer. At various shipyards along the Hudson River, *Nautilus* was given brief trials to test some of the new equipment, but nothing like the thorough trials Wilkins had hoped for. There simply wasn't time. In an unseasonable April snowstorm, Wilkins showed off the converted sub for the cameras. Pathé's newsreel went round the globe, breathlessly reporting him as 'the most daring man in the world!'[30] If they had known how fragile the old vessel really was under its coat of fresh paint, they might have added that he was also a world-class optimist. Back in Adelaide, the hometown paper was convinced that, win or lose, its famous son was heading for glory: 'Experts tell him that the *Nautilus* is going to take him to his doom. If he does fail, what a death!'[31]

All New York came out to see *Nautilus* make its way down the Hudson. Wilkins felt the heavy burden of months of struggle fall away in the wake, his heart beating fast with excitement and the coiled energy of a man headed towards destiny. Old Glory fluttered from the stern in a black cloud of diesel fumes and the crowd on Battery Park, Lady Wilkins among them, rang out a lusty cheer as they passed. Good wishes from the Staten Island ferries sounded on the breeze, and aeroplanes circled above, carrying newsreel men seeking the iconic image of *Nautilus* dwarfed by Manhattan's skyline. Behind them, blazing like a beacon in the afternoon sun, was the newly finished Empire State Building, standing tall amid the mid-town towers. In that grim year of the Great Depression, with five million unemployed and the banks closing their doors, the giant skyscraper and the brave little submarine were symbols of a brighter world where man's imagination could reach for the impossible. Like the great explorers before him, Wilkins knew the deep satisfaction of finally being on his way, beyond the reach of creditors, meddlesome sponsors and critics. There was only one answer for all of them now: success.

14

—

The voyage of the Nautilus

I estimated this adventurous course of the Nautilus *to have lasted fifteen or twenty days. And I know not how much longer it might have lasted, had it not been for the catastrophe which ended this voyage.*
    – from Jules Verne, *Twenty Thousand Leagues under the Sea*

I n the early months of 1931 the world became considerably smaller. It began in January when Sir Douglas Mawson raised the British flag above a pile of rocks on a blizzard-swept Antarctic bay. In the name of King George, he laid claim to nearly half the continent. In February a former postal worker named Bertram Thomas walked out of the Rub al Khali, finally conquering the world's greatest sand desert. In crossing the uninhabited 'Empty Quarter', Thomas added 600 000 square kilometres to the map, an area larger than France.

A few weeks later, Auguste Piccard sat suspended in a tiny aluminium sphere beneath a vast hydrogen balloon as it rose 16 000 metres over the dairy cows of Bavaria to the edge of the stratosphere. Little by little, the world had succumbed to humanity's curiosity and revealed its secrets. Only the polar interiors and some empty scraps of desert had yet to be tramped by a good pair of leather boots.

Hubert Wilkins had done more than most to leave his footprints in those previously unknown places. At that point, however, he was having trouble getting out of the mud of Long Island Sound.

Like so much of his grand submarine adventure, the stirring departure from New York had been created for the cameras and Hearst's newspapers. It was a ceremonial event, and the dangerous work of testing the *Nautilus* in real conditions remained. Since the departure from Brooklyn she had been undergoing a series of trial dives off the Navy base at New London, Connecticut, far from the gaze of the world's press. During the test dives, each crewman was given a piece of coloured chalk to mark any signs of leaks. Everyone was on the lookout for telltale 'teardrops' that might appear on rivets in the bulkheads and soon the interior of the *Nautilus* looked like it had a serious case of measles. Back in the yard caulkers were kept busy plugging each hole.

Perhaps unwisely, Commander Danenhower believed her ready for a deep dive and headed for sea with the submarine rescue ship *Falcon* standing by. The O class submarines were designed to stand pressure to a depth of 70 metres, much less than the deep eastern end of the Long Island Sound where Danenhower ordered all tanks flooded and a cautious descent. Heavy with all her modifications and equipment, the *Nautilus* plunged out of control.

Uncontrolled descent is the most terrifying experience any submariner can encounter. As the pressure builds the entire vessel groans like a wounded beast, light bulbs explode, rivets shoot out of their mountings like bullets. It is only a matter of time before small leaks become gushing torrents. *Nautilus* plummeted deeper than she had ever been, the depth gauges shooting into the red zone. Then a violent thud tossed everyone off their feet. She'd come to rest at a depth of more than 80 metres, her keel deeply embedded in the muddy bottom of the sound.

Engineer Ralph Shaw made a swift inspection and his damage report showed the old sub was holding – for now. Knowing that crushing pressure now pushed against every square centimetre of the superstructure, Danenhower immediately gave the order to blow all tanks to gain maximum buoyancy. The crew eyed each other nervously and no one dared make a sound as they listened for signs of movement. Nothing happened. *Nautilus* lay trapped on the bottom.

The crew was ordered forward, then back, then from side to side, anything they could think of to try to dislodge the keel from the sucking mud. It was useless. Radio operator Ray Meyers sent a message by the submarine oscillator telling the *Falcon* to stand by and remain clear – if she did break free, they would shoot to the surface and Danenhower was fearful of a collision if the rescue ship were directly overhead.

The senior men held a conference in the control room to consider the options. It was just possible that a diver from the *Falcon* might be able to reach them and be able to lay charges to shake her free. Then there was the possibility that one of Lake's innovations, the pressurised diving chamber with its trapdoor, might allow them to nudge themselves off the surface. In reality neither plan offered much hope of success.

Then, as Meyer remembered it, someone yelled, 'My God! – look at the depth gauge!'[1]

While they'd been talking, the submarine had broken loose by itself and was rising rapidly to the surface. The crew rushed to their stations to take control of the ascent.

Back at the New London dock the cause of the near-disastrous dive was discovered to be rubbish stuck in the vent valve of one of the ballast tanks. The seas they faced ahead were considerably deeper than the Connecticut coast and such small oversights could cost them their lives if repeated. For good reason, it was better to put such thoughts out of one's mind. 'The Arctic Ocean is deep,' Wilkins wrote. 'We do not of course care to dwell on the thought of the vast dark depths which will generally lie beneath us.'[2] With no time to lose and unwilling to tempt fate with further tests, he ordered their departure for the trans-Atlantic crossing to Britain.

On the morning of 4 June, two months behind schedule, *Nautilus* left the United States from Provincetown, landing place of the Pilgrim Fathers. Escorting them was a Coast Guard cutter, the *Hunt*, with Lady Wilkins aboard. She and Hubert exchanged a final radio message of love and luck, and *Nautilus* headed out into a grey and choppy sea.

All on board were happy to be away at last. Down below at his tiny desk Wilkins, still formally dressed in his suit and tie, bashed away on a typewriter, producing the initial 1000-word report he was required to send the Hearst newspapers each day.

For three days she made good progress, but on the afternoon of 7 June the seas began to rise and storm clouds lay ahead. Designed for coastal waters, the submarine bucked and rolled furiously, twisting like a log on the high seas. She listed leeward, and water poured through the open hatch into the control room. Closing it meant being cooped up inside the poorly ventilated tube – not a pleasant choice with every stomach churning badly.

Wilkins had ridden the roughest seas without ever suffering from seasickness, but this was different. Soon there was a steel bucket by his feet as he sat at his desk pumping out his daily grind of words for Hearst. Everyone on board was suffering badly, and it was later discovered that the drinking water had been inadvertently poisoned by workers who had coated the fresh-water tanks with lead paint.

The bad luck continued when the generators were flooded with sea water. Danenhower ordered 'All stop' and the engines and bilges were pumped. Sir Hubert, bilious but determined, joined the work crew with a monkey wrench in one hand and his bucket in the other. Fumes from the chemicals used to clear salt from the wiring added to their discomfort. After hours of work they were ready to try to restart, unaware that sea water had also seeped into one of the two engines.

As the starboard engine turned over, even before it had gained speed, a cylinder lifted clean from the crankcase with a massive thump. Shaw hit the kill-switch just in time to prevent further serious damage. If the engine had been in full swing it is likely the cylinder would have blown right through the hull of the vessel. Wilkins knew they had come within moments of disaster: 'It would doubtless have meant the end of the *Nautilus* and all the crew. There were no lifeboats carried [because] there was [no] room for any and no one could have escaped from the sinking vessel.'[3]

As *Nautilus* was making its fitful progress across the Atlantic, the British submarine *Poseidon* collided with a merchant ship off the coast of China and sank within four minutes. The men on deck at the time were saved, but eighteen others were trapped. Four of them eventually made it to the surface using a new hand-held oxygen container and mouthpiece, the Davis Escape Apparatus. The *Nautilus* crew, with no emergency devices, were doomed if they sank.

On one uncertain engine they headed into a rising gale. The waves were slapping over the long narrow deck while Danenhower did his best to ride her through the troughs. Suddenly a giant wave came from nowhere and crashed across the bow, carrying away the bridge and screens and hitting the commander with such force that it doubled him over in pain and smashed the spectacles in his pocket. The force had slammed the conning tower hatch closed, but luckily a forward ventilator was open. Had it not been, the giant diesel engine would soon have sucked in all the air in the boat, creating a vacuum that would have sealed the hatches – suffocating the occupants.

Meyers recommended sending a distress signal while they still had the power for it, but Danenhower, dripping wet and defiant, told him emphatically there was no need. Radio communications were reduced to conserve battery power and all lights save the eerie blue auxiliaries were switched off.

Now they were rolling worse than ever, 47 degrees to either side. Inside it was impossible to stand upright without gripping on solidly with both hands. There was no alternative but to shut down the ventilation system to preserve the batteries, and with the hatches battened down the air quickly fouled. They could not operate the bilge pump, so used oil, sewage and sea water swilled around their feet mixing with the fumes from the batteries. One of the engineers working in the engine room passed out. The evil smells in the compartment were joined by the aroma of eighteen men vomiting, 'creating conditions,' wrote Wilkins, 'where it was almost impossible to exist yet there was no relief and we dared not open the hatches and clear the vessel.'[4] The cook and cabin boy were among the most sick and those with any appetite simply took their fill of whatever they could find in the abandoned galley. Soon the vile odour of raw onion and gorgonzola cheese began blending with the stench from the bilge.

Even this horror was not the final torment. As if to confirm their utter helplessness, the port engine spluttered, and then halted. There was no power to restart it. Wilkins was rueing not taking heed of the note scrawled above the engines on that first inspection back in Philadelphia. He had ordered new cylinders, but they were now on their way to Europe waiting to be fitted on their arrival. *Nautilus* was adrift in the mid-Atlantic in bad weather and low visibility, invisible to any approaching steamers on the busiest sea route in the world.

Now, after three days of radio silence and the battery nearly dead, Danenhower finally ordered Meyers to send an SOS.

'Are you a spiritualist?' Meyers replied.

'What's that got to do with it?'

'That's the only way I can think of getting a radio message off.'

'That's your problem!' barked the Captain. 'You're the engineer!'[5]

Under flashlight in the pitching sub Meyers went to work on his radio gear, turning his heterodyne receiver into a crude but effective low-powered transmitter. It emitted a whistle he could control with his key. For the next eighteen hours, working without a break, he tapped out SOS, SOS, SOS on the quarter-hour silent periods reserved for ships in distress at sea.

'Who are you?' finally came as the reply from the cargo ship SS *Independence Hall*.

Meyers tensed with excitement. His efforts on the jury-rigged gear had finally paid off, and the dim dots and dashes could be understood.[6] He logged the conversation:

'THIS IS THE SUBMARINE *NAUTILUS*.'

'WE PASSED YOU ABOUT 1900 BUT NOBODY ON DECK.'

'THERE'S GOOD REASON. WE CAN'T GET UP ON DECK WITH SAFETY, AND WE'RE JUST ABOUT TO START WALKING.'

The radio operator on board the *Independence Hall* relayed the weak signals to other ships at sea, and they were able to home in on *Nautilus*'s position. The battleship USS *Wyoming*, en route to Sweden, turned about and steamed at full speed towards the stricken submarine, while a second battleship, the *Arkansas*, also came to her aid through what was now a full-blown gale.

At one point while they waited nervously for rescue, a huge wave smashed the *Nautilus* so violently that the force tore away the bunks in the forward battery compartment, blocking Meyers from leaving his tiny radio room. Fumes from a broken bottle of ammonia nearly overwhelmed him, but he kept working as the rescue ships made an 80-kilometre dash through fog and churning seas to reach them. What power they had left was used to turn a single propeller to keep the bow toward the storm and minimise the risk of being rolled over. They watched in dismay as the battery discharged towards the red line. Once it emptied they were literally powerless, at the whim of the worsening weather.

The electrician, Arthur Blumburg, said what they were all feeling: 'We never expected to reach the other side alive. We actually abandoned all hope . . . a leak would have meant quick despatch to never-never lands . . . It was the frailest and most vulnerable craft I have ever been on.'[7]

When the great grey battleship finally appeared out of the fog on the afternoon of 14 June, Meyers was first to spot it. 'I served five years aboard the *Wyoming* and she never looked so wonderful as thru [sic] the periscope of the *Nautilus* that stormy day.'[8] But it was not the end of danger. The little submarine could easily be crushed by the huge warship, so it dared not come too close. Drenched by the heavy seas which threatened to sweep them from the deck, the men of the *Nautilus* struggled for seven hours in failing light to secure a towline.

They worked late into the night, trying to stay in the searchlight beams from the *Wyoming*, but often drifting into darkness. Several times they were able to haul in the ropes, only for the two vessels to drift apart. There was no choice but to let go or be dragged into the green swell. In their clumsy life preservers and exposed for hours to the wind and water, they didn't have the strength to hold it.

Finally they managed to secure the hawser and they fell exhausted into the cabin.

Nautilus was 1600 kilometres from the Irish coast and it would take several days to haul them there. Inside, the crew huddled like rats in whatever space they could find, the dim blue night lights giving those in their bunks a deathly hue. The few who could manage food survived on a diet of canned oysters and cold beans washed down with water from the contaminated tanks. The following morning a brave boatload of sailors battled their way over from the *Wyoming* with a welcome load of fresh bread and apples.

Towed by tug on the last stretch to Cork, they arrived on 22 June to the sound of church bells playing 'The Star Spangled Banner'. On board Wilkins gave written instructions to everyone, thanking them for their efforts under 'sustained and trying conditions' and reminding them of their contracts to say nothing to the press.

Wilkins emerged from the *Nautilus* wearing a neat suit but showing unmistakable weariness from the vicious crossing. Some men couldn't stand up properly for three days, and those who could inflicted new agonies in late-night drinking sessions at the local pubs. Meyers and Crilley journeyed to Blarney Castle and each kissed the famous stone. Meyers remembers wishing for a change in their luck.[9]

Under tow to England there were more mechanical problems, and *Nautilus* was placed in dry dock at the Admiralty submarine base at Devonport in Plymouth for repairs. Two crew members immediately quit, and two more would depart before they left for Norway. Others among the crew were heard to grumble about the ability of the frail little vessel to reach its objective.

The troublesome second mate from Chicago, John Janson, would later complain: 'I am not ashamed to say that from the time we met the storm in the Atlantic . . . every man on the vessel was scared. We all knew of the poor condition of the *Nautilus* for the work she had ahead.'[10]

As optimistic as ever, Wilkins expected the repairs to take just two weeks and 'thereafter we expect little trouble'.[11] In fact they would be delayed a month and the submarine would never perform reliably. With the Arctic summer rapidly fading, he travelled to Bergen for an urgent meeting with his science officer, Sverdrup. They agreed to push on, if only to make preliminary investigations. For now Wilkins kept news of their reduced ambitions to himself.

At Plymouth they were cheered by a visit on 15 July from a curious Prince of Wales (later King Edward VIII). Wilkins had met him in the last weeks of the war, and they shared an avid interest in technology. The Prince had been the first British Royal to fly and later went on to gain his pilot's licence. He emerged from a forty-five minute tour of the submarine with a battered hat and blackened hands.

Buoyed by the support, Wilkins set about making as many modifications to the submarine as he could afford, including removing the two-tonne hydraulic arm, which he considered a heavy and useless addition, but crucially there was neither time nor money to replace the troublesome engines. They would have to accept makeshift repairs and hope for the best.

The delays were maddening and the first casualty was the planned rendezvous with the *Graf Zeppelin*. Dr Eckener wrote: 'Even though I had delayed, I had to depart without [Wilkins], as visibility conditions in the Arctic deteriorate with advancing summer, and I could not wait any longer.'[12] It was a hint of the dangers that lay ahead for the submarine.

The day before *Nautilus* left Plymouth, the *Graf* departed from Berlin on her own epic journey north. Among its crew was a young newspaper reporter: the intriguing Hungarian-born Jew, German communist, naturalised Palestinian and British author, Arthur Koestler[13] and, surprisingly, the biggest individual sponsor of the *Nautilus* expedition, Lincoln Ellsworth.

Despite having devoted a small fortune to the submarine venture, Ellsworth had voted with his feet and decided instead to accompany the airship north – once again paying handsomely for the privilege.

Beneath the Zeppelin's silvery derrière hung a rubber pontoon capable of displacing six tonnes of water, allowing her to land at sea. Ballast water with anti-freeze coursed through her tubes like blood and central heating now warmed her interior. She was the perfect vessel for polar travel.

Now that there would be no money from Hearst, Eckener had turned to other sponsors to cover the cost of the trip, and she carried 50 000 items of mail to exchange in the far north with a Russian icebreaker. Today these letters are among the most valued in all philately. A German publisher, Ullstein, acquired the news rights from Hearst, and Koestler, writing in German for his home market and in English for the *New York Times*, sent back finely crafted descriptions of what turned out to be a hugely successful flight.

While the *Graf Zeppelin* was making its way north, Wilkins was finally preparing to make his own voyage towards the ice, planning a stop in Bergen to collect the scientists and then heading for Spitsbergen. On the eve of departing Britain, Wilkins was interviewed by his old paper, the *News Chronicle*, once again setting out his reasons for the journey and making a far-too-honest appraisal of their chances. It was an admission that would later cost him dearly, though at the time, buried deep in the report, no one seemed to notice its significance:

We have traced the connection between the tides and the moon, and we believe there is a connection between the sun and the air. But we don't really know. Fifty billion tons of air moves from the north to the south – the quantity is a figure of speech, but it serves. What causes it to move? Possibly solar activity; but again, we don't know.

We've certainly had a lot of bad luck, but maybe we've now had all that was coming to us, and it was certainly better to have it here than in the Polar seas.

Due to the lateness of the season we shall be confronted with greater difficulties than we hoped for and perhaps this year's effort will not be the best criterion of the usefulness of submarines in Arctic waters.

It is naturally a disappointment that we cannot expect to carry out the voyage completely across the top of the world, but from the beginning of our plans it has been the opinion of our scientific associates that a journey confined to Arctic waters between Spitsbergen and the pole is of greater scientific value than anything we could achieve in a hurried dash from side to side.[14]

His media sponsors would later use this admission of only a limited expedition to discredit him, and Wilkins, with increasing insincerity, would continue to insist that he was headed to the pole regardless. It lay the seeds for the drama that followed, and damaged the reputation of a man whose noble search for knowledge was incompatible with the needs of newspaper magnates.

On 27 July, from the same dock where Drake had departed to conquer the world, *Nautilus* left Plymouth, reaching Norway four days later. There was an urgency in Wilkins' comments: 'Things must be hurried . . . every hour now counts.'[15]

In Bergen he brought the scientists on board for a look at their home for the next four months: 'The first words I heard from one of them as he viewed the scientists' compartment was that he did not think it was possible to construct such a marvel of inconvenience.' Three scientists and their additional equipment now crowded into a tiny room holding the radio gear and the main ice drill. Meyers complained good-naturedly: 'Well, I don't know how we are going to get on now. Even before you came on board I hardly had room to change my mind.'[16]

One of the new arrivals was the cameraman Emile Dored, who three years earlier had been the first newsreel man to bring the world images of Wilkins after his record-breaking polar flight. Dored had seen almost as many wars and narrow escapes as Sir Hubert, and the two were kindred spirits in many ways. Employed only to film as far as the crossing to Spitsbergen, Dored volunteered to stay for the entire journey.

He kept his own journal of the expedition, and it proved to be the most straightforward and plain-spoken of all the accounts:

AUGUST 5 1931. IT WAS FAR TOO LATE IN THE YEAR TO START A POLAR EXPEDITION, BUT I BELIEVED IN WILKINS AND WAS LOOKING FORWARD TO THE TRIP. LEAVING WAS VERY MOVING. AT LEAST 300

PEOPLE WERE ON THE QUAYSIDE, AND I THINK MOST OF THEM WERE SURE WE WOULD NEVER COME BACK HOME AGAIN.[17]

In an experimental radio broadcast relayed around the globe in six languages, *Nautilus* sent a final message: 'We are now in sight of new fields in science. We shall soon be in the hands of the Gods of the Arctic.'[18]

As they left Bergen, Meyers handed his leader a confidential cable from William Randolph Hearst. It professed deep concern for the safety of the crew, and recommended the expedition be postponed:

NOTIFY WILKINS THAT I'M VIGOROUSLY OPPOSED TO HIS TRYING TO REACH POLE IN PRESENT *NAUTILUS* WHICH HAS PROVED UNSEAWORTHY AND DANGEROUSLY UNRELIABLE EVERY WAY STOP URGE POSTPONEMENT TRIP MEANWHILE SECURING BEST POSSIBLE SUBMARINE AND MAKING ADEQUATE TESTS SIGNED HEARST[19]

In light of what was to happen, it proved to be extraordinarily insincere, even for a master manipulator like Hearst.

Wilkins was not about to quit. Perhaps he had come too far to turn back, perhaps he believed he owed Hearst and Ellsworth and his other sponsors for their support. Whatever the reason, it seems he went ahead although in his heart he had already accepted the task was beyond his old submarine. In a confidential radiogram sent to London on the morning of 7 August, he summed up their chances:

WILL PROCEED NORTH FROM SPITSBERGEN FAR AS CONDITIONS AND BEHAVIOUR OF THE VESSEL PERMITS IF VESSEL FUNCTIONS AS REQUIRED MIGHT REACH POLE TWO WEEKS AFTER LEAVING SPITSBERGEN STOP CONFIDENTIAL HAVE LITTLE CONFIDENCE IN THIS VESSEL AND ITS OPERATIONS AS SUBMARINE BUT HOPEFUL IT WILL PROVE BETTER THAN NOW APPEARS. WILKINS[20]

Disarmed by Hearst's plea for delay, it was an honest report, but naïve. This was not the news his press sponsors wished to hear.

They were hardly at sea again before being battered by another violent storm. Once more the canvas bridge was washed away and the vessel began its ghastly rolling, this time swinging through 57 degrees – almost to the brink of capsizing. Shelves were torn from their lashings; the decks were littered with heavy objects crashing from side to side. Men in the starboard bunks were flattened against the steel walls of their compartment, while those on the port side spilled from the berths until they roped themselves to their bunks around their ankles and chests. Like most sailors, the crew were superstitious, and the sudden storm seemed like an omen warning them not to venture further north. Wilkins wasn't for turning.

They limped through a snowstorm and near gale into the sheltered port of Longyearbyen on Spitsbergen for a last taste of civilisation. After all the months of delay Wilkins had hoped for some luck, but it wasn't to be. The weather had been his passion since he was a boy, and as a man it had been his constant antagonist. Now it threw down yet another challenge.

On 18 August *Nautilus* left Longyearbyen with food for six months, snowshoes, tents, knives and sleds in case of emergency. Each man was issued with a Boy Scout mess kit, four pairs of socks and underwear, a pair of leather boots, a pocket compass and a pack of waterproof matches. Collectively it offered little hope of survival should they be forced to abandon ship. The darkness was already beginning to intrude upon the midnight sun and Wilkins estimated they were at least six weeks late in departing. Despite the daunting odds, he felt the familiar excitement in setting off for great adventure. He lived for these sweet moments of freedom and his spirit, quickened by the icy nip in the air, was infectious. The crew came on deck to watch the magnificent sight of the late summer glow on the snow-clad mountains of Spitsbergen. As *Nautilus* headed for the pack ice there was still hope she may yet take them to glory.

The excitement of leaving still fresh in his mind, that night Wilkins composed his most florid report yet: 'We eagerly wait to try our skill against the Icelord Borealis. Success depends largely on our choice of weapon. We believe it is the most advantageous type but can we with this particular shield of steel slip through the Icelord's fingers? Within the week our fate will be known.'[21]

Whalers had warned them to expect poor conditions ahead and ominously, just a day after leaving Spitsbergen, they encountered the first pack ice. Danenhower's navigator, Ike Schlossbach, was the first to jump onto the solid ice, while Sverdrup cracked a fine bottle of 1921 *Liebfrauenstift* to celebrate. All day snow squalls drifted in the strong northerly breeze, and occasionally they glimpsed the smothered line of a distant horizon. The temperature fell and the snow turned to tiny ice shots which audibly peppered the decks. The solid flakes stung the hands and faces of the men working outside.

The greatest concern was the heavy drifting ice menacing the propellers and diving rudders. But they made good progress inside the pack as Danenhower carefully manoeuvred them through the leads. On 20 August Wilkins wrote: 'If weather clears, we dive tomorrow.' Preparations were made and the superstructure was cleared of obstructions, but once again the vessel let them down with problems. Lake's complicated ice drill would not fully lower, and a blocked valve in the exhaust system made diving impossible until the problem could be repaired. The engineering crew worked through the night while *Nautilus* drifted with the floes.

As there was no heating in the vessel there was a pint of rum a day for every man who wanted it, but this did little to keep out the chill. The crew slept in shifts in camel-hair sleeping bags: great long fetid envelopes in which they huddled to dress and undress. The condensation, dripping off the thin-skinned hull, first soaked the bags then froze, so that they had to be attacked with a hammer to win freedom. 'The ventilation system was outrageous,' complained electrician Arthur Blumberg. 'Why we didn't all perish from suffocation will remain a mystery to me for ever. Somehow or other no one had thought of an adequate ventilation scheme, or at least they failed to foresee the uselessness of the one we had.'[22]

The foul-tasting drinking water only added to their discomfort. Sverdrup was so desperate that he confessed to drinking from the supply of distilled water that was meant for the experiments. Yet perfectly fresh water was drifting past them in the larger ice blocks. Water, water everywhere, but not a drop to drink. The perfunctory meals were prepared on an electric stove and delivered lukewarm in the galley, where the crew took turns to eat standing up.

Wilkins had his bunk in the scientific compartment above his radio operator, Ray Meyers. A veteran submariner, Meyers had decided early on that he liked and trusted Wilkins, and had effectively become his assistant and confidant. As others before, the radioman was amazed by Wilkins' uncanny ability to detect radio signals without the aid of a receiver. When he had trouble for several days making contact with the Hearst radio stations, Wilkins told him it was because the operators were busy relaying signals after a devastating earthquake in Honduras. 'Figuring the midnight sun had touched the old boy in the head, I still kept my schedules but without success.'[23] The boss seemed certain of his information, however. 'Wilkins told me that he had word as to when the station would answer me and darned if he didn't hit it right on the head.'[24]

The weather continued to worsen, and on 22 August, with heaving ice-cakes all around threatening to pierce their flimsy shell, Danen-hower took them east out of the pack to open water. Sverdrup was checking his echo-sounding equipment and he noticed a steady increase in depth. By the afternoon it had reached 2200 metres, meaning *Nautilus* had left the continental shelf and was now in the deep Arctic Basin. He was thrilled. For six years he had drifted with Amundsen on the *Maud* without ever reaching the deepest ocean. Now it had been achieved in just four days. It vindicated Wilkins' belief that the submarine was a viable platform for serious scientific research. Sverdrup, however, began to wonder if the risks justified the results. Looking back on these trying days, he admitted to a growing sense of unease: 'We didn't know what we were up against. I was convinced we would return in one piece, but I confess most openly that my conviction was based on nothing substantial . . . If I had known what the next few days would bring, I would have been singing a different tune.'[25]

The newspapers certainly weren't interested in arcane scientific data. They wanted exciting achievements to justify their sponsorship, and above all they wanted the *Nautilus* to try for the pole. That evening Wilkins received a threatening cable from Hearst's editorial manager, TV Ranck, suggesting that neither Hearst nor the *News Chronicle* in London believed he was making a serious effort to proceed north. They therefore refused to make the payment that was due to the expedition on reaching Spitsbergen.

NEWS CHRONICLE ASKS FORMALLY . . . WHETHER OR NOT YOU'LL BE ABLEOUTCARRY TERMS CONTRACT THIS YEAR . . . OF COURSE IT'S CLEARLY SPECIFIED IN CONTRACT THAT SUBMARINE ON LEAVING SPITSBERGEN WOULD DEFINITELY ATTEMPT CROSS ARCTIC TO ALASKA VIAPOLE STOP NOW APPEARS POSSIBLE THAT WILKINS CONTEMPLATES NOT VOYAGE THIS KIND BUT SIMPLY SORT LIMITED

SCIENTIFIC CRUISE . . . IT CANNOT BE SERIOUSLY ARGUED THAT THIS
WOULD BE FULFILLMENT BY WILKINS OF TERMS CONTRACT . . . NEWS
CHRONICLE UNDOUBTEDLY RIGHT AS TO CONDITIONS UNDER WHICH
PAYMENTS ARE TO BE MADE. AS OUR PAYMENTS TO YOU ARE GOVERNED
BY SAME SET OF CONDITIONS . . . WOULD BE GRATEFUL FOR STATEMENT
FROM YOU AS TO YOUR DEFINITE PLANS AND INTENTIONS REGARDS
RANCK[26]

From thousands of kilometres away the editors presumed to know what conditions were being confronted in the high Arctic. Their lack of concern for the safety of the expedition was staggering, and to withhold payment was little more than blackmail. Given that no Hearst editor would take such a decision without the boss's approval, it showed Hearst's earlier professed concern cabled to Spitsbergen was little more than a cruel charade.

Wilkins replied with some restraint directly to New York and London:

YOU WERE ASSURED WHEN WE TOGETHER THAT EVERY EFFORT MADE
REACH POLE THIS YEAR. THESE PLANS HELD SO DEPENDING ON YOUR
HONOUR EXPECT YOU MAKE SPITSBERGEN PAYMENT.[27]

For Wilkins to rely on the honour of such men seemed pointless, but equally it is difficult to believe he still intended a genuine attack on the pole – so late in the summer it would be suicidal. In any event we shall never know his true intentions, for later that day any chance he had of living up to this promise was shattered.

With the pressure mounting, Wilkins was determined to go under the ice. The weather conditions had not improved, and all day they had been battered by large chunks of ice. Danenhower insisted on moving the vessel to the edge of the pack, but Wilkins felt they would be safer deeper into the floes where the ice was more stable and less likely to trouble them. Their greatest concern was a collision that might damage the control surfaces or the propellers. Sverdrup, the only other man aboard with experience in the ice, wisely kept his head down over his instruments and stayed out of the discussion.

At 4.35 in the afternoon, the winds suddenly dropped and the swells calmed. All around them was low, even ice, not the threatening blocks they had seen in the morning. Ahead, they could see the next large opening in the ice, just 200 metres away. These were, briefly, perfect conditions for diving.

Danenhower had no intention of continuing the family tradition of tragedy in the ice. He ordered a thorough check of all the gear. The batteries had been giving trouble, but this time they had power to start the engines. The freshwater tanks had been frozen in the bitter cold, but the ballasts tanks appeared to be fine. The rudder moved freely and the bow planes were set. The stern planes, the horizontal diving surfaces by the propellers usually ran freely, but on testing the controls were impossible to shift. The commander went up and peered over the stern. To his shock, the planes appeared to be missing.

The ghastly news that the submarine had lost its diving planes flashed around the vessel. Sverdrup heard the whispers. 'I don't know how the rumour reached us – I only remember Meyers came from aft and climbed past the ice drill, the blood drained from his face. He almost did not dare to repeat the news out loud: "Doc, we've lost the diving rudders." I didn't grasp the full meaning of it at first so I just repeated: "Have we lost the rudder?" "Yes, it's gone, we can't dive – we can't get under the ice. I have to tell Wilkins." And Meyers elbowed his way forward: "Captain, we've lost the diving rudders."

'At first Wilkins didn't want to believe him: "It isn't possible."

' "Yes," choked Meyers, "Danenhower has been looking at it, and it's gone." '[28]

Sverdrup could barely bring himself to look at his friend and colleague's face. Together they had hoped for great things, to pave the way for science in a place it had never before reached. It was too cruel. Yet Wilkins showed no emotion. 'Not one muscle indicated that all of his plans had collapsed. He just put on his mittens and slowly went astern alone.'[29]

The *Nautilus* fell silent. There was just an occasional screech from a curious kittiwake flying above. No one knew what to say or do. Without its rudders, the submarine was like a car without a steering wheel, capable of movement but totally uncontrollable under water. The remaining vertical rudder meant it was still possible to navigate on the surface, but travelling further north in the thick ice would be impossible, leaving retreat as the only option. They had come thousands of kilometres, endured weeks of gut-wrenching storms and bitter cold for nothing.

Finally, the diver Frank Crilley volunteered to take a look, and with Ray Meyers feeding his line, dropped over the side into the frigid waters to inspect the damage. Meyers was concerned about the ice which was moving back towards them and might crush the diver against the hull. He gave the signal to come back up, but Crilley sent back the signal that he was all right. Meyers was still worried and gave him a second warning. This time Crilley yanked the line hard, indicating firmly that he was fine. Just as the ice began to look truly threatening, Crilley signalled to be pulled up.

As they unfastened his helmet the escaping air made a rushing sound. They knew from the look on his face what he had found, but Meyers asked the question anyway. 'How about the diving plane?'

'It's gone.'[30]

The official logs recalling this event say merely that the diving planes were 'lost', presumably broken off in a collision with the ice. To the day he died, Sir Hubert Wilkins said little about the cause of the loss, though much about its consequences. There are cryptic references over the years to the extraordinary coincidence that the planes on either side were sheered off while the vertical rudder and propellers were left undamaged; Wilkins even noted that judging by the shiny surfaces left behind, it appeared the planes had been worked up and down before breaking off. All he would say for the record was, 'It may never be told just when and how we lost our horizontal rudder.'[31] But there is little doubt about his true belief. Others on board *Nautilus* that day were not reticent about the cause or where to lay the blame. The submarine was deliberately damaged by at least one, and probably more, of the crew. Sometime before they left for the floes, probably at Spitsbergen, a hacksaw had been taken to the rudders on either side and they had been weakened with the intention of ensuring Wilkins did not proceed far into the ice.

It was a gross act of disloyalty, made by frightened men convinced that the unreliable submarine and its unstoppable leader would carry them all to their deaths. And in that judgment, the saboteurs may well have been right.

The Chief Engineer, Ralph Shaw, quite openly named the young Chicago second mate, John Janson, as the perpetrator. In a colourful report to Wilkins written in the language of a lifetime navy man, Shaw says his problems with Janson began from the first moment the former naval rating was hired in Yonkers. He called him 'an evil influence on the crew'. On the frightening Atlantic crossing, 'the only voice of dissention [sic] was that of Janson, characteristically being raised in the momentary absence of the writer, but being caught in the act, subsided immediately by just a look in the eye . . . I [was] not quite decided what to do, bust him in the jaw or send him forward for the remainder of the cruise.'[32]

Ray Meyers also believed Janson to be part of the 'black gang' of dissenters, along with 'the fellow who wound up in gaol for murder in Connecticut'.[33] This it seems is a reference to Janson's friend on board, the carpenter Harry Zoeller. We are left with no evidence of Zoeller's involvement in the sabotage, but he certainly had the character for it. In 1949 he was charged with the murder of a New York lawyer, shot during an attempted robbery.[34]

Wilkins, too, believed Janson to be the culprit, though he never named him publicly.[35] In a handwritten note the year before he died, Wilkins wrote: 'Crilley and Meyers were not the saboteurs but they knew before we returned who the three were who were not willing to go beneath the ice.'[36] The third man remains a mystery. Though it was as much an act against his leadership as against the ship itself, Wilkins seems not to have carried a personal grudge against the men. In his long years of war and exploration, he had often seen colleagues pushed beyond their limits. 'If men break under trial and strain, they must be replaced. I don't blame such men. They can't help it. I don't think I ever pity them. It's just that they're not suited.'[37]

Despite his forbearance, the discovery of the lost diving planes was for Wilkins 'the most crushing disappointment of the entire maddening trip.'[38] It meant the end of his dream with no possibility of any kind of serious dive, let alone an attempt on the pole. Yet to turn back defeated, tail between his legs, without any knowledge of the suitability of submarines for Arctic exploration, would mean utter failure. He could stand the humiliation, even the financial ruin, but this time there were many others who would also suffer.

In his efforts to fund the expedition, Wilkins had invested all his own money, more than $100 000, with personal liability for considerably more. He was prepared to lose his cash, for after all it had been spent in pursuit of his own dreams and no one had forced him to take on the risks. Lincoln Ellsworth had been exceptionally generous, but could afford to be. Wilkins was more concerned about the money he had raised from ordinary citizens who, in difficult times, had made what small contributions they could afford. He now deeply regretted the visits to Chicago schools where he had accepted pennies from children. Shackleton had once counselled him never to accept money from anyone but the rich, for they were the ones who never felt cheated. The great man had ignored his own advice and it made his failures cut all the more deeply. Now Wilkins too would pay the price. Desperate for cash to pay the mounting shipyard bills, Wilkins had called on his friends and many had come to his aid. His lawyer Harold Clark had even taken out a bank loan for $5000 on Wilkins' behalf and had apologised for not being able to offer more. The scientific institutions had been generous. All were relying on him to succeed. It was inconceivable that he would not do his best for them.

He also knew that to some extent the newspapers were right not to pay him the full amounts, though they were getting their fill of news and would likely sell even more papers on the back of his humiliation. He had been less than forthright about his intentions of going all the way to the pole and had agreed to the conditional payments. While he might have felt Hearst's plea to return had absolved him of responsibility, he had supped with the Devil and knew there would be a price to pay.

Standing alone on the bow, numb to the vicious winds, he considered the options. He must have replayed all the false steps in his mind. How could he have allowed Lake such a free hand in the reconstruction? And once the delays had made the trip to the pole impossible, he should have postponed for a year. He should have intervened in the selection of the crew. Now all their lives were in his hands, and it was clear some of them had lost faith in him.

In an eerie foretelling of his predicament, Wilkins seems to have imagined this very situation when he wrote an article for a popular magazine more than two years before departing aboard *Nautilus*:

These really vital hazards are those moments of indecision that threaten the lives of the party. At times the leader of experience will consult his men and seek their opinions, but he can never afford to be without an opinion of his own. That would be too great a hazard. Fortunately for me I have usually worked alone or with few companions, and therefore have never found it necessary to face fatal moments of indecision.[39]

This time he had many companions, though he'd never felt more alone. In those years on the ice with Stefansson he had learnt an Inuit phrase, *perlerorneq*. It described the depression many succumbed to in the emptiness of the Arctic, the overwhelming *weight of life*; to look ahead into that endless waste knowing all that needed to be accomplished and to feel defeated before even starting. He could give in to it, or he could go on. His reputation, his hopes for science, even his place in history hung suspended like the crystals of his frozen breath. All rested on that millisecond of indecision.

The moment passed. His mind was made up. The *Nautilus* would not turn back.

The crew were called to assemble on the ice and, true to his word, Wilkins asked each their opinion, though he knew their likely answer. Sverdrup remembers the reaction. 'I can, I believe, safely state that on 22 August everyone on board except Wilkins would have been willing to return acknowledging complete defeat, but he did not for one moment consider the possibility of returning . . .'[40] He meant it as a tribute, but it might just as easily be read as an indictment.

Sir Hubert's dream of crossing the Arctic Ocean was gone. At best they could now travel no further north than intrepid sailors had managed in the past. Even if he attempted to dive there was no chance of travelling any significant distance – unless he intended to die trying. Yet there was still much important data to be garnered so Wilkins reorganised the expedition to give science precedence over exploration. He could at least ensure Sverdrup was given every opportunity to complete his work. Together they spent many hours taking deep-sea oceanographic observations from the former torpedo room, converted into a pressurised diving chamber and laboratory. In here the air pressure could be equalised with the ocean pressure, and a heavy steel door dropped open to reveal the calm pool of opalescent sea beneath the sub. It sank more than 1500 metres into the abyss. 'We were unable to control [our] astonishment at seeing the bottom of the ship drop out leaving only water beneath. At such times we realize the need for trusty comrades at the controls.'

In the pressurised chamber it was necessary to keep moving the jaw and forcing a yawn, which Sverdrup found difficult, but Wilkins was used to it from his days of high altitude flying. Sverdrup described the experience: 'We went in and the substantial door was hammered down with eight blows. Crilley opened a vent and let the air pour in, to increase the pressure. I immediately felt the pressure against my eardrums, and as the pressure increased, the sensation grew worse and worse. It dinned in my ears and hurt so much that I could have shrieked.'[41]

Both of them felt their bodies swell and their senses become acute to sound and sight. They carefully lowered a metre-long steel-encased glass tube to the bottom to sample the undersea surface. Even in these ice-covered seas, they could watch its progress for hundreds of metres before it disappeared into the velvet black depths below. These were the first records ever made of the deep polar waters and they would be just part of the rich mine of information collected on the voyage. Sverdrup's reports from the expedition, which one renowned oceanographer has called a landmark in science, would later fill volumes of data, the first publications of the Woods Hole Oceanographic Institute. In vision, if not execution, the expedition was twenty-five years ahead of any other investigation in polar regions.

Mud samples from the Arctic sea bed and samples of strange sea creatures were of little interest to the general public and although Sverdrup had reason to be pleased with the results, Wilkins knew it would not help sell newspapers. Perhaps to appease his critics, he began to embellish their achievements. On 25 August he sent a despatch, printed in the *New York American* and other Hearst papers, telling the world they were 'about 350 miles from the North Pole'.[42] It was an exaggeration, placing them some 300 kilometres closer to their goal than they ever achieved. He later corrected the claim, but the mistake would be used against him by those who claimed the expedition was little more than a publicity stunt.

If so, it was certainly an uncomfortable way to gain notoriety. Ice gripped the boat inside and out. Frozen water pipes from the battery and galley tanks meant endless work for the electricians and cooks working to thaw their equipment. Above, the deck officers were exposed to the miserable, chilling winds. When the hatch opened biting blasts of air rushed into the control room and galley. Inside, shrouded in ice crystals, the *Nautilus* looked like a salt cave. The men now slept in their clothes in the sleeping bags, and even with two blankets dragged over them it was never warm. To add to their discomfort, a leak had sprung in the diving compartment and water seeped slowly through. Even Wilkins, usually impervious to such conditions, was feeling it. 'We are colder in our compartments than I have ever been in a snowhouse at fifty below zero.'[43]

He and Danenhower were searching for a break in the ice that would allow at least an attempt at diving. Together they agreed on a risky plan to take the crippled vessel into the pack, flood the forward tanks and charge the floe, forcing the nose and hopefully the rest of the sub beneath the ice-edge. It was pathetic when compared to his original hopes of travelling thousands of kilometres under the ice, but it might at least prove the feasibility of under-ice operations.

The weather continued to deny them. Wild, choppy waves rode high about the ship, carrying great chunks of steely blue ice speckled with myriad small white fragments. They were in the spawn of the solid pack ice. Ahead they could see the hard edge, glinting in the brief moments of sunshine as it rose and fell in the swell. Under motor power they moved along the barrier, turning north at every opportunity, looking for a sheltered area where they might push under the floes.

With their drills they took soundings and bottom samples, but the lashing seas rushed over the superstructure from stem to stern, making it impossible to spend any length of time on the deck. A frustrated Wilkins wrote: 'Our batteries are full and air flasks charged but even in a submarine [it is] impossible to do anything in this weather. Tonight with engines stop [we] will lie to heaving with waves hoping for improvement.'

On 29 August they were caught in dense fog and radio communications became unreliable. They traced the edge of the pack for the next three days until finally managing to find broken ice. It was the first time since the discovery of the lost rudders that they had calm seas, a chance at last to attempt a dive. Then bad luck struck once more: the main ice drill would not lower. Protruding from the deck it would prevent the submarine from sliding under the ice.

Wilkins was suspicious of sabotage: 'Again, as was the breaking of the rudder, the sticking of the drill is a "mystery" and some on board wanted to use it as an excuse for not attempting to go under the ice.'[44] But he was determined to dive, almost regardless of the consequences. The command was given to flood the main ballast. 'The floes were quiet,' Danenhower recalled, 'and the only sounds were the mewing of the seagulls and the occasional splash of a seal, as we lay between the floes ready for our first Arctic dive.'

Wilkins wrote: 'We took turns watching the water line rise up to meet our eyes through the conning tower eye ports. I could see beautiful colouring in the crystal-clear blue water. We took our time settling down . . . and after jockeying her into what Danenhower thought was the right trim, with the bow down by two degrees and our heavy glass eye ports well awash, he gave the order: "Ahead!"'

'Her bow cleaved the water like a gigantic wedge; as we neared the floe we all unconsciously braced ourselves for a shock. Crunch! Bang! Crack! She was under! Down by the bow three degrees – then four and a half, six, seven and a half!"'[45]

The noise of the ice pounding the superstructure of the boat was fearsome, leaving Wilkins 'more full of awe than anything I had ever experienced . . . It sounded like continuous thunder and the vessel trembled as if subjected to a giant earthquake. Through the portholes the water colour changed from grey to pale blue, then deep blue and violet.'[46]

The rest of the crew were terrified. Meyers recalled: 'About that time my mind was on prayers – I was repeating everything I had heard from "Now I lay me down to sleep" to the latest I had learned. Crilley shouted out in his hay-shaker drawl that he'd forgotten the most important spare part of all, "a spare set of rosary beads – I just pulled mine apart!" He was that sort of guy and knew what to say to settle a guy when the going got rough.'[47]

Those who could witness the view from the crystal eye ports were fascinated. Dored's camera rolled as they passed the jagged under-ice while the floes let loose great strings of pearl-like bubbles. The filtered light turned clear ice into massive diamonds and opals. Jellyfish floated past like tiny airships while small black fish were startled from their ice-holes by the presence of the vast, lumbering steel whale.

'Stop the motor!' Danenhower yelled. Silence, and she came to rest. As far as one could see in the crystal-blue water stretched the flat under-surface of the floe with occasional peaks and valleys. As the clouds moved across the sun above, the light changed with it, and, like some giant kaleidoscope, the colours. 'No human eyes had ever looked on this sight,' wrote Wilkins proudly.

> At last we were under the Arctic Ice, with our depth gauge reading 37 feet . . . We were under all right, for the first time in history, but could we get out again? The ice was too thick to think of breaking through it. Could we back out clear into the open water? With our periscope frozen and fogged, and without our diving rudder, we dared not keep on going ahead because if we sank too deep for our hull strength, we could not blow our tanks and we might come up against the thick ice in an unstable condition which would capsize us.
>
> 'Full astern!' Danenhower ordered. We waited breathless moments, our eyes glued to the ports. Slowly, steadily, the fascinating undersea panorama glided by as *Nautilus* picked up momentum and rose by the stern . . . suddenly brilliant sunlight flooded in through the dripping ports and we were clear of the ice.[48]

The outside world heard no more from the *Nautilus* as the radio masts had been damaged in the dive. They could, however, receive signals and could monitor the reports from the outside world. 'They gave up hope for us,' said Second Engineer Vadim Stavrakov, 'Lowell Thomas's broadcasts got progressively less optimistic.'[49] While trying out the emergency radio on an ice floe, Meyers could just make out a broadcast announcing that the *Nautilus* had not been heard from for six days and last reports said she had prepared to dive.

The Norwegian government ordered a Coast Guard icebreaker, the *Fridtjof Nansen*, to Spitsbergen to be ready for a search at short notice, and two famous Arctic flyers, Hjalmar Riiser-Larsen and Bjørn Helland-Hansen, both friends of Wilkins, were preparing to launch a dangerous aerial search from Bergen. Meyers rushed to repair the radio mast so they could send a message that all was well. The vagaries of shortwave radio, especially from such high latitudes, were still little understood and communication was a haphazard affair. It took some time to get the message through.

Two Danish ships were sent out to begin searching and all ships and amateur radio operators were asked to listen for signals from the submarine.[50] The next evening, the Norwegian Meteorological Radio Service announced that a clear message had been received from Wilkins reporting all was well aboard the *Nautilus*. In the United States the first signs of repercussions for the failed attempt at the pole were emerging. The *New York Times* reported: 'Considerable irritation was connected with the rescue preparations. The Wilkins expedition is characterized openly in Norway as a hazardous gamble with lives and . . . a daredevil stunt. The risk of sending relief expeditions was not underestimated, especially as the Arctic days are growing rapidly shorter.'[51]

For the next few days the *Nautilus* threaded its way through the pack, looking for suitable areas to make more dives, as much for the cameras as for science. Wilkins needed photographic evidence of their efforts so he and Dored rowed themselves out to a solid flow in a little collapsible dinghy and set up the cameras. They took dramatic film of *Nautilus* charging the floes and forcing her nose under the edge. With some justification some of the crew felt abandoned by their leader – though if the *Nautilus* had failed to surface Dored and Wilkins would themselves have little chance of survival.

Most of the diaries and official reports are coy about the amount of actual diving that took place. But it was clearly not very much. The electrician, Arthur Blumberg, was probably closest to the truth: 'As to actually penetrating underneath the ice? – don't let your fancy run away with your reason. The only time we really went under was once when motion pictures and still photos were planned and made . . . At no point were we submerged for any length of time during our stay in the Arctic. It was always a matter of minutes.'[52] For the most part, *Nautilus* merely parked itself beneath the drifting floes. Below them was 2000 metres of water, around them was crunching ice and above them an Arctic storm was gathering. Rolling uncomfortably in the swell, winter snowstorms closed in on them and on 4 September, Wilkins called a halt to the adventure.

'I would have liked to continue further, scraping beneath the scattered ice, but to continue to do so was considered by some on board to be too risky and too dangerous, so we pulled up beside a heavy floe, blew tanks and let the men ashore for exercise . . . An inspection of the vessel showed that some of the light superstructure forward had been dented.'[53] Vadim Stavrakov had a different opinion of the damage: 'The thin-skinned submarine couldn't take such punishment, despite the $500 000 that had been spent on her . . . Another million dollars wouldn't have made a ship of her.'[54]

What are we to make of this affair?

No one could doubt Sir Hubert's courage, but it was his judgment that had failed him this time. From the beginning of the project he had made decisions which, against his own experience, he knew would compromise the chances of success. He had let others run the planning even though this same mistake had cost him so many years of lost opportunity in his Arctic flights. He had let the demands of the press influence his choices, knowing his greatest achievements had come when he ignored them. He had put the lives of others at serious risk in pursuit of his own goals. Most unwisely of all, he had ignored the capricious power of the Arctic to crush the desires of humanity.

He had forgotten the agonising lessons of his first trip to the ice in 1913. Suffering then from a severe bout of snow blindness, he had pushed on instead of taking rest, against the wishes of his Eskimo companion, Natkusiak.

'I was young and foolish and determined to kick against the conditions and fight it out. For seven days I pigheadedly stumbled on and I don't know how I could have been so foolish as to withstand the pain.' It left him weeping with rage at being beaten by the conditions.

In retrospect it is perhaps too easy to criticise Wilkins' decision to go on with his crippled boat. In many ways he faced an impossible choice, damned which ever way he turned. Submariners share a special bond, brought on by the unique risks they face every time the hatches are sealed and the boat dives into the depths. So perhaps it is best left to a submariner to pass judgment on his actions.

James Calvert entered the submarine corps as a young man in the opening days of World War II and trained on claustrophobic pig boats like the *Nautilus*, then saw action on submarine patrols in the Pacific.

Eventually he rose to command one of the US Navy's first nuclear-powered submarines and he took it to the Arctic before retiring as an Admiral. He knew and greatly admired Wilkins. He believes Sir Hubert was wrong.

Sitting in the wood-panelled parlour of the Explorers Club in New York, a place they both enjoyed, surrounded by mementos of Wilkins' extraordinary career, Calvert shakes his head when asked the question.

'I've never understood why he decided to push on. He was just indomitable and I'm sure that to survive some of the things he did while exploring he probably had to have that personality. But most of the time he was either by himself or with two or three others. This time he had a number of lives he had to be responsible for and it was a somewhat irresponsible thing to do, to push forward – even though he may have been convinced in his own mind it would work.'[55]

Wilkins had lived and worked with great leaders like Shackleton and Eckener, and seen the folly of poor ones like Stefansson. He knew the limits of his men and the machine that carried them and was in no doubt they had been exceeded. In putting the crew's life unnecessarily at risk, Wilkins had failed the cardinal test of leadership. Though he brought his crew back alive, it was an error that cost him dearly.

On 5 September William Randolph Hearst sent another of his disingenuous messages, publishing it on the front page of the papers that were simultaneously refusing to pay Wilkins the remainder of his fee:

DEAR SIR HUBERT

I AM EXCEEDINGLY HAPPY TO HEAR GOOD NEWS FROM YOU BUT I FEEL CONTINUED CONCERN ABOUT THE WELFARE OF YOURSELF AND YOUR CREW. I MOST URGENTLY BEG YOU TO RETURN PROMPTLY TO SAFETY AND TO DEFER ANY FURTHER ADVENTURE UNTIL ANOTHER AND MORE FAVORABLE TIME AND WITH A BETTER BOAT. THE SEASON IS LATE. THE ICE IS CLOSING IN. THE NAUTILUS HAS BEEN INJURED ACCORDING TO YOUR OWN REPORT. WE ARE ALL ALARMED ABOUT THE DANGERS YOU ARE INCURRING WHICH SEEMS TO US NEEDLESS. WILL YOU NOT PLEASE COME BACK NOW AND DEVOTE YOUR ENERGIES

TO PREPARATIONS FOR ANOTHER EXPEDITION AT A BETTER TIME AND
IN A BETTER VESSEL.[56]

Wilkins ordered the *Nautilus* south, ending their three weeks in the ice. He was already dreaming of the future: 'Recognizing the lateness of the season and the fact that we required a newly equipped ship, we regretfully turned the *Nautilus* back toward Norway . . . There was no doubt in my mind that ours was but the first of a great submarine fleet that would one day cruise at will beneath the Arctic ice cap, the shortest distance between the great American and Eurasian land masses.'[57]

A fierce storm was blowing as *Nautilus* made the passage back to Spitsbergen, the worst storm since the Atlantic crossing, and the submarine, now much lighter than when it entered the ice, was again tossed fearfully about, ripping equipment, bunks and fittings from their mounts. Wilkins was thrown from his bunk in the middle of the night, hitting the steel wall with a fearful bump. The next day his ribs and left arm were black with bruises. The Arctic seemed unwilling to let them escape.

They passed through this gale, but as they returned to civilisation, another storm was awaiting Sir Hubert Wilkins. There would be consequences from this brave but failed expedition.

15
—

King of the Antarctic

The Polar regions leave a terrible restlessness in a man. You simply cannot settle down to a humdrum existence.[1]

— Lincoln Ellsworth

T he crippled *Nautilus* limped into Bergen harbour in Norway, her paintwork stripped bare by tentacles of ice, the hull battered and scarred. She made it with just a single day's fuel left in the tanks. The exhausted crew were looking forward to a warm bath and bed after five months of cold steel but before they could relax, a rumour went around that the expedition was broke and they might not be paid. There was talk of downing tools. Sir Hubert paid them out plus a month's bonus from his own pocket. It left him with $30 in his account and an accumulating mountain of debt.[2]

Wilkins intended to take the *Nautilus* back to the United States via Iceland, but Danenhower cautioned against the journey. Neither the crew nor the vessel was up to it. Unable to deliver the submarine back to the US Navy, there was no option but to scuttle it in deep water outside Bergen. While Wilkins waited for approval from the Shipping Board, the crew left for home aboard a visiting cruise liner, still divided over whether the venture had been a fiasco or a triumph. For Ray Meyers it was a sad farewell. The radioman wrote a long final despatch to ham operators all over the world: 'As I look back at our whale or long black coffin as so many pessimists called her . . . I feel like I'm deserting the best friend in the world. Goodbye *Nautilus* with all your discomforts. There will always be a warm spot in the heart of your radioman for the first submarine to penetrate the arctic ice.'[3]

Press reports about the expedition concentrated on its failure to get within 800 kilometres of the North Pole. Its considerable scientific achievements were ignored. The expedition was called a 'harebrained farce'.[4] A sarcastic article appeared in *Literary Digest* ridiculing the mission as 'Captain Nemo and his merry men'.[5] The submarine was called 'Jonah's prison', and the newspaper cartoonists were merciless. One popular magazine, which had previously touted the undertaking, now dismissed it blithely: 'There is no question that the *Nautilus*, aptly termed a "floating coffin", proved itself woefully unfitted for the purpose.'[6]

Paramount Pictures, like Hearst, refused to make the final payment on its newsreel contract, claiming Wilkins had never intended to take the submarine to the North Pole and implying the expedition had been little more than a publicity stunt. It was bizarre criticism from an organisation that intended to make money out of the expedition's newsworthiness.

To add to Wilkins' financial pressures, the US Shipping Board advised him that while it approved the plan to scuttle the *Nautilus* it required the expedition to pay $10 000 for not returning the vessel to New York.[7] There were no friends left in Washington to influence the decision. Even worse, despite Wilkins' entreaties, the board insisted on holding the hefty bond from the expedition for two years to protect itself against any legal claims.

Stripped of its useful equipment, the old submarine was towed to a deep fjord outside Bergen – where it stubbornly refused to sink. Eventually, after several attempts, its bow rose one last time and it was sent to the bottom in 350 metres of frigid water.[8] Wilkins had gambled his reputation on the rusty boat – and lost. His agents at NBC Artists Service wrote to advise him they had cancelled the planned lecture tour from which he had hoped to earn his first income in more than two years: 'In the face of the news published in the newspapers . . . relative to the failure of the Expedition in the *Nautilus*, we could no longer proceed with the booking of your tour according to our original agreement.'[9]

Despite the reaction, Wilkins remained unbowed. 'There is great satisfaction,' he wrote in his journal, 'of having done your darnedest against tremendous odds . . . even if you are beaten in the end.'[10] He immediately began planning a new journey to the Arctic in a specially built submarine. These plans, never fulfilled, were to occupy him on and off for the next decade. At times the funding seemed just within his grasp, but someone would always recall the *Nautilus* and the promises would evaporate.

Suzanne was waiting for him in London, perhaps concerned that he might have been downhearted. She found him much his usual self, already planning ahead: 'After hearing that he was lost, I was content to have him back. Because of his "failure" Wilkins went through a great deal of unnecessary suspicion, if not vilification, but it rolled off his back pretty much, as he busied himself with cutting the films he'd brought back, showing the degree of success he'd had, proving at the very least that a submarine could do what he expected and better the next time.'[11]

Wilkins' luck had not entirely deserted him. On the journey back to the United States aboard the liner *Bremen* he was invited to join two young German pilots for a flight in their catapult-launched aeroplane, part of an experiment by Lufthansa to speed up airmail deliveries. The bright red Heinkel would be launched when the ship reached within 1600 kilometres of the coast, cutting back delivery times by two days. Wilkins was keen to go but Suzanne objected. She was right. On 10 October 1931 the plane crashed into Cobequid Bay, Nova Scotia, and both pilots were killed.

A year later the expedition accounts were still heavily in the red, the majority of the money owed to Wilkins himself. Somehow he repaid the outstanding debts, leaving only a personal loan of $20 000 owed to his millionaire friend, Lincoln Ellsworth. On Christmas Day 1931, Ellsworth wrote by hand from his Fifth Avenue club, thanking Sir Hubert and Suzanne for their gift of an amber-stemmed pipe. 'I am appreciative because a pipe is about the most intimate thing there is.' He added, as if in afterthought: 'It is my desire to cancel the debt owed to me by the submarine exped. Therefore I propose that the $20,000 be transferred . . . from me to you so that the money will go to your personal account . . . I am doing it so that any money coming in . . .

will go to your use as you may desire other than submarine debts, for I do not want either Danenhower or Lake to profit by it.'[12]

It was a generous gesture, though Ellsworth had his own motives for helping to get Wilkins back on his feet financially. Their common rival Byrd, with his dubious claim to have flown to the North Pole, had robbed them both of recognition. The millionaire was convinced Wilkins was the man who could make him famous.

All his life Ellsworth had struggled for a sense of purpose in the shadow of his overbearing father. He'd had an unhappy childhood, a lonely youth, and at middle age found himself with vast amounts of money but no closer to a significant achievement of his own making. Though he had no passion for flying, the last great prize in exploration would be a trans-continental flight across the Antarctic. It now became Ellsworth's expensive obsession.

He was a poor pilot, an unproven navigator and had never seen Antarctica. He had no patience for the myriad details involved in putting together a major expedition. With Amundsen now dead, the only man alive skilled in all areas was Sir Hubert. For the next six years, Wilkins was the hired gun who prepared, sustained and delivered the millionaire to his destiny.

We shall never know precisely how the two men came together and on what terms. The crucial correspondence does not appear in their archives. We can be sure, however, that it was never a partnership of equals. Wilkins was broke and deeply indebted to Ellsworth's generosity. He needed a job and was in no position to bargain for a share of the glory. Despite personal differences and what at times became a farcical battle of competing national interests, Wilkins swallowed his pride without complaint and did all in his power to help Ellsworth succeed.

When Ellsworth departed the United States early in 1933 on a luxurious South Pacific honeymoon with his new bride, Wilkins was left to travel the world putting together the expedition. His first act was to hire Bernt Balchen as the main pilot and to supervise the preparation of a startling Northrop monoplane, the *Polar Star*. Its snub-nosed but slender body was purposeful rather than beautiful and its massive wingspan, far wider than the plane was long, gave it the look of a giant seabird. Filled to capacity, the wings held sufficient fuel for an 8000-kilometre flight – twice as long as the *Vega* could manage, and at twice the speed. Ellsworth had no interest in the details of the aeroplane, and Balchen had no interest in exploration except that explorers needed pilots. Wilkins was the glue that held this strange combination together.

With Ellsworth still on holiday, Sir Hubert went to Norway to buy the expedition's ship, an old wooden seal catcher, the *Fanefjord*. She had a small diesel motor, but retained sails fore and aft. A tiny vessel, just 400 tonnes dead weight, the only communal space was the mess room which could hold six people. Crew meetings would have to be held in the corridor. The ship was renamed the *Wyatt Earp* after the famous gun-fighting marshal.

While in Norway, Wilkins also selected the crew to take south. There was no shortage of experienced whalers happy to sail under an American flag. He also engaged the team's assistant pilot, an accomplished flying officer cadet in the Norwegian Navy, Magnus Olsen. Just nineteen, Olsen spent most of the next three years under Wilkins' direction and came to see him as something of a father figure. 'While Sir Hubert was around, there was always a feeling of security,' he wrote, and unashamedly came to call him 'The King of the Antarctic'.[13]

The *Wyatt Earp* slipped away from Cape Town on her first journey south in October 1933, heading into the foul storms of the great Southern Ocean, a test of every sailor's stomach. Heavily laden, the little ship rode violently through the canyons of spume-topped waves. She was solid, though – and once among the icebergs proved herself able. With efficient radio and a small plane to make observation flights, technology had reduced many of the dangers of polar exploration. The worst moment came when the ship was overrun by an army of fleas. It took an old sailor's trick – sewing oakum threads into the armpits and waist of garments – to force them off.

Early in the New Year, they reached the Bay of Whales at the foot of the Ross Ice Shelf. Named by Shackleton, this indentation in the massive ice cliffs of the Shelf had long been the favoured starting point for expeditions. Both Amundsen and Byrd had reached the pole from here. The *Polar Star* was winched gently onto the ice as they waited for a break in the fog to set off on the long flight.

In the early hours of 13 January, the *Wyatt Earp* began to vibrate, slowly at first, then growing in intensity. The unearthly rumbling, like thunder, confused shouts and emergency whistles brought everyone on deck. To Magnus Olsen 'ominous sounds like the tuning of a mighty orchestra' came from beneath the surface, the noise of 'cracking, ripping and breaking of miles of thickly packed ice'.[14] Glacial ice, some of it thousands of years old, was smashed to pieces like a broken plate as part of the shelf broke off, and in an instant the flat surface had become a churning tumult of shattered blocks.

The ice beneath the *Polar Star* first lifted then fell away and the plane dropped, held up only by her wings. Men tumbled over the rails into a dinghy and dragged themselves across the smashed ice to open water, then hauled the boat once again across the next chunk of ice, in a desperate bid to reach the *Polar Star* before it sank.

They were finally able to secure lines and haul it, inch by inch, towards the ship. 'There was a deathly silence as the plane was lifted up – its wings bent, skis smashed like a shattered bird. Hardly one member of the expedition was without tears in his eyes,' wrote Olsen.[15]

Once they had settled, Sir Hubert Wilkins gathered the crew into the corridor and told the men they were not to break their hearts over 'that thing on deck with the broken wings'. With his usual extraordinary optimism he added, 'So, let us say "Skol" to that and drink to our success in champagne.'

Recalled Olsen: 'The mess boy was quick to act on his cue, and suddenly appeared on the scene with bottles of champagne and enough glasses, cups and beakers to go around.'[16]

Hopes of flying that summer were dashed, but Wilkins began planning for their return. He called the men together the following day and asked for volunteers to haul a cache of fuel and supplies onto the plateau in preparation for a flight in the spring. 'He was a wonderful leader,' wrote Olsen, 'and never made decisions without giving us the opportunity either of making suggestions or of declining to undertake tasks if we felt unable to carry them out. But I think that most of us trusted Sir Hubert so implicitly that we gladly followed his ideas.'[17]

The plan meant dragging heavy barrels on sledges for 100 kilometres, a thankless, exhausting task. Wilkins would lead the party himself, and Olsen was first to put his hand up. 'My joy knew no bounds at the prospect of following this great man on the barrier . . . He rarely laughed, but when he smiled his little beard suddenly shot outwards, and then we were assured of his approval. I did not care if I had been the only volunteer; I looked up to Sir Hubert as a dog does to his master. It was a tremendous honour to serve under such a great explorer.'[18]

The history books have long forgotten this insignificant footnote in Antarctic exploration, but the journals of Magnus Olsen have left us with a wonderful portrait of Wilkins at work in difficult conditions. For ten hours each day, in temperatures 30 degrees below, they hauled the heavy sledges against the biting south-westerly wind. Hard, sand-dry drift whipped their faces and bodies. It was a gruelling struggle in the dry air and rising altitude. Five of them fanned out, with the leader pulling from the centre well out in front on a 50-metre rope. If he fell through a crevasse this left the others time to halt before being dragged in. They were four fit young Norwegians and Wilkins, at forty-seven, was more than twice their age. 'When it was the turn of Sir Hubert to lead,' said Olsen, 'we Norwegians, accustomed though we were to ski-ing, had to beg him to reduce speed as we could not keep up with him under the strain of pulling the heavy load. His strength was phenomenal . . . Sir Hubert glided along, apparently unaware of the weight dragging from his shoulders.'[19]

To save energy they barely talked. In the early evening they stopped to pitch a tent and prepare a simple meal. Warm and cosy after their tough march, the young men were keen to hear Wilkins' tales of exploring. 'I am a citizen of the Antarctic,' he told them, and unfolded the story of his struggles and triumphs in that vast southern land.

Olsen, writing many years later, recalled:

Sir Hubert Wilkins was a taciturn man, but on the rare occasions when he did talk, it was always worth listening to him. He spoke of his expedition in the *Nautilus*. Sometime, someone else, with financial backing, will succeed in carrying out the project . . . His philosophy was that every person had ideas which appeared crazy to others, and while they might be laughed at and brushed aside at the time, someone else was sure to bring it forth as his own idea, and be given the chance to carry it out.

Before he bade us good night and dropped off to sleep, he gave me a piece of advice which should be followed by all aspiring explorers.

'Remember, Magnus, you will never gain anything without either personal wealth or government backing.'[20]

Was this advice an unguarded moment of regret? He was now effectively a rich man's servant. He knew that in the United States Byrd was preparing a massive expedition, more like an assault, with the backing of the Navy. Wilkins had achieved much on his own, but the days of the privateer explorer were drawing to a close.

The expedition returned in November with a rebuilt plane, this time landing at Deception Island which, like Point Barrow in the north, had become as close to a home port as Sir Hubert Wilkins ever had. Bad weather and bad luck again prevented any chance of flying.

Ellsworth was set to give up and return home, while Wilkins, patient as always, saw the possibility of staying on to complete the flight he had not been able to achieve in 1928. All he needed was money. He secretly radioed a message to Bowman at the American Geographical Society asking him to see if finance could be found:

> December 29, 1934 CONFIDENTIAL; Ellsworth tired waiting and is packing to return tomorrow. Have not yet proposed anything to him and not sure that he would agree to any proposal, also apart from what I might personally subscribe would need about $20,000 to carry on another year or $10,000 for the rest of the season.[21]

Nothing came of the plan. In what must have been a difficult conversation, he raised the possibility with Ellsworth but the millionaire flatly rejected it, preferring to see the project abandoned rather than someone else take the glory.

The next morning the skies were clear. Ellsworth, spurred on by Wilkins' audacity, decided to chance his luck. He sent a message to the American press: 'The great adventure so long awaited is at hand . . . The opening of a continent for the last time in human history.'[22] Sadly, the outcome was an anti-climax. After two and a half hours, Balchen feared bad weather ahead and turned the *Polar Star* about against his boss's wishes. 'Ellsworth can commit suicide if he likes,' grumbled Balchen, 'but he can't take me with him.'[23] The two men would never fly together again and the expedition retreated with little to show for twelve months of work.

Wilkins had no desire to spend a further year on Ellsworth's egotistical project, and tried to talk him out of another attempt, without success. 'It has been a long drag for me,' he wrote to a friend, 'and I would be more than happy to be released from duties in connection with Ellsworth's attempt in order that I could again set about my own affairs and the building of a new submarine for arctic work. However, I gave Ellsworth my word that I would help him do the job and it is not yet done and a promise is a promise after all . . .'[24]

In November 1935 the *Wyatt Earp* returned south. Wilkins had recruited an old friend, Canadian Herbert Hollick-Kenyon, as a replacement pilot and the expedition established its base on Dundee Island at the northern tip of the Antarctic Peninsula. Twice the *Polar Star* started on its long journey, and twice it was forced back.

Keeping a promise to his young friend, Wilkins took Olsen up for a test flight in the plane. The great craft skied across the runway like an errant albatross and soared up into the air in a perfect take-off. They circled the *Wyatt Earp* and made a short hop to Snow Hill Island while Wilkins put the plane through its paces. It responded well, and he gave instructions over the radio that on return the plane should be prepared for Ellsworth and Hollick-Kenyon to leave the next day. They must have been difficult words – he knew he had the skills to take the *Polar Star* clear across Antarctica, but the honour would go to others.

After he brought the plane down, a smiling Ellsworth greeted them. He was 'so excited about the coming flight that he could hardly wait until the following day to climb into the *Polar Star*,' said Olsen.[25] The next morning at precisely 10.00 am local time, 23 November 1935, Ellsworth finally took off on his flight into history. Planned to take fourteen hours, it lasted twenty-two days, coming to an end 20 kilometres short of the Bay of Whales. After a ten-day trek, the two flyers reached Byrd's old camp at Little America and waited to be picked up. An Australian 'rescue ship' arrived just days before Wilkins brought the *Wyatt Earp* more than 8000 kilometres from Dundee Island. Help came just in time as the two pilots, although in no danger, couldn't stand one another and had passed the days of waiting in virtual silence. They were of different stuff – Ellsworth would holiday in his inherited castle in Switzerland, while Hollick-Kenyon preferred a simple log cabin without running water or electricity. Try as he may, the millionaire could never understand the lives of ordinary people. The famous Northrop plane was recovered and, being of no further use to Ellsworth, was given away. It now sits in the National Air and Space Museum in Washington DC.

Returning to the United States, Wilkins busied himself once more with preparations for a renewed submarine venture in the Arctic Ocean, even going as far as to commission plans for a purpose-built sub, which he dubbed *Poseidon*. He was desperate enough to swallow his pride and reopen communication with Randolph Hearst, sending the magnate some aerial pictures of the plateau in Antarctica he had named Hearst Land. Hearst, perhaps suspecting a request for a handout might follow, wrote back cautiously: 'It is a very pleasing plateau, but it does not seem to be a very good location for oranges. I think I prefer California as a homeland. I wish you would visit us here.'[26] They never met again.

Ellsworth meanwhile was suffering from the curse of polar explorers: the empty feeling that came after achievement. The success of the flight had done nothing to satisfy the need to prove himself, as he wrote often to Wilkins: 'The thing is I can find nothing else and so I just keep clinging on hoping for better but it doesn't seem to come . . .'[27] Wilkins, recognising the symptoms of this peculiar madness, urged Ellsworth to continue with plans for a return trip, adding, 'I can no more see you settling down and tied to a "home" for the next year or so than I can see my way to be content in "civilization".'[28] It seems both of them were at something of a loss about what to do next. Just two weeks after penning his reply, fate was to draw Wilkins into his next great adventure.

Since his astounding flight almost a decade earlier, only two planes had followed Wilkins' trail across the Arctic, both of them commanded by Russians. In June 1937 a plane whipped out of Moscow and landed, almost before the world knew it had started, in Washington State. Only a few weeks later another plane flew a record distance over the North Pole and landed in California. The Soviets had now established the lead in the Arctic and on 12 August their greatest aviator, Sigismund

Levanevsky, taxied a giant four-engined Tupolev heavy bomber down a Moscow runway headed for New York. On board were five crewmates. It was a flight the Russians hoped would be the precursor of regular passenger services between the great cities of the Northern Hemisphere.

The next day, Levanevsky's plane disappeared, leaving behind only a faint radio message that indicated engine trouble. For days Moscow bluffed, hoping to receive news from its missing aviators. On Sunday the 16th, Sir Hubert Wilkins received word from the Soviet Embassy in Washington DC: would he be prepared to lead a search for the men from the American side of the Arctic? Within a day he had secured a big twin-engined Catalina flying boat for the search, by Tuesday he had a crew and by Thursday he was in the air headed for Alaska. Over the next seven months he led the most sustained and difficult aerial search ever conducted, a campaign that must be considered equal to any of his other achievements, on behalf of six men he never knew.

Between September 1937 and March 1938 Wilkins flew over 70 000 kilometres under what he described as 'heartbreaking conditions of almost continuously bad weather'.[29] Much of the time he and his men were flying over uncharted ocean through the perpetual dark of an Arctic winter. For hundreds of hours they navigated by moonlight, something never before attempted let alone accomplished. In the diamond clarity of the Arctic air, the full moon was reflected from the frozen sea with enough intensity to illuminate their charts. It cast strange shadows on the lifeless ice and left the eyes feeling oddly numb – whether from fatigue or fear, they never knew. If the weather was clear, they could risk ten flying nights a month in the spectral lunar light. As one commentator put it, they were searching for one needle in ten thousand haystacks.

These flights were among the most dangerous of Wilkins' career. The search team faced not only the unknown conditions but also their own limits of endurance. On 14 March Wilkins and his friend Herbert Hollick-Kenyon flew a mission of almost twenty hours over 4500 kilometres on instruments alone – a distance greater than his record flight across the Arctic. They made it back home with fuel for just ten more minutes of flight.

Alone in New York with little news, Suzanne was more worried than ever before. She received occasional shortwave messages through

New York Times radio operator Reginald Iversen but they did little to calm her nerves. In a speech she titled 'Is It Worth It?' Suzanne wrote of the tension of being alone and expecting the worst: 'No waiting was as nerve-racking and as tense as my waiting here in the apartment . . . I realized that every hour might spell the doom of the Russian flyers, yet my heart was weeping with the worry lest my husband take a blind chance against insurmountable difficulties and add his name to the long list of martyrs devoured by that capricious tyrant – the Arctic.'[30]

On days when they could not fly because of the weather, Wilkins would impatiently pace the snow gazing into the stormy skies, hoping for a break through which they might risk taking off. He knew what it was to be lost on that ice, with the world giving up hope of safe return. These leaden hours dragged by in slow agony. Somewhere out there the Russians may be injured or starving, cradling dying colleagues in their arms, suffering the vicious bite of unimaginable cold. The slow murderous cramps of hunger might be driving them towards madness. As the months went by without any sightings, he could only hope they had been delivered a merciful death.

At home, Suzanne understood the torments Hubert must be enduring. 'Oh, how I wished that I could be there and at least touch the hand of my husband and comfort him, tell him about the ever returning dear guest: the morrow . . . How many times I have awakened Mr Iverson [*sic*], that trusty and ever alert wireless operator of the *New York Times* . . . "Any news? Any hope?" "No".'

Despite the Herculean efforts of Sir Hubert and his men, no sign of the Russians was ever found. Their disappearance remains one of the many unsolved mysteries of Arctic exploration.[31] In June 1938, Wilkins was invited to Moscow by Stalin, and at the Kremlin received the Soviet Union's highest honours from its most powerful diplomat, the Commissar for Foreign Affairs, Maxim Litvinov. Sir Hubert addressed the Soviet Academy of Sciences and was given a grand tour of the capital and Leningrad, travelling on one of the first Intourist vouchers (no. 53) – a souvenir he kept. It entitled him to a room in the best hotel (with private bath where available) three meals and afternoon tea in first-class restaurants, all transportation and the services of a guide–interpreter. This time there was no record of him engaging in 'unorthodox' activities as on his last visit to the Kremlin.

*   *   *

The search for Levanevsky was notable for another reason: it marked the beginning of Wilkin's experiments with the paranormal. He had long been intrigued by the possibility of what today we would call extra sensory perception. As a boy among Aboriginal people he had noticed they seemed capable 'of knowing of some event which was taking place miles beyond their range of sight and hearing'.[32] He had met and talked with Sir Arthur Conan Doyle about spiritualism, and had witnessed demonstrations of clairvoyance. So when an acquaintance in New York, the writer Harold Sherman, approached him with the idea of conducting a controlled experiment on thought transference, he was intrigued.

As Wilkins prepared for the Arctic search flights, Sherman proposed that he try an experiment in transmitting his thoughts back to New York by means of telepathy. Sherman would record the flyer's impressions as he received them, seal them and send them to an independent party for later comparison with Wilkins' diary.

'Fantastic?' wrote Wilkins. 'I thought not. I had long pondered over the possibility of the civilized mind, after determined exercise and development, responding at will to the thought and influences of others. Here was an opportunity to throw some light on these little understood powers of the mind.'[33]

Three nights a week, between the hours of 11.30 and midnight New York time, 'I would, wherever I might be, attempt to project thought impressions of what was happening to me . . .' Sherman in New York sat in the darkened study of his apartment on Riverside Drive and wrote down his 'readings'.

'It soon became apparent that Sherman, in some manner not understood by us, was picking up quite a number of thought forms – strong thoughts emitted by me,' wrote Wilkins.

The experiment continued for months, and various psychic investigators came to watch the proceedings, among them Dr Alexander Edmund Ronald Strath-Gordon: a scholar, soldier, doctor, diplomat, linguist and Egyptologist. In a statutory declaration submitted as part of the evidence of the experiment, he wrote:

In many years of study and research all over the world, in the field of mental and psychic phenomena, I have never observed such continued clarity and exactness of telepathic vision as that demonstrated by Harold Sherman. To witness his receiving and recording thoughts or thought forms, is to give one the feeling that Mr Sherman is taking what amounts to dictation from some invisible intelligence.[34]

Wilkins, too, was impressed by some of the remarkable coincidences contained in Sherman's records. 'When we finally were able to compare notes, what did we find? An amazing number of impressions recorded by Sherman of expedition happenings, and personal experiences, reactions and thoughts of mine. Too many of them were approximately correct and synchronized with the very day of the occurrences to have been "guesswork".'[35]

The full results of this fascinating experiment were published in 1942 in a book jointly authored by Wilkins and Sherman, *Thoughts through Space: A Remarkable Adventure in the Realm of the Mind*.[36] Largely because of the war, it went unnoticed at the time; however, since then it has become something of a cult classic. The authors claim to have achieved more than 60 per cent of coincidence in their accounts of the expedition.

Whatever we make of them, the examples amount to the first detailed account of a sustained telepathy experiment. Each night, Sherman sealed his impressions and sent them to Dr Gardner Murphy, a psychologist at Columbia University. Murphy had long been interested in the subject and had initiated the first telepathic experiments through wireless in Chicago and Newark. He found the Wilkins–Sherman results intriguing, amenable to coincidences but with marked exceptions that were inexplicable. Among them:

On Armistice Day, 1937, Wilkins attended a formal ball in Saskatchewan after being forced to land in Canada by bad weather. Always fastidious in his dress, Wilkins was troubled about the borrowed dress suit he had to wear, for the waistcoat did not quite meet his trousers. Those at the ball included army men, Mounties and provincial leaders and their wives.

That night, Sherman recorded the following message: 'You in company with men in military attire – some women – evening dress – social occasion – important people present – much conversation – you appear to be in evening dress yourself.'

On the night of 7 December Wilkins was at his old haunt of Point Barrow when an alarm rang. One of the houses was on fire. He went to the window to see it blazing in the night. That evening, 5000 kilometres away in New York, Sherman recorded: 'Don't know why, but I seem to see a crackling fire shining out in the darkness – get a definite fire impression as though a house burning – you can see it from your location on the ice . . .'

Two days later, Wilkins gave a talk to Barrow schoolchildren. Sherman's notes accurately recorded the scene.

These and many other instances show a pattern that seems beyond coincidence. 'We may not have proved that telepathy between two people at some distance apart is beyond doubt,' wrote Wilkins, 'but I was personally pleased to have been engaged in the experiment, and feel that we have proved that the subject is entirely worthy of much further attention.'[37]

Sherman, who would go on to publish many books about telepathy, wrote:

> The laws of chance against my exactly determining at any given moment what was happening to Wilkins, of what event he might be witnessing, were astronomical. Yet, to the increasing surprise of both Wilkins and myself, as our experiments progressed, it was found that my recorded impressions were maintaining a high degree of accuracy.[38] Our experiments convinced Wilkins and myself that humans are still in the kindergarten of their own mental processes – that few of us yet begin to sense our possibilities for development and attainment – that Man has a much higher destiny than he has realized or imagined.[39]

Such studies were certainly beyond the scientific pale then, and would be considered even more so today. It is a mark of Wilkins' courage that he pursued and published the results despite having little to gain and much to lose by involving himself in the experiment.

*   *   *

At the Imperial Conference of 1937 to mark the coronation of Britain's new king, a Polar Committee under the chairmanship of the Australian treasurer, Richard Casey, recommended that the Dominions cooperate in establishing permanent weather stations in the Antarctic. According to polar historian RA Swan, 'the idea of setting up permanent meteorological stations was a triumph for Sir Hubert Wilkins who had long advocated such action.'[40] It was vindication at last for his many years of work and he might have hoped that it would help garner financial support for his new submarine venture. The world, however, was more concerned with the gathering clouds of war and Wilkins found no takers. So when Lincoln Ellsworth came calling for another expedition, Wilkins once more agreed to arrange it for him.

This final trip together was never an easy affair. Ellsworth had no real objective other than making a grand flight via the South Pole. It had all the hallmarks of Shackleton's pointless last expedition aboard the *Quest*, with the additional problem that Ellsworth was jealous of Wilkins' ability to garner his own headlines. The heroic mission in search of the Russian flyers had gone some way to re-establishing Wilkins' reputation, and the favourable press he received irritated Ellsworth. According to records found by Ellsworth's biographer, Beekman Pool, the American was not pleased. 'Please stop press notices and photographs of yourself in connection [my] expedition,' he cabled indignantly.[41] When Wilkins thought it best not to reply, another cable followed: 'Think advisable we do not stay in the same hotel.'[42] Wilkins' reply was diplomatic: 'Having much work *Wyatt Earp*, propose living aboard.'[43]

As before, Sir Hubert got on with the complex job of preparing a polar expedition while the millionaire went on holiday, this time a five-week safari to Kenya, before joining the *Wyatt Earp* in Cape Town. Behind the scenes, however, events were taking place that would see both men on opposite sides of a diplomatic standoff just as the world was moving towards global conflict. At stake was the question of who owned Antarctica.

The status of the southern continent had long remained unresolved. Many nations had claimed territory there, but these claims went unacknowledged by rival powers. As a relative latecomer, the United States made no official claims nor recognised any others. It reserved the right to go wherever it wished on the continent without restriction.

But in the charged diplomatic atmosphere of the late 1930s, the situation changed. A fourteen-page US State Department memorandum, so delicate that it remained classified for nearly twenty years, proposed that the United States join the race in spite of existing international laws.[44] The American Consul in Cape Town advised Ellsworth he was to assert claims to any unexplored land on behalf of the United States, regardless of whether or not it lay in territory already claimed by another nation. However, he was told the government's involvement must remain secret and it would disavow any knowledge of his actions should they be discovered in advance. Ellsworth was not even given a copy of the instructions for fear they may become known to a foreigner.[45] It is clear they meant Wilkins, for the land in question had already been claimed by Australia.

Ellsworth accepted his clandestine assignment with enthusiasm. As his biographer and friend Pool put it: 'Thus, with secret State Department encouragement, private citizen Lincoln Ellsworth set out to assert claims on land that he knew his Australian shipmate and expedition adviser Hubert Wilkins regarded as Australian.'[46]

Sir Douglas Mawson had claimed the territory on the Davis Sea coast of eastern Antarctica for Australia and the Empire, though heavy pack ice prevented him stepping ashore. It was from here, near the present Australian base of Davis, that Ellsworth intended to launch his flight across the diameter of the Antarctic Circle.

As they headed south into the foaming seas of the Southern Ocean, they battled furious storms for sixty-five straight days, the worst weather any of them had ever encountered. Ellsworth carried his secret with increasing discomfort. Wilkins had, after all, been his loyal adviser. On 7 January the American finally unburdened himself, showing Wilkins the copper cylinder he had prepared at Cape Town, admitting he intended to set foot and claim the land Mawson had only seen from the coast.

Wilkins now faced his own dilemma, having to balance his allegiance to his country with his role as paid adviser to an American expedition. Patriotism took precedence over practicality, as Wilkins too had secret instructions from his government to enter, explore and report on 'Australian territory'. The day after Ellsworth's disclosure he took the initiative, going ashore on some small islands supposedly looking for geological specimens. Here, with the assistant pilot JH

Lymburner as witness, he raised the Australian flag. The next day he took a small boat fitted with an outboard motor and landed on the mainland at the western end of the Vestfold Hills and repeated the ceremony, leaving a record of his visit wrapped in a copy of *Walkabout* magazine.[47]

Meanwhile the weather made it impossible for Ellsworth to attempt anything but a short flight in which he dropped an American flag and made a claim for the United States. On 12 January Wilkins radioed a confidential message to government officials in Canberra, urging Australia to establish a winter base in order to challenge Ellsworth's claims. He sought £15 000 to purchase all Ellsworth's equipment, and offered, without consulting Suzanne, to set up the base himself. The government found the idea of bases too expensive, but at Wilkins' suggestion agreed to make an offer to purchase the *Wyatt Earp* to raise the Australian flag over Antarctica in a more permanent sense.

These battles over empty icelands, conducted within the claustro-phobic confines of a little ship at the end of the Earth, seem slightly ridiculous when set against the events sweeping the world to war. In Europe the Spanish Civil War was reaching its bloody climax and Hitler openly called for the annihilation of Jews. In Asia, Japan declared a New Order and strengthened its occupation of China. Yet even distant Antarctica could not escape the gathering storm.

Norway, suspicious of Ellsworth's claims and worried about its whaling fleet, laid claim to 20 per cent of the Antarctic coastline. Wilkins' once jovial host in Berlin, now Air Chief Marshal Hermann Goering, cast his opportunistic eyes on the map of Antarctica and sent a Nazi expedition in search of new territory. Just days after Ellsworth's last flight, two Dornier flying boats reached the coast of Queen Maud Land and in a single week surveyed more than 600 000 square kilometres, dropping aluminium darts topped with swastikas over what they called 'Neu Shwabenland'.

The Nazi expedition marked the end of the land grab in the Antarctic. The world was consumed by crisis and the *Wyatt Earp*, instead of returning to raise an Australian flag, was put to use as a munitions ship. The days of the private expedition were over. When exploration resumed after the war, the expeditions were government financed and supported, more interested in science than subjugation. Slowly the world moved towards one of the triumphs of international governance, the Antarctic Treaty of 1961, which ensured the peaceful scientific management of the continent on behalf of all.

In March 1939 an Australian diplomat visited the State Department in Washington and commented, only half in jest, that he hoped Wilkins wouldn't be tried for high treason.[48] In fact after the war the United States embraced Sir Hubert, welcoming his unparalleled experience.

The post-war years were less kind to Lincoln Ellsworth. Well into his sixties and sliding into dementia, he dreamed of returning to the Antarctic, and continued to seek Wilkins' help in organising phantom expeditions that would never start.

Ellsworth's sad decline – he was a victim of the peculiar polar obsession that had killed Scott, ruined Shackleton, and gripped Amundsen and Byrd – was example enough to Wilkins. Perhaps it was his spiritual dimension which helped fill the void that left the others so emotionally hollow. He ended his days still exploring and travelling, busy to his final moments, at peace with himself and the world.

Restless years

Let us, then, be up and doing,
With a heart for any fate;
Still achieving, still pursuing,
Learn to labor and to wait.
               – from 'A Psalm of Life', Henry Wadsworth Longfellow

H e was an elderly man with tired, milk-blue eyes, thinning grey hair and a slow, soft way of talking. At seventy-three, Dr Frederick A Cook's days of exploring were long gone, lost in a fog of controversy and rancour that still simmers even today, nearly a century after it began. Depending on where you stand, he is either the great martyr of exploration or its greatest fraudster. Cook's career of fine achievements is completely overshadowed by his role in two magnificent hoaxes.

Wilkins had long wanted to meet Dr Cook, and their lunch together in November 1939 marked something of rehabilitation for the old man. It was organised by several members of the Explorers Club, which had banished Cook thirty years earlier for his claim to have climbed the tallest peak in North America, Alaska's Mt McKinley. It was harsh treatment for a former president of the club, but among explorers the crime was great. There is little convincing evidence to suggest Cook got within 3000 metres of that awesome summit. Cook was given the chance to defend himself before a committee of his peers, delayed, then disappeared, only to emerge two years later with an even more astounding claim: that he had been first to reach the North Pole. This time he threatened the reputation of the club's new president, Admiral Robert E Peary, the man whom history says won the race to the pole. Cook said he beat Peary by a year, though once again had scant evidence to prove it. A long and bitter argument ensued, fought by zealous partisans on both sides. Eventually it was the Admiral who won, though skirmishes continue to this day. As long as the fearsome Peary breathed, the disgraced doctor would never again set foot in the Explorers Club.

Peary needn't have fretted. For seven years Cook went no further than the cells of Leavenworth Federal Penitentiary. Gaoled for financial fraud, his wife divorced him and his ruin was complete.[1] Even on the day of the luncheon with Wilkins, a decade after his parole, he was still not forgiven and the meeting was held on neutral ground in the dining room of the New York Athletic Club's summer house on Long Island. Peary had been dead for nearly twenty years, and a couple of the Admiral's former crew were finally prepared to meet with Cook and discuss old times. He'd been living in poverty for years, supported by his fanatically loyal daughter Helene, and Wilkins had come to tell him that it was time to bury the past. Cook's portrait and that of Peary, two men forever linked with the North Pole, were now hung side by side in the Explorers Club in recognition of their genuine contributions as Arctic pioneers.

The old man was gratified, but unrepentant. 'I reached the Pole. I climbed Mount McKinley. The controversy from my angle is at an end,' was all he would say on the matter.[2] He wanted to move on in the little time he had left. Exploration would continue to the end of time, 'but most of all we have got to explore this area,' he said, tapping the top of his head. 'This area here – that lies back of the eyes and between the ears. When the cranial sphere is fully explored men will have no reason to fight wars.'[3]

Cook's words struck a deep and resonant chord in Wilkins. Even before his experiments in ESP he had spent much time pondering humanity's long journey to consciousness. His studies in philosophy and his observations of the spiritual dimension of ancient races had forced him to ponder long-forgotten powers of the human mind – and what lay beyond. How many times had he confronted the mysterious force of nature and felt the presence of something much greater than himself? Increasingly he came to see the borders of traditional science as barriers to the progress of humanity. Having conquered the hidden places, it is hardly surprising that his endless curiosity would take him on a journey well beyond the known world.

In the 1920s these questions began to coalesce around the strange events taking place inside the walls of a dull three-storey greystone in the genteel streets of Lincoln Park in Chicago. A short walk from the zoo and the beaches of Lake Michigan, this was the home and office of a well-respected surgeon and professor of psychiatry, Dr William S Sadler. Every Sunday afternoon a group of people, many of them well known in the city, gathered here to discuss a remarkable finding Dr Sadler had been investigating for years.

Sadler was well known as a debunker of the so-called psychics and mediums who claimed to be in touch with the spirit world. He consulted experts, magicians and even Harry Houdini to prove these mystics were either dishonest frauds or deluded. However, there was one case he had been studying whose authenticity he could not shake, no matter how he and others tried to disprove it. In a secret location in the city, there was a man who often fell into a deep sleep, and began speaking and writing a complex and deeply philosophical story about the origins of humans and our place in the universe.

Sadler never revealed the identity of the man, though some have speculated it was his brother-in-law. The man himself, however, was seemingly irrelevant, as he had no memory of the events taking place while he slept; it was the wisdom he revealed while in his trance that was significant. 'Its philosophy is consistent,' Sadler wrote. 'It is essentially Christian, and is, on the whole, entirely harmonious with the known scientific facts and truths of this age. In fact, the case is so unusual and extraordinary that it establishes itself immediately, as far as my experience goes, in a class by itself, one which has thus far resisted all my efforts to prove it to be of auto-psychic origin.'

The communications appeared to come from 'a vast order of alleged beings who claim to come from other planets to visit this world, to stop here as student visitors for study and observation when they are en route from one universe to another or from one planet to another.'[4]

Over 200 sessions and eighteen years Sadler collected the hand-written notes the man produced while under the influence of these celestial visitors. He had these typed out and locked the originals in a safe. Yet every time he returned to the safe, the original notes had disappeared. In total he collected many hundreds of pages of typescript and it was these that the Sunday meeting group came to discuss. Sworn to secrecy, this gathering came to be known as 'the Forum'. Each week they would ask questions about the meaning of the text, and, sure enough, the answers from the visitors came back in the next lot of handwritten notes.

In 1939 an inner circle of the Forum, known as 'the Seventy', volunteered to study the papers in more detail. Sir Hubert Wilkins was one of them. Over a period of years, the Seventy received several more written communications from a personality calling itself 'the Seraphim of Progress attached to the superhuman Planetary Government of Urantia'. Wilkins, like the others, kept these discussions confidential. No notes on the papers could be taken from the Chicago house, and Wilkins would return many times over the years to add comments and questions in the notebook he stored there. Not even Suzanne was aware of his work. Eventually from these long years of study *The Urantia Book* emerged in 1955, weighing more than two kilograms, it runs to 2097 mind-numbingly complex pages. It is a rich and complex moral narrative, equal parts Tolkein and St Paul. It does not lend itself easily to a brief summary.

The Urantia Book does not present a complete religion or a creed one is required to believe in. It is, in short, a story that explains the origin of our universe and the activities of the advanced beings that populate it. From these stories, there are meanings to be found for humans. It includes descriptions of an interplanetary community replete with complex history, mythology, philosophy and guidance from the 'superhuman Planetary Government of Urantia'. There are many narratives, even discussion of a court case between Gabriel and Lucifer. To sceptics, the chapters read like the most colourful science fiction, while for believers they provide a kind of space-age Gnosticism, updating Christianity and other world religions.

The Urantian movement, which still exists, does not actively proselytise beyond a brotherhood of community organisations that meets to discuss its findings and revelations. It is active on the fringes of the Internet, though it has had its share of internal disagreements, including some lengthy court proceedings over copyright ownership of the book (now determined to be in the public domain). If it is a cult, then it is a benign one. There is no coercion, no authoritarian personalities growing rich on the donations of followers, no hidden retreats or doomsday mongering. Its main appeal is intellectual: a colourful philosophy that seeks the peaceful development of society. Even its harshest critics, like the arch-sceptic Martin Gardner, conclude its worst sin may be plagiarism.[5]

Sir Hubert Wilkins became a steadfast supporter of the Urantia movement, and his cheque for $1000 was the first money to go towards the publication costs of *The Urantia Book*. According to Dr Sadler, it became 'Sir Hubert's personal religious philosophy. He came to see us [in Chicago] every year or two, spending two or three weeks reading, studying and making notes.' Wilkins would read for up to ten hours a day then spend long evenings with Dr Sadler and his wife in 'very deliberate discussions of the teachings of the Urantia Papers'.[6] Asked once by a Urantia devotee how he tested the validity of the book, he responded succinctly: 'Its utter consistency with itself.'[7]

The movement's lack of a formal structure appealed to him. It required solitary contemplation to absorb the huge book, and that suited his nature and increasingly deaf ears. In the few years he lived after the publication of the book, Wilkins carried the massive work on his long travels, even to the Antarctic. In 1957, visiting the US base at Little America during the major exercise Operation Deep Freeze, Wilkins bunked with a navy helicopter pilot, James Waldron.

'He always seemed to be reading from a Bible-sized book,' recalled Waldron, 'and when I questioned him about it he told me that he belonged to a "religion" that welcomed only a handful of members from each world throughout the universe. He considered himself to be one of the fortunate few who had been selected to belong to this extraordinary cult. He believed that the various members of this "religion" communicated telepathically over the vastness of space. He was more than convinced that this "religion" was no hoax. Of course, I didn't challenge his beliefs.'[8]

Wilkins' interest in the inexplicable origin of humanity may have had a far greater consequence than he could ever have imagined. Just two weeks after his lunch of reconciliation with Dr Cook, Wilkins was holding court in the wood-panelled lounge of the Explorers Club.

Though never prone to boasting, and generally reluctant to talk about his beliefs, in the confines of the club he was happy to answer questions when asked. Listening eagerly to his many stories was a likeable former Eagle Scout and promising writer of adventure stories for magazines like *Thrilling Westerns* and *Super Science Stories*, Lafayette Ronald Hubbard.

The young adventurer recorded in December 1939 that he was thrilled to meet the famous explorer and his colleagues who 'made me much at home'.[9] It began a long association with those who, in Hubbard's words, 'had to be big or made to fall before the unknown'.[10] He became a full member of the exclusive club the following year.

L Ron Hubbard later became famous as the author of bestselling science fiction novels full of . . . well, religious philosophy, all-knowing celestial beings, colourful cosmology and titanic inter-galactic struggles. However, he is better known today as the founder of the Church of Scientology.

An intriguing comparison can be drawn between the teachings of Urantia and what is publicly known about the beliefs of higher-level Scientologists. Both seek to explain the contemporary human condition in terms of an ancient struggle that was waged across universes whose geography and history each belief system describes in great detail. Scientologists claim the crucial moment came at the 'Fourth Dynamic Engram', when an evil galactic emperor called Xenu used Earth – called Teegeack – as a dumping ground for billions of excess citizens, freezing their inner spirit – Thetans – and burying them inside volcanoes. Urantians call the revelations of their book the 'Fifth Epochal Revelation'. Earth is Urantia, presided over by a planetary prince called Michael, and humans contain a fragment of God within them, called the 'thought adjustor'.

There are many parallels between the two beliefs, not the least of which is their emergence in the eastern United States in the years after World War II. The Urantians came first, but differ from the Church of Scientology in some important ways. *The Urantia Book* offers no church, does not claim to be the received wisdom of one man, nor hides its mysteries in a set of teachings that are costly to acquire. The book is freely available on the Internet and its followers have only sued each other, not outsiders. Today Scientology is a hugely profitable enterprise with a global infrastructure, while the Urantia movement has not moved far from Dr Sadler's house in Chicago, which remains its headquarters. What Sir Hubert Wilkins and the attentive L Ron Hubbard discussed about religious philosophy will never be known for sure. It's clear, though, that the young acolyte didn't need to learn about making money.

When Wilkins returned from a trip to South Africa in the summer of 1939, Suzanne had a surprise for him. She had heard of an abandoned farm for sale in the north-east corner of Pennsylvania, deep among the maple forests of the Endless Mountains in Susquehanna County. The little house was at the end of a dirt track, standing on 43 hectares of undulating hills with not a neighbour in sight. It reminded her of the countryside where she had grown up in Victoria and she bought it after one look. 'I handed him the Deed as a welcome home present and hoped for the best.'

Woodchucks and field mice had taken over the living room, there were no windows and sunlight poured through the roof. It had never been connected to electricity or the telephone. 'But it was a house on a hill and there was lots of water all around,' said Suzanne. 'It was an ideal place to store all of Wilkins' treasurers, books, odds and ends of exploring equipment, and Lord knows what else. It had a wonderful smell, some ghosts I'm sure, and absolute serenity.'

Sir Hubert liked it immediately and it became the only house he ever owned. 'The world had been his home for forty years, and a rented apartment and a club. This was a home, or soon to be one,' wrote Suzanne.[11] They named it Walhalla after her home town, and that autumn, as the hills turned a blazing red and the swallows and purple martins began gathering in flocks for their migration, they rebuilt it together. He'd always enjoyed the sweat of good labour and found he had a talent for carpentry that came as easily as his sureness with machines. Friends came to visit and help, and in the still evenings Suzanne dressed up and acted out pantomimes and games to keep them amused. It was as close to peace as he had ever known.

Wilkins was sitting atop a hired bulldozer, gouging out the five-hectare lake he planned in the narrow valley running down from the house, when Suzanne arrived from New York with the newspapers.

She ran towards him crying, for she knew the news would end their brief idyll. The world was at war.

It was inevitable that Wilkins would volunteer for service in Australia or Britain, and equally inevitable that at fifty-one he would be politely turned down. As ever, he refused to give up and turned his efforts towards encouraging Americans to support Britain. With prominent aviators such as Lindbergh deeply opposed to the United States becoming involved in the war and a heated presidential election under way, it was a difficult task which he approached with his usual ambition and imagination. In Detroit he met again with the auto industrialists who had helped him in the 1920s and won their support for a mission to Europe to investigate how their factories could be used to supply the British war effort.

Europe was burning as Wilkins boarded a Boeing Clipper flying boat in Baltimore bound for Lisbon. He arrived with the Nazi Blitzkrieg at its most furious. Norway, Denmark, Holland and Luxembourg had fallen and five German divisions were bearing down on Paris. Armed with a letter of introduction from the American air attaché in Lisbon, on 10 June 1940, the day Italy entered the war, Wilkins entered what remained of free France.

The countryside was in chaos, the roads choked with refugees and retreating soldiers. It was the madness of Passchendaele repeated. The Channel ports had already fallen to the German Army, blocking Wilkins' escape by sea. On 14 June Paris fell without a shot being fired and the French Government collapsed. His only chance now was to get out by air, and he managed to talk his way onto a French aircraft transport fleeing to Britain. It was an unexpectedly short flight.

For Suzanne, the news came as a shock. 'It was only through the Press that I learned that he had been shot down, flying as a passenger with some French officers, by a German fighter.' The plane came down in a field and Wilkins spilled out with a load of silver and the personal loot the fliers were hoping to take with them. Suzanne later recounted:

He brushed this off as a great lark, as though he hadn't had another near miss, managing to see the pathetic humour of the French officer marooned in the field with considerable wealth but no way out. Wilkins helped them to collect it and hid it in a ditch when the Germans came back to strafe them. Then, being more intent on

getting to England, Wilkins paid his respects, wished them luck and
went off on a bicycle he commandeered, later arriving in England by
RAF plane.[12]

He got out of France on 16 June aboard one of the last RAF aircraft
operating from French soil, the same day General de Gaulle escaped to
England to become the exiled leader of the Free French Government.
Wilkins' only recorded comment on this narrow escape was written
after the war, in a few blithely dismissive lines written in his résumé:
'Visited Europe on behalf of the US Aviation Industry. Was entrapped
by the Germans when they captured the city of Paris. Crashed in
French airplane while attempting to escape; later walked and cycled
through German lines to Nantes and eventually reached England.'[13]

In London he met with Lord Beaverbrook, then serving as a Cabinet
Minister for aircraft production. He'd known Wilkins since World
War I when, with Hurley, Wilkins had been taking pictures on the
Western Front. The minister arranged for Wilkins to get passage back
to the United States with a message for the air companies: Britain was
desperate and needed planes, or the war was lost.

Wilkins returned on a refugee ship under threat from submarine
attack. It was a repeat of his epic journey to the frontlines in the Great
War, except this time he was travelling in the opposite direction.
Among those on board were some of the Jewish scientists who would
go on to work on the top-secret Manhattan project to build an atomic
bomb.

When he returned to the United States, he undertook work for the
US intelligence services, although in what capacity is not certain.
Later in the war he admitted to a secondment to the Office of
Strategic Services, forerunner of the CIA. His archives include a
photo ID for the OSS: member no. 59, making him one of the US
Government's first international spies, a unique position for a foreign
national. His intelligence work before the United States entered the
war was cloaked by his work for the aviation industry, and as a
world-famous aviator he was still welcome almost everywhere. Suzanne only once asked about this work. By her account, he replied:
'Can you keep a secret? So can I.'[14]

Shortly after returning in 1938 from his last expedition with Ellsworth, Wilkins had met Winston Ross who, with his brother, was a

well-known musician and performer. They became friends, and by Ross's account he became a 'mother's helper'. In practice he became Sir Hubert's private secretary for nearly twenty years, organising his papers and official engagements, helping Suzanne when he travelled.

One day in the summer of 1940, Wilkins asked Ross to drive him to LaGuardia Airport. 'He told me as if he was going to the corner for cigarettes: I have to go to China. I asked him on the way, what are you really doing? The cover was that he was doing an economic survey and he was going to China, Burma, Dutch East Indies [Indonesia] Australia and Singapore.' In fact Wilkins was on an intelligence mission, and the itinerary included Japan.

Ross was not as discreet as Suzanne: 'I asked him what he'd do if he fell into the wrong hands and was put up against a wall and shot. He said "nothing, as long as it's a good stout wall"! I knew the "economic survey" was nothing less than a spy mission dressed up.'[15]

The eye of a catastrophic cyclone hung briefly over Asia in those last calm months before it unleashed a war everyone knew was coming and was powerless to prevent. It was a dangerous mission, strange from the very onset. Wilkins left Los Angeles for Japan on a steamer carrying a cargo of cotton and lubricating oil, for the US was still happily exporting to its greatest potential enemy. On board, the intriguing company included the Italian Ambassador to Moscow and 125 German nationals, transiting through the United States on their way to jobs as advisers with their Axis partner.

In Tokyo the Imperial Hotel was also crowded with Germans – and mosquitoes. The city was sombre, preparing for war, and extravagance was discouraged. It was very different to the exuberant town he had visited during the triumphant visit of the *Graf Zeppelin*. 'Department store windows are tastefully dressed but no luxuries are displayed,' he wrote. 'Hotels and restaurants no longer publicly serve expensive meals and no liquor is served before 5 p.m. Taxis are not permitted to carry people to places of amusement.'

Remarkably, Wilkins was permitted to travel widely in Japan, and his observant eye captured many telling details. He noticed there was no rubber on the heels of a Japanese soldier's boots, that there were long queues at bread shops and that lemonade cost more than beer. None of it spoke well for the rubber and fruit plantations of Malaysia or the wheat fields of Australia. In the mountains he stayed with a

Japanese family, and, like any tourist, had his picture taken with them. He knew very soon his gracious hosts would be his enemies.

The officials he met did not disguise their certainty that war was coming. Tosu Shiratoi, adviser to the Foreign Minster and a former ambassador to Rome, detailed a long list of grievances Japan had against the Western powers: 'The memories of these anti-Japanese acts will never be effaced from the minds of the Japanese nation . . . We can not expect that this conflict will soon be over. The war may continue for a period of 20 or 30 years.'[16]

The Japanese had a right to pursue their so-called 'co-prosperity sphere' in Asia, he told Wilkins. The diplomat 'only smiled when I suggested that their plan seemed to me to be one in which East Asia would be the "co" and Japan the "prosperity".'

Wilkins agreed with the outcome if not the analysis. 'If a breakdown of diplomatic relations becomes inevitable both sides must be prepared to wage a long war lasting, possibly, a score of years . . . Japan and America are moving in opposite directions and there is every prospect of a clash.'

He had a foretaste of the conflict while travelling through Japanese-occupied Manchuria. The invasion had been marked by numerous atrocities, met with remarkable forbearance by the Chinese.

'Here in China I have seen an example of fortitude enacted to a degree incomprehensible to anyone who has not seen it with their own eyes.'

In Chunking he witnessed the Japanese air raids that bombed the city 'extravagantly, ridiculously and futilely . . . Just to give you an impression, I am permitted to say that no less than 63 bombing planes circled over the city in the few hours after my arrival last Thursday.' Doing the arithmetic he estimated it was the equivalent of eighty bombs dropped on an area equivalent to just three New York city blocks. 'With such an intensity of bombing carried out over a period of four years, you may imagine the devastating effect.'[17]

Wilkins travelled by convoy along the miserable muddy track of the Burma Road, its grim truck-stops full of gambling shops and opium dens – sixty American cents for a smoke. One of the drivers in his group had his throat cut, and when violence wasn't threatening disease was. For days he lolled half-conscious in the back of the truck with some mysterious ailment. 'I had been suffering from [a] disease which caused yellow viscous matter to ooze continuously from my nose and throat and with considerable fever. I was miserable but with usual mental control it did not worry me.'[18]

Though his intelligence assessments remain hidden, he wrote a detailed 165-page economic report on his Asian travels which was unsparing in its criticism of the rapacious colonial administrations – and fearful of the consequences: 'The difference in living standards of the West and East cannot be explained by the difference in intelligence or diligence. Fundamentally it can only be explained by the subordination of the Eastern economy . . . this in part has brought about the present world disturbance.'

In Singapore, he found the administrators ridiculously casual about the growing threat, having convinced themselves that Japan's success in China could never be repeated against British troops. If his reports had been read more closely, there is the tantalising chance they may have even altered history, for it seems beyond doubt that Wilkins provided intelligence that predicted the attack on Pearl Harbor.

At Raffles Hotel he met with the Japanese Consul General, a man he had met during the visit of the *Graf Zeppelin* to Tokyo. Much sake was drunk and, according to Winston Ross, the consul told Wilkins: 'I know what you're doing here, you're pretending to do an economic survey but you're really on assignment for the US Government. Now, I'll tell you something you don't know.' Ross recalled, 'He said sometime eighteen months from now, around the middle of December 1941, the Japanese will attack Pearl Harbor. And Wilkins said, "Where did you get such a fantastic idea? Why do you tell me this?" And he said go back and make a report to your government and they'll laugh you out of the room, because it's such a preposterous idea, you couldn't tell them. They'll think you're crazy.'[19]

Suzanne also wrote an account of the conversation, saying: 'They knew Wilkins was an Intelligence Agent, but nobody would believe a man who was crazy enough to take a submarine up to the North Pole, especially if he didn't quite get there. Wilkins told me good-humoredly that this was adding insult to injury.'[20]

The report is not as outlandish as it may seem, as Wilkins had a direct personal connection with the events that brought the United States into the war. One of the Japanese guests aboard the round-the-world *Graf Zeppelin* trip had been Lieutenant Commander Ryunosuke Kusaka, and he and Wilkins had got along well, staying in touch after the flight. That Wilkins was so well treated on his visit to Tokyo is evidence that he was well respected by the Japanese. Throughout the 1930s, Ryunosuke rose through the ranks of the military elite, and even before he travelled on the *Graf* had written a proposal describing a Japanese aerial attack on Pearl Harbor. On the morning of 7 December 1941, as a rear admiral and chief of staff of the Japanese armada, he stood on the bridge of the Japanese carrier *Akagi* shouting '*Banzai!*' as his attack squadrons took off for Hawaii.

After Wilkins' return from Asia, the newly installed telephone at the farm began ringing with voices asking endless questions about his trip. Exasperated, one day Suzanne told the unnamed caller: 'If you value his opinion so much, you should stop picking his brains and give him a job instead.' There was a pause and then the words: 'That's not a bad idea.'[21] A week later Wilkins was appointed as a consultant to the Military Planning Division, a new organisation charged with rapidly updating the United States' armed forces. During the war years he had various roles in geography and meteorology, but his most important job was in completely redesigning military equipment for desert, cold-weather and jungle conditions.

When the United States entered the war its soldiers were hopelessly ill-equipped for their mission. Tents in the South Pacific disintegrated in just two weeks because their fire-resistant finish encouraged mildew. Food shipments were dumped at sea after the cans rusted, and when American troops invaded the icy Aleutian Islands wearing leather boots, they suffered more injuries from trench foot and exposure than from the enemy. With his expertise in extreme conditions and survival, Wilkins was the perfect man to design the new uniforms for fighting men.

Glaciologist Walter Wood, President of the American Geographical Society, witnessed the gusto with which Wilkins approached his wartime work:

Wilkins was indefatigable and his love for high latitudes was insatiable . . . we shared a number of aerial missions over the Arctic. One of these was a flight of more than 26 hours, which ended at Fairbanks in the late afternoon of a spring day. During the entire time we were airborne Sir Hubert never left his observation station, and he filled two notebooks with data. Nor did his eyelids ever droop. In Fairbanks, aware of a scheduled take-off early on the following morning, he passed the intervening time talking with military personnel and with friends of earlier days. With not a minute's sleep he boarded a plane for the next mission – this time a flight of only 22 hours – and repeated his performance of the preceding flight. The last I saw of him, he was shouldering a pack that contained 50 pounds of experimental survival gear and was marching off toward the railway station, undisturbed by at least 60 hours without sleep.[22]

Though no longer making headlines, from time to time Wilkins appeared in the press. The *New Yorker* wrote an endearing portrait of him at work in 1943:

He is a peripatetic consultant. He got back recently after two and a half months in Alaska where he had been testing combat clothes . . . In fourteen years of marriage he's never been home for over two months in any one year. Last year it was only 12 days. When sighted by us, he was wearing his customary beard and dark blue suit made by Norton and Sons of London, but we wouldn't want to guess what he will be wearing as you read this. As he remarked to us, 'I may be *anywhere* next week.'[23]

The restless travel continued, with Suzanne accumulating a collection of intriguing stamps.

The surviving letters from their twenty-nine-year correspondence give a hint to the marriage: cheerful, occasionally romantic, always optimistic. Each began with a trademark 'Hello Hello'. Often he apologised for not coming back as he had expected, and usually there was advice for things to deal with on the farm in his absence. Occasionally there was a revealing insight into the life of a man often alone, but never lonely: 'Hope you had a good New Year's Eve. It was quiet on the train, no one even mentioned it.' Usually they ended with words like: 'Will let you know when I leave and will send a list of addresses where I may be found. Hubert.'[24]

Despite the separations that would destroy a less committed relationship, Suzanne remained unwavering in her support and acceptance of the life they had chosen. 'What shall I bless Wilkins for, and whom shall I thank for a man like that?' she wrote, with no hint of bitterness for what often must have been difficult times. 'I think ingratitude is the worst sin. Wilkins has my undying gratitude for the education being married to him afforded me. His severest word, if it ever came, was a lesson and his unselfishness an example. He was the kindest man I ever knew and in his simplicity a saint . . . He wasn't really very interested in fame or money, a fact that may seem incongruous to some. He sought neither, as they were not his criteria.'

The constant movement continued after the war, when Wilkins became the resident expert at what must surely be the most unusual laboratory in the United States, the Quartermaster Research Command, today known as the Army Soldier Systems Center at Natick, west of Boston. Over the years it has developed everything from chicken nuggets and space food in toothpaste tubes to radioactive cockroaches and an inflatable chapel. Wilkins had found a professional home for his peculiar obsessions and a free ride on military aircraft anywhere in the world his interests took him.

He threw himself into the work with the usual disregard for his own safety. During his studies on clothing for fighting aircraft crashes, he tested his own prototype by walking into a blazing petrol fire. On another occasion a policeman discovered what he thought to be an old vagrant asleep in the snow during the depths of a Massachusetts winter. Fearing the hobo might freeze to death, he prodded him awake with his nightstick. It turned out to be Sir Hubert, testing a new sleeping bag filled with chicken feathers.[25]

Dr Ralph Goldman, an environmental physiologist, did extensive research with Wilkins on the effects of harsh environments on the performance of soldiers. Even fifty years later, his impressions of the man remained vivid: 'I remember Sir Hubert well, mostly for his rather unusual life style – he lived in a furnished room at a run down hotel near the Framingham Rail Road Station, drove Natick's pay office wild because he seldom cashed his paychecks, told what we thought were wild stories about barely escaping with his life from a Sultan's harem . . . He was one of the last of his kind.'[26]

In the field, his prowess became legendary. Well into his sixties he was embarrassing much younger men with his stamina and skill. One of Sir Hubert's associates on a research expedition in Alaska recalled a typical instance: 'The crew were hand picked military and civilian men, most of whom were on skis, he was on snow-shoes. Not only did he stay well in advance of us, but following his tracks, we saw how he repeatedly went off the trail and returned, making side studies. To top off everything, he beat us back to the bivouac area . . . and had time to film the young soldiers straggling back in his wake.'[27]

In 1952 Wilkins undertook an arduous journey through Pakistan, the Middle East and North Africa, studying various articles of military equipment to see how they performed in the local climate and terrain. He produced a 200-page report, unremarkable until one realises he had intentionally chosen to travel in the height of mid-summer. A random entry gives a sense of it: 'We went beyond Hyderabad and spent the night at Sulkur where the temperature in daylight hours was never less than 122 degrees F.'[28] He was sixty-four and had no intention of retiring, and the dream of returning to the North Pole by submarine still shimmered like a mirage.

In 1952 he wrote to Winston Ross:

You were right in your feeling that there was something more or less final in my recent trip to the Arctic. It was one I had looked forward to for several years since it culminated in my circumnavigation of all the continents and large islands of the world and gave me a look at the high snow plateau of Greenland . . . I am not much concerned about any further geographical activities in the far north and do not much care whether I visit that area again. Of course if Army duties call for other visits I am not unwilling to go, but the only thing I would really like to do up there is to again demonstrate the use of a submersible under the Arctic ice, for scientific, defense, or offensive operations . . . there is not much chance of drumming up enough private capital for the building of a special submarine.[29]

While the submarine remained for him unfinished business, his lifelong passion for polar meteorological research was vindicated in 1957 with the massive Antarctic research effort, the International Geophysical Year. Twelve nations established fifty stations on the continent, involving more than 5000 personnel. The United States and USSR cooperated despite the chill of the Cold War and it led directly to internationalisation of the southern continent under the Antarctic Treaty as a global zone for peace and science.

It would be unthinkable for him not to participate, and he did it in style, travelling first to the North Pole and then completing a polar circumnavigation a few weeks later in the south. Suzanne took him to the airport as he left for the trip: 'I looked at the big plane that was to convey him to the Antipodes and then south, and suddenly I felt sad, hoping desperately that he'd return safely from the Antarctic. He was sixty-nine, and there couldn't be too many "adventures" left for him now, except one. He had learned to master pain, and death was an adventure he was not afraid to embrace.'[30]

17

Ninety degrees north, 3 August 1958

James Calvert's long journey to the North Pole began in the spring of 1955 as he stepped out of the gloom of Union Station into one of the perfect blue-sky days that helps disguise Washington DC's other sins. It would be curiously linked to a man he didn't yet know and could only vaguely recall from childhood memories. But the story of Sir Hubert Wilkins would become his inspiration and the blueprint for one of the most important missions in US Navy history.

The young naval commander decided to walk to his appointment under the shady trees lining Constitution Avenue, hoping it might steady his nerves. Although he had survived eight submarine patrols off the Japanese coast and was one of the most decorated naval officers of the war, Calvert could not remember ever being quite so on edge. There was no doubt his appointment in the capitol that afternoon would be the turning point of his career, whatever its outcome.

He had been summoned to a meeting with the Director of Naval Atomic Operations, Admiral Hyman G Rickover. Although not sent as an order, it was not an invitation to be refused. Rickover was already a legend within the submarine force and well on his way to becoming the most feared officer ever to wear a uniform. Which was all the more remarkable considering he wore it as little as possible, preferring the civilian clothes of the engineer he had trained to be. Though Rickover didn't salute and claimed not to have read a rule book, the US Navy had never known quite so imperial a figure. In a naval career lasting sixty-four years in the service of thirteen presidents, Rickover's authority was at its zenith that May. He had just overseen the successful launch of his obsession, the most significant peace-time development in the history of the US Navy: nuclear power.

Already at sea on its shakedown cruise was the first atom-powered submarine, the ugly but revolutionary USS *Nautilus*. Overnight *Nautilus* changed not only submarine warfare, but the geo-political balance of the Cold War. Prior to her launch, every submarine needed to come to the surface, usually daily, to recharge batteries and replenish air supplies, just as Wilkins had in 1931. By doing so they revealed their position and usually their intentions. Yet *Nautilus*, with virtually unlimited power from its reactor, was able to restore its own oxygen, distil its own water and, if necessary, circumnavigate the globe without surfacing. It carried enough food for months of submerged operations, including round-the-clock supplies of ice-cream and coffee, and forty Hollywood movies to keep the 111-man crew amused.

In its centre, a lump of enriched uranium no bigger than a golf ball sat inside an atomic pile, nearly seven metres tall, humming away behind lead-glass windows. The reactor itself was a jug-shaped steel vessel containing a grid of uranium plates filled with water under such intense pressure it would not boil even when reaching temperatures exceeding 300 degrees Celsius. When metal rods in the grid were pulled out, a controlled fission chain reaction was unleashed, generating intense heat. This was transferred to a separate loop of water, converted into high-pressure steam, and sent along heavy steel pipes to the engine room where it spun the turbines which drove the ship.

Naval vessels were literally *steaming* once more, replacing the diesel engines and racks of batteries that had propelled submarines for the past fifty years. That this immensely complex reactor could be reduced to the size of a squash court, well before the opening of the first commercial nuclear power plant, was a technological leap that rewrote military history.

Even on the first tentative mission, *Nautilus* displayed the awesome capability of the pressure cooker in her midships. She travelled submerged from her base at New London, Connecticut, to San Juan, Puerto Rico, steaming over 2000 kilometres in eighty-four hours – ten times further than any submarine had ever gone without surfacing. She moved at an average speed of nearly 20 knots, faster than any homing torpedo and so swift that sonar could not fix her position.

Nautilus's creation, from conception to launch, in little more than five years, overcoming both scientific obstacles and entrenched opposition, was the work of thousands of highly trained technicians and specialists. But above all it was the achievement of one man, an unshakeably determined Polish immigrant, the son of a tailor who grew up in a Chicago ghetto.

Hyman Rickover hadn't heard a word of English before arriving at Ellis Island as a six-year-old, yet as a teenager he managed to gain entrance to the exclusive Annapolis Naval Academy. There he outlasted the vicious hazing meted out to the only Jew in class and with an engineer's clear logic proceeded to push himself between the cracks of the naval establishment like ivy climbing a stone wall. In his passionate conviction that atomic energy could free the submarine from its technical limitations, he had bullied, cajoled, bluffed and outsmarted the considerable opponents of his grand plan.[1]

Rickover *was* the Nuclear Navy and he would personally interview every ranking officer in his fleet. What awaited them was a gruelling battle of wits that might last hours – or a summary execution dispensed in seconds. He would use extreme tactics to throw his candidates off track, including shortening the legs on the front of the interview chair to make it impossible to sit comfortably, dazzling them with lamps, and even locking them in a janitor's cupboard for hours at a time 'to help them think better if they gave me stupid answers'.

A young ensign from Georgia escaped the broom cupboard but never forgot his grilling by Rickover. He was castigated for not coming top of his class at Naval Academy. The future president of the United States, Jimmy Carter, was forced to admit that he had not tried hard enough.

Rickover asked 'Why not?' and Carter was speechless, unable to give a sensible answer to a logical question. Many years later Carter called his autobiography *Why Not the Best?*. Despite being President and Commander-in-Chief, Carter admitted that he never really felt like Rickover's boss, and he doubted Rickover considered it that way either. Asked about his authority over the Admiral, Carter replied: 'I'm not sure he ever acknowledged it deep down in his heart.'[2]

*   *   *

So when James Calvert entered the shabby, grey temporary building of the Atomic Energy Commission, he knew what to expect. Ushered into a bare anteroom, he sat and waited for two hours, the delay only adding to the tension, as was no doubt intended.

Finally he was sent down a long corridor covered in patched, bilious brown linoleum and into Rickover's carpetless office. The Admiral was white-haired and small, dressed as usual in a nondescript civilian suit that hung loosely off his slight frame. His features were fine, and his thin mouth seemed unsuited to smiling. Calvert was asked his age – thirty-four – about his education at a small Ohio high school, his two years at Oberlin College and, inevitably, his class standing at Annapolis.

'About one hundredth out of a class of six hundred,' he answered with some pride. It was not unwarranted, given that Calvert's family had suffered during the Depression and he had been forced to give up medical studies for lack of money.

'Why so low?' snapped Rickover.

As he began to answer, Calvert was cut off. 'I'll tell you why,' Rickover said, answering his own question. 'You're either dumb or lazy. Which is it?'

And so it proceeded, so vicious that almost fifty years later, Calvert could still remember the intensity of it.[3] He returned home that night drained by the experience and certain that his chance of joining the Nuclear Navy was dashed. The next morning as he stepped aboard USS *Trigger*, the diesel submarine he had commanded for more than two years, the duty officer handed him a message from the Navy Department. It read:

WHEN RELIEVED OF COMMAND OF USS TRIGGER YOU WILL PROCEED TO WASHINGTON DC AND REPORT TO THE CHIEF OF THE NAVAL REACTORS BRANCH US ATOMIC ENERGY COMMISSION FOR DUTY

In the years that followed, James Calvert was progressively schooled in the skills he would need to take command of the most destructive weapons ever built, cut off from normal human existence for months at a time, hundreds of feet below the surface. In the worst circumstances, after the devastation of nuclear war, he would need to operate independently without further orders or guidance. He would have to take decisions that not only affected the lives of his crew, but possibly the lives of tens of thousands of civilians as well.[4]

Amid the hectic rounds of seminars and lectures there was one conversation early in his training that Calvert remembers as the most important of his life, even more significant than that day he was interviewed by Rickover. Before it he was merely making steady progress through a naval career; after it, he had a mission, a goal against which he could test his abilities and focus his aim. It started with a visit from a friend, the first skipper of the *Nautilus*, Commander Eugene Wilkinson.

For some reason, everyone called him Dennis. Tall, energetic and engaging, Wilkinson had the enthusiasm of a pioneer settler, and with a nuclear submarine under his command, the wagon to take him anywhere. He noticed a chart on Calvert's wall and jabbed at it with his finger.

'There are only four oceans in the world, and this one is the most important. Just look where it is.'

Calvert understood the point. The Arctic Ocean was the threshold to three continents, the smallest ocean but still five times the size of the Mediterranean. It was entered on one side by the narrow strait that separated the United States and USSR, while on the other it opened wide into the North Atlantic. Its strategic importance was beyond doubt, but for the Navy, it seemed impenetrable.

Mostly covered in thick ice, the Arctic Ocean was effectively closed to naval operations. These men with their nuclear vessels understood little more about it than the Vikings did centuries ago. Their greatest concern as submariners was the plunging ice ridges: giant spikes forced downwards when the massive floes collided.

Wilkinson admitted there was little real knowledge of how deep the ridges went. 'Probably not more than 100 feet. But I think we could get under them,' he said, smiling.

Calvert dismissed the idea. 'What are you going to do if something goes wrong when you're 200 miles inside the ice?'

'You're missing the point of the whole thing,' Wilkinson responded. 'This icepack isn't one solid piece. It's filled with lakes that open and close as the ice floes shift. Listen, this isn't a brand new idea. Do you remember Sir Hubert Wilkins?' his friend asked. 'He went up there at least twenty-five years ago in a converted Navy submarine. Had to turn back because the ship gave out.'

Calvert thought back to his boyhood in the early 1930s and could dimly recall newspaper stories about the expedition. And when he entered submarine school in 1942, some of the old chiefs teaching there would tell stories about the courageous journey that had seen a submarine pioneer a route to an unexplored ocean.

'I vaguely remember it,' he answered. 'They had a pretty tough time of it didn't they?' His friend knew the story well.

Wilkinson went on to describe the stops and starts that followed the original attempt to operate a submarine in the Arctic. Here was an entire ocean that was virtually unexplored, and with its nuclear submarines, the Navy finally had a way discover its secrets. He had given the idea much thought, and by the time he left Calvert's office that afternoon, the *Nautilus* skipper had made another convert to the cause of polar submarining. What neither of them knew was how significant that earlier, long-forgotten trip by Sir Hubert Wilkins would become for both *Nautilus* and for James Calvert.

As interested as the Navy was in exploring unknown oceans, its fascination for the Arctic was not based on a desire for better maps. Those they had already told them all they needed to know. In the simple arithmetic of the Cold War, the USSR could only be restrained if the United States could credibly threaten its major cities and supply routes.

In the mid-1950s the explorer's quest for knowledge had been replaced by the soldier's fear of war. Intercontinental missiles were still in their infancy, and military strategists worried that such fixed weapon sites only invited a first strike. So plans for submarine-launched nuclear missiles were accelerated. A hidden submarine force armed with its own missiles and able to patrol the Soviet Arctic coastline would be a potent deterrent. The only problem was, nobody knew the first thing about operating submarines in the Arctic.

And so in the summer of 1957, the US Navy's first nuclear submarine was sent on a secret mission. USS *Nautilus* was attempting to travel under the Arctic Ocean – the last unconquered stretch of ice and water.

Dennis Wilkinson's ideas had found favour, although with his promotion to a desk job Commander William Anderson was now in charge of *Nautilus*. Also patrolling the edge of the pack for its turn under the ice was USS *Skate*, a new nuclear sub now under the command of James Calvert. Since that meeting in his office, Calvert had spent almost three years waiting for his chance to explore the icy frontier at the top of the world.

Commander Anderson had passed Iceland and was soon cruising north into little-known waters. On the evening of 1 September the men on the bridge took their last look at the white mass spread before them and dived deep beneath the edge of the icepack. Sonar revealed the profile of the thick cap overhead, the first anyone had seen of the heavy floes since Sir Hubert Wilkins looked through the small quartz windows of that other *Nautilus* twenty-six years earlier.

Travelling smoothly, with no sensation of movement except the almost imperceptible vibration of the propellers, the magnetic compasses soon began to behave erratically, as was expected to happen the further north they headed. The old-fashioned gyro, designed for accuracy only as far as 70 degrees north latitude, also wavered abnormally. But it had recently been joined by a newer model installed especially for the trip, which was performing well.

Nautilus crossed 87 degrees north with the pole just 300 kilometres ahead. Then, just as Calvert had feared in his conversation with Wilkinson two years before, potential disaster struck. A cheap fuse blew and took with it the most critical equipment on the vessel: its twin gyroscopic compasses. Though power was soon restored, it would take hours to reset the gyros. The pride of the US Navy was effectively blind, in uncharted waters, deep beneath the frozen icepack.

Commander Anderson could no longer be certain of his precise position and now had no more accurate means of navigation than that used by sailors for centuries: dead reckoning. Speed could be calculated by pit log, and distance by clock time, but they were unreliable measures.

Though the Russians and Americans had both made cautious forays to the fringes of Arctic Ocean with conventional submarines, very little was known about the conditions if they ventured beyond. The entrance to the deep Arctic basin could only be made through shallow channels where the narrow margin between ocean floor and ice cap made submarine navigation extremely hazardous. No one had yet found a secure path to the inner ocean.

Anderson dared not proceed further and ordered a long slow turn south that he hoped would bring them to the safety of a fixed position. But hours later the atmosphere in the Control Centre became tense. Anderson looked across the low room as his Quarter-master-of-the-Watch charted their position and intently studied a grey metal box suspended at eye level in the corner. Inside, a metal stylus inscribed two irregular patterns across a slowly moving paper tape. It made a familiar sound in the otherwise quiet room, like a polishing brush against leather, but what it was drawing was not expected. The pattern on the paper tape looked like a mountain range drawn upside down.

The tape recorded the outline of plunging ice hundreds of metres deep, jagged pinnacles that could tear through the steel hull of the submarine. These were not the conditions they were expecting at this time of year, and it was far too thick for their estimated position. Bottom soundings of the ocean floor were not making much sense either. They were in water much deeper than expected. *Nautilus* was lost in the middle of an uncharted ocean.

Only one man aboard had any real experience of these conditions. Its ice pilot was a civilian scientist, Dr Waldo Lyon, who in his ten years with the Navy's Electronics Laboratory had been a key member of earlier tentative ventures into the Arctic. Lyon knew more about polar ice conditions than anyone. As well as his personal experience, Lyon, like Dennis Wilkinson, knew something of the journey of the only other submarine to have come this far north.

Wilkins' choice of the diligent Harald Sverdrup as his scientific officer was about to save the US Navy a major embarrassment and potential disaster. Despite the difficult conditions on the decrepit sub, Dr Sverdrup had compiled valuable data on the journey. These were the first measurements of the deep Arctic basin, its water temperature, salinity, currents and ocean depth. Lyon had often sought advice from the Norwegian, and almost as an afterthought had brought his friend's old charts along with him. To an oceanographer they could be read much like a navigator reads a map.

In theory, the modern *Nautilus* should have been in much the same position as the old submarine on its earlier journey, and Lyon had faith enough in Sverdrup to feel confident of the accuracy of the old charts. The readings should correspond with Lyon's own data, but it was clear they were divergent. Poring over the tables made nearly three decades earlier, he found the clue to their real position.

Dr Lyon recalled the moment: 'The water temperature in particular didn't check with the data of Sverdrup's measurements, both in regard to depth and temperature.' In the cautious understatement learned from decades of scientific report writing, he added, 'Those data were most valuable to us.' Aided by the information from the old tables, he was able to estimate their true position. Lyon recognised they were most likely in the outgoing Greenland current and advised his skipper that they were well off course. Anderson ordered a correction and *Nautilus* headed to open water and safety.

Just six weeks after the *Nautilus*'s aborted mission, the world changed. An aluminium alloy sphere, little bigger than a basketball, destroyed the myth of the United States' technological and scientific superiority.

Sputnik 1 circled the Earth, the first artificial satellite in space. Inside, a converted tractor battery powered a small transmitter which for twenty-three days sent a rude beep that reverberated deep within the Eisenhower administration and across the world. The launch was announced by a few terse paragraphs in *Pravda* but by a rare triple-row headline in the *New York Times*. Sputnik's arrival set off a panicked scramble for a response that could re-establish American prestige.

America's own space science efforts were hopelessly divided between military and civilian programs, and early efforts to send a rocket aloft were embarrassing failures. Sputnik ll was soon launched, this time carrying its canine passenger, Laika, on a simultaneous journey into history and oblivion. For the United States, the crisis of confidence deepened.

The aborted excursion by the *Nautilus* to the Arctic Ocean was not well known outside a small group of naval commanders. But on a visit to the Pentagon, President Eisenhower's naval aide, Captain Peter Aurand, met quite by chance with Commander Anderson and listened intently to the exciting story of a near miss heading for the North Pole. Aurand knew the administration would be interested and the *Nautilus* skipper and Waldo Lyon were invited to brief a small White House group that included Eisenhower's Press Secretary, James Hagarty. The story Anderson told, including the narrow escape using the old Wilkins charts, stirred them all.

'Everyone was interested,' remembered Captain Aurand, 'particularly Jim Hagarty. Jim and I were both interested in doing something that would take the curse off the Sputnik scare. We wanted some technological development that the United States could make.'

Within days of the meeting, instructions came from the National Security Council that *Nautilus* was to be prepared for a journey across the Arctic Ocean. Hagarty planned that if successful, the trip would be announced to the world by an elaborate scheme that would get Commander Anderson back to the White House even before *Nautilus* made it back to a friendly port. But because of the high risk of failure and the severe embarrassment it would cause, the mission was to be prepared in the deepest secrecy.

So much had changed since the days of Wilkins and the loud trumpeting of his expeditions by Hearst's newspapers. Governments owned science now, and most of it was driven by strategic needs. In this environment it would have been inconceivable for the Navy to have ever leased one of its submarines to an amateur privateer, any more than a Shackleton or Amundsen would have been encouraged to go tramping where the military had not.

With the President's approval 'Operation Sunshine', implying a leisurely cruise through the tropics, set about preparing *Nautilus* for its dangerous crossing from the Pacific to the Atlantic via the North Pole. The mission was so secret that even the Commander-in-Chief of the Pacific Fleet was not informed of the plans. When *Nautilus* left its base in Groton, Connecticut, in April 1958, her crew were expecting a pleasant cruise to Panama. Instead, they headed through the canal towards San Diego, en route to the Northwest Passage.

Nautilus attempted two different routes into the Arctic basin, but both were blocked by deep ice. Trying to return, the sub had barely a metre to spare beneath its keel as it plunged beneath the ice. Anderson sent a message to the Chief of Naval Operations that he would have to return unsuccessful. *Nautilus* had escaped by the narrowest of margins, and President Eisenhower was to be frustrated once again.

'It took a lot of moral courage,' recalled Captain Aurand. 'Here was a presidential-directed project. Turning around was probably just as tough as going ahead.'[5]

Even before *Nautilus* made it back to Pearl Harbor, the American public was treated to the unscheduled fireworks display of yet another Vanguard rocket blowing itself to pieces on the launch pad at Cape Canaveral.[6] What was worse, Vanguard belonged to the Navy. One way or another, the submarines were going to have to make it to the North Pole.

It would be several weeks before *Nautilus* would be ready for another attempt. Everyone in the crew now knew what their real objectives were and the President's press secretary wagered a bet with Captain Aurand that the mission would leak.

While *Nautilus* was going through its final preparations, another submarine was being readied for an attempt on the Pole. Once again, only its Commander, James Calvert, knew the true purpose of the mission. *Skate* would follow *Nautilus* regardless of whether it succeeded.

Calvert waited in half hope that he would be the first to make the undersea crossing via the pole. But *Nautilus* was not to be denied its triumph. On 1 August 1958 she found what she was looking for – a deep undersea valley east of Point Barrow in Alaska. Plunging 100 metres and getting deeper as it headed north, the valley proved to be the perfect path into the Arctic basin. Two days later, moving swiftly with more than 4000 metres of water below, *Nautilus* crossed the geographic North Pole. On 5 August she emerged into open water after crossing the Arctic Ocean on almost the same route beneath the ice that Wilkins had flown above it. *Nautilus* sent a coded message via a Navy radio station in Japan: nautilus-90-north. ninety-six hours. point barrow to the greeneland sea.

By an elaborate scheme involving helicopters and a flight from the US Air Force base in Iceland, Commander Anderson was delivered to Washington while *Nautilus* was still steaming towards Britain.

With no time to sleep, Anderson faced the White House press corp at a hastily announced conference in the Fish Room. Peter Aurand revealed the charts he had prepared showing the route *Nautilus* had taken. As hoped, the news had every bit as much of an impact as the Sputnik launch.

William Anderson, still wearing his freshly minted Legion of Merit, flew back to Britain in time to be winched aboard his submarine before it reached Portsmouth, to a huge welcome.

The day after *Nautilus* reached Britain, James Calvert took USS *Skate* under the North Pole. Though understandably disappointed at not being first, he already knew an even greater challenge lay ahead: to bring a submarine to the surface through the ice. Wilkins had been convinced it would be possible to surface through thin ice, but the US nuclear fleet captains were not so sure. USS *Nautilus* had damaged its periscopes trying on its first mission, and *Skate* had fired torpedoes at the surface to see if they would break through – but they had made no impression at all. Calvert did, however, succeed in coming up through the small lakes between the ice known by their Russian name, poly-nyas, and as he headed on to open water he began to believe it might just be possible to break through the ice as Wilkins had predicted. By a strange coincidence, *Skate* returned to the North Atlantic and made for the port of Bergen in Norway. As she entered the harbour, she passed directly over the rusting hulk of the old *Nautilus* that had once sailed proudly for the North Pole.

Many people came to congratulate Calvert while *Skate* was in Bergen, among them an old friend of Sir Hubert, Dr Odd Dahl. He left Calvert a well-thumbed copy of *Under the North Pole* – the book written by Wilkins in 1931 to raise money for his grand expedition, and a statement of intent that others might follow in case they never returned. In it were all the plans and ideas of the 'Suicide Club'.

Calvert was riveted by its predictions. 'I was unable to put it down until I finished it. Here was a work, written when I was eleven years old, which again and again forecast accurately what we had just experienced.'

That night he drafted a message to Sir Hubert:

The experiences of this summer followed by conversations with your old associates in Bergen have left us deeply aware of the accuracy of your insight and vision in regard to the use of submarines in the Arctic. The majority of your aims of nearly thirty years ago were realized this summer. The men of *Skate* send a sincere salute to a man who has many times shown the way.

As *Skate* crossed the Atlantic on its way back to Boston, Calvert received Wilkins' reply:

Sir Hubert Wilkins sincerely appreciates the message from the men of the *Skate* and extends to them hearty congratulations upon their skilful and efficient accomplishment of a measure which no doubt will lead to new and far reaching developments in science, economics and defense.[7]

In the autumn of 1958 *Skate* returned to moor at the place she had been built, the Electric Boat docks, near the Navy's submarine headquarters in Groton, Connecticut. The docks belonged to a private company founded by the backers of John P Holland, a brilliant Irishman and rival of that other submarine pioneer, Simon Lake. Holland's dock became the centre of submarine construction for the next century.

Just down Thames Street on the east side of the river, a naval car headed towards Electric Boat, passing as it went the modest memorial marking the fifty-two submarines and their crews lost during World War II, many of them friends of James Calvert.[8] He was now aboard *Skate* awaiting a special guest.

Sir Hubert Wilkins stepped carefully out of the car. He was seventy now, and though he hid it well under his usual smart double-breasted dark suit, there were many aches and pains on a body that had survived air crashes, shrapnel hits and the agonies of frostbite. He was quite deaf in the right ear from explosions and had lost much of the hearing in the left from countless hours spent inside the roaring cockpits of those primitive aeroplanes. Calvert remembers he still had a firm handshake and the mellifluous voice was unaffected. People would often comment how pleasing it sounded, and in the few recordings which still survive, it remains gently persuasive. It would be hard to argue with a voice so innately reasonable.

As Calvert listened, he began to appreciate how this man could have convinced an experienced submarine crew to risk their lives on his venture to the North Pole. His enthusiasm and curiosity made him very attractive, and Calvert knew enough about his exceptional courage to imagine that others would be willing to follow him, even into extreme danger.

Wilkins spent the entire afternoon aboard *Skate*, and Calvert was a little ashamed of its technical sophistication, so much more advanced than anything aboard the old *Nautilus*. With no need to accommodate the huge batteries and diesel tanks of a conventional sub, there was much more room for crew comforts. Its wealth of mechanical and electronic devices bore little resemblance to the primitive equipment Wilkins had relied upon.

'Now that you have everything you need to do the job,' said the old explorer suddenly, 'you must go in wintertime.'[9]

Calvert was startled, but he knew what he meant. All previous attempts had been made in summer when the ice was at its thinnest and open polynyas were abundant. The pole would not be truly conquered until vessels could operate there in winter darkness and thick ice.

'Not much use in going if we can't get to the surface,' Calvert answered.

'I think you can,' Wilkins replied. 'Maybe you'll have to bore a hole, maybe blast. I don't know but you'll find a way.'

Calvert recalls that Wilkins then let out a long sigh and sat down with a half-smile and a distant look in his eyes. 'I'm sure he found it hard to face the fact that the years were past when he could take active part in such an adventure.'

A few days after the visit, Calvert received a letter of thanks from the gallant explorer, appreciative of the hospitality and offering some advice: 'I . . . have given considerable thought to the idea of a winter expedition. You must attempt to bring this about. Do not be discouraged by apathy and resistance, press for it . . .'

A week after visiting the *Skate*, on 31 October, his seventieth birthday, Sir Hubert received a letter from his old friends at the Explorers Club, inviting him to be the guest of honour at their annual dinner. It was always a big event and more than 650 people would be gathered at the Biltmore Hotel to honour him. That was amusing. The Biltmore was where Byrd had kept his offices back in the 1920s when they were racing each other down in the Antarctic. Could it be thirty years ago? For the most part these dinners became a wake, the few who could remember reminiscing about the many who'd been forgotten. Byrd was gone now, so were all the others except Stefansson and himself. He'd like to make the event, though he wasn't looking forward to any kind of fuss being made. The difficulty was confirming – who knew where he would be next March? Suzanne was planning a long visit to the West Indies where he was hoping to find time to get started on the books long promised to publishers. There was always so much to complete and so little time.

A month later Wilkins was back at Framingham at the little hotel he used when visiting the nearby army research laboratory. He was working outdoors on the car engine despite the nasty wind and a soft covering of snow on the ground. He'd always taken pleasure in motors, enjoying the mechanical certainty of cause and effect, the slow process of elimination that meant you could eventually fix anything or at least know the reason it wasn't working. Before going back to his ram-shackle hotel room he called Suzanne. *The Herald Tribune* had devoted an entire supplement to Australia that day, which they had both read. The two expatriate Aussies shared a tinge of homesickness. Hubert was glad his homeland had turned out a little better than he expected back in 1925. It was now a prosperous place, invigorated by the immigrants who had arrived after the war, though still ravaged by droughts. He told his wife he expected to be home before Christmas and looked forward to going up to the farm. With those thoughts in mind and Suzanne's sweet goodnight in his one useful ear, he washed engine grease off his hands. Suddenly he felt a sharp pain in his chest. Probably he knew what it meant. He lay down on his bed, still in his suit with the tie neatly knotted, closed his eyes and waited for the moment of that last great adventure.

He was gone. The last of his family, the last of his kind. The last explorer. Lady Suzanne reported he died smiling.

18

The final journey, 17 March 1959

Who has known heights and depths shall not again
Know peace – not as the calm heart knows
And though he tread the humble ways of men
He shall not speak the common tongue again.
Who once has trodden stars seeks peace no more.

– Mary Brent Whiteside

S he lifted like a mythical beast from the deep, a Kraken woken from
its dreamless slumber. The conning tower rose sharply until the
hull broke through, the sharp crack of fractured ice echoing across the
frozen landscape until it was lost in the gale. It was a black hump in the
featureless white, great blocks of ice strewn across the bow. The
nuclear submarine USS *Skate* had surfaced at the North Pole.

From the bridge, *Skate*'s officers looked out in the dim twilight of a polar
winter across the barren ice, a lifeless sheet stretched thin across the deep
ocean. There were no shadows and no point to fix the eye. In the distance
just the palest rose tint marked out the sky, the first signs of the sun that
would soon rise above the horizon and not set again for 187 days. It was
south in every direction and the whole Earth turned slowly beneath them.

Commander James Calvert wondered how such a featureless waste-
land could have so inspired humanity's imagination. When Robert
Peary had dragged himself here exactly fifty years before *Skate*, he had
tried to describe his emotions but could not. Later he wrote: 'If it were
possible for a man to arrive at 90 degrees north latitude without being
utterly exhausted, body and brain, he would doubtless enjoy a series of

unique sensations and reflections . . .' Yet Peary never found the language to capture his feelings. The bitter struggles had drained any joy, and the bleakness of what he found was too empty for words.

Calvert, by contrast, had arrived well-fed and in airconditioned comfort with the added satisfaction of knowing he was the last in the line of a seafaring tradition stretching back beyond recorded history. He had entered an unknown sea with no charts to guide him and no certain knowledge of what lay ahead, and in surfacing at the pole, he had finally conquered the most mysterious ocean of all. Bringing a submarine to this point was not without military significance. It proved that the US Navy could raise its flag anywhere on any ocean, even a frozen one, and at the height of the Cold War it sent a warning message to the USSR that there was nowhere to hide from the American fleet. Back home, Calvert's success would help calm the panic that had followed Russia's Sputnik launch.

The *Skate*'s crew, however, had another, more personal, mission at the pole. They had come to honour one of their own, a submariner like themselves, a visionary, eccentric pioneer who had attempted this perilous journey a generation earlier. In a small wooden box in his stateroom, Calvert carried the ashes of the man who had first imagined a submarine voyage to the pole was possible.

Most people had forgotten about George Hubert Wilkins by now, but not the submarine fleet. Though Wilkins was never in the Navy and was not even an American, Calvert and his fellow officers had been so inspired by his story that they were determined to honour him on this historic day. It was 26 degrees below zero, and in the stiff gale it felt even colder. The winds were shifting the ice floes ominously against *Skate*'s hull, more than enough reason not to linger. But the Navy had come a long way to put Wilkins to rest, and the promise would be kept.

In their few meetings, Calvert had liked Wilkins immensely. 'I had been fascinated by him. I had wondered most of my life how anyone could have been crazy enough to try and do what he attempted. The man was a dreamer, and dreamers are important. They think things that other people would reject immediately as not being possible.'[1]

Only a few old explorers would even have recalled his name and it was hard to imagine that for a short time Wilkins had been one of the most famous men alive. As Calvert prepared a few brief notes in his cabin trying to sum up the man's achievements, he was stunned by the list. In all Wilkins had made thirty-three expeditions in polar regions and explored every continent. He had sledged and flown, sailed and walked across more unknown land than any man in history. He had been knighted by the kings of England and Italy, awarded by the great societies, honoured by Stalin and US presidents. The other giants of the golden age of polar exploration considered him without peer. But the great achievements had ultimately been overshadowed by one sad misadventure aboard a decrepit submarine which had put the lives of twenty men in the gravest danger.

The three flags that marked his career were raised from *Skate*'s masts and periscopes: the Southern Cross of Australia, where he was born; the Union Jack, in whose name he had made many discoveries; and the Stars and Stripes of the United States, where he made his home. Two dozen crew members formed ranks on either side of a little table, as much in the lee of the submarine as possible. It offered scant protection against the 30-knot winds. Their breath froze on the edge of their hoods, making it seem as if they all wore white beards.

The stinging cold made it difficult for Calvert to hold the prayer book, and it was too dark to read unaided, so several of the men held flares on either side of the table where the little bronze urn of ashes stood. Raising his voice over the wind, the *Skate*'s skipper read:

> On this day we pay humble tribute to one of the great men of our century. His indomitable will, his adventurous spirit, his simplicity and his courage have all set high marks for those of us who follow him. He spent his life in the noblest of callings, the attempt to broaden the horizons of the minds of men.
>
> Some of his personality is expressed in this prayer which he himself wrote: 'Our heavenly Father, wouldst thou give us the liberty without license and the power to do good for mankind with the self-restraint to avoid using that power for self aggrandizement . . .

The burial party came to attention and Commander Calvert and the torchbearers walked away from the ship. Under the lurid red glow of the flares he read the committal while an officer sprinkled the ashes to the wind. A rifle report shot out three times in a final salute and the ashes disappeared into the swirling snow and half-darkness. Sir Hubert Wilkins had come to his final resting place in the white ocean that had been the vast stage for his dramas of triumph and defeat.

Epilogue

–

The weatherman

Everybody talks about the weather, but nobody does anything about it.
– Charles D Warner, often attributed to his brother-in-law, Mark Twain

Both Warner and Mark Twain were talking through their hats.
– Sir Hubert Wilkins

The twenty-first century arrived at Mt Bryan East much as the nineteenth century ended. The land is brown and parched. Eddies of dust sweep across the abandoned fields like spectres, while stumpy-tailed lizards and the buzz of blowflies are the only signs of life. A hundred years of human settlement, book-ended by droughts so severe that people and their animals have retreated in despair, has left behind only the peculiar archaeology of natural disaster.

The pioneer houses stand empty, untouched since their broken-hearted owners walked away, defeated by the weather. This place is so remote even vandals haven't found the abandoned homesteads, though mice have taken residence in the rotting wooden floors. Old machinery lies in the fields where it was dropped, the gates to dead gardens swing in the breeze. Windmills, like rusted skeletons, still turn towards the wind but there is nothing left to pump beneath the deadened surface. If anything, history has gone backwards here. Once there were telegraph poles and fenceposts, but the timber was too useful to leave behind and today it's long gone. The school has been empty for decades and the tiny chapel that Harry and Louisa Wilkins could fill with their own large family stands roofless, the stained-glass windows removed.

Ten kilometres down a dirt road, the stone cottage where they raised thirteen children is a pile of tumbled down stones.

Mary Fahey stands at the rusting gate of what remains of *Netfield* on a blistering summer afternoon that seems to hum with waves of heat shifted by the limp breeze. 'To come from *here*,' she says, staring towards the bare tan hills, 'and achieve all that. It's just unbelievable really, like a fairytale.'[1]

A shearer's wife, Mary has lived in this district for most of her life yet only came to know of Wilkins in recent times. With the backing of philanthropic Australian entrepreneur Dick Smith, Mary and other members of the local history society set about rebuilding the Wilkins family home, a millennial project to celebrate the life of the most important man ever to emerge from this part of the world.

Far away across the Southern Ocean, as the millennium dawned over Antarctica, scientists from six different bases ringing the continent sent balloons high into the stratosphere. As part of the Global Atmosphere Watch program their work epitomised what Wilkins had hoped for in cooperative meteorology. In September 2000 they discovered that the ozone hole over the Antarctic had expanded enormously, covering an area larger than the entire landmass of the Unites States. Fifty million tonnes of ozone that shielded Earth from the sun's ultraviolet radiation had gone missing, with potentially devastating consequences for life on the planet.

Meanwhile, at the opposite end of the world, the nuclear submarine USS *Hawkbill* was returning from a mission to the North Pole, on the final cruise of a five-year program taking civilian scientists on journeys into the high Arctic. These scientific ice expeditions, dubbed SCIEX, have accumulated mountains of data on the geology, physics and chemistry of the deep Arctic Ocean. Working in comfort, dozens of scientists investigated more than 160 000 kilometres of ice-covered territory: a priceless opportunity for fieldwork that only a submarine could offer. It was the culmination of everything Wilkins had predicted.

By 2005 the crucial role the poles play in regulating the world's weather had become clear. As we discover more about the serious dangers of global warming, changes at the poles have provided us with warnings we seem reluctant to heed. The world's climate is changing and humans are undeniably implicated. While in the north the glaciers disappear from Iceland and Greenland, in the south the giant ice shelves that once carried the early explorers towards their goals are shattering. High over Antarctica, scientists have measured a 30-kilo-metre-high tornado of swirling winds around the continent. This vortex is a vast engine of weather in the Southern Hemisphere, and as it spins faster under the warming effect of the ozone hole and greenhouse gases, it may well be sucking away the storms that bring rain to southern Australia. The land of Wilkins' birth now faces the prospect of permanent drought, and rainfall in its southern cities has already declined alarmingly.

In the north, oceanographers keep a worried eye on changes to the vital exchange of currents between the Arctic Ocean and the Atlantic. This thermohaline circulation, popularly known as 'the conveyor belt', shifts a flow of warm surface water equivalent to 100 Amazon Rivers north towards the pole. There it cools and sinks and eventually flows back between Greenland and Norway. This massive exchange helps regulate global currents, including the Gulf Stream which keeps Europe several degrees warmer than other maritime regions at similar latitudes. Many scientists are now concerned that global warming may be upsetting the conveyor. Should it weaken, or even shut down, it could perversely plunge the Earth into a new ice age. Standing in the freezing diving chamber of the *Nautilus* with their crude salinity measures and flowmeters, Wilkins and Sverdrup were the first to study the conveyor in the deep Arctic Ocean.

All over the world, and soon above it in a permanently manned international space station, scientists work together on projects that Wilkins predicted would one day concern us all. What he wrote once seemed like science fiction; now reality is catching up with his ideas: 'I can imagine,' he said, 'a time when a radio message from a Polar station will set ten thousand men to set locks to hold water; when a flash of that news will alter the plans of every farmer, manufacturer, businessman and financier; when it will even move whole populations from one area to another, as primitive tribes now move from moun-tains to lowlands because they know that winter is coming.'[2]

As the consequences of climate change and global warming become apparent, Wilkins' eccentric obsession with polar meteorology looks increasingly like the work of a visionary, not a crank. Now, as the scientific consensus confirms that human activity is driving us towards a climate crisis, Wilkins' predictions of vast populations on the move to escape rising oceans begin to have the disquieting sound of prophecy about them. If so, he was a prophet ignored in his own land.*

The low-roofed cottage has risen again now, somewhat dwarfed by its new carpark which, in the Australian way, is optimistically large for the likely number of visitors. The rebuilt *Netfield*, in the shadow of the copper mountain of Mt Bryan, is the only monument anywhere that commemorates Wilkins' life. A sign at the entrance quotes Dick Smith: 'In practically any other country than Australia, his birthplace would be a national shrine. But here, many people don't even know that it exists. Well, we're going to change that.'

Judging by the recognition Wilkins has had in his home city of Adelaide, change will be a long time coming. Along the elegant central boulevard of North Terrace are plaques celebrating the lives of 169 eminent South Australians, the men and women who enriched the state's culture and inspired its people. There's Sir Donald Bradman, of course, the finest cricketer in history, and Sir Douglas Mawson, the famous explorer – though neither was born or raised in the state. There's the first woman constable in the British Empire, along with the soldiers, silversmiths, shopkeepers and surveyors who helped build a fine city from very unpromising material. There is no sign, however, of Sir Hubert Wilkins. This son of the first-born South Australian, the war hero whom the *New York Times* eulogised as joining the firmament of the great explorers, the boy from the bush who conquered the skies above the poles and struggled for years to end the pain of drought that so blighted his countrymen, is forgotten.

The *Wakefield Companion to South Australian History*, fine work that it is, can muster a mere ten lines beneath his name, giving us a travelogue of his early visits to '27 countries in 18 months' and concluding that he was little more than a gypsy, 'a ceaseless wanderer'. The *Australian Dictionary of Biography* dismisses him even more perfunctorily – whereas Mawson's entry occupies three pages, he once adorned the currency and has one of Australia's permanent Antarctic bases named after him. The other two are called Davis and Casey, after

---

* In belated recognition of Wilkins' contribution to polar aviation, the Australian Government has recently decided to name its first permanent airstrip in Antarctica 'Wilkins Ice Runway'. Located near Casey Station it is scheduled to begin operation in 2007.

a mariner and a politician, both of whom knew Wilkins well and appreciated his vital role in establishing Australia's presence in the Antarctic. Today there is no Wilkins base nor is there likely to be one. Sir Hubert has been reduced to those utilitarian ephemera of history, a face on a postage stamp. There are a few places named for him that no one is likely to visit, and additions to the nomenclature of assorted birds, a wallaby and a small lizard. Though it's more than most of us will leave, it's a modest legacy, and in no measure equates with the man whose life must surely rank as one of the more extraordinary of the past century.

How is it he so easily slipped from the pages of history? In part the *Nautilus* expedition had built such high expectations that its failure would have damaged the reputation of any man. If glory were his aim, it would have been better not to return, for dead men make better heroes than surviving failures. Equally, his utter lack of interest in the prizes of exploration did nothing to help his reputation. Twice he stepped aside to allow Byrd to reach the poles by plane, when both times he had started his expeditions ahead of the American and, by any reckoning, was more skilled for the job. Stefansson often complained of Wilkins' 'aggressive modesty', and chastised him for not taking on that trusted aid of modern explorers, the publicity agent. Byrd certainly understood the value of self-promotion and took classes at Harvard Business School to learn what he called the 'hero business'. 'Success depends on more than hard work,' he wrote. 'Fame will help you to success.'[3] Another famous adventurer of the day, Roy Chapman Andrews, remarked that 'unless you have the personality and ability to sell yourself as well as your plan, you are just out of luck.'[4] Wilkins ignored their advice, and did the barest minimum in the press to sustain his expeditions financially. Having worked in Fleet Street and as a newsreel man himself, he was wise to the game but never enjoyed playing it. A pity, for when he did write about his adventures his work was universally admired.

'Several of his associates said he was born 30 years too soon,' wrote Herb Nichols, in an appreciation of Sir Hubert's career in the *Explorers Club Journal*. [5] While it's true that Shackleton and others recognised the Australian had what it takes to be one of the greats of the classic age of polar exploration, he was never cut out for the drudgery of the dog sled. The flimsy aeroplanes and fluky airships he flew too often ended up in a tangle of wires and wood. His submarine venture was so premature that it was nearly thirty years before anyone dared repeat it. When the technology of the time failed him he could imagine what was to come. Twenty-four years before the first man in space he told an audience: 'We really should be able to put ourselves outside this earth of ours and study it as a whole.'[6] Even earlier, he had described the view of the Earth from space with uncanny precision:

> Gradually I could imagine myself apart from this earth situated somewhere out in space watching the whirling winds sweep from the poles to the equator then, heated by the sun's rays, they swept upwards to the stratosphere. Then as they gradually cooled they would sink toward the poles and reach the earth, only to be swept furiously once more toward the equator and upwards again. Visualising the atmosphere, imagining it to be in colour I see the earth as a solid bodied sphere with two circulating systems of atmosphere circulating about its surface. The centre of its air mass was at the polar areas.[7]

It was the view of our planet first seen by the Apollo astronauts.

It's only now that we can begin to appreciate the extent of his vision and the depth of the implacable self-belief that drove him onwards despite so many setbacks. Apsley Cherry-Garrard, a member of Scott's tragic Antarctic expedition, was a man after Wilkins' heart who once risked his life in order to gather a few penguins' eggs. He observed that exploration is but the physical expression of the intellectual passion. It was Wilkins' restless inquisitiveness about the weather that set him apart. It was a goal far more ambitious than the mere attainment of some meaningless geographic spot and it made him very different to the better-known explorers. While they searched breathlessly for location, he sought revelation. He kept to the plan he wrote as a penniless schoolboy and never faltered.

Where did such self-confidence come from? To walk away from one big crash was luck, from two or three was uncanny. What were the odds of escaping a dozen, among them that desperate out-of-fuel descent in pitch dark onto a frozen ocean? From his early experiences in war it seems clear that he stepped beyond the mundane fears that hold back ordinary men. He'd come so close to death on so many occasions that it no longer concerned him. Later, sustained by his peculiar but heartfelt faith, he came to see our life on this Earth as just a passing moment in the great flow of the universe. One of his hidden skills was poetry, and Lady Suzanne liked one in particular that she felt best expressed the qualities that she loved in him:

Not twice may any stand by the same stream,
Not twice possess the years that hasten on;
Something there was we looked on, loved, 'tis gone
Or stays but as the shadow of a dream.
Hands that we touched clasp ours no more, and eyes
That shone for us as stars withdrew their light;
Voices beloved pass out into the night;
The gift of yesterday, today denies.
Yet must we hold it for a deeper truth,
Nothing that is, but only that which seems
Shall find its dwelling in the place of dreams;
The soul's possession is eternal youth.
Swift flows the stream, but in it as it flows
The same unchanging stars are mirrored bright.
Swift fly the years, but heedless of their flight
The touch of time, not love nor friendship knows.[8]

Suzanne and Sir Hubert somehow managed to freeze the swift flow of time and were reunited beneath the stars. Though Lady Wilkins outlived her husband by sixteen years, when the time came the US Navy also carried her ashes to the North Pole, where they were spread to the winds to join those of her husband – united after a lifetime of separations.

After her husband's death, Suzanne received tributes from all over the world. One of the finest came in a personal note from the legendary science editor of the *New York Times*, Walter Sullivan, who had first met Sir Hubert at Point Barrow: 'He was a great man, and quite unlike so many polar explorers whose principal motivation seems to be a craving for publicity rather than solid, scientific achievement. Sir Hubert was a charming, modest, brilliant and highly skilled explorer whose mark on polar history, at both ends of the world, will always be a deep one.'[9]

Richard Byrd Jr, son of his great rival, had served briefly under

Wilkins during World War II and was more than happy to put to rest any lasting ill-feeling. He reminded Lady Wilkins how proud he was that Sir Hubert had graciously named a cape after Byrd in the Antarctic. Evidence, he wrote, of 'his thoughtfulness and generosity'.[10]

Merle Tuve, of the Carnegie Institution, said: 'His life was like epic poetry full of struggle and partial fulfilment. Both his victories and defeats pushed back the frontiers of knowledge, and often he was the only one pushing.'

Of his contemporaries, only Stefansson outlived him, but he belonged to a previous age of explorers and eschewed anything modern. Wilkins was the shining link from the heroic age of Nansen, Amundsen and Scott, the only one to travel from the age of sailing ship and dog sled to jet planes and submarines.

James Calvert, a good sailor and ultimately a famous one, admired him and, I suspect, was left with a touch of envy for the man's easy freedom and unwillingness to conform to any rule book.

'People like Wilkins,' he told me, 'take us to places we might not otherwise go and reveal the truths that might otherwise stay hidden.'

Wilkins was unmoved by working-class revolutions, unshackled by dogma; his optimism was left unbroken by the ferocity of wars or the blind cruelties of nature. His talent was to see beyond the horizons of our limitations or the vicissitudes of fate. He sought a licence to dream, to imagine, to go where we had not ventured with our feet or our minds. Ultimately he believed in the power of the human spirit to walk into unknown territory and make good, for ourselves and our world. His legacy was this sanguine, unshakeable faith in our power to progress. Where would we be without his kind?

Notes

A note on sources

Not surprisingly for a man with such a varied career, the remnants of Sir Hubert Wilkins' colourful life are spread around the world, in many libraries and scientific archives and especially in the collection of the Byrd Polar Research Center at the Ohio State University. (References from this collection are cited as follows: author, description, BPRC, box number–folder number.)

Wilkins' long career attracted many journalists over the years and the *New York Times* was, as ever, an important starting point for research. A bibliography of key books, including of course Sir Hubert's own, follows.

Abbreviations

AWM   Australian War Memorial, Canberra
BPRC   Byrd Polar Research Center, Ohio State University, USA
CAE   Canadian Arctic Expedition, 1913–1917
ML   Mitchell Library, Sydney
NHM   Natural History Museum, London
OSU   Ohio State University
SHW   Captain Sir George Hubert Wilkins
Stefansson Collection – Rauner Library, Dartmouth College, New Hampshire, USA

Prologue

1 In fact they were probably just short of the record of 82 70' set by the steamship *Roosevelt* under the command of Admiral Peary in 1908.
2 Sir Hubert Wilkins, 'I Was Afraid', *The Country Gentleman*, February 1929 (American Geographical Library, University of Wisconsin) p. 153.
3 Sir Hubert Wilkins' Diary, 22 August 1931. *Wilkins-Ellsworth Trans Arctic Submarine Expedition: Reports – May-September, 1931*, BPRC, 15–30.

Chapter 1

1 *Adelaide Advertiser*, 30 December 1908.
2 Sir Hubert Wilkins would later claim he was descended from the great scientific figure Bishop John Wilkins (1614–1672), one of the founders of the Royal Society, whose astounding predictions would include the use of submarines in polar exploration. See Chapter 12.
3 No full list of the first South Australian settlers remains, probably due to the loss of records in the same fire that destroyed William Wilkins' papers. However extensive research work has been done by the Pioneers' Association of South Australia and the information used here draws heavily on its various publications.
4 *The Complete Newgate Calendar*, Vol. V.
5 Edward Gibbon Wakefield, 'A letter from Sydney', *London Morning Chronicle*, 21 August 1829.
6 Giancarlo de Vivo, *Collected Works of Robert Torrens*, University of Naples, Volume 4 Introduction Colonisation of South Australia (2nd edition, 1836); Minute on the Evidence given by Mr Wakefield, before the Committee on the Affairs of South Australia (1841).
7 Adelaide eventually became the centre of the Australian wool industry, the world's biggest producer and exporter.
8 The Kaurna began rapidly disappearing after white settlement began. Within 35 years the last full-blood tribal member would be dead
9 The term *wowser* – surely one of the most expressive in the Australian vernacular – is used to express healthy contempt for those who try to force their own morality on others. Australia's leading nineteenth-century poet CJ Dennis defined the term: 'Wowser: an ineffably pious person who mistakes this world for a penitentiary and himself for a warder.'
10 Fifty years after his birth, Sir Hubert would initiate a search to try to discover his birth records. In an apologetic letter dated 26 October 1938, the Deputy Registrar of South Australia would write to him, saying that despite his efforts, 'no trace of your birth could be found', and respectfully returned a refund of two shillings for the unsuccessful search.
11 SHW, unpublished, undated manuscript, BPRC, p. 4.
12 SHW, *Under the North Pole* (New York, Brewer Warren and Putnam, 1931) p. 77.
13 ibid., p. 79.

Chapter 2

1 SHW, *Biographical sketches*, undated, unpublished BPRC, 1–15.
2 SHW, *Outline for an Autobiography*, undated, unpublished, BPRC, 1–14, p. 2.
3 SHW, *Under the North Pole*, op cit., p. 82.
4 SHW, *Outline*, op. cit., p. 8.
5 SHW, Diary, 1911, BPRC, 2–6.
6 SHW, *Outline*, op. cit., p. 11.
7 *True Adventure Thrills*, unpublished, undated radio scripts, BPRC, Episode 2, p. 3.
8 Prest, Round and Fort (Ed.), *The Wakefield Companion to South Australian History* (Adelaide, Wakefield Press, 2001).
9 G Edgar (Ed), *Careers for Men, Women and Children* (London, 1911), Vol. I, pp. 106–7: 'How to Become a Bioscope Photographer': *Bioscope*, 12 December 1912, pp. 800–801. I am indebted to the invaluable research into the early newsreel done by Nicholas Hiley, former Head of Information at the British Universities Film & Video Council.

10 Paul Desdemaines Hugon, *Hints to Newsfilm Cameramen*, (New Jersey, Pathé, 1915). The author was managing editor of the American Pathé News, but he had spent the previous three years at the company's London branch.

11 John Grierson, *Sir Hubert Wilkins, Enigma of Exploration* (London, Robert Hale, 1960) p. 23. The amount seems an exaggeration given that other newsreel men at the time were so poorly remunerated.

12 David Oliver, *Hendon Aerodrome – A History* (London, Airlife, 1994).

13 SHW, *Early Flying Experiences*, script for public lecture, undated. BPRC, 1–15, p. 1. 14 Hamel, winner of many of the early air races, disappeared over the English Channel in 1914. Hucks, the first Englishman to fly upside down, lasted until 1918. Grahame-White was the exception. He died in 1959 at the highly advanced aviator's age of 80.

15 As colourful as any of the early flyers, the former cabaret singer Deperdussin made and lost a fortune in flying. In 1917 he was jailed for embezzling millions of francs from his aviation company.

16 SHW *Early Flying Experiences*, op. cit., p. 2.

17 SHW, 'I Was Afraid' op cit.

18 SHW, *Under the North Pole*, op. cit., p. 86.

19 *True Adventure Thrills*, op. cit., Episode 3, p. 3.

20 ibid., p. 1.

21 Philip Gibbs and Bernard Grant, *Adventures of War With Cross and Crescent*, (London, Methuen, 1912) p. 165.

22 ibid., p. 189.

23 *True Adventure Thrills*, op. cit., Episode 6, p. 2.

24 SHW, *Balkan War Reports*, unpublished, undated handwritten manuscript, BPRC, 13–8, p.3.

25 *True Adventure Thrills*, op. cit., Episode 7 p. 2.

26 ibid., Chapter 10 p. 2.

27 Reported conversation with Walter Wood, former president of the American Geographical Society, *The Geographical Review*, No 3, 1959, p. 411.

28 SHW, *Lecture for the Gaumont Company Cinematographers*, 1912 Unpublished typescript, BPRC, 13–8, p. 7.

Chapter 3

1 Cablegram, West India and Panama Telegraph Company, 16 April 1913, BPRC, 17–11.

2 SHW, undated manuscript, *From a Hundred Above to Fifty Below*, Stefansson Collection, Dartmouth College Library, 62, 1:2.

3 SHW, undated manuscript: *Christmas Candy and a Runaway Balloon*, BPRC, 13–9.

4 Harold Noice, *With Stefansson in the Arctic* (London, Harrap, 1925) p. 24.

5 Quoted in DM LeBourdaid, *Sir Hubert Wilkins in the Canadian Arctic*, *Canadian Geographical Review*, May 1926, pp. 161–167.

6 These diaries and notes, some typed and others handwritten in Wilkins' frustratingly difficult script, reside today among the papers of the Stefansson Collection at the Baker Library, Dartmouth College, New Hampshire. Wilkins himself began a book based on them, but eventually abandoned the project. They remained unpublished until 2004 when Stuart Jenness, son of CAE scientist Diamond Jenness, painstakingly reconstructed them for his book *The Making of an Explorer*, for which the author is greatly indebted.

7 William Laird McKinlay, *The Last Voyage of the Karluk*, (London, Weidenfeld and Nicolson, 1976) p. 29.

8 Eskimo is an inclusive term covering many linguistic groups of Artic people. It is preferred to the term Inuit, which is specific to a language group of people inhabiting Artic Canada and parts of Greenland. For the most part, Wilkins was in contact with non-Inuit speaking people during his travels with the CAE and during his later flying expeditions.

9 Vilhjalmur Stefansson, *The Friendly Arctic*, (London, Macmillan, 1921) p. 291.

10 SHW, *CAE diaries*, 29 October, 1913.

11 SHW, *True Adventure Thrills*, op cit., Episode 20

12 ibid.

13 ibid.

14 SHW, *CAE diaries*, 31 October 1913.

15 Stuart Jenness, *The Making of an Explorer*, (Toronto, McGill-Queen's University Press, 2004) p. 41.

16 SHW, *True Adventure Thrills*, op cit., Episode 21.

17 Wilkins went back to his rifle after his lucky escape. Two bear cubs he and his regular indigenous travelling companion, Natkusiak, collected near Kellett Base in December 1914 were made into museum skins and sent to Ottawa. For thirty years they were on display as part of a museum diorama and one of the cubs has been part of a travelling exhibition on climate change since 2003.

18 Herbert Nicholls, *Explorers Journal*, December 1964, p. 203.

19 Wilkins was gradually able to restore his photographic equipment from various pieces he purchased. He has left a remarkable archive of nearly 1000 images and more than 2000 metres of moving pictures, much of which survives today. Sadly, almost half his film was lost in a fire at the National Film Board of Canada in 1967. Many of the surviving moving picures and photos may be viewed online at the Canadian Museum of Civilization: http://www.civilization.ca

20 SHW, *CAE diaries*, 6 June 1914.

21 Vilhjalmur Stefansson, 'The Most Unforgettable Character I've met,' (Nomad Publications, New York, 1925).

22 SHW, *CAE diaries*, 18 June 1914.

23 McConnell Papers, *Arctic Diaries*, 9 July 1914, folder 28, Stefansson Collection, Dartmouth.

24 SHW *CAE diaries*, 11 August 1914.

25 Vilhjalmur Stefansson, *The Friendly Arctic*, loc. cit.

26 SHW, *Under the North Pole*, op. cit., p. 4.

27 SHW, unpublished manuscript, undated but likely to be circa 1930/1931, BPRC, 1–15.

28 Stuart Jenness, *The Making of an Explorer*, op. cit., p. 332.

29 Neither man needed have worried about the widow Wilkins' health. She still had many years left, and Stefansson in fact met her on a visit to Australia in 1923.

30 Vilhjalmur Stefansson, 1920, National Archives of Canada. http://www.civilization.ca

Chapter 4

1 The most complete record of Wilkins' diaries and reports from the expedition is held in the Stefansson Collection at Dartmouth College, New Hampshire. Stefansson added many corrections and comments to the Wilkins accounts, but uncharacteristically appears to have left unchallenged many of Wilkins' more critical observations. As they were already known to Canadian authorities, perhaps he felt the damage had been done.

2 Following this disastrous convoy, the practice of allowing Canadian families to travel to Britain was discontinued.

3 SHW, *True Adventure Thrills*, op cit., episode 29, p. 1.
4 Sadly, today there is not a single monument or recognition of this favoured son anywhere in the state, although a private group raised funds to rebuild the simple stone cottage where Wilkins was born.
5 SHW, *Early Flying Experiences*, op cit., 1–15, p. 8.
6 Dennis Winter (Ed.), *Making the Legend, The War Writings of CEW Bean.* (University of Queensland Press, 1992).
7 CEW Bean, *The Gallipoli Mission* (Australian War Memorial, 1948), p. 20.
8 Frank Hurley, *Diaries, August 1917 to August 1918*, Official War Photographer, 1st AIF, Mitchell Library MSS389/5, diary entry for 23 August 1917.
9 As told to Lowell Thomas in *Sir Hubert Wilkins: His World of Adventure*, (New York, McGraw Hill, 1961), p. 103.
10 Casualty Form, War Service Records, GH Wilkins, National Archives of Australia, B2455.
11 Charles F Horne (Ed.), *Records of the Great War, Vol. VI,*(National Alumni, 1923).
12 Frank Hurley diary, op cit., 23 August 1917.
13 ibid., 26 August 1917.
14 SHW, unpublished biographical sketch, BPRC, 1–15, p. 9.
15 Frank Hurley diary, op cit., 28 October 1917.
16 ibid., 26 September 1917.
17 CEW Bean (Ed.), *Official History of Australia in the War of 1914–18, Vol. IV* (Sydney, Angus and Robertson, 1933).
18 John Grierson, *Enigma of Exploration*, op cit., p. 63.
19 SHW, *True Adventure Thrills*, op cit., Episode 30.
20 ibid.
21 Lowell Thomas, Unpublished biography, notes, p. 190, BPRC, 2–1.
22 Frank Hurley diary, op cit., 12 October 1917.
23 ibid., 10 November 1917.
24 *War Memoirs of David Lloyd George, Vol. IV*, (London, 1933-36), p. 2110.
25 Winston Churchill, *The World Crisis, 1911–1918, Vol. IV*, (Thornton Butterworth, 1923) p. 1177.

Chapter 5

1 SHW, *Early Flying Experiences*, op cit., p. 8.
2 John Grierson, *Enigma of Exploration*, op cit., p. 59.
3 CEW Bean, *Diaries and Notes Concerning the War of 1914–18*, 21 April 1918, AWM, 3DRL, 606/107/2 p. 54.
4 SHW, letter to CEW Bean, 20 November 1923, AWM, 38 3DRL6673/468.
5 CEW Bean, *The Gallipoli Mission*, loc cit.
6 CEW Bean, Notice of Commendation for Military Cross, undated, AWM, 3000 6673/57.
7 Balloons were considered a legitimate 'kill' and were added to the tally of aces of all air forces.
8 SHW, *True Adventure Thrills*, op cit., Episode 32.
9 Lowell Thomas, *Sir Hubert Wilkins: His World of Adventure* (New York, McGraw-Hill, 1961), p. 105.
10 SHW, *True Adventure Thrills*, op cit., Episode 31.
11 CEW Bean, *Diaries and Notes Concerning the War of 1914–18*, 19 April 1918, op cit., p. 38.
12 SHW, *Under the North Pole*, op cit., p. 103.
13 SHW, *True Adventure Thrills*, op cit., Episode 30.

14 SHW, *Biographical sketches*, undated, unpublished, BPRC, 1–15, p. 11.
15 Australian military records differ on the precise date Wilkins received his MC. Both June and July are given for his award. Similar imprecision surrounds the date he was awarded a bar to his MC though it appears to have been awarded in September 1918. Such confusion was not uncommon.
16 Both Wilkins and Hurley had pioneered the use of colour photography. Using an early Paget process they captured the first images of battle ever taken in colour. These were the subject of a major exhibition at the Australian War Memorial, Canberra, in 2004.
17 Gaumont Graphic No. 873 of July 31, 1919 summarised as 'His Majesty Invests Captain GH Wilkins with MC and Bar and Arctic Medal: Captain Wilkins Was Formerly on the Staff of the Gaumont Co'. Sadly, no copy of the film survives.
18 The conversation is related in a newspaper article by Stefansson written for the Australian press: *Adelaide Register*, 12 July 1924.
19 CEW Bean, as quoted by the official website of the Australian War Memorial exhibition 'Captured in Colour'.
      http://www.awm.gov.au/captured/official/gallipoli/index.asp
20 CEW Bean, 'A Great Australian – Sir Hubert Wilkins', *Reveille Magazine*, 1 April 1939.

Chapter 6

1 John Grierson, *Enigma of Exploration*, op cit., p. 63.
2 SHW, *Flying the Arctic* (New York, George Putnam, 1928) p. 6.
3 John Grierson, *Enigma of Exploration*, loc cit.
4 ibid.
5 Hughes cable as quoted in Nelson Eustis, *The Greatest Air Race*, (Adelaide, Rigby, 1968). I acknowledge a great debt to the late Hamilton Nelson Eustis, the doyen of Australian philately, who was the acknowledged expert on international air races and supplied much of the information for this chapter.
6 ibid., p. 4
7 *Manchester Guardian*, 28 May 1919.
8 Nelson Eustis, *The Greatest Air Race*, op cit., p. 16
9 Kingsford Smith was not the only great aviator excluded from the race. Despite months of intensive preparation, Bert Hinkler was also refused a start because he intended to fly solo. In 1928, Hinkler broke all records for the England–Australia route – flying solo, and went on to become one of the finest long-distance flyers of all time.
10 SHW, *True Adventure Thrills*, op cit., Episode 33, p. 2.
11 Wilkins' war-time friend Frank Hurley released a successful film on the race in 1920. It was based on film shot with competitors Ross and Keith Smith, as they flew across Australia at the end of the race. By inserting old footage he'd shot in the Middle East during the war, and adding some wobbly stills, Hurley was able to re-create the entire journey convincingly.
12 *New York Times*, 19 October 1919.
13 SHW, *True Adventure Thrills*, loc cit. Episode 33.
14 The problems of flying through fog were so intractable in the early days of aviation that airmail pilots caught in sudden fog often bailed out, apparently gathering the mailbags from the crashed remains of their aircraft.
15 *New York Times* editorial, 18 October 1919. Unfortunately, in its first mention of Wilkins this venerable paper misspelt his name as 'Watkins'. But they got it right in the following years and he became something of a favourite, writing many

articles and always being favourably reviewed. The *New York Times* archive holds
more than 700 references to him.

16 SHW, *England to Australia Air Race*, BPRC, 13–12.
17 *The Sun*, Sydney, 23 November 1919.
18 SHW, *True Adventure Thrills*, loc cit. Episode 33.
19 SHW, 'I Was Afraid', op cit.
20 SHW, *True Adventure Thrills*, op cit., Episode 33, p. 4.
21 SHW, *True Adventure Thrills*, op cit., Episode 33.
22 ibid.
23 SHW, *True Adventure Thrills*, op cit., Episode 33, p. 6.

Chapter 7

1 JC Beaglehole (Ed.), *The Journals of James Cook*, Volume II, (Cambridge, The Hakluyt Society, 1961).
2 The estimate of the number of scientific expeditions is derived from Dr Michael Rosove's monumental bibliography, *Antarctica, 1772–1922* (Santa Monica, Free-standing Publications, 1999).
3 Letter from Cope to the Royal Aeronautical Society, 3 May 1920, which was already promising Wilkins' involvement, BPRC, 13–13. This was by no means the most grandiose of his descriptions of the plan.
4 SHW, *Under the North Pole*, op cit., p. 106.
5 *The Geographical Journal*, Volume 55, 1920, p. 327.
6 SHW, *The Economic Value of Antarctic Meteorology to the Agriculturists of Australia*, MS 1920, BPRC, 13–3.
7 SHW, *Under the North Pole*, op cit., p. 107.
8 *New York Evening Post*, 11 December 1920.
9 Christensen later became something of a friendly rival to Wilkins in polar aviation. In 1937 his wife was the first woman to fly in Antarctica.
10 Also aboard the *Solstrejf* was another noted adventurer, the Danish writer Aage Krarup Nielsen, whose photos of the forlorn Cope party were published in one of his many travel books, *En Hvalfangerfaerd gennem Troperne til Sydishavet* (Copenhagen, H Aschehoug & Co., 1921).
11 SHW, *True Adventure Thrills*, op cit., Episode 38, p. 2.
12 ibid., p. 3.
13 *The Geographical Journal* Volume 57, 2 February 1921, p. 151.
14 Claude Cowan, *John Lachlan Cope's Expedition to Graham Land, 1920–22*, Scott Polar Research Institute, online summary. www.spri.cam.ac.uk/resources/expeditions/blax/
15 Lowell Thomas, *Sir Hubert Wilkins: His World of Adventure*, op cit., p. 138.
16 Thomas Bagshawe, *Two Men in the Antarctic* (Cambridge, Cambridge University Press, 1939) p. 114.
17 David McGonigal and Dr Lynn Woodworth, *Antarctica and the Arctic* (Willondale, Ont., Firefly Books, 2001) p. 479.
18 SHW, *Under the North Pole*, op cit., p. 107.
19 In the small circle of polar expeditioners, Marr and Wilkins would become part of a closely linked network. Not only did Marr go on to travel on the 1931 BANZARE voyages with Wilkins' war-time colleague Frank Hurley, his success as the scouting-explorer inspired Wilkins' rival in Antarctic aviation, Robert Byrd, to take an American scout on one of his expeditions.
   Like Marr, that teenage recruit, Paul Siple, went on to an illustrious career in polar science, inventing the concept of wind-chill, founding America's permanent

base at the South Pole and in the late 1950s, working as a colleague of Sir Hubert Wilkins.

20 SHW, letter, 7 August 1921, BPRC, 13–14.
21 Macklin in Frank Wild, *Shackleton's Last Voyage* (London, Cassell, 1923) p. 141–142.
22 SHW, letter, 7 August 1921, loc cit.
23 James Marr, *The Western Mail*, 12 April 1922.
24 SHW, *Notes of GH Wilkins, Naturalist*, manuscript, BPRC, 13–17, p. 20.
25 ibid., p. 30.
26 ibid., p. 35.
27 SHW, *True Adventure Thrills*, op cit., Episode 40, p. 2.
28 *New York Times*, 22 April, 1928.
29 ibid.

Chapter 8

1 John Ruskin, *Remarks on the Present State of Meteorological Science* (London, Transactions Meteorological Society, Smith Elder and Co., 1839) p. 56–59.
2 ibid.
3 Though the records of the Royal Meteorological Society no longer contain Wilkins' proposal, its receipt was acknowledged in the minutes of its Governing Council, 21 February 1923. Wilkins made many written references to the plan, including a seven-page undated letter written in London (BPRC, 13–15) from which the quotation and other details are drawn.
4 Wilkins proudly kept his certificate of election, dated 21 March 1923, all his life. It remains in his papers at the Byrd Polar Research Centre, Ohio State University.
5 In one of the many curious coincidences surrounding Wilkins, Lucita Squier would in 1925 write the screenplay adaptation of *City of Temptation*, written by Wilkins' Balkan war friend Philip Gibbs. The film was directed by a fellow war correspondent, Walter Niebuhr.
6 Williams was eulogised in the USSR and decried in the USA. While *Pravda* praised him, his *New York Times* obituary (28 February 1962) described him as a Soviet apologist.
7 The films are held today in the archives of the British Film Institute, London, and graphically capture the devastation and poverty of this dark and largely forgotten period in recent European history.
8 SHW, *Notes on Conditions Existing in Soviet Russia*, December 1922, BPRC, 13–18, p. 6.
9 Estimate taken from a detailed review of the famine years with much background on the work of the American Relief Administration: Bertrand Patenaude, *The Big Show in Bololand*, (Stanford, Stanford University Press, 2002).
10 SHW, *Notes on Conditions* op. cit., p. 7.
11 Telegram from Nansen to Red Cross Headquarters, 9 December 1921. Nansen Electronic Photographic Archive, Norwegian National Library
http://www.nb.no/baser/nansen/english.html
12 Bertrand Patenaude, *The Big Show in Bololand*, op cit., quoting former Hoover Institution director Harold Fisher.
13 SHW, *True Adventure Thrills*, Episode 43, p. 2.
14 SHW, *Mark Twain Was Dead Wrong*, undated manuscript, BPRC, 22–22.
15 SHW, *Notes on Conditions*, op.cit., p. 11.

Chapter 9

1 Charles Darwin, 'Journey Across the Blue Mountains to Bathurst in January 1836, in Fourteen Journeys', cited in Allan Fox and Steve Parish, *Australia's Wilderness Experience* (Adelaide, Rigby, 1984) p. 68.

2 *Nature*, Volume 105, No 2644, 1 July 1920, p. 558.

3 SHW, *Undiscovered Australia*, (New York, Brewer, Warren and Putnam, 1929) Appendix, p. 319.

4 *Brisbane Courier*, 9 April 1923.

5 A useful discussion concerning the various means of estimating can be found in Gordon Briscoe, *Disease, Health and Healing: Aspects of Indigenous Health in Western Australia and Queensland, 1900–1940*, thesis submitted for the degree of Doctor of Philosophy, Australian National University, September 1996
http://histrsss.anu.edu.au/briscoe/1.html

6 For a depressing assessment of Australia's environmental degradation, see Michael Archer and Bob Beale, *Going Native* (Sydney, Hodder Headline, 2004), Chapter 4.

7 SHW, *Undiscovered Australia*, op cit., p. 10.

8 ibid., p. 40.

9 ibid., Foreword.

10 ibid., p. 49.

11 SHW, letter to Dr Herbert Smith, British Museum, 9 July 1923, NHM.

12 SHW, letter to Dr Herbert Smith, British Museum, 22 November 1923, NHM.

13 SHW, *Undiscovered Australia*, op cit., p. 160.

14 The railway would take another 80 years to complete.

15 SHW, *Undiscovered Australia*, op cit., p. 247.

16 ibid.

17 ibid., p. 130.

18 The only contemporary, corroborating reference the author can find to this story by Wilkins is by a local historian Leo Carpenter, in *Livingstone: A History of Livingstone Shire* (Brisbane, Boolarong Publications, 1991): 'An entire tribe was chased back into the hills and finally onto the cliff edge of Mt Wheeler . . . there the native troopers "did not waste their ammunition" and the blacks were stampeded and driven over the side of the cliff.'

19 Australian marine archaeologist Michael Tracey has spent many years studying the fate of the *Douglas Mawson* and is one of the few to have read the Royal Commission's final report. He believes it adds little to solving the mystery of what actually happened.

20 SHW, *Undiscovered Australia*, op cit., p. 258.

21 White Australia was slow to learn. In this precise spot in 1932, five Japanese fishermen were killed in a dispute over Indigenous women. A police constable was later speared after handcuffing the wife of the tribal leader, Dhakiyarr Wirrpanda. In a celebrated case that went to Australia's High Court, Dhakiyarr's murder conviction was overthrown. The night before his release from prison, he disappeared, believed murdered by local police.

22 *Daily Mail*, Brisbane, 19 May 1925.

23 SHW, *Undiscovered Australia*, op cit., p. 286.

24 SHW, 'I Was Afraid', op cit., p. 154.

25 *The Adelaide Chronicle*, 28 March 1925.

26 SHW, 'I Was Afraid', op cit.

27 A comprehensive study of 400 claims of Aboriginal cannibalism has shown that less than 1 per cent claimed to be from first-hand observations. See Michael Pickering, *Cannibalism amongst Aborigines? A critical review of the literary evidence.*

Litt. B. Thesis, Department of Prehistory and Anthropology, Australian National University, 1985.

28 What other evidence we have does little to substantiate his account. Several years before Wilkins arrived in Carpentaria, a young etymologist, Norman Tindale, spent 20 months recording his observations there in rigorous detail. It was his first expedition and the beginning of a remarkable career in several branches of science including anthropology. Tindale lived peacefully with the 'savage' tribes that Wilkins described as 'man-eaters'. His extensive expedition diaries confirm the potential dangers of working alone in tribal country, but there is no suggestion of cannibalism. Tindale's diaries, collected over nearly fifty years of field work, are held in the South Australian Museum. Like Wilkins, he eventually left Australia for the United States and his unique contributions in several scientific fields have been largely overlooked in his homeland.

29 *The Daily News and Westminster Gazette*, 5 October 1928.

30 One paragraph in his book, *Undiscovered Australia*, had mentioned that several people observed at Milingimbi exhibited a protrusion on their lower vertebrae, not unusual perhaps in a region of endemic leprosy. It became the basis of numerous newspaper stories about 'men with tails'.

31 SHW, *Undiscovered Australia*, op cit., p. 311.

32 Unidentified newspaper clipping, Adelaide, April 1925, BPRC, 31–15.

33 SHW, *Undiscovered Australia*, op cit., p. 315.

34 SF Harmer, letter to British Museum (Natural History) Trustees, 21 October 1925, NHM.

35 The rock wallaby *Petrogale wilkinsi* and the short-limbed lizard *Lerista wilkins*. The wallaby is on Queensland's endangered species list.

36 SHW, letter to Dr Herbert Smith, British Museum, 23 October 1924, NHM.

37 *New York Times*, 24 February 1929.

Chapter 10

1 SHW, letter to Dr Herbert Smith, 28 November 1928, NHM.

2 SHW, *Flying the Arctic*, op cit., p. 16.

3 Richard Byrd, telegram to Detroit Arctic Expedition, via Bowman, 9 January 1926, American Geographical Society.

4 Richard Byrd, letter to SHW, 22 January 1926, BPRC, 14–9.

5 SHW, *Flying the Arctic*, op cit., 1928, p. 24.

6 Bert and Margie Webber, *I Shoot the News – The Adventures of Will E Hudson*, (Oregon, Webb Research Group, 1999), p. 169.

7 SHW, *True Adventure Thrills*, op cit., Episode 51, BPRC, 1–13.

8 SHW, *Flying the Arctic*, op cit., p. 45.

9 ibid., p. 54.

10 ibid., p. 56.

11 Bert and Margie Webber, *I Shoot the News*, op cit., p. 175.

12 ibid.

13 Richard Byrd, *Skyward* (New York, Putnam and Co, 1928) p. 175.

14 See the excellent summary of the controversy in Beekman Pool, *Polar Extremes, The World of Lincoln Ellsworth* (Fairbanks, University of Alaska Press, 2002), chapter 4.

15 Given that they loathed each other, it remains one of the sad ironies of polar history that in 1928 Amundsen would eventually disappear while flying on a search and rescue mission in support of Nobile's crashed airship, the *Italia*.

16 As brave as they were neither Byrd's nor Ellsworth's efforts were initially recognised as having made much contribution to science in the United States. The Langley Medal, the highest award of the Smithsonian Institution, was denied both of them. Ellsworth's cousin, Vice President Charles G Dawes, appointed a special committee of distinguished experts who came to the same conclusion – there was nothing about the flights that had significantly advanced science. A year later however, the committee for some reason changed its mind. Byrd got his medal, though Ellsworth was overlooked.

17 Press statement by WB Mayo, 30 December 1926, BPRC, 14–11.

18 SHW, *Under the North Pole*, op cit., p. 143.

19 SHW, *True Adventure Thrills*, op cit., Episode 52, p. 3.

20 Richard Byrd and Vilhjalmur Stefansson, *Science*, Volume LXV, No. 1691, 27 May 1929.

21 ibid.

22 SHW, *Under the North Pole*, op cit., p. 147.

23 SHW, 'I Was Afraid', op cit., p. 156.

24 SHW, *True Adventure Thrills*, op cit., Episode 53, p. 1.

25 In fact the remaining members of the team ignored his instructions and launched a series of unsuccessful search flights. Snippets of Wilkins' radio messages had been received, though not his location report. The team remained in Barrow waiting for their leader's return.

26 Lt Ben Eielson, comments, Barrow, 2 May 1927, as communicated to AM Smith, *Detroit News* correspondent, BPRC, 14–21.

27 SHW, *True Adventure Thrills*, op cit., Episode 54, p. 2.

28 SHW, letter to AM Smith, *Detroit News* Correspondent, 14/15 April 1927, BPRC, 14–8.

29 *The Times*, London, 2 December 1958.

Chapter 11

1 SHW, *Flying the Arctic*, op cit., p. 202.

2 In 1998 two commemorative small aeroplane flights attempted to recreate the Wilkins/Eielson flight. One made it, one did not. Both had the benefit of modern GPS navigation systems.

3 Lowell Thomas, *Sir Hubert Wilkins: His World of Adventure*, op cit., p. 200.

4 SHW, *Flying the Arctic*, op cit., p. 232.

5 SHW, letter to Dr Herbert Smith, 19 March 1928, NHM, p. 207.

6 SHW, *Flying the Arctic*, op cit., p. 249.

7 ibid., p. 270.

8 *Quarterly Journal of the Royal Meteorological Society*, XIII (1887) p. 163.

9 SHW, *Flying the Arctic*, op cit., p. 289.

10 SHW, 'Flying Over the Top of the World', *Blue Book Magazine*, Volume 62, No 1, November 1935.

11 OM Miller, *The Geographical Review*, Volume XVIII no. 4, October 1928, p. 552.

12 SHW, *Flying the Arctic*, op cit., p. 325.

13 ibid., p. 301.

14 Leon S Vincent, letter to Lura Shreck, 30 April 30 1928, republished in *Flying the Arctic*, op cit., p. 333.

15 SHW, *Flying the Arctic*, op cit., p. 316.

16 ibid., p. 331.

17 Arthur Hays Sulzberger, letter to SHW, 2 May, year unknown, BPRC, 13–7.

18 The *New York Times* syndicated the story on his behalf around the world; eventually it earned him nearly $20 000, a huge amount for the era.
19 Burt M McConnell, 'Wilkins Goes Over the Top', *The Elks Magazine*, June 1928.
20 Herbert Nichols, *Explorers Journal*, December 1964, p. 209.
21 Lady Suzanne Wilkins, unpublished draft of chapter for Lowell Thomas, BPRC, 1–16, p. 5.
22 Wilkins later also received a knighthood from the Italian monarch.
23 *The Times*, London, 8 June 1928.
24 Mawson, letter to JP Thomson, 1 July 1929, Mawson Antarctic Collection, Adelaide. A detailed examination of the difficult relations between Australia's two polar knights, Wilkins and Mawson, is found in Philip Ayres' *Mawson, A Life*, (Melbourne, Melbourne University Press, 1999).
25 Lowell Thomas, op cit., p. 285.
26 Lady Suzanne Wilkins, unpublished draft chapter, op cit., p. 5.
27 *New York Times*, 7 July 1927.
28 TV Ranck, cable to WR Hearst, 5 July 1928, BPRC, 14–26.
29 Richard Montague, *Oceans, Poles and Airmen* (New York, Random House, 1971) p. 221.
30 Ellis to Amery, Dominions Office, diplomatic cable, 21 November 1928, Public Records Office UK, CO 78/182/9.
31 As the SS *Medic* she had sailed the route between Liverpool and Australia since 1898 and carried Australian soldiers to the Boer War . . . The *Hektoria* ended its days as a British oil carrier, sent to the bottom by a U-boat torpedo in 1942.
32 *The Times*, London, 21 December 1928.
33 ibid.
34 SHW, 'Illustrated Record of the Wilkins-Hearst Antarctic Expedition', Article 2, March 1929, manuscript, BPRC, 13–34, p. 18.

Chapter 12

1 A Scott Berg, *Lindbergh*, (New York, Putnam, 1998) p. 5.
2 ibid., p. 163.
3 Douglas Botting, *Dr Eckener's Dream Machine*, (London, HarperCollins, 2001) p. 143.
4 *New York Times*, 21 March 1929.
5 SHW, *True Adventure Thrills*, op cit., Episode 56.
6 *New York Times*, 11 August 1929.
7 Their aeroplane, the *City of New York*, is now in the collection of the Smithsonian Institution museum in Washington DC. It was Mears' second circumnavigation. In 1913, he had cut Nellie Bly's time to thirty-six days. Collyer was killed later in 1928 attempting the transcontinental flight record across the United States.
8 *New York Times*, 13 August 1929.
9 Hugo Eckener, *My Zeppelins*, translated by Douglas H Robinson, (London, Putnam and Co, 1958).
10 Sadly this unique film, given to the US airforce in the 1960s by Wilkins' widow, has been lost.
11 Douglas Botting, op cit., p. 170.
12 ibid., p. 184
13 SHW, *True Adventure Thrills*, op cit., Episode 56.
14 ibid.
15 Bert and Margie Webber, *I Shoot the News*, op cit., p. 195.
16 *New York Times*, 30 August 1929.

17 Herbert Nichols, *Explorers Journal*, December 1964, p. 210.
18 Unidentified newspaper clipping, 'Wilkins Treks to Happiness via Matrimony', 31 August 1929, BPRC, 28–20.
19 Lady Suzanne Wilkins, manuscript of public address, 'The Loneliest Wife in the World', undated, circa 1937, BPRC, 21–12.
20 Eugene Rogers, *Beyond the Barrier* (Maryland, Naval Institute Press, 1990) p. 156.
21 Byrd to Hilton Railey, radiogram, 5 August 1929, in Byrd's diary. Reprinted in Eugene Rogers, *Beyond the Barrier*, op cit., p. 157.
22 ibid.
23 Royal Commission dated 29 August 1929, Public Records Office, UK, C 235/1 105163.
24 Lowell Thomas, *Sir Hubert Wilkins: His World of Adventure*, op cit., p. 251.
25 Associated Press report, 27 January 1930, republished in Dorothy Page, *Polar Pilot*, (Detroit, 1992) p. 372.
26 *New York Times*, 8 February 1930.
27 *New York Times*, 23 March 1930.
28 The only other recorded flight the couple took together was several years later on the maiden voyage of the even more luxurious Zeppelin, the *Hindenburg*. Suzanne performed a song broadcast around the world, and also took the first shower ever made.
29 Lady Suzanne Wilkins, unpublished draft chapter, op cit., p. 9.

Chapter 13

I gratefully acknowledge the work on the *Nautilus* expedition done by Emily Wichman in 'Two Routes to the Arctic: Under the Ice with the *Nautilus* and through the Air with the Graf Zeppelin', in *Archive: A Journal of Undergraduate History*, University Of Wisconsin-Madison, Volume 4, May 2001; the thesis by Maria Pia Casarini-Wadhams, *By Submarine to the Arctic*, Scott Polar Research Institute, University of Cambridge, 1989; and the substantial research made by Trond Elliasen, co-director on the documentary film *Voyage of the Nautilus*, AS Videomaker, 2001.

 1 *New York Times*, 24 June 1930.
 2 SHW, 'Manuscript for Circulation to Fulfill an Agreement made with Hearst Enterprises', Part 1, 1931, BPRC, 15–27, p. 12.
 3 SHW, 'Wilkins Soon to Build Submarine', *New York Times*, 7 June 1936.
 4 SHW, unpublished manuscript, undated but likely to be circa 1930/31, BPRC, 15–19, p. 4.
 5 Lady Suzanne Wilkins, unpublished draft chapter for Lowell Thomas, op cit., p. 11.
 6 Jules Verne, telegram to Simon Lake, 21 August 1898, as reprinted in Lake, *Underneath the North Pole* (New York, Putnam, 1931) p. 230.
 7 Admiral James Calvert, US Navy (Ret.), interview with author, Explorers Club, New York, 8 March 2000.
 8 SHW, unpublished manuscript, undated but likely to be 1930/31, op cit.
 9 Lt Commander Sloan Danenhower, *Syracuse American News Paper*, 1 March 1931.
10 Editorial, *Washington Post*, 6 June 1931.
11 *New York Times*, 11 April 1931.
12 *New York Times*, 3 May 1931.
13 Memorandum of Agreement between SHW and Hearst Enterprises, undated, unsigned draft, BPRC, 15–7.

14 Admiral Hugh Rodman, syndicated article, 17 April 1931. This version quoted from *Knoxville News-Sentinel* by Beekman Pool, *Polar Extremes*, op cit., p. 153.
15 SHW, 'Manuscript for Circulation to Fulfill an Agreement made with Hearst Enterprises', Part 1, 1931, BPRC, 15–27, p. 5.
16 Sverdrup would eventually be appointed head of the Scripps Institute in La Jolla, California. It is one of the scandals of American science that during World War II he was unjustly excluded from sensitive US Government research after a jealous colleague implied Sverdrup was too close to the Nazis.
17 Lincoln Ellsworth, *Beyond Horizons* (New York, Doubleday, 1938) p. 246.
18 ibid.
19 SHW, 'Report, *Nautilus* Submarine Expedition', prepared for the US Navy, Washington DC, 1947, p. 32, BPRC, 15–28.
20 See Brayton Harris, *The Navy Times Book of Submarines: A Political, Social and Military History* (New York, Berkley Books, 1997).
21 Hugo Eckener, *My Zeppelins*, translated by Douglas Robinson (New York, Arno Press, 1958), p. 120–121.
22 SHW, unpublished manuscript, undated but likely to be circa 1930/31, BPRC, 15–19.
23 Letter to SHW from RR Pritchard, 4 February 1931, BPRC, 15–1.
24 Undated telegram to Wilkins-Ellsworth Trans-Arctic Expedition, BPRC, 14–43.
25 *New York American*, 15 April 1931.
26 'General Release of Crew', 25 February 1931, BPRC, 15–17.
27 Grimmer's family lived in hope for more than a year that he might have been picked up by a passing ship. Several bodies were found washed up in the area in that time, and one tentatively recorded as that of Grimmer. However, the family and authorities were not satisfied and it was decided later to disinter the body for examination. All crewmen on the *Nautilus* had been given dental checks, and these records made it possible to positively identify the body. It was one of the first legally binding uses of dental records in this way.
28 Ray Meyers, journal as republished in Marion D Williams, *Submarines Under Ice*, (Annapolis, Naval Press Institute, 1998) p. 8.
29 Transcribed from the contemporary newsreel, Grinberg Library, New York.
30 *Pathé News*, intertitle, 2 April 1931.
31 *The Mail*, Adelaide, 20 June 1931.

Chapter 14

1 Marion D Williams, *Submarines Under Ice*, op cit., p. 12.
2 SHW, 'Manuscript for Circulation to Fulfill an Agreement made with Hearst Enterprises', loc cit.
3 SHW, 'Draft Account of the Journey of the *Nautilus*', undated, BPRC, 22–22.
4 SHW, cablegram typescript, undated, BPRC, 15–25.
5 Marion D Williams, *Submarines Under Ice*, op cit., p. 15.
6 Meyers was later awarded the International Guild Medal of the Wireless Operators' Association for his Herculean efforts in successfully sending messages on his improvised radio transmitter.
7 Alfred Albelli, 'The Real Truth', *Modern Mechanics and Inventions*, January 1932, p. 43. From the collection of the American Philosophical Society Library.
8 Ray Meyers, radiogram, 20 September 1931, p. 2, BPRC, 15–25.
9 Marion D Williams, *Submarines Under Ice*, op cit., p. 19.
10 'Nautilus Voyage Criticised', *Adelaide News*, 12 July 1932.
11 SHW quoted in *New York Journal*, 26 June 1931.

12 Hugo Eckener, *My Zeppelins*, op cit.

13 Koestler, of course, would later become better known as the fiercely anti-communist British citizen and author of such works as *Darkness at Noon*.

14 Wilkins was interviewed by the *News Chronicle* on 25 July 1931, but the full report, and its admission that he would not be attempting to reach the Pole, was not published in full until the *Adelaide News* reported it on 5 September that year.

15 SHW, radiogram, 1 August 1931, BPRC, 15–25.

16 SHW, 'Draft Account of the Journey of the *Nautilus*', op cit.

17 Elisabeth Dored, *For meg er jorden rund*, ('To me the earth is round'), (Oslo, H Aschehoug & Co, 1955).

18 SHW, undated radiogram, BPRC, 15–25.

19 SHW, telegram, 8 August 1931, BPRC, 15–25.

20 SHW, radiogram, BPRC, 15–25.

21 SHW, cablegram, 18 August 1931, BPRC, 15–25.

22 Alfred Albelli, 'The Real Truth', *Modern Mechanics and Inventions*, op cit., p. 44. From the collection of the American Philosophical Society Library.

23 *Spark Gap Times*, August–September 1981.

24 Ray Meyers, letter to Winston Ross, 20 October 1989, BPRC, 18–4.

25 Harald Ulrik Sverdrup, *Hvorledes og Hvorfor med* Nautilus (How and Why with *Nautilus*), translated by Trond Eeliassen, (Oslo, Gyldendal Norsk Forlag, 1931), p. 91.

26 TV Ranck, Hearst Enterprises, radiogram to SHW, 23 August 1931, BPRC, 15–25.

27 SHW to Tom Clarke, *News Chronicle*, London, 23 August 1931, BPRC, 15–25.

28 Harald Ulrik Sverdrup, *Hvorledes og Hvorfor med Nautilus*, op cit., p. 106.

29 ibid.

30 Marion D Williams, *Submarines Under Ice*, op cit., p. 26.

31 SHW, report, 8 September 1931, BPRC, 15–31.

32 Ralph D Shaw, letter to SHW, 30 March 1933, BPRC, 15–7.

33 Ray E Meyers, letter to Winston Ross, 23 August 1983, BPRC, 18–4.

34 *New York Times*, 3 November 1949, p. 34.

35 Janson did not return the favour. On a visit to Wilkins' hometown of Adelaide in 1932 he accused Sir Hubert of outright cowardice. Wilkins' outraged brothers wrote letters defending him from the slur. The most telling response came from an old war colleague, Major EA Wisdom, who had witnessed many acts of courage by Wilkins on the Western Front: 'He did not know the meaning of the word fear . . . I . . . considered it a privilege to know one of Australia's greatest sons.' *Adelaide News*, 13 July 1932.

36 John Grierson, *Enigma of Exploration*, op cit., p. 145.

37 SHW, handwritten note to Winston Ross, undated, BPRC, 15–16.

38 SHW, untitled, undated manuscript, BPRC, 22–22, p. 427.

39 SHW, 'I Was Afraid', op cit.

40 Harald Ulrik Sverdrup, 'Scientific Results of the *Nautilus* Expedition', Papers in Physical Oceanography and Meteorology, published by Massachusetts Institute of Technology and Woods Hole Oceanographic Institute, Volume 2, No 1, Part 1, p. 11.

41 GK Randby, 1935 translation from the Norwegian of HU Sverdrup, *Hvorledes og hvorfor med* Nautilus (How and Why With *Nautilus*), Oslo, 1931. Typescript, Stefansson Collection, Dartmouth College Library, New Hampshire, p. 62.

42 Maria Pia Casarini-Wadhams, 'By Submarine to the Arctic', thesis, Scott Polar Research Institute, Cambridge University, 1989, p. 48.

43 SHW, Radiogram, 25 August 1931, BPRC, 15–25.

44 SHW, Report to US Navy, '*Nautilus* submarine expedition', unpublished, 1947, BPRC, 15–28.

45 SHW, 'Draft Account of the Journey of the *Nautilus*', undated, p. 432, BPRC, 22–22.
46 ibid.
47 Ray Meyers, 'Adventure, Excitement and Nostalgia Plus . . .' *Spark Gap Times*, June–July 1981.
48 SHW, 'Draft Account of the Journey of the *Nautilus*, undated, p. 433, BPRC 22–22.
49 'Stavrakov Boys Follow the Sea', *The Daily Colonist*, 12 March 1961.
50 *New York Times*, 4 September 1931.
51 *New York Times*, 5 September 1931.
52 Alfred Albelli, 'The Real Truth', op cit., p. 192.
53 SHW, 'Ship's Log and Personal Diary', 4 September 1931, p. 77, BPRC, 15–28.
54 'Stavrakov Boys Follow the Sea', op cit.
55 Admiral James Calvert, interview with author, New York, 8 March 2000.
56 William Randolph Hearst, radiogram to SHW, 5 September 1931, BPRC, 15–25.
57 SHW, 'Draft account of the Journey of the *Nautilus*', undated, p. 435, BPRC, 22–22.

Chapter 15

1 Lincoln Ellsworth, *Antarctic Lures Ellsworth Again*, copyright *New York Times* and North American News Agency, *Polar Times*, 6 March 1938.
2 SHW, handwritten corrections to manuscript by *Life* editor Wilbur Cross III, 8 October 1957, BPRC, 1–14, p. 20.
3 Ray Meyers, radiogram, 20 September, 1931, BPRC, 15–25.
4 'The Wilkins Expedition', *Outlook*, 1 July 1931, p. 263–264.
5 'A Thousand Leagues Under the Ice with Wilkins', *Literary Digest*, 21 March 1931, p. 31–33.
6 *Modern Mechanics and Inventions*, January 1932.
7 Elmer E. Crowley, President, United States Shipping Board Merchant Fleet Corporation, letter to W Herbert Adams, 30 September 1931, BPRC, 15–6.
8 In 1981 a team of Norwegian divers located the wreck of the *Nautilus* in Byfjorden, just 5 kilometres from Bergen. On the seventieth anniversary of its sinking, a television documentary crew led by Trond Elliasen returned to the site and a submersible sent back video images of the craft. It remains in good shape.
9 NBC Artist Services, correspondence to SHW, 14 October 1931, BPRC, 15–6.
10 SHW, manuscript for unfinished book, BPRC, 15–19, p. 17.
11 Lady Suzanne Wilkins, unpublished draft chapter for Thomas, op cit., p 11.
12 Lincoln Ellsworth, letter to SHW, 25 December 1931, BPRC, 15–5.
13 Magnus Olsen, *Saga of the White Horizon* (Lymington, Nautical Publishing Company, 1972) p. 125.
14 ibid., p. 99.
15 ibid., p. 104.
16 ibid., p. 106.
17 ibid., p. 113.
18 ibid., p. 114.
19 ibid., p. 124.
20 ibid., p. 124–127.
21 SHW, radiogram to Bowman, 29 December 1934, American Geographical Society, quoted in Beekman Pool, *Polar Extremes*, op cit., p. 185.
22 Lincoln Ellsworth, *Beyond Horizons*, op cit., p. 292.
23 ibid., p. 294.
24 SHW, letter to Aksel Holm, 5 April 1935, BPRC, 15–39.

25 Magnus Olsen, *Saga of the White Horizon*, op cit., p. 124.
26 William Randolph Hearst, letter to SHW, 22 May 1936, BPRC, 15–40.
27 Lincoln Ellsworth, letter to SHW, 25 July 1937, BPRC, 15–41.
28 SHW, letter to Lincoln Ellsworth, 31 July 1937, BPRC, 15–41.
29 SHW, 'The Time I Tried Telepathy', *Coronet* magazine, October 1942, p. 127, BPRC, 22–17.
30 Lady Suzanne Wilkins, *Is It Worth It?* manuscript, p.3, BPRC 21–21.
31 In March 1999, an Alaskan mineralogist, Dennis Thurston, noticed an unusual shape on a sonar image of the sea floor in the shallows of Camden Bay, between Prudhoe Bay and Kaktovik, Alaska. Thurston thought the unusual object might be the fuselage of an aeroplane. Subsequent searches have not confirmed the discovery.
32 SHW and Harold Sherman, *Thoughts Through Space: A Remarkable Adventure in the Realm of the Mind*, 2nd edition (New York, C&R Anthony, 1951) p. 34.
33 SHW, 'The Time I Tried Telepathy', op cit., p. 125–130.
34 SHW and Harold Sherman, *Thoughts Through Space*, op cit., p. 288.
35 SHW, 'The Time I Tried Telepathy', loc cit.
36 This book has been through various printings and publishers. A revised 1951 edition, with a second edition by C&R Anthony, New York, is the source of the quotations here. The latest edition was published in 2004.
37 SHW and Harold Sherman, *Thoughts Through Space*, op cit., p. 192.
38 ibid., p. 12.
39 ibid., p. 19.
40 RA Swan, *Australians in the Antarctic*, (Melbourne, Melbourne University Press, 1961) p. 224.
41 Lincoln Ellsworth, cable to SHW, 7 September 1938, quoted in Beekman Pool, op cit., p. 226.
42 ibid.
43 SHW, reply to Lincoln Ellsworth, quoted in Beekman Pool, op cit.
44 Memorandum America Policy Relating to the Polar Regions, Department of State, Division of European Affairs, 28 July 1938 (declassified 4 April 1984), 2, National Archives.
45 State Department telegram to American Consul, Cape Town, 22 October 1938, Claims 800.014 (129) Doc. File National Archives.
46 Beekman Pool, *Polar Extremes* op cit., p. 229.
47 In May 1957, a party of Australian scientists rediscovered Sir Hubert's records beneath a small cairn. The area has been known as Walkabout Rocks ever since.
48 Pierpont Moffatt, memorandum of conversation, 3 March 1939, National Archives, Washington DC quoted in Beekman Pool, op cit., p. 237.

Chapter 16

1 On his death bed, less than a year after meeting with Wilkins, Cook received a pardon from President Roosevelt.
2 Frederick Cook, unpublished manuscript, *Hell is a Cold Place*, as quoted in David Roberts, *Great Exploration Hoaxes* (New York, The Modern Library, 2001).
3 'Wilkins and Cook Discuss the Arctic', *New York Times*, 22 November 1939.
4 William S Sadler, *The Mind at Mischief* (New York, Funk & Wagnalls Company, 1929) p. 382–384.
5 See Martin Gardner's *Urantia: The Great Cult Mystery* (Amherst NY, Prometheus Books, 1995). Gardner concludes the Urantia Book includes incorporates the work of Bertrand Russell among others.

6 William S Sadler, letter to Mrs Nancy Hildick, secretary of Stefansson, 14 August 1959. http://www.urantiabook.org/index_history.htm

7 JC Mills, *The Urantia Book: An Evaluation*, 1970 see: http://urantiabook.org/archive/readers/doc994.htm

8 Commander James Waldron, US Navy (Ret.), *Flight of the Puckered Penguins*, http://www.anta.canterbury.ac.nz/resources/flight/

9 See http://adventurer.lronhubbard.org/page58.htm

10 ibid.

11 Lady Suzanne Wilkins, unpublished draft chapter for Thomas, op cit., p. 20.

12 ibid., p. 14.

13 SHW, curriculum vitae, undated, BPRC, 1–15.

14 Lady Suzanne Wilkins, *Epilogue*, in Thomas, *Sir Hubert Wilkins, A Biography*, op cit., p. 293.

15 Lady Suzanne Wilkins, unpublished draft chapter for Lowell Thomas op cit., p. 13.

16 SHW, 'Report on a Visit to Asia', unpublished manuscript, BPRC, 22–37, p. 6.

17 ibid., p. 3.

18 ibid., p. 20.

19 Oral history interview, Winston Ross with Peter J Anderson, Ohio State University, BPRC, 2–29.

20 Lady Suzanne Wilkins, unpublished draft chapter for Thomas op cit., p. 23.

21 ibid., p. 13

22 Walter A Wood, 'George Hubert Wilkins', *The Geographical Review*, No 3, 1959, p. 415.

23 *New Yorker*, 20 March 1943.

24 Only a few dozen of his letters remain, and today form part of the considerable Wilkins archive at the Byrd Polar Research Center at Ohio Sate University, filed in 1–16.

25 *The Los Angeles Times*, 25 August 2002.

26 Dr Ralph Goldman, email correspondence with author, February 2004.

27 Jack B. Chambers, geographer, Environment Protection Research Division, article, *Research and Engineering Command*, 1960, p. 6.

28 SHW, 'A Journey Through Hot Climates', June–August 1952, BPRC, 127–1-6.

29 SHW, letter to Winston Ross, 1 April 1953, BPRC, 18–8.

31 Lady Suzanne Wilkins, unpublished draft chapter for Thomas, op cit., p. 28.

Chapter 17

1 Rickover's opponents would battle him all the way. Despite the success of the *Nautilus*, Rickover was not promoted to full Admiral until three years after *Nautilus* was launched, and only then after the intervention of Congress. However, he convinced five US presidents to extend his service beyond retirement age, before finally being dismissed at eighty-four by the Reagan Administration, ostensibly for accepting gifts from a naval contractor, General Dynamics. The gifts totalled more than $67 000 but it seems that the company was wasting its money. Before he was sacked, Rickover declared war on General Dynamics. He accused them and other contractors of trying to cheat the government of a billion dollars.

2 Interview with Diane Sawyer, CBS Network, '60 Minutes', transcript at http://www.people.vcu.edu/~rsleeth/Rickover.html

3 The job interview, in all its embarrassing detail, is revealed in Calvert's account of his nuclear submarine career, *Surface at the Pole*, (London, Hutchinson and Co, 1961). Despite his supposed underachievement at Annapolis, Calvert would

eventually return to run it as Superintendent before taking command of the US Pacific Fleet.

4 Decades later, British Prime Minister John Major would reveal the crushing responsibility he felt while composing the handwritten notes to be stored in each of his nuclear-armed submarines. A personal message from commander to his captain ordering retaliation against the enemy, it would only be read after a nuclear armageddon. US Navy subs also carry these personal orders from the President.

5 Marion D Williams, *Submarines Under Ice*, op cit., p. 118.

6 A military rocket hastily converted to carrying satellites, Vanguard would explode with alarming regularity. Between December 1957 and the end of 1958 it would fail in seven out of eight attempted launches.

7 Calvert, *Surface at the Pole*, op cit., p. 134.

8 A much more substantial and permanent memorial now commemorates the lost World War II crews.

9 The full conversation is quoted in James Calvert's *Surface at the Pole*, op cit., p. 135–144.

Chapter 18

1 James Calvert interview with author, New York, 8 March 2000.

Epilogue

1 Interview with author, Mt Bryan East, December 2000.

2 Lowell Thomas, unpublished manuscript for chapters of biography, p. 89, BPRC, 2–1.

3 Eugene Rogers, *Beyond the Barrier*, op cit., p. 23.

4 Andrews, *The Business of Exploring*, (GP Putnam, New York, 1935) p. 14.

5 Herbert B Nichols, *Explorers Journal*, December 1964, p. 203.

6 SHW, address to the Canadian Club, 'Sixteen Years of Polar Exploration', 15 March 1937, BPRC, 22–39.

7 SHW, unpublished manuscript, undated but likely to be circa 1930/31, BPRC, 15–19, p. 10.

8 SHW, poem quoted by Lady Suzanne Wilkins in *Epilogue*, Thomas, op cit., p. 296.

9 Walter Sullivan, letter to Lady Suzanne Wilkins, 23 December 1958, BPRC, 20–27.

10 Richard Byrd Jr, letter to Lady Suzanne Wilkins, 2 December 1958, BPRC, 20–27.

Bibliography

Michael Archer and Bob Beale, *Going Native, Living in the Australian Environment* (Sydney, Hodder, 2004).

Philip Ayres, *Mawson, A Life* (Melbourne, Melbourne University Press, 1999).

Thomas Wyatt Bagshawe, *Two Men in the Antarctic, An Expedition to Graham Land 1920–1922* (Cambridge, Cambridge University Press, 1939).

Bess Balchen, *Poles Apart, The Admiral Richard E Byrd and Colonel Bernt Balchen Odyssey* (Oakland OR, Red Anvil Press, 2004).

A Scott Berg, *Lindbergh* (New York, Putnam, 1998).

Douglas Botting, *Dr Eckener's Dream Machine* (London, HarperCollins, 2001).

Commander James Calvert, *Surface at the Pole, The Extraordinary Voyages of the USS Skate* (London, Hutchinson, 1961).

Peter Cochrane, *The Western Front 1916–1918* (Sydney, ABC Books, 2004).

Hugo Eckener, *My Zeppelins*, translated by Douglas H Robinson (London, Putnam and Co, 1958).

Lincoln Ellsworth, *Beyond Horizons* (New York, Doubleday, 1937).

Nelson Eustis, *The Greatest Air Race England–Australia 1919* (Adelaide, Rigby, 1969).

John Robert Francis, *Shackleton's Last Voyage, The Story of the 'Quest'* (London, Cassell and Company, 1923).

Philip Gibbs and Bernard Grant, *Adventures of War with Cross and Crescent* (London, Methuen, 1913).

John Grierson, *Sir Hubert Wilkins, Enigma of Exploration* (London, Robert Hale, 1960).

——*Challenges to the Pole, Highlights of Arctic and Antarctic Aviation* (London, Foulis, 1964).

Richard Hamblyn, *The Invention of Clouds* (New York, Picador, 2002).

Stuart E Jenness, *The Making of an Explorer, George Hubert Wilkins and the Canadian Arctic Expedition 1913–16*, (Montreal, McGill-Queen's University Press, 2004).

Barry Lopez, *Arctic Dreams* (London, Picador, 1987).

David McGonigal and Dr Lyn Woodworth, *Antarctica and the Arctic, The Complete Encyclopedia* (Ontario, Firefly Books, 2001).

William Laird McKinlay, *Karluk* (London, Weidenfeld and Nicolson, 1976).

Stephen Martin, *A History of Antarctica* (Sydney, State Library of NSW Press, 1996).

Richard Montague, *Oceans, Poles and Airmen, The First Flights over Wide Waters and Desolate Ice* (New York, Random House, 1971).

Bibliography

Jennifer Niven, *The Ice Master, The Doomed 1913 Voyage of the Karluk* (New York, Hyperion, 2000).

Magnus L Olsen, *Saga of the White Horizon* (Lymington, Nautical Publishing, 1971).

Dorothy G Page, *Polar Pilot: The Carl Ben Eielson Story* (Danville IL, Interstate Publishers, 1992).

Beekman Pool, *Polar Extremes, The World of Lincoln Ellsworth* (Fairbanks, University of Alaska Press, 2002).

David Roberts, *Great Exploration Hoaxes* (New York, Random House, 2001).

Eugene Rodgers, *Beyond the Barrier, The Story of Byrd's First Expedition to Antarctica* (Annapolis, Naval Institute Press, 1990).

Michael H Rosvoe, *Let Heroes Speak, Antarctic Explorers 1772–1922* (New York, Berkley, 2000).

Swan, RA, *Australia in the Antarctic* (Melbourne, Melbourne University Press, 1961).

Lowell Thomas, *Sir Hubert Wilkins: His World of Adventure* (New York, McGraw-Hill, 1961).

Bert and Margie Webber, *I Shoot the News, The Adventures of Will E Hudson* (Oregon, Webb Research Group, 1999).

Captain Sir George Hubert Wilkins, *Flying the Arctic* (New York, Putnam, 1928).

——*Undiscovered Australia: Being an Account of an Expedition to Tropical Australia to Collect Specimens of the Rarer Fauna for the British Museum, 1923–1925* (London, Putnam, 1929).

——*Under the North Pole, The Wilkins-Ellsworth Submarine Expedition* (New York, Brewer, Warren and Putnam, 1931).

——with Harold M Sherman, *Thoughts through Space, A Remarkable Adventure in the Realm of the Mind* (New York, C&R Anthony, 1951).

Marion D Williams, *Submarines Under Ice, The US Navy's Polar Operations* (Annapolis, Naval Institute Press, 1998).

Index

338